Readings in
Public Policy

Readings in Public Policy

Edited by J. M. Pogodzinski

San Jose State University

First published 1995

Blackwell Publishers, a publishing imprint of
Basil Blackwell, Inc.
238 Main Street
Cambridge, Massachusetts 02142
USA

Basil Blackwell Ltd.
108 Cowley Road
Oxford OX4 1JF
UK

Library of Congress Cataloging-in-Publication Data
Readings in public policy / [edited by] J.M. Pogodzinski.
        p.   cm.
    Includes bibliographical references
    ISBN 1-55786-521-3 ✓
    1. Policy sciences. 2. Social policy. I. Pogodzinski, J.M.
H97.R432   1995
321'.6—dc20   94-26134
                                                               CIP

British Library Cataloguing in Publication Data

A CIP catalogue record for this book is available from the British Library.

Typeset by Cornerstone Composition Services.

Printed in the USA by BookCrafters.
This book is printed on acid-free paper.

Chapters

Contents

Introduction

This collection of readings is addressed to students and practitioners of public policy. The elasticity of that term is evident from the range of topics discussed in the collection: AIDS, child care, mortgage markets, the Americans with Disabilities Act, and much more. All of the contributions collected here except one were specially prepared for this reader, and all of the contributions meet the basic standard that was enunciated at the beginning. Each contribution teaches a lesson in economics, takes a stand on an issue of public policy, and tries to expose as fully as possible the methods economists use in addressing public policy issues. While interesting topics are considered, the thrust of the collection as a totality is to constitute a sort of "learning by example" for public policy analysis. The contributors have tried to make their contributions as accessible as possible while also being fully faithful to the research on the topic under discussion.

While the contributions have been loosely ordered topically, I should emphasize that there is considerable overlap among the contributions at a more basic level. For example, each contribution considers (whether implicitly or explicitly) the idea of *market failure*. I would like to take the occasion of this preface to point to some other interconnections. This is by way of encouraging those readers who may start out only, say, with an interest in health care issues to delve into some other areas.

Health Care Issues. This is perhaps the area of public policy debate that would come most immediately to mind from today's headlines. The contribution by Alain Enthoven provides a framework for the other readings on health issues and also gives an important conception of the idea of managed competition. One of the important points to consider from the public policy perspective, and one that has become obscured in the most recent political debates about health care, is the role of "purchasing alliances" (referred to as Health Insurance Purchasing Cooperatives (HIPCs) by Enthoven).

The contribution by Thomas Getzen is a good companion to the paper by Enthoven. Getzen's paper considers broadly the factors that account for health care expenditures, both in the United States and in other developed countries, and also considers the U.S. experience of price controls in health care. The thrust of Getzen's argument is that it is important to correctly identify the causes of the increase in health care spending. Misperception of the causes of the increase results in policy recommendations that may exacerbate the problem.

Paul Farnham considers the question of measuring the cost of AIDS. Measuring the cost of AIDS, or of any disease, is a difficult task. The difficulties are both practical and methodological. At the same time, cost estimates of AIDS and of other diseases are important for proper public policy analysis. Farnham also considers the incidence of AIDS costs, an even more difficult and arguably more important area of policy analysis.

Labor Market Issues. The contribution by Carolyn Weaver should be of special interest to those whose initial interest is in health care issues. Such laws as the Americans with Disabilities Act (ADA) are addressed, it would seem, at least partly to people who have some kind of medical condition. Weaver focuses on the incentives created by mandated job accommodation under the ADA. She argues that the ADA creates both costs and benefits, and that while some benefits accrue to some people with disabilities, costs may also be imposed on some people with disabilities, as well as upon society as a whole, by the job accommodation provisions of the ADA. Weaver contrasts the "rights-based" approach of the ADA with an "incentive-based" approach.

David Sjoquist considers the differential between wage rates and employment rates of blacks and whites. These differentials have been increasing in recent times, notwithstanding governmental efforts to close the gap. While acknowledging that there are several competing explanations for the increase in these differentials, Sjoquist examines the spatial mismatch hypothesis (and the related skills mismatch hypothesis) formulated more than 25 years ago. This hypothesis holds that the underlying factors accounting for the increase in the wage and employment differentials are the changing structure of the economy and the persistent barriers to adjustment that prevent blacks from attaining the wage and employment levels of whites. The spatial mismatch hypothesis carries with it specific policy recommendations for addressing the problem of the increasing differentials.

Housing, Public Finance, and Infrastructure. My paper is addressed to the basic question: What is the appropriate locus for decision making about land use? The paper is an outgrowth of several factors. First, I have studied several aspects of zoning in a series of review papers and in a series of empirical papers (with Tim Sass). Second, thanks to Fannie Mae, I attended a roundtable where the newly released report of the Advisory Commission on Regulatory Barriers was debated. Finally, I was exposed to some of William Fischel's ideas in a recent series of papers and manuscripts. Out of this maelstrom arose the idea that the Advisory Commission had not got it quite right.

Ellen Roche's paper on secondary mortgage markets provides a clear introduction to an important topic. The operation of secondary mortgage markets is, of course, important to the housing industry, but the idea of providing increased liquidity is one that is applicable to many situations. Yet such secondary markets may fail to emerge or to operate efficiently without government sponsorship. Whether government intervention is warranted, and if so what the appropriate kind of intervention might be, is discussed in the paper.

Charles Hulten and Robert Schwab's paper on public infrastructure is one that is also addressed to a topic from today's headlines. It is often suggested that U.S. productivity decline can be traced to the decline in public sector infrastructure investment. Some people view this proposition as axiomatic. Yet there is considerable debate among economists about the validity of this hypothesis. Hulten and Schwab are among the skeptics. They review a variety of evidence concerning the productivity of infrastructure and also outline their own approach to the isssue, examining the relationship between multifactor productivity (MFP) and public capital.

Youth Issues. Joseph Cordes, Sheila Kirby, and Richard Buddin address the contentious issue of school vouchers. Various voucher schemes have been proposed. The general line of argument in favor of school vouchers is that schools that are forced to compete will improve, and parents will be more satisfied with their children's schooling if they have a greater scope of choice about schools. Opponents of vouchers cite numerous objections, among them that voucher schools will undermine public education and result in lower-quality schooling for low income students. Cordes, Kirby, and Buddin point out that many of the arguments, both pro and con, make suppositions about facts that are not supported by evidence. One of the central issues addressed in this paper is: Who would choose to accept a voucher? Wild estimates are often made by partisans in the debate. Cordes, Kirby, and Buddin provide a theoretical framework and review empirical estimates of private/public school choice.

Ellen Magenheim's paper on the child-care market is addressed primarily to the structure of that market and the role of government in addressing potential market failures. She eschews the more traditional analyses addressed to the effect of child care on the labor supply decisions of women. Magenheim uses the theory of monopolistic competition to analyse the child-care market. The focus is on the welfare evaluation of the market. Informational asymmetries play a central role in the analysis. A wide variety of empirical literature is reviewed.

This book was completed while I was on sabbatical leave from San Jose State University. Parts of the book were written while I was a fellow of the

Lusk Center for Real Estate Development at the University of Southern California, and a Visiting Scholar in the Department of Economics at George Washington University in Washington, DC. I wish to thank my colleagues at those institutions for their expressions of support and helpful comments.

I have enjoyed editing this book. It forced me to move from a familiar but narrow perspective to a broader field. I did not know most of the contributors to this book when I started, and it has been a pleasure to work with them and to get to know them and their work. I would also like to thank our editors at Blackwell, including Rolf Janke, executive editor; Mary Riso, development editor; Jan Leahy, production manager; and Paul Bodine, copy editor.

Part 1

Health Care Issues

The History and Principles of Managed Competition

Alain C. Enthoven

Introduction

The continuing health care debate has brought numerous issues before the public: managed care, managed competition, employer mandates, price controls, and purchasing alliances. However, these are not independent pieces that can be brought in or tossed away without reference to the other parts of the reform package. Public discussion has tended to focus on aspects of a particular piece but not on the interrelationship among the pieces. As will become clear from the following reading, not all the pieces mentioned fit together.

The public discussion health care tends to focus, if that term can even be applied, on too many of the problems with the health care system at once. There are many problems of the health care system, but solutions to these problems may involve trade-offs among desirable goals. The public discussion of health care seems to reject solutions that fail to address all problems of health care.

Enthoven's paper provides a framework for policy analysis of health care reform. Enthoven gives a particular conception of managed competition. It is not everyone's conception nor is any version of managed competition everyone's conception of reformed health care. Nonetheless, Enthoven's is an important voice in the health care debate, and his careful analysis of the interrelationships among goals and policies deserves serious attention.

One key idea of managed competition as presented here is that the competition among insurers should be channeled into price competition. Price competition does not necessarily occur in the market for health insur-

ance now. The channeling of activity by health insurers into other than price competition can be construed as a market failure.

Such ideas as price competition do not fit well with ideas for governmental price controls, even, as sometimes proposed, those that would be triggered if competition failed to halt the increase in health care expenditures. Enthoven presents a variety of arguments against direct governmental control. Essentially, such governmental controls always have undesirable incentive effects and tend to slow needed adjustment to change.

In keeping with the spirit of this collection of readings, Enthoven calls upon empirical work in his analysis. It is noteworthy, for example, that research supports the idea that only a small portion of total variation in individual annual health expenditures is explainable even with complete knowledge of patient characteristics.

To understand the procompetition movement and the idea of managed competition, one must first understand the history of the noncompetitive system we have today. The word *competition* as used by economists, if not qualified by some phrase indicating the contrary (such as *nonprice competition*), means price competition. When there is price competition, suppliers compete to serve customers who are using their own money or are otherwise motivated to obtain maximum value for money. *Price competition* does not mean that price is the only factor influencing the customer's choice. Quality and product features also enter in. It simply means that price is one of the factors. Perhaps *value-for-money competition* would be a more apt phrase. One of the striking features of the U.S. health care economy to date is how little value-for-money competition there is.

Charles Weller has described our traditional system of fee-for-service, solo (or small, single-specialty group) practice, free choice of provider, and payment by a remote third party as "guild free choice."[1] The principles of this system and their economic consequences are as follows: (1) Free choice of doctor by the patient, which means that the insurer has no bargaining power with the doctor; (2) free choice of prescription by the doctor, which prevents the insurer from applying quality assurance or review of appropriateness; (3) direct negotiation between doctor and patient regarding fees, which excludes the third-party payer, who would be likely to have information, bargaining power, and an incentive to negotiate to hold down fees; (4) fee-for-service payment, which allows physicians maximum control over their incomes by increasing the services provided; and (5) solo practice, because multispecialty group practice constitutes a break in the seamless web of mutual coercion through control of referrals that the medical profession has used to enforce the guild system.[2]

These principles dominated the U.S. health care system until well into the

1980s, and their effects are still important today. They were enforced by legislation (for example, guild principles were built into all state insurance codes until the 1980s and into Title XVIII of the Social Security Act), boycotts (for example, by doctors against hospitals contracting with health mainte-nance organizations [HMOs]), professional ostracism (for example, from county medical societies and hospital staffs), denial of medical staff privi-leges, and harassment.[3] Blue Cross and Blue Shield were created, respec-tively, by hospital associations and medical societies as chosen instruments to apply the guild principles to health care financing. For example, hospitals subsidized Blue Cross plans by giving them discounts. Only in fairly recent years have providers been forced to yield controlling positions on Blue Cross and Blue Shield boards.[4] Commercial insurance companies offered coverage based on the casualty insurance model. They comfortably ac-cepted the guild principles because they were and, with a few important exceptions, remain financial intermediaries with expertise in underwriting risk, not in organizing, managing, or purchasing medical care.

Employers also fit into this model. A few attempted to contract selectively with doctors for the care of their employees. But for the most part, this was beaten down by organized medicine.[5] An overwhelming majority of em-ployers offered traditional "guild free choice" coverage of either the Blue Cross/Blue Shield or the commercial variety because that was all there was. The typical pattern was virtually 100 percent employer-paid coverage. This pattern spread rapidly because health insurance was an attractive fringe benefit, it was cheap, it was tax deductible to the employer and tax free to the employee, employment groups could buy coverage at much less than the cost of individual coverage, and employer-paid health benefits were a great source of bargaining prizes for unions. In the minds of many employees, fee-for-service coverage fully paid by the employer became normal, an entitlement. Employment-based insurance spread to small employers. Roughly half of the privately employed labor force is either self-employed or in groups of 100 or fewer. This added another element of noncompetition: Such groups are too small to offer individual employees a choice of health care plans. I return to this point later.

When HMOs entered the scene in large numbers in the 1970s and employers were required to offer them, employers usually agreed to pay HMO premiums in full as long as they did not exceed the cost of the traditional coverage. Thus, HMOs were placed in the noncompetitive system created by the guild model. Medicare and Medicaid also adopted the dominant guild model. Section 1801 of the Social Security Act prohibits any federal interference in the practice of medicine; section 1802 is entitled "free choice by patient guaranteed."

All of this created a system dominated by the cost-increasing incentives of fee-for-service payment combined with the cost-unconscious demand of insured patients. This in turn inspired greatly increased numbers of people to choose careers in medicine, especially in highly paid specialties. This was fueled by federal grants to induce medical schools to expand. This open-ended, cost-unconscious demand, combined with large increases in federal funding for biomedical research, led to a huge outpouring of costly new medical technologies.

Finally, most well-functioning markets contain an adequate supply of information to assist purchasers in making decisions. In health care, there is no regulation to require the uniform production of health outcomes information. In fact, providers have been active and successful in political activities to block access to such information.[6]

The Beginnings of "Competition"

The precursors of competition are many.[7] But the origins of today's competitors are in prepaid group practice: multispecialty group practices that contracted with employment groups and individuals to provide a comprehensive set of health care services in exchange for a periodic per capita payment set in advance. The pioneers of the prepaid group practice movement introduced the "limited-provider" or "closed-panel" plan as a significant competing alternative. They survived strong opposition by organized medicine and proved the acceptability of prepaid group practice and its economic superiority over the traditional model.[8] They successfully advocated dual or multiple choice by individual subscribers of closed-panel plans as an alternative to guild free choice. The flagships of this movement included Ross Loos in Los Angeles (1929), Group Health Association in the District of Columbia (1935), Group Health Cooperative of Puget Sound (1945), and Kaiser Permanente, with roots in the 1930s.

In 1960 the federal government adopted health insurance for its employees. The Blues and commercial insurers sought a noncompetitive guild model. But federal employees who were members of prepaid group practices were sufficiently numerous and vocal that a compromise was adopted under which the federal government would offer a range of plans for individuals to choose from and a defined contribution. The Federal Employees Health Benefits Program (FEHBP) that emerged had both good and bad design features.[9] On the good side was price-conscious individual choice; on the bad, nonstandard benefits and lack of a design to manage biased risk selection. But it did demonstrate on a large scale that choice-of-plan arrangements were feasible and comparatively economical.

These practical achievements, which were of fundamental importance, came to be reflected in the writings of scholars and public policy analysts. Paul Ellwood, Walter McClure, and colleagues proposed a national "health maintenance strategy" in 1970 that would deal with the crisis in health care cost and distribution by promoting "a health maintenance industry that is largely self-regulatory."[10] Their work led directly to the HMO Act of 1973. In 1972 and 1973, while serving in the Department of Health, Education, and Welfare (HEW), Scott Fleming designed and recommended a proposal for national health insurance that he called "Structured Competition within the Private Sector."[11] His proposal emphasized practical ways of extending the successful experience of the FEHBP to the entire population. In 1977 I designed the Consumer Choice Health Plan (CCHP), "a national health insurance proposal based on regulated competition in the private sector," and recommended it to the Carter administration.[12] CCHP built on the ideas of Ellwood, McClure, and Fleming and added design proposals to deal with such issues as financing, biased selection, market segmentation, information costs, and equity. In 1978 Clark Havighurst attacked "professional restraints on innovation in health care financing" from the perspective of antitrust law.[13] By the end of the 1970s the idea of a competitive health care economy had attained intellectual respectability and a significant following in Congress.

An additional departure from the guild free choice model occurred in the 1980s, starting with enactment of A.B. 3480 by the California legislature in 1982. A.B. 3480 overturned the previous prohibition on selective contracting with providers by insurers and authorized preferred provider insurance (PPI). Under PPI, the patient obtains better coverage if he or she receives services from contracting "preferred" providers. This creates an incentive for providers to accept the insurer's fee schedule and utilization controls under contract. Many other states followed California in subsequent years.

From Early Competition to Managed Competition

Experience has shown that Fleming's "structured competition" and my "regulated competition" did not quite describe what we had in mind. Under our inflexible form of government, it is difficult and time-consuming to change such things as the Medicare law and regulations, which have been negotiated with financially and politically powerful interest groups that can block efficiency-improving changes that are to their disadvantage. Civil servants are not allowed to use judgment; they are supposed to administer regulations, and they can act only on evidence that can stand up in court. The intent of both of our terms was interpreted as structuring the market by a set of rules laid down once and for all, with purchasing by individual consumers and a passive regulatory agency. Whatever set of rules one proposes, critics could and did dream up ways for health plans to get around them to their advantage. As critics identified actual or hypothetical problems,

I would often reply, "I think that problem could be managed using the following tools. . . ." This led me to believe that a more accurate characterization of what actually works would be *managed competition*.

Managed competition must involve intelligent, active collective purchasing agents contracting with health care plans on behalf of a large group of subscribers and continuously structuring and adjusting the market to overcome attempts to avoid price competition. I call these agents "sponsors"; they play a central role in managed competition. A sponsor is an agency that contracts with health plans concerning benefits covered, prices, enrollment procedures, and other conditions of participation. Managed competition also connotes the ability to use judgment to achieve goals in the face of uncertainty, to be able to negotiate, and to make decisions on the basis of imperfect information. It takes more than mere passive administration of inflexible rules to make this market work.

Managed Competition Defined

Managed competition is a purchasing strategy to obtain maximum value for money for employers and consumers. It uses rules for competition, derived from rational microeconomic principles, to reward with more subscribers and revenue those health plans that do the best job of improving quality, cutting cost, and satisfying patients. The "best job" is in the judgment of both the sponsor, armed with data and expert advice, and informed, cost-conscious consumers. The rules of competition must be designed and administered so as not to reward health plans for selecting good risks, segmenting markets, or otherwise defeating the goals of managed competition. Managed competition occurs at the level of integrated financing and delivery plans, not at the individual provider level. Its goal is to divide providers in each community into competing economic units and to use market forces to motivate them to develop efficient delivery systems.

Managed competition is price competition, but the price it focuses on is the annual premium for comprehensive health care services, not the price for individual services. There are several reasons for this. First, the annual premium encodes the total annual cost per person. It gives the subscriber an incentive to choose the health plan that minimizes total cost. Second, it is the price that people can understand and respond to most effectively, during the annual enrollment, when they have information, choices, and time for consideration. Third, sick, nonexpert patients and their families are in a particularly poor position to make wise decisions about long lists of individual services they might or might not need. They need to rely on their doctors to advise what services are appropriate and on their health plans to get good prices. For economical behavior to occur, doctors must be motivated to prescribe economically. Managed competition is compatible with selected copayments and deductibles for individual services that can influence patients to do their part in using resources wisely and that are price signals patients can understand and to which they can respond.

Sponsors and Managed Competition

To understand managed competition, one must begin with the concept of a sponsor. Markets for most goods and services are normally made up of suppliers on one side and individual purchasers on the other. This is not the model that actually works in most of private health insurance in the United States, and in my view, this model is not workable at the individual level in health insurance for a number of reasons.

First, insurers have strong incentives to group their customers by expected medical costs and to charge people in each group a premium that reflects their expected costs. This practice is known as *experience rating* or *underwriting*. The consequence is that those people having high predicted medical costs face high premiums. Many sick people find such premiums unaffordable and may go without insurance, taking their chances that they will receive free care. Second, healthy individuals face strong incentives to ride free–that is, to go without insurance or with minimal coverage until they get sick, at which point they seek to buy comprehensive coverage. Consumers are more likely than insurers to know more about their prospective medical needs. Third, partly because of the behaviors induced by these incentives and partly because of high marketing costs to reach individuals or small groups, the administrative costs of individual health insurance policies are very high–40 percent of medical claims or more. This creates more of an incentive for relatively healthy people to go without insurance. Rather than bearing the risks and expenses of covering individuals who are sick, even at a high price that would cover their expected costs, most insurers choose not to cover them at any price. Fourth, health insurance contracts are extremely complex and difficult to understand and administer. Insurers deliberately make them even more complex to segment markets and to make it difficult for consumers to compare prices.

The model of private health insurance that works–the one that covers most employed people–is group insurance with a sponsor. Most sponsors are employers, but the federal Medicare program and labor/management health and welfare trusts are also sponsors. Examples of large employers that offer their employees such a multiple choice of health care coverage include the federal government; many states, including California, Wisconsin, and Minnesota; and Stanford University. While some HMOs and some PPI carriers compete for unsponsored individuals, most of their business is in sponsored groups. Sponsors set the rules for competition among them.

Sponsors Establish Rules of Equity

The sponsor has several important functions in managed competition. First, through contracts with the participating health plans, it establishes and enforces principles of equity such as the following:

(1) Every eligible person is covered or at least is offered coverage on terms that make it attractive, even for persons with low expected medical costs, and at a moderate financial cost. Health plans accept all eligible persons who choose them.

(2) Every eligible person has subsidized access to the lowest-priced plan meeting acceptable standards of quality and coverage. Persons choosing a plan priced above the lowest-priced plan must pay the full premium difference with their own money.

(3) Coverage is continuous; that is, once a person is enrolled, coverage cannot be cancelled (except for nonpayment of premium or serious noncompliance with reasonable norms of patient behavior). Moreover, everyone can re-enroll during the annual enrollment period.

(4) Community rating (or limited departures from it) is established, whereby the same premium is paid for the same coverage regardless of the health status of the individual or small group. (This might be blended with, for example, age rating if it is felt that pure community rating requires excessive subsidies of the old by the young.)

(5) No exclusions or limitations are placed on coverage for preexisting conditions. Obviously, some of these principles may have to be compromised with other practical considerations, depending on the circumstances.

Sponsors Select Participating Plans

The freedom of the sponsor in selecting participating plans will depend on the circumstances. A private employer will have more freedom of action than a public employer. And a public employer will be able to exercise more freedom than will a health insurance purchasing cooperative (HIPC) that serves as the gatekeeper for much or all of the market in a geographic area.

Sponsors Manage Enrollment Process

In managing enrollment, the sponsor should serve as the single point of entry to all participating health plans. Subscribers notify the sponsor of their choice of plan (probably through the employer), and the sponsor notifies the health plan. This is normal in large employment groups but, unfortunately, is not the usual practice with such public programs as Medicare and Medicaid. The purpose is to create an institutional embodiment of the principle that health plans take all who apply and to obviate what would otherwise be a large set of opportunities for screening and selecting applicants. The sponsor must define the enrollment procedures, such as giving each subscriber an annual opportunity to switch plans. It also must establish procedures to enroll newcomers and to deal with changes in address or family composition. The sponsor also should prepare informative materials about the benefits covered, the characteristics of the health plans and locations of their providers, and the quality controls in place. The sponsor establishes contractual payment terms with participating employers and individuals. And the sponsor runs a clearinghouse for the money.

Sponsors Create Price-Elastic Demand

Next, the sponsor must seek to create price-elastic demand. (A seller faces inelastic demand if the seller can increase revenue by raising price and elastic demand if the seller increases revenue by reducing price.) For there to be an incentive for health plans to cut price, demand must be so elastic that the additional revenue gained exceeds the additional cost of serving more subscribers. Managed competition is about creating such price elasticity.[14] The following are some of the main tools for accomplishing this.

1. **Employer/Sponsor Contributions**. The key point here is that the sponsor's contribution to the premiums must not exceed the price of the lowest-priced plan. An essential component of managed competition is that it must always be possible for the lowest-priced plan to take business away from higher-priced plans by cutting premiums more. The lowest-priced plan must be able to widen the gap between its price and the next lowest by cutting price. Premiums of course are quoted in the context of annual enrollments. The sponsor sets its contribution after the health plans have submitted their quotes.

2. **Standardized Coverage Contract**. Standardization should deter product differentiation, facilitate price comparisons, and counter market segmentation. There are powerful reasons for as much standardization as possible within each sponsored group. The first is to facilitate value-for-money comparisons and to focus comparison on price and quality. The second is to combat market segmentation–the division of the market into groups of subscribers who make choices based on what each plan covers (such as mental health or vision care) rather than on price. The third is to reassure people that it is financially safe to switch plans for a lower price with the knowledge that the lower-priced plans did not realize savings by creating hidden gaps in coverage. The fourth is that biased risk selection can reduce demand elasticity for health plans that enroll a favorable mix of risks.

3. **Quality-related Information**. People will be reluctant to switch from Plan A to Plan B to save $20 per month if they have no information that Plan B is safe for their health. The *Jackson Hole Group* proposes creation of a national Outcomes Management Standards Board that would set standards for outcomes reporting.[15] Sponsors should play a role in making

such information accessible to the local market. Sponsors are also the appropriate agencies to survey their sponsored populations regarding experience with health plans and to publish the results for consumers.

4. Choice of Plans at Individual Level. Sponsors should structure the market to offer annual choice of plan at the individual subscriber level, not the employment group level. Limitation of choice to the group level is a major barrier to price-elastic demand. (Effective managed care plans are linked to specific doctors. Because some people have strong attachments to their doctors, it is much harder to persuade a whole group to change plans and doctors to obtain lower premiums than to allow individuals who are willing to change to choose to do so.)

There are other opportunities for sponsors to exercise ingenuity in making demand curves for health plans more price elastic. For example, an alert sponsor might create a system to inform all patients of primary care physicians who contract with more than one health plan about which plan has the lowest premium so that patients can switch to the lowest-priced plan covering their doctor's services. Combined with standardized benefits, this could greatly increase people's willingness to switch plans to save money.

Finally, current income and payroll tax laws create a heavy tax on cost containment. These laws must be changed so that a health plan that cuts its premium by a dollar sees the full dollar transmitted to the subscriber as an incentive to select that plan. This gives the health plan the full marketplace reward (more subscribers) for cutting price. Thus there must be a limit on tax-free employer contributions at a level that does not exceed the premium of the lowest-priced plan. This is beyond the scope of the sponsor and is mentioned here only for the sake of completeness.

Sponsors Manage Risk Selection

Finally, in managed competition, the sponsor must manage the problem of biased risk selection. The goal here is to create powerful incentives for health plans to succeed by improving quality and patient satisfaction, not by selecting good risks and avoiding bad ones. This is a crucial and complex issue. Here I describe the general outlines without getting into technical detail.

Joseph Newhouse has noted that in the RAND Health Insurance Experiment, the 1 percent of patients with the highest costs in a given year accounted for 28 percent of total costs on average.[16] Most of these patients could not be identified in advance. But such concentration suggests that it could be very profitable for a health plan to find ways to avoid enrolling or retaining such patients.

To accomplish the goal of managed risk selection, the sponsor should follow a coordinated strategy with the following elements:

1. *Single point of entry*—Subscribers notify the sponsor of their choice and the sponsor notifies the health plan. The health plan must accept all enrollees. This should be combined with continuity of enrollment; that is, patients cannot be dropped from enrollment, and they must be allowed to reenroll during the periodic open enrollment in the plan of their choice.

2. *Standardized coverage contract*—Coverage contract features can be a powerful tool for selecting risks.

3. *Risk-adjusted premiums*—The general idea is as follows. Health risks are likely to fall differently among the different plans, either by design or by accident. The characteristics of the population enrolled in the different plans (for example, age, sex, family composition, retiree or disability status, and diagnosis) should be measured and translated into estimates of expected relative medical costs, independent of plan. Each plan can be assigned a relative risk index–for example, 1.01 for a plan with unfavorable selection that makes its expected costs 1 percent above the whole group average. Then a dollar value is assigned to one percentage point of risk. For example, that might be 1 percent of the premium of the lowest-priced plan or the average-priced plan. This is a policy choice; there is no single mathematically correct answer. Surcharges are then applied to premiums of plans that received favorable selection; subsidies are given to plans that received unfavorable selection to compensate for risk selection This takes selection out of the competition.[17]

    The natural starting point is the available demographic variables (age, sex, family composition, and retiree status). Unfortunately, these do not explain much of the variation in individual annual expenditures. Newhouse found that of the total variation in individual expenditures, only about 15 percent is explainable even with complete knowledge of patient characteristics.[18] Demographic variables might explain 2 to 3 of the 15 percentage points.

    There is research under way to develop better risk-adjustment models, based on diagnostic information. It turns out to be much harder than one might think to turn available diagnostic information into good "risk adjusters." For example, among patients diagnosed in one year to have breast cancer or human immunode-ficiency virus (HIV), there will be a very wide variation in medical costs the next year. But it seems reasonable to suppose that diagnosis-based models eventually will be available. Another approach may be to fund treatment of some conditions by fixed payments per case outside the capitation payments, or to use specific capitation payments on behalf of people with very costly diseases such as acquired immunodeficiency syndrome (AIDS).

In the Jackson Hole proposal, sponsors are the final arbiters of risk selection. An interesting paper by Harold Luft casts the sponsor in the role of expert mediator among health plans that are in a "zero-sum game" over risk selection.[19] This suggests periodic face-to-face meetings with the marketing directors of all participating health plans, with the sponsor serving as honest broker. If Plan A is skimming, that hurts the other plans. The sponsor should lead a discussion on how risk selection can be defined, measured, and compensated for. This is an ongoing process, not a single event.

Since the sponsor must be seen as an impartial broker, not a biased participant, it should not have its own plan. Medicare's management of competition among HMOs has been seriously impaired by the Health Care Financing Administration's (HCFAs) preoccupation with protecting fee-for-service Medicare, which HCFA considers to be "its plan" that should be protected from HMOs. Similar problems occur in the private sector.

4. *Monitoring of enrollment patterns*—Sponsors should monitor voluntary disenrollments for evidence of risk-selecting behavior. With a brief questionnaire, sponsors can ask people why they switched plans. The box to watch would be one such as, "They told me Plan B was better at treating my kind of cancer."

5. *Monitoring of specialty care and quality*—Sponsors need to examine the quality of tertiary care arrangements and also monitor access to specialty care. A good way to avoid enrolling diabetics is to have no endocrinologists on staff in the county. A good way to avoid cancer patients is to have a poor oncology department. HMO regulation now monitors such aspects. These are subtle matters in which judgment must be applied.

Health Insurance Purchasing Cooperatives

Large employers of, say, 10,000 or more employees in one geographic area have the size needed to perform the functions of sponsorships with reasonable effectiveness, especially if they collaborate with other large employers. But over 40 percent of the employed population is in groups of 100 or fewer workers. Such groups (and even much larger ones) are too small to spread risks. Thus we observe wide variations–tenfold and more–in the premiums paid by small groups, depending on their claims experience. They also cannot achieve economies of scale in administration. Thus administrative expense reaches 35 percent of claims in groups of 5 to 9 and

40 percent in groups of 1 to 4, compared with 5.5 percent in groups of 10,000 and more.[20] Small groups cannot acquire needed information and expertise to function effectively in this market. In theory, agents and brokers perform this function. In practice, agents and brokers have their own interests, related to the commissions carriers pay, and they lack competence regarding quality or value of medical care.

The Jackson Hole initiative proposes to solve these problems by establishment of a new national system of sponsor organizations–HIPCs–to function as a collective purchasing agent on behalf of all small employers and individuals in a geographic area.[21] HIPCs are designed to correct the problems of market failure in the small-group market and to cut employers' administrative burdens to a minimum (for example, administering for them the requirements of mandated continuity of coverage and public subsidies). They provide a solid basis for determining the competitive costs of covering uniform benefits that could be used to establish a tax-exclusion limitation for each market area.

HIPCs would be nonprofit membership corporations whose boards would be elected by participating employers. HIPCs would contract with participating employers and would accept all qualifying employment groups in their area. They would not be allowed to exclude groups or individuals because of health status. HIPCs would manage competition, applying business judgment in determining the numbers and identities of competitors, and would carry out all of the sponsor functions described above.

HIPCs would select the participating health plans. Some would favor a rule that a HIPC must offer all health plans that achieve federal certification and that wish to be offered in the HIPCs' territory. Whether or not market forces would resolve the problems arising from this arrangement is a debatable proposition about which reasonable people can differ. I would prefer to see that HIPCs have some authority to select and drop health plans. The presumption should favor competition. Thus it would make sense for a HIPC to encourage participation by all provider groups in the territory, but some discretion might be appropriate for the following reasons. First, federal qualification and state regulation do not guarantee financial solvency. Second, many "managed care" plans offer overlapping provider networks (that is, many providers contracting with many plans). Some overlap may not be undesirable. But too many carriers all offering essentially the same set of providers can add to administrative costs and weaken the sponsor's purchasing power with providers. As noted above, managed competition seeks to motivate providers to create efficient delivery systems. Third, HIPCs should be able to drop health plans that persistently achieve very low market penetration. Fourth, HIPCs should be able to drop carriers that are persistently uncooperative with the HIPC's risk management program.

HIPCs would administer health benefit contracts. The HIPC should act like a competent, effective employee benefits office servicing beneficiary inquiries and complaints. It should interpret the contracts for beneficiaries, stand behind patients in disputes with health plans, and resolve disputes on terms that are fair to beneficiaries. This should be much more efficient than taking disputes to litigation. The HIPC also should monitor what is happening in the health care settings. It should survey consumer experience and make the information available for consumers. It should investigate complaints and should aggregate complaint data to identify problem areas.

HIPCs should not bear risk. Health plans should bear all risk for medical expenses, for several reasons. First, if HIPCs were to bear risk, we would have a whole new class of risk-bearing entities that would have to be capitalized and regulated, and we have more than enough of them now. Second, HIPCs should be unbiased, honest brokers among risk-bearing entities. Third, providers–doctors and hospitals–must be at risk for the cost of care to give them powerful incentives to reduce cost. Finally, HIPCs could contract with government agencies to cover publicly sponsored populations, such as Medicaid, the otherwise uninsured, and public employees.

Creating HIPCs means that persons and groups with low health care costs in a given year share in the costs of persons and groups with high costs. If given a choice, people expecting low costs are not likely to do so voluntarily. Once the HIPC is operating at a large scale, there will be important benefits for small employers, even those with good health risks–including economies of scale, stable rates, competition, and individual choice of plan. But to get HIPCs going and to prevent a spiral of adverse selection, there must be compelling incentives or legal requirements for all small employers to participate. In the Jackson Hole initiative, small-group participation in a HIPC would be a condition for exclusion of employer contributions from employees' taxable income.

One large and successful HIPC is the health benefits program of the California Public Employees Retirement System (CalPERS). CalPERS arranges coverage and manages competition for more than 870,000 people who are employees, retirees, and dependents of the state and more than 750 public agencies, some of which have as few as two employees. CalPERS offers each subscriber a choice of plan: 23 HMOs, 4 preferred provider organizations (PPOs) offered to employee association members, and a statewide PPO.

Role of Organized Systems of Care

Managed competition is not based on a mere hope that the market will somehow generate better models of care. It is based on demonstrations of successful, high-quality, cost-effective, organized systems of care that have existed for years. To date, the strongest evidence of their economic superiority relates to prepaid multispecialty group practices. For example, the RAND Health Insurance Experiment found that the Group Health Cooperative of Puget Sound cared for its randomly assigned patients for a cost 28 percent below that for comparable patients assigned to a fee-for-service plan whose care was paid for entirely by insurance or with 25 percent coinsurance (up to an annual out-of-pocket limit of $1,000).[22] The evident marketplace success of Kaiser Permanente, now serving over 6.5 million people, reinforces this finding. Successful large-scale HMOs based on individual practice styles have emerged in recent years. These HMOs carefully select participating physicians and arm physicians and management with strong information systems about practice patterns. These models can expand rapidly, and they offer a practice style that is familiar to many doctors and patients. While we do not have proof of their efficacy in the form of a randomized controlled trial, we do know that some of them now compete effectively with Kaiser Permanente and Group Health Cooperative.

Compared to the traditional fee-for-service model, there are many things such organizations can do–and, if appropriately motivated, will do–to improve quality and cut cost. (1) Fee-for-service has created a costly adversarial relationship between doctors and payers. Organized systems can attract the loyalty, commitment, and responsible participation of doctors. They can align the incentives of doctors and the interests of patients in high-quality economical care by appropriate risk-sharing arrangements. (2) Fee-for-service has failed to create accountability for health outcomes and the outcomes information systems doctors need to evaluate and improve practice patterns. Organized systems can gather data on outcomes, treatments, and resource use; evaluate practice patterns; and motivate doctors to choose economical practices that produce good outcomes.

(3) Fee-for-service "free choice" leaves patients to make remarkably poorly informed choices of doctor. Organized systems select doctors for quality and efficient practice patterns, monitor performance, and take corrective action where needed. (4) Fee-for-service has left us with excess supply in many specialties. Organized systems can match the numbers and types of doctors to the needs of enrolled populations. (5) Fee-for-service has left us with major excesses in hospital beds, high-tech equipment, and open-heart surgery facilities. At least some systems can match all resources used to the needs of the enrolled population.

(6) Our present system is characterized by major misallocations of resources. Organized systems can allocate all resources–capital and operating–across the total spectrum of care, including less costly settings. (7) Fee-for-service has little or no capability to plan and manage processes of care across the total spectrum (inpatient, outpatient, office, and home);

organized systems do. (8) Organizations that integrate financing and delivery as well as doctors and hospitals can practice total quality management/continuous quality improvement, the powerful management philosophy employed by the most successful world-class industrial companies.[23] This cannot be done effectively with doctors who are in fee-for-service practice in several hospitals and are attached to none.

(9) Fee-for-service has led to a costly and dangerous proliferation in facilities for such complex procedures as open-heart surgery. Such surgery done in low volumes has higher costs and higher death rates than when done in high volumes.[24] Organized systems concentrate open-heart surgery in regional centers with low mortality rates and low costs. Such regional concentration in the most cost-effective hospitals could save a great deal of money. (10) Systems can organize ongoing technology assessment and facilitate a rational response to the results. (11) HMOs emphasize prevention, early diagnosis and treatment, and effective management of chronic conditions. Traditional third-party coverage is usually based on the casualty insurance model: It pays very generously for costly inpatient episodes but not for the preventive services and management of chronic conditions that can reduce the need for inpatient care. Organized systems can use systematic management processes to make sure these services are actually delivered, not merely covered. And they can be held accountable for their enrolled populations.

Managed Competition in Sparsely Populated Areas

People do not find it hard to visualize managed competition in San Francisco or Boston. What about Wyoming, Vermont, or southern Texas, where there are not enough people to support competing systems?

Creation of a HIPC in such states would consolidate purchasing power so that it could be used more effectively to meet the needs of the covered population. There is such a thing as "competition for the field" where there cannot be "competition in the field." HIPCs might request proposals from established urban comprehensive care organizations to establish and operate a network of primary care outposts, paying doctors and nurse practitioners what is needed to attract them to provide high-quality ambulatory care in rural locations, while giving them professional support in the form of telephone consultations, temporary replacements, continuing education, and transportation and referral arrangements. Organized systems are needed to accomplish this; traditional fee-for-service solo practice has not produced satisfactory results.

In a state with a small population but with perhaps two or three competing health plans, no one plan might be large enough to purchase tertiary care effectively. A HIPC might "reach through" and "carve out" tertiary care and contract for it on a competitive basis with one or another regional center. A doctor with a monopoly in a small town might refuse to contract with any of the health plans on terms acceptable to doctors in other areas. Or, no one of several health plans might have enough patients in town to be able to support its own doctor. The HIPC might "reach through" the health plans, consolidate their purchasing power, and recruit a willing doctor from the outside to contract with all health plans and be the only contracting doctor. The HIPC in a small state might contract with a single HMO based on a primary care network to cover the state in an ongoing bilateral customer/supplier relationship. The HIPC might use "benchmarking" techniques as a substitute for ongoing competition in the field. The vision of competition in such circumstances should not be limited to large medical center–based prepaid group practices. That is but one model. But, as noted earlier, modern information technology has enabled primary care individual practice networks to perform management functions that previously required physical proximity.

Why Competition?

Why attempt to bring about these changes through competition and market forces? Why not expect the government simply to order them? First, we have an extremely wasteful and inefficient system that has been bathed in cost-increasing incentives for over 50 years. We badly need a radically more efficient system. That will mean closing hospitals and putting surgeons out of work. As Charles Schultze has written, "Under the social arrangements of the private market, those who may suffer losses are not usually able to stand in the way of change. As a consequence, efficiency-creating changes are not seriously impeded."[25] Government controls, on the other hand, tend to freeze industries in place. Thus we find it extraordinarily difficult to close an unneeded school or air base. Government action is constrained by what Schultze calls the rule to "do no direct harm."

Second, to offset the expenditure-increasing effects of an aging population and an expanding array of medical technologies, we need to foster a process of continuing productivity improvement and the development of cost-reducing technologies. Only ongoing competition to provide value for money can do this. Third, as medical technology and social and economic conditions of the population change, we need a health care system that is flexible and can come up with entirely new ways of organizing and delivering care. Fourth, we need and want a system that is user-friendly. Government monopoly public service agencies are notoriously user-unfriendly.

Fifth, our society needs to make cost/quality trade-off judgments. These should be made by consumers who are using their own money at the margin. For example, given a choice, many might prefer a much less costly style of care, based on limited access in tightly controlled facilities, with more use of physician-extenders, and so on. They might have other worthy uses for their money, such as their children's education. Others may be happy to pay more for wider access and greater convenience. (Note that under managed competition, consumers would be exercising this preference with their own net after-tax dollars, not with pretax dollars and substantial tax subsidies for the more costly choice as happens today.) In this country we are now spending nearly 14 percent of gross domestic product (GDP) on health care services. It is altogether possible that a very efficient competitive system could get us back to 9 or 10 percent. This would free up resources that are badly needed for education and other investments in long-term economic growth. In theory, a government-imposed "global budget" might be seen as a way to reduce national health expenditures as a share of GDP. In practice, this would be extremely difficult to do if all of the cost-increasing incentives of fee-for-service and all of the wastefulness of the present system were to remain in place. The reduced spending would mean care denied to people who need it and a sustained barrage of complaints by health care providers. The global budget would be hard for our government to sustain politically. Finally, competition is the way to achieve a system that is driven by the informed choices of consumers who are responsible for the cost consequences of their choices. A government-controlled system is driven by political forces.

Why Universal Coverage?

Today, millions of Americans either have no health care coverage or have coverage that will disappear or become extremely costly when they need it. Nobody defends the proposition that people without coverage or money to pay should go without necessary medical care or should be allowed to suffer, be disabled, or die for lack of reasonable care. For this reason our society has developed a complex patchwork of institutions to care for and finance the care of the uninsured. These institutions are extremely wasteful and often unfair, permitting preventable medical bankruptcies and disabilities. They lead to delayed care, which can often mean serious and costly illness that could have been prevented by early treatment. They lead to care in costly settings–particularly, hospital emergency departments–when care could have been delivered at much lower cost in the primary care physician's office. They permit epidemics of communicable diseases that could have been prevented. They generate requirements for costly eligibility determinations. They lead to cost shifting from those who do not pay and those who provide free care to those who do pay for health insurance. They lead to the closing of hospital emergency departments, which are the major point of entry for patients who cannot pay. This, in turn, deprives whole communities of an important resource.

By putting market pressure on providers to cut costs, market reforms promoting competition–if not accompanied by universal coverage–could exacerbate access problems. (This would be true of any serious cost containment program.) It would be more humane, economical, and rational simply to adopt a policy providing coverage to virtually everybody through an integrated financing and delivery organization that provides primary and preventive care as a part of a comprehensive benefit package.

A necessary condition for universal coverage is that everybody who can contribute to financing the system must do so. A system of universal coverage will not work if everybody is covered, but only those who voluntarily choose to do so pay for it. Such a system would be destroyed by free riders.

Universal contributions might be achieved in a variety of ways that are compatible with managed competition: (1) a requirement that employers and full-time employees jointly buy coverage ("employer mandate"), combined with payroll taxes on part-time employees and taxes on nonpoor nonemployed (such as early retirees), with revenues used to subsidize purchase of coverage for them through a HIPC; (2) a requirement that every household buy coverage through a HIPC or pay an equivalent tax ("individual mandate"), with subsidies to assist low-income households; and (3) payroll taxes or more broadly based taxes.

Managed Competition or Top-Down Global Budgets?

The level and growth of tax-supported and tax-subsidized national health expenditures is an appropriate object of public concern. Excessive growth in these expenditures, relative to other priorities, crowds out other programs important to our nation's future. Managed competition offers the most powerful force for reducing national health expenditure; that is, it makes economical decisions about health resource use in everybody's personal interest–an almost complete reversal of the cost-increasing incentives that drive the present system. However, as is the case with any other policy, there is no guarantee that managed competition will automatically hold spending growth to acceptable levels, even if implemented optimally as I have proposed here. Patients would be insured, thus not using their own money when demanding care. The health insurance and health services industries have an extensive history of market imperfections, not all of which will be corrected by managed competition. Very costly technologies might emerge. And directly or indirectly (through tax subsidies), government pays about half the bill.

What should government do if national health expenditure growth is excessive under managed competition? "Top-down," government-imposed global budgets are not likely to work well. Such global budgets today would have to be imposed on sectors such as hospitals, doctors, and pharmacies and enforced by price controls. The most plausible candidate for price controls would be Medicare payment methods and volume performance standards, which penalize sectors that increase volume by offsetting reductions in next year's prices. Such controls block efficiency-improving reallocations across sectors, such as doctors working harder to keep people out of the hospital. They create a "tragedy of the commons," penalizing the most economical doctors. They leave all of the cost-increasing incentives in place and even intensify them as providers struggle to maintain target incomes.

Top-down global budgets, if imposed on capitation rates of integrated financing and delivery organizations, would avoid some of the worst inefficiencies and disincentives. But they would focus the whole health services industry on political efforts to raise or maintain the ceiling as a percentage of gross national product (GNP). The British refer to the likely behavior as "shroud waving." Regulatory authorities are held responsible for the economic survival of the regulated entities. Hospital rate regulators are notoriously unwilling to force unneeded or inefficient hospitals to close. Insurance rate regulators are responsible for the solvency of insurers. So such regulation becomes cost reimbursement. Only impersonal market forces can close down unneeded, inefficient activities. Thus the history of such regulation is that it does not really lower the cost to consumers.

Moreover, regulatory authorities are not czars. They must observe the due process requirements of the Administrative Procedures Act and the Fifth Amendment. They must hold hearings, consider arguments, and base conclusions on evidence–all of which can be costly. Such global budgets would raise a whole maze of paradoxes and conundrums: Would they be equal per capita across states, and if unequal, on what basis? How would one deal with high- versus low-cost states? Could one justify locking Massachusetts and Arkansas, with a nearly twofold difference in per capita spending, into the same percentage rate of increase forever? Who decides?

Finally, for managed competition to work well, the managed care industry must make a great deal of investment in corporate restructuring, service expansion, and information and reporting systems, all of which are much less likely to appear attractive if government threatens to set prices and expropriate the return on investment.

How then should government respond? The answer is that the managed competition framework gives government a number of tools to use to influence the outcome. First, government could define as the "global budget" the lowest capitation rate in each HIPC, multiplied by the number of people residing in each HIPC area, added up over all HIPCs. These would be market-determined global budgets and would encompass all publicly supported and tax-subsidized national health expenditures. Government could then decide on a public policy that sets a target for this global budget relative to GNP. If the global budget grows faster than the target, the president and Congress should direct the National Health Board to develop and implement a set of targeted interventions designed to reduce health spending based on solid and current data. The list might include, for example, reducing covered benefits; raising copayments and deductibles (except for the poor); removing from coverage and inclusion in the uniform effective covered benefit package those drugs and other technologies of very high cost in relation to the benefits produced (with protection against tort litigation for providers who comply); antitrust action against local cartels; and possibly taxing the excess of premiums over the premiums of the low-cost bench-mark plan in each area. In other words, government should examine the causes of excess spending and apply specific remedies, rather than trying to sweep the problems under the carpet of a national global budget.

What Managed Competition Is Not

Managed competition is not a lot of things it has been called by people who do not understand it or who prefer central governmental controls to decentralized markets. (1) Managed competition is not a free market. A free market does not and cannot work in health insurance and health care. If not corrected by a careful design, this market is plagued by problems of free riders, biased risk selection, segmentation, and other sources of market failure. Managed competition uses market forces within a framework of carefully drawn rules. (2) Managed competition is not merely a "voucher" system (giving people a certificate and seeing if they can find insurance). In managed competition sponsors work actively to perfect the market. Everyone is given an opportunity to enroll. (3) Managed competition is not deregulation. It is new rules, not no rules. (4) Managed competition is not what we have had for the past 10 or 50 years.

(5) Managed competition is not forcing everyone into large clinic-style HMOs or other types of care they do not like. On the contrary, managed competition emphasizes the importance of individual (not employer) choice of plans. Many systems and styles would be able to compete effectively, including familiar solo doctor styles in some selective individual practice models. However, managed competition *does* make people bear the economic consequences of their choices. (6) Managed competition is not a

reduction in the quality of care. On the contrary, far more often than not, quality and economy in medical care go hand-in-hand. The correct diagnosis done promptly, and the appropriate procedure done by someone very proficient, without errors or complications, is best for the patient and the payer. Competing managed care plans would have powerful incentives to improve the quality of care.

(7) Managed competition is not blind faith in an untested economic theory. We know that some types of managed care can cut cost substantially. We know that there are wide variations in costs for many procedures and that the best producers have the lower costs. We know that when given responsible choices and information most people choose value for money. We know that HIPC-like arrangements work well. All of the pieces of the managed care/managed competition model are in actual successful practice somewhere. The challenge is to put these best practices together into one complete managed competition system. The rest is extrapolation based on generally accepted principles of rational economic behavior. All reform proposals must rely on similar extrapolation. (8) Managed competition is not just the latest buzzword that anybody should feel free to appropriate. It has been explained, developed, and debated in the academic literature for more than a decade.[26] Also, managed competition does not exist in Canada. Managed competition is not just a grab bag of ideas that sound good. It is an integrated framework that combines rational principles of microeconomics with careful observation and analysis of what works.

(9) Managed competition is not a panacea. Its authors do not claim that it can solve America's problems of racism, poverty, hopelessness, the frail elderly, and others. It cannot be counted on to bring comprehensive care to Nome, Alaska. Managed competition is aimed at care for the 90 to 95 percent of Americans whose medical needs can be met by programs that look like prevailing employment-based coverage. For most Americans managed competition can mean higher-quality care at a much lower cost, organized and delivered in a much more coherent and satisfactory way. Special programs, usually publicly sponsored, will be needed for special populations. If managed competition is successful, more public money will be available for them.

(10) Managed competition will not take until the year 2010 to transform health care financing and delivery in this country. It does not depend merely on the steady growth of existing prepaid group practices. In response to managed competition, thousands of hospitals and their medical staffs could quickly form integrated organizations and begin accepting capitation con-tracts. Many individual practice and network HMOs could expand very rapidly. And Blue Cross and/or Blue Shield plans must now have statewide preferred provider networks in existence in practically every state.

Managed Competition and the American Way

The managed competition idea attracted widespread support in 1992 in recognition of the urgent need to do something serious about costs and as an alternative to federal price controls. Paul Tsongas adopted it as his health platform during his presidential bid. In developing its proposal, the Bush administration began with a managed competition model.[27] Unfortunately, for political reasons, it withdrew some of the essential features needed to make it effective, especially the limit on tax-free employer contributions to employee health care and the powerful tax incentive needed to motivate small employers to join HIPCs. In April 1992 the 60-member Conservative Democratic Forum (CDF) in the House of Representatives announced its support for the Jackson Hole initiative. The CDF introduced a bill, the Managed Competition Act of 1992, in September 1992.[28] A similar bill was introduced in the Senate and drew bipartisan support. In October 1992 presidential candidate Bill Clinton said, "Managed competition, not price controls, will make the budget work and maintain quality."[29]

Managed competition is compatible with a variety of ways of financing universal coverage–from a tax-financed approach as in the proposal of California Insurance Commissioner John Garamendi and my 1977 proposal to the Carter administration, to an employer/employee mandate plus an individual mandate and subsidies for the nonemployed as in the Jackson Hole initiative, to an individual mandate.[30] Thus, it can appeal to liberals, whose main concern is universal access, and to conservatives, who have strong preferences for decentralized private markets and against centralized governmental power.[31]

Like any serious reform proposal, attempts to enact a national managed competition model will be controversial. Some of the most powerful congressional leaders distrust market mechanisms and prefer direct government price controls. Many of the specific features of managed competition will be opposed by private-sector interests seeking to hold onto the present market imperfections that favor them. However, recent months have seen considerable movement in the private sector toward support of real managed competition as it becomes apparent that government will be forced to act decisively to contain costs.

In the coming debate, managed competition has the important advantage of being compatible with strong American cultural preferences, as articulated by Alexis de Tocqueville, for limited government, voluntary action, decentralized decision making, individual choice, multiple competing approaches, pluralism, and personal and local responsibility.[32]

Notes

1. C. D. Weller, " 'Free Choice' as a Restraint of Trade in American Health Care Delivery and Insurance," *Iowa Law Review* (July 1984): 1351–92.

2. A. C. Enthoven, *Theory and Practice of Managed Competition in Health Care Finance* (1987 Professor Dr. F. de Vries Lectures, North-Holland/American Elsevier, 1988).

3. L. G. Goldberg and W. Greenberg, "The Emergence of Physician-Sponsored Health Insurance: A Historical Perspective," in *Competition in the Health Care Sector: Past, Present, and Future.* Edited by W. Greenberg (Germantown, MD: Aspen, 1978); and J. G. Smillie, *Can Physicians Manage the Quality and Costs of Healthcare? The Story of the Permanente Medical Group* (New York: McGraw-Hill, 1991).

4. Weller, " 'Free Choice' as a Restraint of Trade."

5. Goldberg and Greenberg, "The Emergence of Physician-Sponsored Health Insurance."

6. S. J. Singer, "Problems in Gaining Access to Hospital Information," *Health Affairs* (summer 1991): 148–51.

7. See P. Starr, *The Social Transformation of American Medicine* (New York: Basic Books, 1982); and R. Stevens, *American Medicine and the Public Interest* (New Haven, CT: Yale University Press, 1971).

8. W. G. Manning et al., "A Controlled Trial of the Effect of a Prepaid Group Practice on Use of Services," *The New England Journal of Medicine* (7 June 1984): 1505–10; and E. M. Sloss et al., "Effect of a Health Maintenance Organization on Physiologic Health,"*Annals of Internal Medicine* (January 1987): 1–9.

9. A. C. Enthoven, "Effective Management of Competition in the FEHBP," *Health Affairs* (fall 1989): 33–50.

10. P. M. Ellwood et al., "Health Maintenance Strategy," *Medical Care* (May 1971): 250–56.

11. S. Fleming, "Structured Competition within the Private Sector" (Unpublished memorandum within the Department of Health, Education, and Welfare, by the Deputy Assistant Secretary for Health Policy Development, Washington, D.C., May 1973).

12. A. C. Enthoven, "Consumer Choice Health Plan: A National Health Insurance Proposal" (Memorandum to HEW Secretary Joseph Califano, 22 September 1977), reprinted in R. D. Luke and J. D. Bauer, *Issues in Health Economics* (Rockville, MD.: Aspen, 1982), 509–32; and A. C. Enthoven, "Consumer Choice Health Plan: A National Health Insurance Proposal Based on Regulated Competition in the Private Sector," *The New England Journal of Medicine* (23 and 30 March 1978): 650–58 and 709–20.

13. C. Havighurst, "Professional Restraints on Innovation in Health Care Financing," *Duke Law Journal* 1978, no. 2 (1978): 304–88.

14. A. C. Enthoven, "Why 'Competition' in Health Care Has Failed: What Would It Take to Make It Work?" (The 1992 Clemens Lecture, St. John's University, Collegeville, Minnesota, 17 September 1992).

15. P. M. Ellwood, A. C. Enthoven, and L. Etheredge, "The Jackson Hole Initiatives for a Twenty-First Century American Health Care System," *Health Economics* 1 (1992): 149–68. The Jackson Hole Group is an informal collection of health industry leaders, public officials, and health services researchers that started meeting in the mid-1970s in Paul Ellwood's living room in Jackson Hole, Wyoming.

16. J. Newhouse, "Rate Adjusters for Medicare under Capitation," *Health Care Financing Review* (1986 Annual Supplement): 45–56.

17. For recent literature, see M. C. Hornbrook, "Risk-Based Contributions to Private Health Insurance," *Advances in Health Economics and Health Services Research* (Greenwich, CT.: JAI Press, 1991).

18. Newhouse, "Rate Adjusters for Medicare."

19. H. S. Luft, "Compensating for Biased Selection in Health Insurance," *The Milbank Quarterly* 64, no. 4 (1986): 566–89.

20. "Private Health Insurance: Options for Reform," House Ways and Means Committee on Health, 101st Cong., 2d sess., Committee Print 101–35 (Washington, D.C.: U.S. Government Printing Office, 1990).

21. Ellwood et al., "The Jackson Hole Initiatives."

22. Manning et al., "A Controlled Trial of the Effect of a Prepaid Group Practice."

23. D. Berwick, A. B. Godfrey, and J. Roessner, *Curing Health Care* (San Francisco: Jossey-Bass, 1990).

24. H. S. Luft, J. Bunker, and A. C. Enthoven, "Should Operations Be Regionalized?" *The New England Journal of Medicine* (20 December 1979): 1364–69.

25. C. L. Schultze, *The Public Use of Private Interest* (Washington: The Brookings Institution, 1977); and Enthoven, "Consumer Choice Health Plan."

26. A. C. Enthoven, *Health Plan: The Only Practical Solution to the Soaring Cost of Medical Care* (Reading, MA: Addison-Wesley, 1980); A. C. Enthoven, "Managed Competition in Health Care and the Unfinished Agenda," *Health Care Financing Review* (1986 Annual Supplement): 105–19; A. C. Enthoven, "Managed Competition: An Agenda for Action," *Health Affairs* (summer 1988): 25–47; Enthoven, *Theory and Practice of Managed Competition in Health Care Finance;* A. C. Enthoven and R. Kronick, "A Consumer Choice Health Plan for the 1990s: Universal Health Insurance in a System Designed to Promote Quality and Economy," *The New England Journal of Medicine* (5 and 12 January 1989): 29–37 and 94–101; and A. C. Enthoven and R. Kronick, "Universal Health Insurance through Incentives Reform," *Journal of the American Medical Association* (15 May 1991): 2532–36.

27. *The President's Comprehensive Health Reform Program* (The White House, 6 February 1992).

28. The Managed Competition Act of 1992, H.R. 5936, 102d Cong., 2d sess., 15 September 1992.

29. Press release, Clinton/Gore '92 Committee (Little Rock, Arkansas, 8 October 1992).

30. J. Garamendi, "California Health Care in the 21st Century: A Vision for Reform" (Sacramento, CA: California Department of Insurance, February 1992); and Enthoven, "Consumer Choice Health Plan: A National Health Insurance Proposal."

31. P. Starr, *The Logic of Health-Care Reform* (Knoxville, TN: Whittle Direct Books, 1992).

32. A. de Tocqueville, *Democracy in America* (New York: Alfred A. Knopf, 1948).

2

Macroeconomics and Health Care Spending: The Policy Implications of Delayed Response

Thomas E. Getzen

Introduction

The current health care debate is dominated by numerous slogans: cost containment, universal coverage, managed care, competition, price con- trols, *and many others. The health care debate raises difficult questions of public policy, and is hard for policymakers and others to understand because so many of the issues are interrelated. Proposed solutions, like the "managed competition" scheme of Alain Enthoven (see Chapter 1) are sensitive to a number of assumptions. The "building blocks" of a health care system (or other economic system) cannot be mixed and matched at will. Moreover, we are often confronted in health care (and also in other policy areas) with "stylized facts" that upon closer inspection may not be facts at all or at least may not have the obvious interpretation we often assume at first blush.*

One example is the increase in health care expenditures in the United States over recent decades. Has there been a substantial increase in health care expenditures, say, as a percent of GNP? The answer is "yes," but the reason for the increase may be both less obvious and in some ways simpler than we might think. That is the thrust of Thomas Getzen's paper. Getzen argues that we can explain much of the increase in health expenditures by examining two related variables, income and income growth. U.S. health care expendi- tures respond to both income and income growth but with a lag or delay. The result, according to Getzen, is that we perceive a crisis "late" in the cycle of adjustment, and, by the time we respond to it, our response is no longer appropriate.

One of the main examples of this is the U.S. experience with various regimes of cost controls. The United States has experimented with such controls since the 1970s, and Getzen traces the outcome of such interventions. Likewise, cost control regimes have been enacted by states, and Getzen reviews the results of these efforts.

The reading provides several lessons in the economics of policy analysis. The macroeconomic effects upon health care spending are demonstrated using regression analysis, and likewise the effects of alternative price control regimes are evaluated using regression analysis. The reading also compares U.S. health expenditures with those of other countries (and provides a host of caveats about interpreting such statistics). One of the main policy lessons is that one needs to know the causes of a problem before prescribing a solution.

Change takes time. It takes time for a legislature to make up its mind and vote for a new policy. Once the legislature has voted, it takes time for an agency to make up an implementation plan. Once the implementation process has been decided, it takes time to hire staff. Even after the program is up and running, every change in the environment requires adjustments that take time. If inflation makes it necessary to revise wage schedules, that change in personnel policies does not occur immediately, or in two weeks when the latest CPI (Consumer Price Index) is published, but only after a new contract is negotiated, which may be as much as several years later. Major policy decisions must sometimes be made years in advance and have effects for many years into the future. The responses of any organization to a change in the environment are thus always to some extent delayed and therefore potentially inappropriate. Only if the future has been perfectly anticipated with precisely accurate forecasts would every adjustment be smooth and error-free.

Health care is funded primarily through employer insurance pools and public taxation. Health employment is dominated by professional licensure rather than free market entry. Quality is a life-or-death matter, placing the patient's welfare directly in the hands of the hospital and the doctor. An unequal exchange of "trusting" dependence that the physician will act as an agent on behalf of the patient replaces informed purchases by sovereign consumers. All of these factors lead to heavy regulation, strong social sanctions on behavior—and a great resistance to change. Such a system cannot easily be altered by an administrator's decision; it requires the development of a broad public and political consensus as well. The need to change social perceptions, constructs of professional behavior, and regulatory structures means that organizational decisions take longer and last longer in health care than in most other sectors of the economy.

In this chapter we examine two main issues, (1) the determinants of national health care spending and (2) the effectiveness of public policy interventions to control spending. By analyzing expenditures in the United States over the period 1960 to 1990 and expenditures in other developed countries, we are able to see that aggregate per capita income is by far the most important determinant of the level of a country's health care expenditures. However, since it takes so long for the health care system to adjust, any changes in national income create changes in national health expenditures only after a *delay* or *lag*. Furthermore, delayed adjustment to unanticipated inflation may create sharp short-term fluctuations in spending. Lags in the health care financing system mean that any overall macroeconomic disturbances are apt to create undesirable state or federal budget deficits, labor shortages, and other visible problems that legislatures are urged to respond to. Our examination of the second issue–public policy–begins with a recognition that regulations do not arise from nowhere but are crafted in response to external forces, including macroeconomics. The same forces that change spending also tend to create new legislation. Since cost controls usually arise when delayed budgetary adjustment has made fiscal distress most acute, they are often followed by a period of improvement that would have occurred no matter what action was or was not taken. A superficial analysis of cost controls thus makes them seem very effective in reducing spending, while a more careful analysis shows that new regulations in 1971, 1978, and 1983 made only a small difference in actual spending relative to what would have been expected once the effects of the macroeconomic disturbances that helped to create them were factored in. The main theme of this chapter is that the dynamics of public spending, the adjustment of expenditures to economic growth and inflation over time, may be more important for health care policy than the level of spending at any one point in time.

Budgeting and Macroeconomic Adjustment

Every governmental entity must ultimately bring expenditures into line with revenues. This is difficult both practically and politically. Practically, the difficulty lies in forecasting revenues for the year to come when so many things are unknown and in forecasting expenditures when so many decisions are still to be made by line administrators over the course of the year. Such practical difficulties lead to random fluctuations–a variable budget surplus or shortfall that will net out on average. The political difficulties arise from the fact that in general people would rather spend than pay. This leads to a nonrandom upward bias or "structural deficit" that is often worked out indirectly in ways that are invisible to many voters. Maintenance is deferred until a crisis occurs, pensions are un- or underfunded, legislation is passed that uses mandates or guarantees to take expenditures "off budget," and so on. Most popularly, more money is printed, inducing inflation, which erodes the purchasing power of future generations. This inflation is like a tax that is used to pay off the deficit. It is important to recognize that adjustment is not automatic and takes some political will so it will frequently be put off until the last possible moment–a game of denial that makes adjustment more painful and, in the end, may destroy the credibility of government. Anything that hides the true costs of health care or is able to shift the bills to some future period and thus mask the painful consequences of overspending is apt to further delay the adjustment process.

There are two elements to budgeting: real and nominal. The real budget is the one stated in terms of the programs, labor, equipment, and the like that are actually required. One aspect of the technical process of budgeting is to convert these real resources into dollar amounts that can be authorized for expenditure. While an accountant might initially have thought that the "real" budget was the one stated in dollars, an economist familiar with inflation and money illusion would quickly convince him or her that it is people and supplies that count, not IOUs from a government bank. Given the ambiguity of dollars, it is natural to ask why budgets are not presented for approval in real rather than monetary terms. One reason is that there are so many different kinds of labor and supplies that some common measure–money–must be used to get an overall picture of the resources required. Another is that the employees and vendors want to be paid in dollars rather than mixed baskets of real goods (unless you happen to be in present-day Russia or post–World War I Germany, where hyperinflation has truly destroyed the value of money). In the next sections, we will examine the process of macroeconomic adjustment and response to forecasting errors in both real and nominal terms.

Adjustment to Inflation

It has long been recognized that inflation (that is, the rate of change in the general level of prices) is responsible for most of the nominal growth in health expenditures for all countries but has little real effect in the long run as both costs and revenues rise by similar percentages. Dividing income and expenditures by a price index such as the GDP deflator provides an estimate of real (constant-dollar) amounts that can be compared over time.[1] However, short-term (one- to three-year) budget commitments such as salaries and construction contracts are not made in terms of real resources but are stated in nominal currency amounts. Expected inflation is implicitly or explicitly factored in, but if actual inflation turns out to be less than anticipated, then the amount budgeted will be too large; that is, more generous than intended. Conversely, excess inflation will create a spending shortfall since the budgeted amount is worth less in real terms (supplies, labor, equipment) and will be a smaller percentage of the tax revenues than intended (excess inflation having made nominal tax receipts larger). Some adjustments will occur, but they will be incomplete and tardy since administrators are responding to unanticipated changes in the inflation rate—changes that are often not even fully perceived or measured until several months after the fact.

Consider table 2.1: budgets are made assuming that the number of nurses (the only input) will remain constant, inflation will be 5 percent, and wage contracts will be renegotiated each December. In 1997 everything goes according to plan, but in 1998 inflation is, unexpectedly, 12 percent. The excess unanticipated inflation in 1998 causes a temporary decline in "real" deflated health expenditures. The deficit is made up during the next year by a wage increase larger than the rate of inflation, so the "inflation effect" is entirely transitory.

Any anticipated changes in inflation are already built in to existing budgets and wage contracts. How can the effects of "unanticipated" changes be determined given that such changes are by definition not known in advance and hence do not exist in any set of government or commercial statistics? The best measure of unanticipated inflation would come from a comparison of actual price changes with the inflation forecasts used to create the budget. Yet such forecasts exist in no clear form. Is the appropriate comparison made with the forecast of 1 year prior, or 18 months, or 24 months? Since the Congressional Budget Office (CBO), Health Care Financing Administration (HCFA), commercial forecasters, and the American Hospital Association (AHA) all have slightly different expectations, which should be used as a standard? It is much easier to say that some forecasting mistakes were made by budgetary decision makers than to determine exactly what they previously thought inflation would be. Also, their expectations of the future changed from day to day and were different for different organizations and for different people within each organization. It is relatively easy to predict inflation. What is hard to predict is changes in inflation. McNees (1988) has shown that for any period longer than 24

TABLE 2.1 Nominal and Real Spending

	1996	1997	1998	1999
Price index	100	105	117	122
Nominal spending	$1,000	$1,050	$1,100	$1,220
Real spending	1,000	1,000	940	1,000

months (and many contracts do run longer), a simple forecast that tomorrow's rate of inflation will be the same as today's works as well as any professional forecast or econometric model. Therefore the change between last year's rate of inflation and this year's (ΔCPI_{0-1}) provides a good first approximation to "unanticipated" inflation.

The delay in the adjustment of health wages can be seen in equation 2.1.[2] This equation estimates the percentage rate of change in the U.S. Bureau of Labor Statistics health care wage index, 1973–1992 ($\Delta Wage$), as a function of inflation (CPI) and the year-to-year changes in the rate of inflation (ΔCPI) over the previous year and the year before that (Getzen and Kendix 1993).

$$\text{DWages} = .016 + .77\, CPI - .59\, \Delta CPI_{0-1} - .13\, \Delta CPI_{1-2} \quad N = 18,\ \overline{R} = .871\ (2.1)$$
$$\quad\ (.007)\ (.07)\qquad (.06)\qquad\qquad (.08)\qquad\quad \text{(standard errors)}$$

On average, health wages rose faster than inflation, at a rate equal to 77 percent of the annual CPI + 1.6 percent, but with a delay. The coefficient on ΔCPI_{0-1} indicates that 59 percent of the rise (or fall) in inflation from one year to the next was not incorporated into health wages until the following year, and 13 percent was still missing after two years. These lag coefficients indicate substantial contractual rigidity in health care wages.

The potential distortion from using nominal spending as a measure of real health expenditures can be seen in table 2.2, which reproduces data on Canada for the inflationary surge of 1972–1975. Real resources, as measured by the number of nurses employed, rose steadily throughout this period. Their wages were rising *but not as rapidly as the general price level*, so that dividing by the GDP deflator made health spending seem to rise very slowly. As a fraction of all nominal spending in GDP, health fell. This "decline" was a transitory illusion since nurse wages eventually had to be brought back up to the level of wages generally. When this was done, in 1975, the apparent jump in health expenditures was in fact just the removal of the earlier distortion.

To the extent that wages are slow to adjust, workers bear the brunt of the decline in real health spending. The number of workers and the quantity

TABLE 2.2 Nominal spending as a Measure of Real Health Expenditures

Canada	Inflation (%)	Employment		Ratio	Health Share of GDP
		Nurses	Total		
1972	5.6	152,005	8,447,000	.0180	7.3
1973	8.9	159,274	8,860,000	.0180	7.0
1974	14.4	168,530	9,220,000	.0183	6.9
1975	9.8	177,182	9,364,000	.0189	7.4

of supplies, equipment, food, and the like are also likely to decline as fixed expenditure budgets buy fewer real resources than anticipated. Some lag in spending appears to occur for most consumption expenditures. Deaton (1977) estimates that one-half of all unanticipated inflation is involuntarily left unspent by consumers in the U.S. and U.K. economies, although with a much shorter quarterly lag. The timing of financial reports can create similar fluctuations in measured spending even if there are no real differences. The inevitable slowness in accumulating national data from local units, changes in format, and other administrative difficulties usually cause some reports to be filed late. This tardiness will make the rate of growth in expenditures appear artificially low during a period of rising inflation, and artificially high during deflation. Over time, health care budgets and prices will catch up to the rest of the economy, reversing these short-run effects. Thus the long-run effect of inflation is neutral. Yet the short-run fluctuations from year to year created by fluctuations in inflation may be larger than the shifts caused by any other variables and may obscure these more fundamental causes unless the dynamic process of temporal adjustment is made explicit in the analysis.

Adjustment to Real Growth in GDP: The Decision Process

It is the real income of a nation that primarily determines how much will be spent on health care. Figure 2.1 shows the health expenditures of seven major countries over 25 years. More than 90 percent of the variation is due to one factor: per capita GDP (that is, average personal income). However, when we look at the growth in health spending from one year to the next, it appears to be entirely unrelated to the growth in per capita GDP (figure 2.2a). How can the discrepancy between figure 2.1 (income determines health spending) and figure 2.2a (income growth unrelated to growth in health spending) be reconciled? The answer lies in the dynamics of slow adjustment. Once we look at growth over the previous seven years, it again becomes clear that spending is caused by income (figure 2.2b). Looking at change over a very short period can be misleading. Just because you get paid on Thursdays does not mean that you will spend 10 times as much that day as on Wednesday or Friday. Analysis of income and spending *per day* might show almost no relationship, while an analysis based on a more appropriate temporal unit of observation, spending and income per year, for example, would show that they are closely related.

A similar distortion occurs if the geographic unit of observation used is too small. The health care spending of an individual is not related to that individual's income (for example, my son gets to have braces and see the pediatrician even though his income is zero) because health care is not

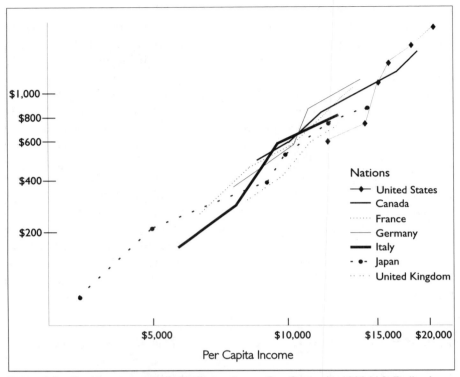

Figure 2.1   Real Income and Health Expenditures Per Capita (in 1990 U.S. Dollars), 1960 – 1985. *Source:* Data are original by author for this chapter.

really a transaction between individuals but a pooled transaction for a group and, more comprehensively, for societies as a whole (which usually means nations). Funds are shared among cities and provinces to purchase health care just as they are shared among members of a family, so that the relevant budget constraint is total national income, not regional or city or household income. In looking at individual health expenditures, medical need is the most important factor. However, it is only the allocation of the total across individuals that is determined by medical need, not how much is available in aggregate. If need determined how much a country spent on health, then people in Bangladesh, because they are sicker, would receive far more care than people in Boston. This is not the case because wealth, not illness, determines the level of national spending, and therefore the people of desperately poor Bangladesh must mostly do without medical care.

The set of decisions that defines the health system is best thought of as a sort of implicit long-term contract between the government, health professions, employers, and the public. Planned levels of national health spending are based on current expectations of what revenues will be in the coming year. Such plans also reflect decisions made in prior years, accu-

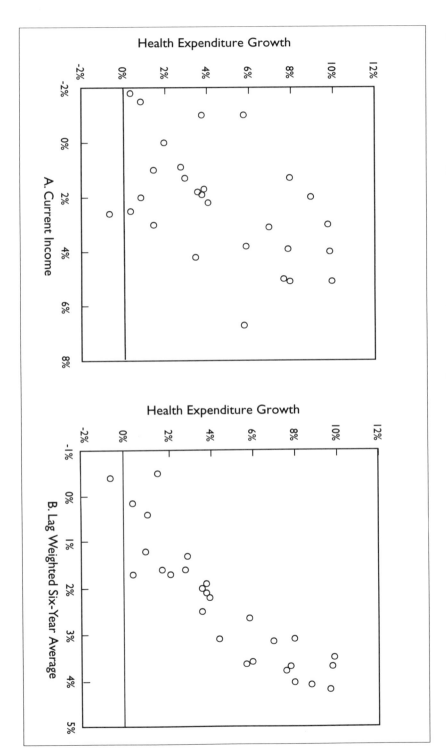

Figure 2.2   Annual Percentage Growth in Health Care Systems Per Capita.

mulated surpluses and deficits, and projections of the likely rates of change in wages and supply costs, technology, and so on. Actual spending will deviate from planned levels due to unanticipated inflation, recession, strikes, epidemics, and the like. Organizational dynamics (layers of management, degree of bureaucratic rigidity, forecasting capability) will determine how fast plans and actual expenditures can be adjusted to changing conditions. Inertia in individual behavior, organizations, financing mechanisms, and government policy creates variable delays between the time when decisions are made and when their consequences arise in national health spending. Empirically, this means that current health expenditures will be a delayed function of GDP growth over several prior years.

While the transitory distortions created by price fluctuations cause much of the short-run noise, it is real economic growth that determines the level of health care spending in the long run. The problematic issue is, how long is the long run? Eventually expenditures must be brought in line with revenues, but a deficit may accumulate for years before it becomes so painful that policymakers must make an honest reckoning. Consider the alternative patterns of real adjustment of health care spending to GDP indicated in figure 2.3. The scenario is the same throughout; a long-run average GDP growth rate of 3 percent is marked by rapid rises in the early years, recession in years 5 and 6, and then stabilization around the long-run average. In each case (A, B, C, and D), the elasticity of health expenditures with respect to GDP is the same over the long run, so that the final expenditure levels are identical, but the short-run adjustments are quite different.[3] With perfect anticipation of the future, shown in figure 2.3, panel A, the long-run growth of health expenditures is maintained from the beginning and held steady throughout. This minimizes adjustment costs, since there are no sudden changes in employment, number of hospital beds built, and so on. Panel B shows a modestly myopic policy: growth in health expenditures parallels growth in GDP in the early years but adjusts quickly to shifts with only a short lag. Panel C shows more foresight, and its long lags are more like the extreme smoothing of the first scenario. Growth of health expenditures in the early years is held down by the realization that current GDP growth rates are above the long-term average, and reductions are moderated during the recession since it is to be expected that normal growth will resume. While there are some adjustment costs under pattern C, they are clearly less than under pattern B. Panel D illustrates fatal optimism. The rise in health expenditures parallels the rapid rise in GDP for periods 1 to 4 and then continues to soar even after the recession has set in. Two periods of mounting deficits are required for reductions to begin, and at that point severe cuts must be made to restore financial equilibrium. Citizens of D pay dearly for their moments of blissful ignorance.

The interaction of imperfect information with organizational rigidity

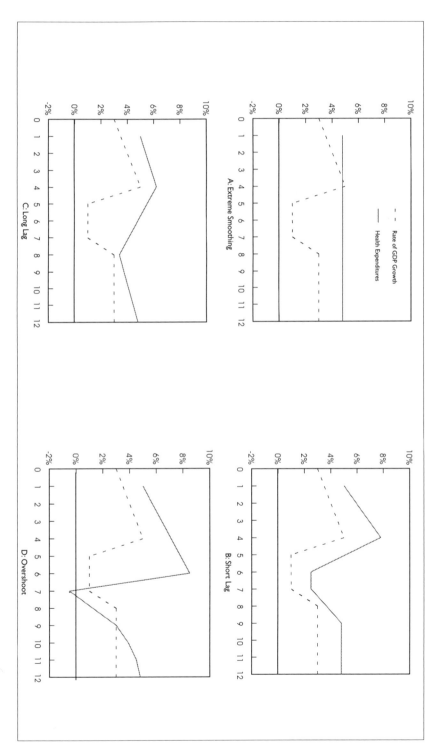

Figure 2.3 Hypothetical Responses to a Change in GDP.

(delayed decision effects) determines the dynamics of adjustment. A decision made five years ago not only has effects today (some intended, some unintended) but was made based upon the expectations that were then current. That is, today's spending depends upon the forecasts made five years ago as well as current, actual, and forecast income and inflation. Those old forecasts continue to influence outcomes for years into the future. In equation 2.2, the percentage rates of growth in real (deflated) U.S. health care spending for the years 1960 to 1991 were estimated as a function of income and inflation during prior years; that is, the coefficient with subscript "t-3" is .20, which means that for every additional 1 percent growth in GDP three years ago, there is an additional 0.2 percent growth in current health spending. This equation is used to forecast expenditures through 1999 and is presented graphically in figure 2.4 (Getzen 1990; Getzen and Poullier 1992).

$$\text{Health\$ \%} = 2.7\% + \overbrace{.14_t + .16_{t-1} + .22_{t-2} + .20_{t-3} + .30_{t-4} + .15_{t-5}}^{\textit{Income effects}} \overbrace{- .52\Delta_{0-1} - .19\Delta_{1-2}}^{\textit{Inflation effects}} \quad (2.2)$$

Similar regressions were run for different types of medical care, and the results showed that the time required for adjustment depended upon the category of spending (Kendix and Getzen 1994). "Average lag" is the average length of time required for one variable to create change in another. The average lag between GDP and health spending was 2.7 years. Hospital spending showed a longer lag, 3.0 years, and the estimated strength (elasticity) of the income effect was larger. Drugs, which are mostly purchased by consumers using their own money, showed a much weaker correlation with national per capita income and a short lag of just 1.3 years.

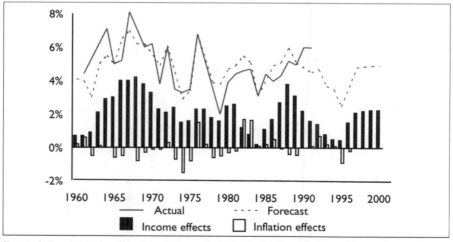

Figure 2.4   Annual percentage Change in U.S. Health Expenditures Econometric Forecast: 1960–1999.

Dental expenditures, which are also mostly consumer paid, showed weak income effects and an average lag. Nursing home expenditures, almost half of which are paid for by the government, showed very strong income effects and an average lag. The longest lag, 3.5 years, was for the construction expenditure category. Since planning and fund-raising for a new building take a long time, it is quite plausible that current construction spending would depend upon decisions and macroeconomic forecasts made many years ago.

Macroeconomic Adjustment in OECD Countries, 1960–1990

The single most pressing macroeconomic issue for national health care systems around the world for the last 30 years can be summed up in two questions: How and how well did each country adjust to the combination of rising prices and weak GDP growth that threatened the global economy in the mid-1970s? Macroeconomic policy was dominated first by the need to control inflation and subsequently by the need to restore productivity growth. These problems were made worse because they followed the 1960s, the decade when it appeared that prosperity would never end. The decision delay model expresses the length of time required to bring national health spending under control as a function of two processes: how long it takes for expectations of future GDP and prices to adjust, and how much rigidity is built in to the system due to *decision delays* (the length of time required for those revised forecasts to diffuse through the institutional structure and influence commitments for wages, labor supply, construction, insurance systems, benefit coverage, and the like).

Comparable data on health care spending and macroeconomic variables are available for the major industrial economies, which belong to an umbrella organization known as the Organization for Economic Co-operation and Development (OECD). Health expenditures increased rapidly throughout the 1960s, averaging 8.7 percent annually in the 17 largest OECD countries, more than 3 percent above the GDP growth rate of 5.5 percent. This 3 percent "surplus expenditure" was not sustainable and was not intended to be. It reflected a deliberate expansion of social spending to compensate for the lean postwar rebuilding years. The 1969–1973 rate, 1 percent to 2 percent above GDP growth, represents a more normal period. After 1973 the world changed, with GDP growth averaging only 2.5 percent for the next 15 years. At first, the oil price shock of 1973 looked like an aberration that would result in only a temporary dislocation, similar in magnitude to a mild recession. Yet the weakness of the global economy post-OPEC was much worse than expected. Prior to the second oil price rise in December 1973, the OECD had forecast 4 percent GDP growth for

1974. The actual result was a decline of 0.1 percent. The year 1975 was even worse, with a fall of 1.2 percent.

Macroeconomic expectations were not substantially revised until 1976. Thus for two years planners were steering toward a goal they would not reach. During this time, commitments were made to train new employees, build hospitals, and expand insurance benefits that would continue to raise costs for years to come. The extent of overspending on health was initially concealed by the lagging adjustment of health care prices, and it is likely that in 1974 the "actual" cost of maintaining the current level of health employment and facilities was understated by 5 to 10 percent in most countries. Then, having trained and hired additional nurses, physicians, and therapists, the cost-of-living increases required to restore the purchasing power of their wages forced total expenditures higher during the following year even if no new workers were added. If the 1.7-year average historical lag estimated in Getzen and Poullier's (1992) pooled time series analysis is added to the two-year lapse before global economic expectations were adjusted, it would imply that health care spending would not have come into alignment with the new economic realities until 1978.

The excess marginal growth in health expenditure above the rate of growth in GDP, 3 percent higher during 1960–1969 on average for the OECD countries, was abnormally large. Conversely, the 1983–1988 margin, just 0.5 percent, was abnormally small and for exactly the opposite reasons. In 1960, health ministers made plans to correct for two decades of deprivation; in 1980 they had to forcibly restrain an industry that for two decades had overindulged. In 1960, a new era of 5 percent GDP growth "forever" was being established; in 1983 many felt that back-to-back recessions confirmed the era of limits. It seemed that growth could, and had, ended. The dynamic is clear. Expectations and institutional arrangements are revised slowly. Many current spending commitments are a result of decisions made long ago when conditions appeared to be, and were, different. Therefore, each turning point creates an imbalance between the health system and its economic base (tax revenues or private insurance premiums) that is only corrected when it is averaged over the entire cycle.

The accumulation of excess spending can be clearly seen in figure 2.5; while GDP growth in Germany began to fall in 1970, the rate of increase in health spending remained high through 1975, and the bulge created by this period of immoderate growth was not worked off until deep cuts were imposed in 1982. Almost all countries made similar adjustments and changed the trend of health spending sometime during this period: Australia in 1979, Austria in 1982, Belgium in 1977 and 1984, Denmark in 1975, Finland in 1974 and 1978, Italy in 1975, Japan in 1976, the Netherlands in 1981, Norway in 1979, Spain in 1978, Sweden in 1981, Switzerland in 1978, and the United Kingdom in 1977 and 1982. Canada had already confronted a health care

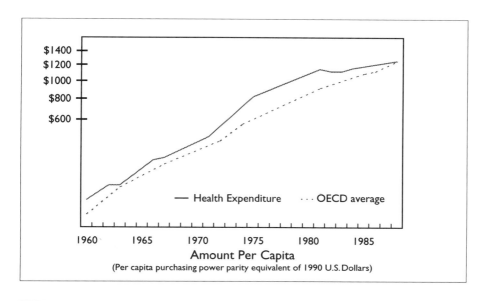

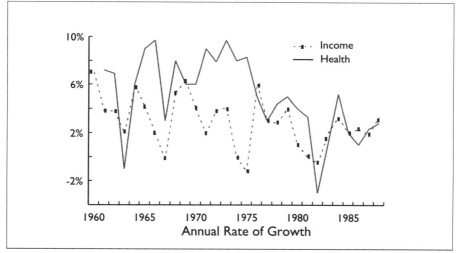

Figure 2.5   Health Care Spending in West Germany

cost crisis in 1971, substantially slowed the rate of health expansion then, and has not imposed significant additional controls since. In general, the longer a country waited to make adjustments, the larger and more difficult were the eventual cuts required to restore prudent fiscal balance. Sweden, for example, has had to continually tighten its belt throughout the 1980s. The United States has yet to make any substantial adjustment and thus faces a continuing crisis in health care funding of its own making.

The diversity in national response reflects historical and institutional characteristics of the health system in each country, most of which are still not well understood. Yet the problem–rising inflation and stagnating productivity–was global in origin and external to the health care sector. From a diagnostic point of view, it was not that health care spending rose too much but that GDP rose too little. It was difficult for health administrators to revise their expectations of economic growth and prices and then to incorporate this awareness of more limited means into fragmented and bureaucratic systems where decisions made many years ago in prosperous times were still being carried forward by organizational inertia.

Why Are U.S. Health Care Expenditures So High?

As can be clearly seen in figure 2.6, U.S. health expenditures are out of line with those of the other OECD countries. Based on an international comparative macroeconomic forecasting model, the United States spends about 30 percent more than it can afford given its per capita GDP. This was not always the case. In 1960, United States spending was below the international average (Getzen and Poullier 1991). The rapid and steady growth of the health care system brought the United States up to a "normal" level in 1972 and has forced spending ever higher since then. The United States has not adapted its health care system to the slower rate of economic growth that has prevailed since 1970. Many of the proposals and adjustments (mandated enrollment and benefits, "play or pay," postretirement funding and catastrophic insurance) are merely attempts to shift the burden and expand off-budget financing so that government spending can be cut without facing the pain of real reductions in labor or facilities. Such cost shifting can divert attention and mask the problem, but cannot solve the recalcitrant dilemma of excess spending in the face of limited revenue growth.

There are many likely reasons why health care spending has grown faster than income in the United States, and no single explanation can possibly encompass all of the responsible factors. However, the dynamics of delayed response suggests a line of reasoning that provides a plausible interpretation of events. The macroeconomic adjustments examined earlier have all been short to medium term, on the order of 1 to 10 years. Yet it is likely that some changes take more than 10, 20, or 30 years to adjust to. The Great Depression influenced the savings and consumption patterns of my parents and grandparents for a full generation. Building a new medical school expands the physician supply for the next 60 years. The consequences of a severe macroeconomic disturbance may last longer than our data series and thus not be directly observable. If the pattern of delayed response can be extrapolated from the medium run to the long run, then the excess spending that has characterized U.S. health care since 1970 can in large part be

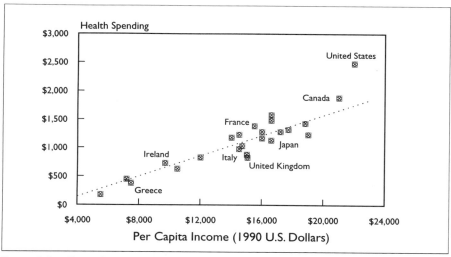

Figure 2.6   Cross-Sectional Analysis of 24 Countries, 1990.

attributed to a failure to come to grips with the end of the postwar boom and the passing of the United States' global economic hegemony.

Since 1945, the United States has enjoyed robust and sustained economic growth. In effect, by 1975 no one in the United States under the age of 30 had known anything else. Given a 30-year expansion interrupted only occasionally, there was no reason to change course. The situation was like that presented hypothetically in figure 2.3, panel C. The strong and lasting expectations that GDP growth would continue carried U.S. health care spending forward for the next 15 years. One by one, all of the easy answers are being tried. Eventually, the nation will bite the bullet and make real cuts in health care costs. Why would the United States persist in the denial of budgetary limits so much longer than other countries? In Europe and Japan, World War II had been a devastating reminder of the fragility of economic growth. In the United States, it created a boom. Small and medium-sized countries almost entirely dependent upon oil imports for energy were acutely aware of the potential threat. The United States struggled, and failed, to accept even a minor cutback in automobile driving and still has the lowest gasoline taxes in the world. In short, the United States thought it was different, that the limitations faced by other governments did not apply, for the quite simple reason that for the last 30 years those limits *had* not applied, the rules *had* been different. It is speculated here that only after the change in global macroeconomic reality has fully penetrated the public consciousness of ordinary Americans will there be sufficient political willpower for the United States to tackle the problem of health care costs.

Cost Controls in the United States

Health care expenditures are never "too high" or "too low" in some timeless absolute sense; rather they are out of line with the level of spending that can be afforded under current economic conditions. Yet there is a fundamental asymmetry in governmental control of health expenditures: it is easier to spend more than to spend less. Rhetorical conventions are revealing in this regard. When a higher level of spending is desired, we speak of "new initiatives" or "program expansion," but when expenditures are growing faster than desired, the word is "regulation." In fact, health expenditures in modern, developed economies are never unregulated (made evident by the thousands of pages of constantly changing rules published in the *Federal Register*), and regulation per se does not serve to either increase or decrease costs–it may do both, or neither, to different segments of the health care system. What policy analysts can observe is the effect of changing regulatory structures on the rate of growth in spending.

Why change regulatory regimes? Substantial public dissatisfaction is required to overcome bureaucratic inertia and craft a new set of rules and procedures. While occasionally a regulatory regime may be brought down by accumulated evidence of failure to achieve stated goals, it is much more common for a set of regulations to be made outdated because conditions have changed. In particular, the assumptions regarding inflation and economic growth used for budgeting may not be realized, creating sufficient fiscal tension to force a change. The preceding section of this paper examined how massive global macroeconomic disorders during the 1970s caused disruptions affecting health care financing in every OECD country. If corrective adjustments were made immediately, such disturbances would matter less. In practice, downward adjustment is an arduous political and administrative task that takes substantial time and governmental willpower (unless done indirectly through failure to keep up with inflation).

National Price Controls

Annual data on U.S. health expenditures are relatively complete and consistent from 1960 on. While pre-1960 data would be helpful to give a more comprehensive picture, the earlier period is less useful for analysis of regulation because the fraction of total spending accounted for by third-party insurance with government or employer financing was much smaller. However, initiatives such as the Shepard-Towner Act in 1922 and the Hill-Burton Act of 1946 were clearly designed to increase total spending and were based on a perceived strength in the economy. It is instructive to start the detailed examination of U.S. federal regulation with a similar but more recent act of expansion before considering the cost-control programs that followed.

The Medicare and Medicaid Expansion

Health expenditures in 1960 were $153 per capita, 5.25 percent of GDP. Over the next year, spending grew in real terms by 4.3 percent, significantly greater than the 1 percent rate of growth in per capita GDP, so the health share of national income was rising (see appendix table). Since these rates are essentially identical to those of the previous five years (4.3 percent health and .50 to 1 percent GDP for 1955–60), the pattern of expenditures and the regulatory structure within which they were generated appear to have been quite stable. While a substantial excess growth in health expenditures over the rate of growth in incomes may have been untenable in the long run, it evidently reflected a strong postwar political consensus that the nation could afford better medical care.

Economic growth accelerated in 1962, with real incomes growing by 4 percent. Strong growth was repeated in 1963, 1964, and 1965, causing a shift of expectations. Planners vowed that the economy would no longer be in thrall to business cycles that interrupted growth but that instead incomes and social welfare would expand smoothly and continuously for decades to come. In light of these revised expectations, a new and more expansionary medical care system was planned and implemented in the Social Security Act of 1965, with coverage for the elderly under Medicare and the indigent under Medicaid. However, no federal funds were actually spent until 1966 and no substantial amounts until 1967. The patterns of spending before and after reveal some differences: in the pre-Medicare period nonhospital expenditures were rising most rapidly, while from 1966 on, hospital expenditures rose most rapidly. An analysis of health employment (Kendix and Getzen 1994) shows that real labor resources followed a similar pattern, with health employment surging two years after passage of the act, in 1967, and tapering off over the next decade.

Health expenditures had already begun to rise in 1963 and 1964 even before Medicare and Medicaid were enacted. This demonstrates that costs may be ratcheted up (or down) within the current regulatory structure. It also shows that the underlying macroeconomic forces and changing public expectations that had been pushing up spending during the prior years were, in fact, the precursors of that legislation. Also notable is the delayed response to policy change. Although Medicare and Medicaid constituted the most massive revision of the U.S. health care system to date, it took two years before they had a discernible effect upon either employment or spending.

Economic Stabilization Program

Growth slowed toward the end of the 1960s, and a recession occurred in 1970. Unlike previous recessions, there was no moderation in prices. "Stagflation" had arrived and pushed aside the dream of endless prosperity. The inflation of the 1950s and 1960s, low and relatively constant, had been perceived as beneficial, a financial lubricant allowing for steadily increasing wages and a reduction in the burden of debt. This was different. "Cost-push" inflation threatened the whole economy with runaway wage and price increases that could destroy economic rationality. President Nixon stepped boldly in to impose shock therapy in the form of wage and price controls with the Economic Stabilization Program (ESP) on August 15, 1971. All prices were frozen for 90 days in Stage I, with rules and procedures for Stages II, III, and IV to follow. In retrospect, the U.S. experience from 1971 to 1975 served mostly to confirm the lessons learned from wage and price controls imposed by other governments around the world over the last 20 centuries. The underlying pressure created by excess monetary growth and the fiscal imprudence of waging a war without raising taxes could not be contained, controls were routinely evaded, and prices shot up as soon as controls ended in April 1974.

What is surprising is not that controls failed but rather the continuing misperception among some health policy analysts that they actually suc- ceeded in constraining health care costs. Three things supported the myth of effective ESP price controls in health care: (1) rudimentary comparisons of before and after that did not control for other factors showed a decline; (2) the dynamics of inflation were not understood and forecast values were left out of the explanatory equation; and (3) it is sometimes more convenient for policymakers to accept superficial evidence that policy works than to design more rigorous studies that show that it does not—who wants to pay an econometric consultant to find out that your legislative committee was ineffectual after all? The first study of ESP by Altman and Eichenholz (1976) was a simple descriptive presentation of data from the Bureau of Labor Statistics showing that the hospital daily room charge component of the CPI, which had increased 13 percent annually in the pre-ESP period, rose by just 6.6 percent in 1972.

Altman and Eichenholz are careful to point that many other factors are involved, that wage and price controls had many harmful distortionary effects, that costs per day and per discharge rose much more rapidly than daily room charges, that short-term restraint was not a valid indicator of long-run control, and that in the brief post-ESP period that they could observe (May 1974–February 1975) room charges rose explosively at a 21.7 percent rate. Yet most subsequent commentators focused on the one line in the study that said that ESP had reduced the rate of inflation in room and board charges by 50 percent and did not report the many caveats that hedge this figure nor any of the other comparisons made by Altman and Eichenholz that suggest much smaller effects.

Ginsburg (1976), who worked with the Price Commission responsible for implementing the ESP, provided a detailed look at the practical difficulties of writing and enforcing regulations. The problems of ambiguity in the definition of "price" (per item, per day, or per admission), crudeness in the construction of adjustment indexes, use of a "fudge factor" for technological change, arbitrariness in implementation, and the inability to provide a consistent and fair mechanism for determining exceptions became cumulatively worse as time went on. Price control rules were frequently changed, became administratively complex, and lost credibility. Ginsburg also pointed out that cost-based reimbursement insulated many hospitals from the effects of controls over charges and that hospital price inflation had already begun to decline even before controls were imposed. His econometric study using a pooled cross-section time-series approach with an ESP dummy variable did not show any significant effect on hospital costs or input use.[4] A broad study of many regulatory programs (CON, ESP, PPS, 1122) by Sloan (1981) found that ESP reduced costs by 2.0 to 3.3 percent per year, but his similar study with Steinwald (1981) found the effects of ESP to be insignificant. It is necessary to look at the data carefully and with an appreciation of what was going on before and after each year to resolve the issue of how well the ESP price controls worked.

Data for the period 1960–1990 are presented in the appendix table and graphically in figure 2.7. There was a clear moderation during 1971 in both nominal (9.3 percent) and real (3.5 percent) health care costs from the 1966–70 trends (11.1 percent and 6.1 percent, respectively). The dip was even more pronounced for the narrower measure–hospital costs–which grew 8.3 percent in 1970 but only 3.4 percent in 1971. In 1972, the rate of cost increase rose to 5.9 percent before falling down to the 3 percent range for 1973, 1974, *and* 1975. The latter is problematic for the hypothesis that ESP controlled cost since if this were the case then costs should have started to rise after the expiration of ESP in April 1974. A truer picture of actual ESP effects is obtained by comparing the actual rate of increase in health care costs with the predicted value (from the dynamic macroeconomic forecasting model given in equation 2.2). Examination of the residuals (that is, actual minus predicted for each year) shows that spending was indeed below expectations in 1971 and that ESP could have been responsible for this decline, but then ESP was in effect only for the last three months of the year. Spending in the year 1972 was slightly above expected, 1973 below, and 1974 and 1975 slightly above again, but none of these differences are significantly different from the residual variation in the series. Expenditure growth in 1973 and 1974 was low due to the delayed adjustment

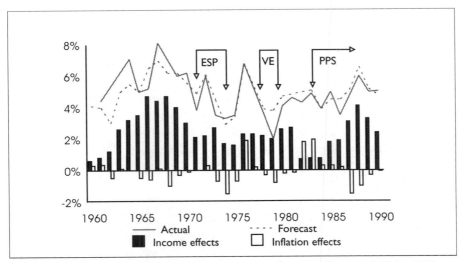

Figure 2.7   Annual Change in Health Expenditures, Actual v. Projected: 1960–1990.

of the health sector to the post-OPEC oil crisis. Expenditures in 1975 were held down not only by delayed adjustment to inflation but, more importantly, by the recession that caused declines in real GDP for 1974 and 1975.

Econometric estimates of the "ESP effect" depend upon whether the dummy variable is for 1972–1973, when ESP was applied for the whole year, or for 1971–1974, so that the years only partially under ESP are included. A regression on annual percentage rates of change in real expenditures from 1960 to 1990 with an ESP dummy variable (taking on the value of one for 1972–1973 and zero in all other years) indicates that, before controlling for lagged income and inflation effects, ESP appears to have reduced costs by 0.4 percent per year (see table 2.3, line 1) but that this estimate falls to 0.2 percent per year and is not significant once a fully specified dynamic model is used for evaluation (see table 2.3, line 5 and Getzen 1990). In sum, it is likely that the ESP had some effect on the rate of growth in health care costs but that its effect was small and that the evidence is inconclusive.

Voluntary Effort

After the expiration of ESP, health care costs were freed from external economywide controls, although they continued to be regulated by the rules of cost reimbursement. Medicare in particular attempted to constrain costs under administrative rule sections 223 and 1122 but without notable success. Then came a period of voluntary hospital regulation known as the Voluntary Effort or VE. Its genesis lay in President Carter's April 1977 legislative proposal to regulate hospital revenues. The hospital industry was strongly opposed to the measure and formed the VE coalition of providers and payers

TABLE 2.3   Time-Series Analysis of U.S. Health Care Cost Controls, 1961–1990

		ΔIncome	ΔInflation	Trend	ESP	VE	PPS	R^2
[1]	Naive Regulatory Comparisons				−.004 (.010)			.000
[2]	Naive Regulatory Comparisons					−.023 (.009)		.156
[3]	Naive Regulatory Comparisons						−.002 (.006)	.000
[4]	Macroeconomic Projection	1.17	−.62	.00045 (.00017)				.657
[5]	Macroeconomic Regulatory Evaluation	1.09 (.17)	−.58 (.11)	.00066 (.00025)	−.002 (.005)	−.012 (.006)	+.006 (.005)	.717

Note: Five regressions on the annual percentage growth in real per capital health expenditures in the United States, 1961–1990. "ΔIncome" is annual percentage growth in real per capita income (PCI) over the previous six years. "ΔInflation" is the change in the rate of inflation. "ESP" is a dummy variable for the ESP taking the value of 1 for the years 1972–1973. "VE" is the dummy for the VE, 1978–1979, and PPS is the dummy for Medicare's Prospective Payment System, 1984–1990. R^2 adjusted for degrees of freedom. (Standard errors) in parentheses.
Source: National Health Expenditure data, HCFA Office of the Actuary.

in December 1977. Flyers and buttons were printed up to promote voluntary efforts to reduce the rate of cost increases. A national target, that cost increases be held to 2 percent less than the previous rate or 3 percent above the rate of inflation (the 1978 target was 13.6 percent), was promulgated. More buttons and flyers were printed as industry representatives lobbied Congress. After several modifications by the legislature, a new version of the Carter bill was voted on by the House in November 1979 and decisively defeated, removing the force that had sustained the VE.

Such an incidental story of voluntary regulation would normally have been forgotten and relegated to footnotes, particularly since the effectiveness of even strongly supported legislation with comprehensive administrative regulations has been difficult to establish. Yet the story lingers because claims of its effectiveness were uncritically accepted even by some industry critics. The reasons for the persistence of the impression that VE worked is that hospital price increases did moderate in 1978 and 1979, the claims of VE's effectiveness were loudly voiced, and these claims were cited by Congress in the debate that led to defeat of the legislation. Davis et al. (1990) argue that the industry was sufficiently frightened by the threat of regulation to actively reduce costs in 1978 and 1979 but that cost increases continued once the threat of regulation was removed by legislative defeat in November 1979. While it is difficult to understand how flyers and buttons could accomplish what administrative rules with the force of law and government reimbursement behind them could not, this political reaction analysis might be plausible—until, that is, the data from the period are examined more carefully.

Hospital costs had already begun falling in 1977 before VE. The rate of increase was still lower in 1978; indeed it was lower than the target (12.8 percent versus a target of 13.6 percent). Even believers at that time referred to the American Hospital Association's luck because the VE program, which was still mostly concepts and exhortations, could not have had time to directly affect hospital behavior. The financial reports upon which the 1978 percentage increase figure was based came mostly from hospitals with July 1, 1977–June 30, 1978 fiscal years. The national VE committee had not been convened until December 1977. Even if hospital planners got right on the job, they would have had to work on the fiscal year 1979 (FY79) budget. For hospitals on a calendar year, the FY78 budget would already have been up and printed. For hospitals on a June 30 budget year, FY78 was already half over. Once the budget is drawn up, allocations made, and labor hired, the ability of administrators to reduce expenses in the current year is very limited.

Luck was but one factor in the fortuitous "success" of VE. The main reason that nominal expenses came in lower than expected was that hospital wages and supply prices, since they lag the CPI, had not yet caught up with the surge of inflation that had begun in 1977. There was no decline in hospitals' use of real inputs (labor FTEs [full-time equivalents], supply items), just a delay in price adjustment that made them temporarily cheap relative to the CPI (just as in the example of Canadian health spending and nurse employment presented earlier). In 1979, however, there was a real decline. Nominal expenditures per capita rose by only 10.8 percent, half a percent less than the year before and, deflated to remove the effect of inflation, rose by just 1.8 percent. This drop placed spending almost 2 percent below the predicted value. Is this the real VE effect? Probably not. VE was a program to control *hospital* expenditures and was promoted by the hospital industry. Therefore, the effect of VE should have been greatest in the hospital sector, so hospitals would have had a lower rate of increase than the nonhospital spending that was not under VE.

In fact, the opposite was the case: nonhospital expenditures rose more slowly in 1979, less than half the rate of hospital expenditures. Therefore, even though a dummy variable for the years 1978–1979 has a coefficient that is negative (−.012) and "significant" (standard error = ±.006) (table 2.3, line 5), it is not credible to accept this coefficient as a reasonable estimate of VE effects for these three reasons: (1) nominal costs were falling prior to

VE, (2) the timing of hospital fiscal reporting makes it implausible that an effect only just begun in December 1977 could significantly affect FY78 results, and (3) reductions were greater in the nonhospital costs that were *not* targeted than in the hospital costs that were under VE.

The explanation for the persistence of the story of VE effectiveness lies not only in its superficial appeal (a simple before-and-after comparison that showed a decline the public and legislators could see and understand) but also in the active involvement of many analysts as participants–an involvement that may have made it hard for them to accept that so much well-intentioned effort could have had so little ultimate effect on outcomes, outcomes that were in fact largely determined by external macroeconomic forces. Davis et al.'s (1990) account is imbued with the detail and drama that comes from the perspective of a player on the field of politics. It may have been difficult for participants to see the forest for the trees and to realize that no matter how many trees they cut or saved from cutting, the size of the forest would still depend mostly on sunlight, rainfall, and other macroconditions.

Prospective Payment System with Diagnostically Related Groups

The implementation of Medicare's prospective payment system (PPS) based on diagnostically related groups (DRGs) for hospital care in October 1983 sent shock waves through the U.S. health care system and the academic research community as well. There are more than 500 papers evaluating the effects of PPS, enough that a consensus can now be reached on most issues but also enough to guarantee that dissenting studies exist for any specific topic. Some of the expected effects were quickly realized, length of stay declined, and there was a real reduction in input use as hospital employment declined. Contrary to expectations however, the number of admissions fell. The change in practice and admitting patterns was diffuse so that non-Medicare patients were also affected, albeit by a lesser amount. There was a substantial regulatory offset as more patients were given home care and outpatient treatment than inpatient stays. However, the extent of cost shifting to private payers was not as great as anticipated and may have been negligible in the long run. PPS was clearly responsible for a significant reduction in the rate of increase in Medicare part A (hospital inpatient) expenses and in hospital expenses generally; yet it failed to achieve global cost-containment goals as total health expenditures per capita continued to rise at historically high rates (Levit and Freeland 1988). Nor did PPS reduce federal health spending despite the fact that deficit reduction was identified by most authors as a major reason for implementing PPS and that significant savings in specific programs and components are identified in several studies. In 1985, 16.9 percent of the $407.2 billion spent on health care was paid for by the federal government, and by 1990 the fraction had actually increased to 17.7 percent of the $643.4 billion spent in that year. The paradox of declining Medicare part A expenditures and increasing total federal expenditures is explained by the shift to part B outpatient and to non-Medicare services like nursing homes that receive substantial federal funding through each state's Medicaid program and the like.

Estimation of a PPS effect using a 1984–1990 dummy variable in the dynamic time-series model (table 2.3, line 5) yields a coefficient that is positive (.006 that is, 0.6 percent higher annual increase in costs per capita) and nonsignificant (t=1.2). The estimate is not particularly sensitive to the period chosen or allowance for "early" versus "mature" regulatory effects. Most of the residuals during this span of time are small and positive. In sum, it is necessary to conclude that PPS had a wide range of substantial effects but failed to reduce the rate of increase in total or federal health care costs. A similar pattern of strong localized effects that failed to add up to any global cost containment is reported by Mitchell, Wedig, and Cromwell (1989) for the Medicare physician fee freeze.

State Rate Regulation

The states of the United States have served as "laboratories of government" under a federal system. The collision between rising costs and straggling revenues during the 1970s provided the impetus for an outburst of state regulatory activity (Davis et al. 1990, 219). Prior to the passage of Medicare and Medicaid, only one state, Indiana, had a health care cost regulation agency. The first of the new wave was New York, which passed legislation in 1969 giving the Department of Health authority to set rates for Medicaid and private payers as well as Blue Cross. Implementation was begun in 1970, although it is generally accepted that the program did not effectively begin to operate until rate formulae were developed and staff were trained in 1972. Rate-setting programs were started in Delaware, Massachusetts, and Rhode Island in 1971; in Arizona, Missouri, and Wisconsin in 1972; in Arkansas, Connecticut, Oregon, and Washington in 1973. By 1975, more than 25 rate-setting programs could be counted.

The methodology for rate setting, despite variations in form and political functioning, has always been to take historical costs and trend them forward. This is known as "prospective reimbursement" since the rate is set in advance of actual service delivery. Under the previous "retrospective" cost-reimbursement methodology used by Medicare and Blue Cross, the rates depended upon actual costs and were not finalized until after the period had ended and a full-cost audit had been completed. In 1980, an influential study in the *New England Journal of Medicine* (Biles, Schramm, and Atkinson 1980) presented graphs showing a lower rate of cost increase in regulated than in nonregulated states, and the Government Accounting Office (GAO) issued a report concluding that regulation could moderate hospital costs (GAO 1980). Numerous studies followed, a sufficiently large number, in fact, that major review articles were prepared by Sloan (1983), Morrisey et al. (1984), and Eby and Cohodes (1985). Studies of state regulation waned after this as attention turned to the nationwide PPS hospital reimbursement plan implemented by HCFA in 1983.

The evolution of studies of state rate regulation follows a common path, from simple tests of straightforward assertions to more detailed assessments of a complex reality. The first studies, exemplified by Biles, Schramm, and Atkinson (1980), compared rates of increase before and after rate regulation or between states with and without regulation. The next stage was to use multiple-regression models to control for potential confounding factors such as state per capita income, physician supply, political structure, and the like (Sloan 1981; Morrisey 1984). Attention was broadened to include multiple measures of outcome (cost per capita or per admission versus per day) and potential side effects (quality, hospital finances, and closure). Closer examination showed that *regulation* was a term covering a wide variety of state activities, and that even within the same agency, the regulatory approach would vary as conditions changed due to an election or a fiscal crisis. By 1985, the consensus among researchers was (1) that state rate regulation did reduce the rate of hospital cost increases but (2) not by as much as early proponents suggested and (3) that the development of regulation took time so that only mature programs were likely to be effective, (4) that motivation and political will mattered more than the language of the legislation, and (5) that regulatory willpower often arose out of a perceived crisis due to rising costs in states where spending was higher than average to begin with, and hence (6) that these results could not necessarily be generalized to project what would have happened in other states facing different fiscal conditions or to what might be the effect of similar regulations in the future.

A major defect of most existing studies of state rate regulation is that they look at too short a time period and do not account for lags in the adjustment of the health care sector to the rest of the economy. Incomplete adjustment to inflation and recession is apt simultaneously to exert pressure on legislatures to "do something" about excessive health care costs and force future spending downward, giving rise to a spurious correlation between regulation and the rate of increase in costs. The history of the state of Washington from 1965 to 1980 provides a particularly clear example of how macroeconomic difficulties can bring about regulation.

In 1965, Washington was a robustly growing state with above average per capita income (PCI), 108 percent of the U.S. average (figure 2.8). Growth continued in 1966 and 1967, with PCI rising above 110 percent of the U.S. average, and state population growing 3 percent a year. Growth slowed in

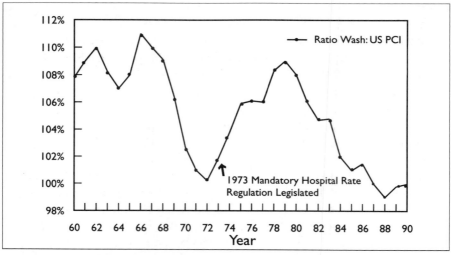

Figure 2.8   Washington State per Capita Income Relative to U.S. per Capita Income.

1968 and again in 1969 before recession caused real PCIs to fall in 1970 and 1971. Instead of migrating in for high-paying jobs in the aerospace industry, workers left to find employment elsewhere. In 1972, state population declined and PCI had fallen to meet the U.S. average. The fiscal crisis created by the loss of tax revenues led to the passage of legislation in 1973 that created a mandatory state Hospital Rate Review Commission, which was among the toughest in the nation. In 1974, hospital expenditures per capita declined 2.8 percent in real terms. The question, however, is whether the decline in hospital costs was due to the newly created rate review commission or to the lagging effects of the sharp 1970–1971 state recession?

Using a dynamic model that incorporates lagged income and inflation effects provides an unambiguous answer: mandatory state rate controls in Washington did not reduce the rate of increase in hospital costs relative to what would have been expected without controls. All of the decline in hospital costs was a delayed response to the severe state recession, not regulation. Eventually, the state legislature came to the same conclusion, and the hospital rate council was disbanded. If the economists responsible for analyzing the program had been able to take a longer view, they would quickly have realized that controls did not cut costs in Washington, since the level of per capita hospital expenditures was essentially unchanged relative to projected levels or the U.S. average in 1990 compared to 1973.

The ineffectiveness of rate controls in Washington does not mean that no state regulatory program can reduce costs. The Maryland cost-containment legislation, passed without the pressure of a severe fiscal crisis, did reduce costs. Prior to implementation, Maryland costs were 111 percent of the U.S. average, and by 1990 they had fallen to just 95 percent of the U.S. average. The controls in New York, Massachusetts, and Connecticut may have had some impact, but the evidence is less clear. What can be learned from a more careful examination of the data is that one-half or more of the regulation effect reported in the initial comparisons was due not to the enactment of regulatory controls but was instead a delayed effect of the adverse macroeconomic conditions that gave rise to regulation.

Potentially just as informative as the experience of the states with legislated cost containment are those where regulatory agencies failed or never came into existence. Colorado passed a hospital cost-containment bill in 1977, and commissioners were appointed on October 1 (Klapper and Harrington 1981). Brutal legislative hearings in 1979 made it clear that the commission had lost most of its support, and all of the original commissioners resigned before the end of the year. New commissioners made a valiant attempt to recruit staff and justify their existence, but in February 1980 the state legislature terminated the agency. Klapper and Harrington attribute the demise of the Colorado Hospital Commission to the opposition from hospitals, a changing political climate, and the fading pressure for federal regulation. They neglect to mention an underlying cause of antiregulation sentiment in Colorado—a state economy growing by more than 8 percent in 1978 in real terms and more than 6 percent in 1979, far outpacing the national economy. Curtailment of hospitals is inconsistent with the expansionary mood generated during the boom years. How can a state build the will to cut costs when everybody has a job and the main problem is how to accommodate all of the newcomers?

This question is not entirely rhetorical, as the experience of California after the passage of Proposition 13 in 1978 placing strict limits on the ability of the state to raise revenue indicates. California has had a mandatory hospital data-reporting program since then, but with no authority to set rates or review budgets, it would not generally be considered to have significant regulatory cost controls. Those constraints have come directly from the fiscal side and have applied to schools, social welfare, and other programs as well as to hospitals. In 1974, California hospital spending per capita stood at 110 percent of the U.S. average. Since then, the cost containment imposed by revenue constraints has had a fiscal effect equivalent to a cumulative reduction of -20 percent relative to projected annual rates, and by 1990 California hospital costs per capita had fallen to just 91 percent of the U.S. average. Given the current condition of the economy in the Golden State, one expects that it has dropped even more by now. The example of California demonstrates that sustained reductions in spending can be brought about through administrative action in the absence of any enabling hospital cost-containment legislation, as long as the prerequisite fiscal and political conditions are present.

Summary

The argument and empirical findings of this paper can be summarized in four key points:

1. The major determinants of total health spending are macroeconomic (inflation, GDP).
2. Health care adjusts slowly to changes in macroeconomic conditions.
3. These delays in response create pressures for regulatory change.
4. Many of the effects associated with the passage of health care cost-control regulations are actually delayed effects of inflation and recession.

A theory of health care cost regulation must start with the realization that shared costs, and governmental expenditures in particular, are always regulated even when no external regulatory agency is in operation. Furthermore, costs can be ratcheted up or down within the existing framework by making administrative procedures tighter or looser even if no legislation has been passed. Regulation is an integral component of health care system management in a modern nation. It is part of the process, not an external shock. What can be evaluated is not regulated versus unregulated health care but a change in the regulatory regime. To do so, one must first ask why the change took place and why at this particular time. Usually cost-containment measures are passed because a sufficiently large portion of the body politic feels that costs are too high. Since there is no absolute standard, what that means in practice is that revenues are less than had been planned for, expenses are greater than planned for, or some fundamental shift in political consciousness has forced plans themselves to change.

Changing macroeconomic conditions are a major reason for the disruption of plans. If corrective action could be taken immediately, such deviations would matter less. In practice, adjustment is delayed so that over or underspending in the long run tends to occur whenever significant turning points come about. Worse, the delays are not symmetric. Downward adjustment (spending less and raising taxes) is harder and therefore takes longer than upward adjustment (spending more and reducing taxes). Fiscal pressures cause deficits to build up painfully over time, not surpluses. If the necessary adjustment of spending is too large to be handled by the buffers within the existing government budgets, a crisis may occur that brings about a legislative mandate for cost control.

Politicians, analysts, and the public need to understand the dynamics by which health care adjusts to the economy if any real progress is to be made in controlling costs. Careful examination of the history of health care spending in the United States and other countries is a necessary antidote to the process by which every failure to live within a budget is blamed on technology, partisan politics, an aging population, AIDS, or some other factor that "is not my fault." A rigorous analysis of the results of previous regulatory efforts reveals that there are no magic answers, that all of the easy solutions have been tried and found wanting. Any real reduction in health care costs is going to hurt someone and probably will hurt most of us. Yet it is necessary and overdue. Excess spending has bought more drugs and therapists and diagnostic equipment for the U.S. public–it has not bought better health. A positive theory of change for the health care system can be the grounds for effective action and a way out of persistent denial and budget deficits.

Appendix: U.S. Health Expenditure and Macroeconomic Data

Year	Health Spending	Share of GNP	Hospital Income (real 1990 $ per cap)		Inflation (GNP deflator)
1950	$458	4.4 %	$141	$10,392	
1955	$516	4.4	$172	$11,743	
1960	$638	5.3	$218	$12,117	1.7 %
1961	$666	5.4	$232	$12,228	1.0
1962	$697	5.5	$239	$12,681	2.2
1963	$738	5.7	$256	$13,013	1.5
1964	$792	5.9	$268	$13,519	1.6
1965 Medicare	$834	5.9	$281	$14,124	2.6
1966 Medicaid	$877	5.9	$302	$14,769	3.5
1967 enacted	$951	6.3	$339	$15,026	2.8
1968	$1,015	6.6	$369	$15,492	5.0
1969	$1,072	6.8	$393	$15,718	5.4
1970	$1,135	7.3	$426	$15,490	5.7
1971 ESP	$1,174	7.5	$441	$15,730	5.6
1972 " "	$1,243	7.6	$468	$16,337	4.8
1973 " "	$1,283	7.5	$488	$17,023	6.5
1974 " "	$1,322	7.9	$517	$16,777	8.9
1975	$1,364	8.3	$538	$16,404	9.9
1976	$1,455	8.5	$579	$17,043	6.3
1977	$1,526	8.6	$608	$17,660	6.7
1978 VE	$1,581	8.6	$630	$18,398	7.3
1979 " "	$1,610	8.6	$653	$18,647	8.8
1980	$1,677	9.1	$690	$18,398	9.1
1981	$1,756	9.5	$727	$18,572	9.6
1982	$1,833	10.2	$769	$17,925	6.4
1983	$1,924	10.5	$795	$18,396	3.9
1984 PPS	$1,998	10.3	$812	$19,473	3.7
1985 " "	$2,100	10.5	$836	$19,946	3.0
1986 " "	$2,183	10.7	$863	$20,307	2.6
1987 " "	$2,278	10.9	$895	$20,816	3.2
1988 " "	$2,414	11.2	$937	$21,548	3.3
1989 " "	$2,537	11.6	$979	$21,885	4.1
1990 " "	$2,666	12.2	$1024	$21,867	4.1

Appendix: U.S. Health Expenditure and Macroeconomic Data (Continued)

Year	ΔHealth	Fitted	Residual	ΔIncome	ΔInflation
1960	(Macroeconomic Projections)			0.6 %	−0.9 %
1961	4.3 %	4.4 %	−0.1 %	0.9	−0.7
1962	4.8	3.8	1.0	3.7	1.3
1963	5.9	5.6	0.3	2.6	−0.8
1964	7.2	6.2	1.1	3.9	0.2
1965 Medicare	5.3	5.7	−0.4	4.5	0.9
1966 Medicaid	5.2	6.5	−1.2	4.6	0.9
1967 enacted	8.4	7.6	0.8	1.7	−0.7
1968	6.8	5.6	1.1	3.1	2.2
1969	5.6	6.5	−0.9	1.5	0.4
1970	5.8	5.5	0.4	−1.4	0.3
1971 ESP	3.5	5.1	−1.5	1.5	−0.1
1972 " "	5.9	5.3	0.5	3.9	−0.8
1973 " "	3.2	4.2	−0.9	4.2	1.8
1974 " "	3.0	2.8	0.2	−1.4	2.4
1975	3.2	2.9	0.3	−2.2	1.0
1976	6.6	6.8	−0.1	3.9	-3.6
1977	4.9	4.7	0.2	3.6	0.3
1978 VE	3.6	4.5	−0.9	4.2	0.7
1979 " "	1.8	3.4	−1.6	1.4	1.5
1980	4.2	4.1	0.1	−1.3	0.3
1981	4.7	4.6	0.1	0.9	0.5
1982	4.4	5.4	−0.9	−3.5	−3.2
1983	4.9	4.7	0.2	2.6	−2.6
1984 PPS	3.9	3.5	0.4	5.9	−0.1
1985 " "	5.1	4.0	1.1	2.4	−0.7
1986 " "	4.0	4.4	−0.4	1.8	−0.4
1987 " "	4.4	4.0	0.3	2.5	0.6
1988 " "	6.0	5.7	0.3	3.5	0.1
1989 " "	5.1	5.0	0.0	1.6	0.8
1990 " "	5.1	4.3	0.8	-0.1	0.0

Source: National Health Expenditure Data from HCFA Office of the Actuary, 1992 and projections.

Notes

1. GDP stands for Gross Domestic Product and is the standard measure of national income used by government, economists, and statistical agencies. The GDP deflator is a price index similar to the CPI but applies to price levels for the national economy as a whole, not just to consumer spending.

2. Regression is a statistical procedure used to estimate the relationships between one variable, the dependent variable (here, the annual percentage change in the wages of health care workers), and some other variables. The best-fitting equation for the given set of data is calculated. The variable coefficients are the numbers by which that variable would be multiplied to predict the value of the dependent variable for that observation and thus is a measure of the correlation between them. However, the correlations between all the variables are all estimated at the same time to provide the best fit. The coefficient of determination, R^2, is usually interpreted as the percentage of variation in the dependent variable *explained* by the other variables. Since a different set of data would give a different estimate of the relationship between the variables, it is usual to report the *standard error* of each estimate. This measure, analogous to the standard deviation of a mean, provides a confidence interval; under certain assumptions, the true value of the variable coefficient would be within one standard error ($\pm$1SE) of the estimated coefficient two-thirds of the time. In this example, wages are estimated to go up by (77% $\pm$ 9%) of the CPI. The variable coefficient divided by its standard error is known as its t-statistic. If the coefficient is more than two standard errors away from 0, it is usual to say that the variable is *statistically significant*.

3. "Elasticity of health expenditures with respect to GDP" is the terminology economists use to mean "the percentage change in health expenditures for each 1 percent change in GDP."

4. A "dummy variable" is a variable that takes on only the values 1 or 0, representing, respectively, the presence or absence of some factor. In this case, the dummy variable was set equal to 1 for the period from August 1971 to April 1974 (representing the presence of the ESP program) and 0 for all other months.

References

Altman, H., and J. Eichenholz. 1976. "Inflation in the Health Care Industry: Causes and Cures." In *Health, a Victim or Cause of Inflation,* Edited by M. Zubkoff. New York: Prodist, 3–30.

Biles, B., C.J. Schramm, and J. G. Atkinson. 1980. "Hospital Cost Inflation under State Rate-Setting Programs." *New England Journal of Medicine* 303: 664–68.

Davis, K., G. Anderson, D. Rowland, and E. Steinberg. 1990. *Health Care Cost Containment.* Baltimore: Johns Hopkins University Press.

Deaton, A. 1977. "Involuntary Savings Through Inflation." *American Economic Review* 67: 899–910.

Eby, C., and D. Cohodes. 1985. "What Do We Know about Rate Setting?" *Journal of Health Politics, Policy & Law* 10: 299–327.

Government Accounting Office [GAO]. 1980. *Rising Hospital Costs Can Be Restrained by Regulating Payments.* U.S. Comptroller General, Report to Congress, 14 September 1980. Washington, D.C.: U.S. Government Printing Office.

Getzen, T. E. 1990. "Macro Forecasting of National Health Expenditures." In *Advances in Health Economics and Health Services Research.* Edited by L. Rossiter and R. Scheffler. Greenwich, CT: JAI Press, 27–48.

———. 1992. "Medical Care Price Indexes: Theory Construction and Empirical Analysis of the U.S. Series, 1927–1990. In *Advances in Health Economics and Health Services Research.* Greenwich, CT: JAI Press, 83–128.

Getzen, T. E., and J. P. Poullier. 1991. "An Income-Weighted International Average for Comparative Analysis of Health Expenditures." *International Journal of Health Planning & Management* 6: 3–22.

———. 1992. "International Health Spending Forecasts: Concepts and Evaluation." *Social Science & Medicine* 34 (9): 1057–68.

Ginsburg, P. 1976. "Evaluation of the ESP Program on Hospitals: An Analysis with Aggregate Data. In *Health, a Victim or Cause of Inflation?* Edited by M. Zubkoff. New York: Prodist, 31–51.

Kendix, M., and T. Getzen. 1994. "U.S. Health Services Employment: A Time-Series Analysis." Paper presented at the Association for Health Services Research Annual Meeting, Washington, D.C.

Klapper, G. H., and R. L. Harrington. 1981. "Viewpoint: The Rise and Fall of Cost Containment in Colorado." *Health Care Management Review* 6 (Spring): 79–83.

Levit, K. R., and M. S. Freeland. 1988. "National Medical Care Spending." *Health Affairs* 7 (4): 124–36.

McNees, S. K. 1988. "How Accurate are Macroeconomic Forecasts?" *New England Economic Review* (July/August): 16–36.

Mitchell, J. B., G. Wedig, and J. Cromwell. 1989. "The Medicare Physician Fee Freeze: What Really Happened?" *Health Affairs* 8 (1): 24–33.

Morrisey, M., D. A. Conrad, S. M. Shortell, and K. S. Cook. 1984. "Hospital Rate Review: A Theory and Empirical Review." *Journal of Health Economics* 3: 25–47.

Sloan, F. 1981. "Regulation and the Rising Cost of Hospital Care." *Review of Economics and Statistics* 63 (4): 479–87.

———. 1983. "Rate Regulation as a Strategy for Hospital Cost Control: Evidence from the Last Decade." *Millbank Memorial Fund Quarterly* 61 (2): 195–221.

Sloan, F., and B. Steinwald. 1981. "Effects of Regulation on Hospital Costs and Input Use." *Journal of Law & Economics* 23: 81–109.

3

The Economic Costs of HIV/AIDS

Paul G. Farnham

Introduction

This paper examines the cost of Human Immunodeficiency Virus (HIV)/Acquired Immunodeficiency Syndrome (AIDS). Paul Farnham, a visiting health economist at the Centers for Disease Control and Prevention, identifies a variety of costs associated with HIV/AIDS and other diseases. Policy makers are concerned with both the overall costs to society of HIV/AIDS and with the distribution of these costs among health care providers, public and private third-party institutions which finance medical care, and individuals affected by the disease. Cost estimates are required for the economic evaluation of HIV prevention and treatment strategies and for developing appropriate public policies regarding the financing of treatment and prevention activites.

Farnham first discusses the societal or social costs of HIV/AIDS. The societal cost approach measures opportunity costs, i.e., the value of resources used in providing health care (direct costs) or foregone to society as a result of the illness (indirect costs). The direct costs of HIV infection include personal medical care costs for diagnosis and treatment as well as nonpersonal costs for biomedical research and prevention programs. Indirect costs are the lost value of market and nonmarket output due to morbidity (illness) and premature mortality (death) from HIV/AIDS.

There are measurement problems with both categories of these costs. For direct costs, data are more readily available on the prices or charges to different payers than on the true opportunity cost of providing the services. For indirect costs, there is a controversy over the use of the human capital approach, which focuses on earnings lost as a result of an illness, and the willingness-to-pay approach, which is a more comprehensive concept, but one which is more difficult to measure accurately.

Farnham reviews a wide variety of literature on the costs of HIV/AIDS. Estimates of the costs of the disease have become more accurate over the last several years given better data and more comprehensive estimation methods. It is also clear that HIV/AIDS costs impact various players differently. Businesses, health care providers, especially public hospitals, and federal government programs such as Medicaid are each impacted significantly by the costs of this disease.

As the HIV/AIDS epidemic enters its second decade, the magnitude and impact of the costs of the illness remain a question of continuing concern to policymakers. Any illness imposes economic costs on both society as a whole and on various groups and individuals within society. Tracing the impact of these costs is always challenging, but this is particularly true for HIV/AIDS, where many of the factors influencing these costs are changing rapidly over time and where the current state of knowledge about these factors may be sketchy in some areas. Moreover, there are conceptual and empirical issues involved in defining "cost" because what is measured depends upon the question to be answered and the perspective taken for the analysis.

Estimates of the costs of HIV/AIDS are needed for several types of public policy decisions. Estimates of the costs to society as a whole are required for the economic evaluation of various HIV prevention and treatment strategies and for comparing HIV interventions with other public sector investments. Some of these illness costs will be saved by society if HIV/AIDS interventions are effective in preventing infections or delaying the onset of disease symptoms. Cost savings are typically considered to be a benefit of a public program in an economic cost-benefit analysis.

The time pattern of these societal cost savings is also important since economic evaluations generally weight costs that are saved now more heavily than costs saved in the future. This factor is important in evaluating and comparing HIV/AIDS treatment programs with those interventions designed to prevent HIV infections. Treatment programs generally result in cost savings in the near future, whereas interventions that prevent HIV infections save costs that would have occurred in the more distant future.

Knowledge of the distribution of HIV/AIDS costs–their incidence or impact on different groups and payers–is needed to develop the appropriate policies for HIV prevention and treatment. For example, if the medical costs of individuals who are HIV-infected but who have not yet developed diagnosed AIDS are covered by private insurance, these individuals are more likely to be able to obtain the benefits of early medical intervention against the disease. If private insurance typically does not cover these costs for certain individuals, there may be a role for public sector programs, such as Medicaid, or other strategies to increase access to these services.

How the costs of HIV/AIDS affect groups such as employers will influence their response to the disease. Business responses could include both positive factors, such as using the workplace for HIV education and information dissemination, and negative factors, such as the development of discriminatory policies against infected employees or those thought to be at risk for the disease. Knowledge of the costs borne by businesses can influence public policy in the development and economic evaluation of workplace education programs and in the design of legislation regarding employment discrimination or the use of other public policy tools such as tax credits and subsidies.

This chapter outlines the issues involved in measuring the economic costs of HIV/AIDS. The first section of the chapter describes the basic characteristics of HIV/AIDS in the United States, while the second section discusses the measurement of the aggregate societal or social costs (direct and indirect) of the illness. This discussion is followed by a description of current research on the lifetime direct personal medical costs of HIV/AIDS. These costs, which are a subset of the aggregate direct costs, are calculated from the societal perspective for an individual. The sensitivity of the estimates to baseline assumptions and changes in these estimates over time will be examined.

The third section discusses the measurement of costs from alternative perspectives. This section focuses on the economic impact or incidence of the illness costs on businesses and individuals, providers of services such as hospitals, and government programs funding health care services, such as Medicaid. Relationships between and among various payers are described. The final section of the chapter discusses implications of cost analysis for current public policy questions, such as the allocation of resources among alternative HIV/AIDS prevention strategies.

The Nature of HIV/AIDS

Human immunodeficiency virus (HIV) infection emerged as a leading cause of death in the United States during the 1980s. In 1992, HIV was the eighth-leading cause of death overall (up from ninth in 1991), accounting for 1.5 percent of all deaths, but the second leading cause of death among persons aged 25 to 44 years (up from third in 1991), accounting for 16.2 percent of deaths in this age group. HIV infection became the leading cause of death among men aged 25 to 44 years in 1992 (up from second in 1991) and the fourth leading cause of death among women in this age group (up from fifth in 1991). While death rates from most other leading causes of death declined or remained relatively stable for both men and women in this age group, the death rate for HIV infection has steadily increased during the past 10 years. From 1982 to 1992, the death rate increased from 0.6 per

100,000 to 52.8 per 100,000 for men aged 25 to 44 years and from 0.1 per 100,000 to 7.8 per 100,000 for women in this age group (CDC 1993a).

Acquired immunodeficiency syndrome (AIDS), which includes a series of illnesses such as *Pneumocystis carinii* pneumonia and Kaposi's sarcoma, represents the end stage of HIV infection. These illnesses develop when a person's immune system is so weakened by HIV infection that he or she cannot fight off these more serious infections or malignancies. The average survival time for a person diagnosed with AIDS is 20 to 25 months (Hellinger 1992, 1993). As of December 1992, a total of 253,448 cases of AIDS had been reported to the Centers for Disease Control and Prevention (CDC). These included 221,714 cases in men, 27,485 cases in women, and 4,249 cases in children. Although gay men still account for the majority of AIDS cases reported each year, AIDS is becoming more prominent in the young and in heterosexual men and women. Forty-seven percent of all reported AIDS cases through 1992 were among blacks and Hispanics, although these population groups represent only 21 percent of the U.S. population (Office of the Surgeon General 1993).

As of December 1992, 76 percent of all AIDS cases were among individuals 25 to 44 years old. As we shall discuss, this fact has a great impact on the calculation of the costs of the epidemic. Over 169,000 deaths have resulted from HIV infection and AIDS since 1981 (CDC 1993b).

An estimated one million people are thought to be infected with HIV (CDC 1990). Because the median time from HIV infection to date of diagnosed AIDS is 10 years (Brookmeyer 1991) and many individuals do not experience any symptoms for much of this period, a large number of these individuals do not know they are infected. Recent evidence from the National Health Interview Survey indicates that approximately 20 percent of the population report that they have been tested for HIV antibodies to learn if they are infected (Anderson et al. 1992).

The Societal Costs of HIV/AIDS

Definitions: Societal Costs

HIV and AIDS have imposed a variety of monetary and nonmonetary costs on society (Pascal 1989; Scitovsky 1988, 1989; Bloom and Carliner 1988; and Sisk 1987). Monetary costs include direct and indirect costs. As shown in figure 3.1, direct costs of HIV infection include personal medical care costs (IA of figure 3.1) for diagnosis and treatment as well as nonpersonal costs (IB) for biomedical research and prevention programs (educational campaigns, blood screening, outreach, and so on). Indirect costs (II of figure 3.1) are the lost value of market (IIA) and nonmarket (IIB) output due to morbidity (illness) and premature mortality (death) from HIV/AIDS. These

I. Direct Costs
    A.   Personal Medical Costs
          Hospitalization
          Physician Visits
          Outpatient Ancillary Services (e.g., Laboratory)
          Nursing Home Days
          Home Care
          Hospice
          Drugs
          Alternative Therapies
    B.   Nonpersonal Costs
          Research
          Screening Programs
          Health Education
          Support Services
II. Indirect Costs
    A.   Lost Value of Market Output (Future Earnings)
          Morbidity and Mortality
    B.   Lost Value of Nonmarket Output (Household Activities)
          Morbidity and Mortality
III. Nonmonetary Costs
    A.   Value Placed on Suffering and Death
    B.   Value Placed on Changing Behavior

FIGURE 3.1   Societal Costs of HIV/AIDS

costs are traditionally measured as the foregone earnings of affected individuals. They are derived either from labor market data or are imputed to estimate the value of household services (household management, child care, cooking, cleaning) affected individuals would have provided in the absence of the illness. Indirect costs could also result from lost productivity and job opportunities related to discriminatory behavior against individuals with or at risk for HIV/AIDS.

Nonmonetary costs (III of figure 3.1), which are less concrete and more difficult to measure, are defined as "the value that AIDS patients, their families and friends, and other members of society place on the suffering and death of AIDS patients and on the need to behave differently to avoid contracting or transmitting AIDS" (Bloom and Carliner 1988, 604). These are very real effects of the illness, although their impact may be impossible to measure in dollar terms.

The societal or social cost approach to cost measurement, which builds on the work of Rice and her associates (Rice 1966; Cooper and Rice 1976; Rice, Hodgson, and Kopstein 1985), is useful for (1) demonstrating the aggregate burden of the illness to society, (2) making comparisons among different types of diseases, and (3) developing cost-effectiveness and cost-benefit analyses of different prevention and treatment programs. The societal approach focuses on measuring opportunity costs–that is, the value of the resources used in providing health care (direct costs) or foregone to society as a result of the illness (indirect costs). This opportunity cost concept is typically used by economists to analyze the allocation of resources among competing activities. The societal cost approach is concerned with measuring the overall impact of the illness on society and *not* with the distribution of the costs among various individuals and groups.

Indirect Costs: Human Capital versus Willingness-to-Pay Approaches

Although the methodology described previously has become fairly standard in health services research, a continuing controversy relates to the measurement of the indirect costs of illness–the costs that result from premature morbidity and mortality. There are two major research approaches to this issue: (1) the human capital approach and (2) the willingness-to-pay methodology.

The health services literature generally uses the human capital approach to measure indirect illness costs (Hodgson and Meiners 1982). This methodology focuses on an individual's foregone stream of earnings measured either directly from market data or imputed for nonmarket activity. This approach has been criticized for incorporating all of the imperfections of the labor market–differential earnings for the young versus the elderly, male versus female, black versus white, and so on. Thus, the indirect costs of an illness would have a lower value for women than for men given the lower earning streams for many women over their lifetimes. The human capital approach also does not include other facets of an illness that may be more important than economic loss: pain and suffering, aversion to risk, and the loss of leisure time (Landefeld and Seskin 1982).

Proponents of the human capital approach clearly recognize the limits of their methodology. "Disease thus creates an undeniable loss to individuals and society, and it is this loss that the human capital approach attempts to measure. The justification for the human capital methodology is not that it measures the value of life, but that it does provide a measure of a cost of disease" (Hodgson and Meiners 1982, 439). Reliable, comparable data are more generally available for the human capital approach than for the willingness-to-pay methodology. Thus, the human capital approach provides "objective numbers based on life expectancy, labor force participation, and projected earnings" (Landefeld and Seskin 1982, 557).

A conceptual alternative to the human capital methodology is the willingness-to-pay approach, which attempts to measure the amount society is willing to pay "to reduce the probability of an event such as death from a certain disease" (Hodgson and Meiners 1982, 443). This approach has a stronger grounding in economic theory since it is based on the concept of a "potential Pareto improvement" that exists when individuals who gain from a social change, such as a public sector program, are able to compensate those who lose from the change and still leave a net gain (Landefeld and Seskin 1982, 557). Gains in this approach are measured by society's willingness to pay for the outcomes of the program. This approach is consistent with the private sector evaluation of goods bought and sold in the marketplace since the private sector demand for a good reflects society's willingness-to-pay for that output.

The willingness-to-pay approach is a more comprehensive concept than the human capital approach because it would ideally incorporate any factors that relate to an individual's well-being such as pain and suffering and the loss of leisure time. However, there are empirical problems in inferring willingness-to-pay values that have led to a substantial range of these estimates.

There are three major approaches to estimating the willingness to pay for reducing the risk of death: (1) wage-risk studies, (2) contingent valuation methods, and (3) consumer market studies (Fisher et al. 1989). Wage-risk studies estimate the wage premium demanded by workers who choose jobs with greater risk of death and injury. These studies assume that workers have freedom of choice among jobs and that they have full knowledge of the risks faced on each job and are able to evaluate this information correctly. All other factors influencing wage differentials must be controlled in these studies to achieve a valid measure of the valuation of risk. In contingent valuation studies, individuals are surveyed about their willingness to pay for various levels of safety in hypothetical market situations. Thus, valuation measures are based on what people say they would do, not on actual behavior. The wording of questions in the surveys may influence the results of this analysis. Consumer market studies examine the risk and benefit trade-offs that individuals make in their actual consumption decisions. Only a relatively small number of these studies have been conducted at present, limiting the ability to generalize their results.

Current estimates of the value of a human life saved based on willingness-to-pay methods range from $1.6 million to $8.5 million in 1986 dollars (Fisher et al. 1989, 96). These are substantially larger than many of the human capital estimates, which range from $300,000 to $800,000 (Landefeld and Seskin 1982; Holtgrave et al. 1993).

At present, there is no firm consensus on which estimates are "better". Usage differs by discipline, with health services researchers favoring the human capital method and economists using the willingness-to-pay methodology. For policymakers, there are basic trade-offs between the two approaches. The willingness-to-pay methodology is better grounded in economic theory. However, the human capital estimates are easier to obtain and to understand conceptually.

Costs versus Charges

There is one other point on which most of the cost-of-illness research remains somewhat ambiguous–that is, the distinction between costs and charges for medical and health care services. Many studies do not make a clear distinction between these two terms. However, as Finkler (1982) and Drummond et al. (1987) point out, such data as hospital charges may bear little relationship to the actual economic costs of providing the service. Hospitals engage in cost shifting both to maximize their revenues from various public and private third-party payers and to provide services for those patients without insurance who are unable to pay. Different individuals or groups may, thus, be charged fees that are more or less than the actual cost of providing the service to them. This cost/charge issue should be kept in mind during the following discussion of HIV/AIDS cost estimates.

Aggregate Societal Costs of AIDS Estimates

Scitovsky and Rice (1987) developed aggregate estimates of the societal costs of AIDS in 1984 and projected these costs to 1985, 1986, and 1991. Their 1991 projection of $10.9 billion in direct costs (see figure 3.1) is composed of (1) $8.6 billion in *personal medical costs* (section IA of figure 3.1) including the costs of hospitalization, inpatient and outpatient physician services, outpatient ancillary services, nursing home care, home care, and hospice care; and (2) $2.3 billion in *nonpersonal costs* (IB of figure 3.1) including the costs of research; blood screening; health education; and a variety of support services provided by local governments and community-based organizations, such as counseling, housing, and help with shopping and transportation. Many of the components of these estimates were based on arbitrary assumptions. Moreover, since these estimates were developed from epidemiologic and cost data in the early 1980s, their current relevance is questionable.

Hellinger (1992) estimated the aggregate societal medical costs of treating people with AIDS (section IA of figure 3.1) to be $6.8 billion in 1992. Using his updated cost estimates (Hellinger 1993) and the number of AIDS cases reported to the CDC between July 1992 and June 1993 (CDC 1993c), this figure would be $5.8 billion.

Scitovsky and Rice (1987) projected the indirect costs of the AIDS epidemic (section II of figure 3.1) to be $55.6 billion in 1991. This estimate is composed of $3.3 billion in morbidity (illness) costs and $52.3 billion in mortality (premature death) costs. These calculations were based on the assumption that persons with AIDS have the same average earnings and labor force participation rates as their corresponding age and sex group in the population since there are no hard national data on the earnings of persons who would have developed AIDS. Indirect costs represent more than 80 percent of the total societal costs of AIDS. The indirect costs are dominated by the mortality costs or lost wages of young workers, given the high prevalence of HIV-illness in the 25-to-44-year-old age group.

There have been no comprehensive updates of these national indirect cost estimates to reflect recent changes in the natural history of the epidemic or new knowledge about the employment patterns of persons with HIV and AIDS. Using the $5.8 billion direct medical cost figure and the assumption that indirect costs are approximately four times the amount of the direct costs of the illness (Scitovsky and Rice 1987), a rough current estimate of indirect costs would be $23.2 billion in 1992. This estimate is substantially smaller than that of Scitovsky and Rice (1987) because (1) revised cost and illness case figures are incorporated into these estimates and (2) the four-to-one ratio is based on direct medical costs only (section IA of figure 3.1) and not all direct costs (section IA and IB of figure 3.1) as in the Scitovsky and Rice study.

Individual Lifetime Costs of AIDS Estimates (Societal Perspective)

The lifetime medical costs of treating a person with AIDS, or the costs incurred from time of diagnosis of AIDS until death, have been estimated to range from $60,000 to over $100,000 (Bloom and Carliner 1988; Scitovsky 1988; Hellinger 1990, 1991, 1992, 1993). Hellinger's estimates of these costs are of great interest because he has developed and refined his methodology over a number of years and he continues to incorporate the most recent data sources as they become available. Given the changing nature of the AIDS epidemic, cost estimates based on illness assumptions more than a few years old are not very useful. Hellinger also attempts to develop national consensus estimates, recognizing that there will be substantial variations by geographic region, type of provider, and progression of the illness. These types of cost estimates are crucial for the economic evaluation of alternative HIV prevention and treatment strategies. Note the following:

Hellinger 1991 and 1992 Results—In his 1991 study, Hellinger estimated the inpatient cost of treating a person with AIDS during any part of a year to be $24,000 (15 days in the hospital × $1,000/day × 1.6 admissions). Outpatient costs were estimated at $8,000 or 25 percent of the total cost of care. These outpatient costs were broken down into the following categories (as a percentage of total care costs): outpatient clinic and physician costs (8.8 percent), long-term care (1 percent), home care (2.5 percent), and outpatient drugs (12.7 percent). Assuming that the average number of months lived by a person alive with the disease during any part of a year is 7.5 months, the monthly cost of treating a person with AIDS is $4,267 ($32,000/7.5) and the lifetime medical cost is $85,333 ($4,267 × 20 months from diagnosis to death) (Hellinger 1991, 215–216).

Hellinger's estimate of the total cost of treating a person with AIDS alive during any part of a year increased slightly to $38,300 in 1992 (Hellinger 1992). This resulted from an increase in the average length of stay to 16.3 days and in the average hospitalization charge to $1,100 per day. Hellinger retained the assumption that outpatient costs were 25 percent of total costs. Using the same epidemiologic assumptions as in 1991, Hellinger estimated the average cost per month of treating a person with AIDS as $5,100 ($38,300/7.5) and the average lifetime cost of treatment at $102,000 ($5,100 × 20) (Hellinger 1992, 360).

Hellinger 1993 Results—In the 1991 and 1992 studies, Hellinger based his estimates on a wide range of existing data sources, most of which provided data from a single insurer or hospital. However, in 1993 he relied primarily on data from the AIDS Cost and Service Utilization Survey (ACSUS), which includes data about the types of care received by persons with various stages of HIV infection from 26 sites (hospital clinics, freestanding clinics, and physicians' offices) in ten cities (Hellinger 1993). Although the data are self-reported, they are obtained directly from respondents and include information about *all* medical services consumed during a given time period.

Drawing on the ACSUS data, Hellinger estimated inpatient monthly costs of $1,890 based on an average length of stay of 13.4 days, an average cost per day of $1,085, and an average number of hospitalizations per month of 0.13. Data on outpatient visits, home health care, drug costs, and long-term care were directly available from ACSUS to estimate a monthly outpatient cost of $874, or 32 percent of the total monthly costs of $2,764. Hellinger projected a mean survival time of persons diagnosed with AIDS in 1993 of 25 months. Thus, his 1993 estimate of the lifetime cost of AIDS was $69,100 ($2,764 × 25) (Hellinger 1993).

Of considerable interest is the *decrease* in this estimate from the previous year's calculation of $102,000. This decrease resulted from lower estimates of both the average length of hospital stay and the frequency of hospitalization based on the ACSUS data (Hellinger 1993, 477–78). However, outpatient costs are a significantly larger fraction of total costs, suggesting that "outpatient services have begun to supplant, rather than simply augment, inpatient hospital care" (Hellinger 1993, 478).

Costs of HIV Infection Prior to Diagnosis of AIDS

All of the cost estimates in the previous section apply *only* to individuals with diagnosed AIDS, which represents the very late stage of HIV infection. Until recently, virtually nothing was known about the costs associated with the estimated one million persons who are HIV-positive but who have not yet developed AIDS. These costs are becoming increasingly significant as more of these individuals begin treatment with antiviral and other prophylactic drugs.

Building on the work of Arno et al. (1989) and others, Hellinger (1991) estimated the annual cost of treating a person infected with the human immunodeficiency virus to be $5,150. This estimate included the cost of (1) AZT, aerosol pentamidine, and other drugs ($2,210); (2) office, outpatient, and clinic visits ($700); (3) laboratory tests ($800); (4) other outpatient expenses such as counseling ($200); and inpatient care ($1,240) (Hellinger 1991, 219).

In 1992, Hellinger increased this estimate to $10,000, which is an average of $13,525 for those with CD4+ lymphocyte (T-cell) counts less than 200 and $6,444 for those with T-cell counts equal to or greater than 200 (Hellinger 1992). Researchers use CD4+ or T-cells as a marker indicating the stage of HIV infection. The number of CD4+ cells drops in an individual as HIV infection progresses and damage to the immune system increases. Fifty-six percent of these estimated costs are for inpatient care for persons with T-cell counts less than 200, whose immune systems are severely compromised, whereas only 36 percent are inpatient costs for those with T-cell counts equal to or greater than 200. The increase in these costs from 1991 to 1992 resulted from changes in both inpatient and outpatient costs for HIV-infected individuals.

Given the availability of the ACSUS data on cost and service utilization and data from the San Francisco Men's Health Study on average occupancy times in various stages of illness, Hellinger (1993) was able to estimate the average cost of treatment from time of infection to time of AIDS diagnosis. This analysis assumed that an individual was identified and treated for HIV immediately following infection. Since this assumption does *not* hold in many cases, these cost calculations are upper-bound estimates. The stages of HIV infection (prediagnosed AIDS) were broken down into three categories for this analysis: (1) T-cell counts greater than 500 (5.6 years); (2) T-cell counts between 200 and 500 (3.7 years); and (3) T-cell counts less than 200 (1.0 year). Given these assumptions, Hellinger estimated the cost of treating a person with HIV from the time of infection to the date of diagnosed AIDS to be $50,174, or approximately $5,000 per year on average (Hellinger 1993, 477). These figures are consistent with his earlier annual estimates if the time pattern for disease stage in the 1993 research is applied to the 1992 estimates.

The Distribution of the Costs of HIV/AIDS

The discussion in the second section of this chapter focused on the estimation of the costs of HIV/AIDS from the societal perspective. The distribution of these costs, or their impact on different groups and payers, is also important for public policy development. Relevant groups include: (1) *business* (the impact of illnesses on health-related employee benefits); (2) *individuals* (the costs of illness paid out of pocket and the indirect costs arising from labor market reactions to the illness); (3) *health care providers* (the illness costs imposed on various types of hospitals, HMOs, or other providers); and (4) the *federal government* (the impact of illness costs on the budgets of specific agencies or on programs such as Medicaid or Medicare, which fund the purchase of health services). It is necessary to use different approaches to cost measurement to analyze the impact of costs on these various groups.

The analysis in this section is similar to the concept of incidence in the economic analysis of taxation (Hyman 1993). The question in that literature is whether the individual or organization upon which a tax is imposed actually pays the tax or whether the tax is shifted to other persons through economic behavior. Thus, although the corporate income tax is imposed upon firms with a particular business structure, the final burden of the tax may rest upon consumers in the form of higher product prices, workers in the form of lower wages, or investors in the form of lower returns on their corporate shares.

The discussion in this section will relate primarily to the *initial* incidence or distributional impact of the costs of HIV/AIDS, given that research on these initial distributional impacts is relatively sparse. Research on the questions of shifting and the ultimate burden of these costs is still to be undertaken. Bloom and Carliner (1988) and Bloom and Glied (1989) have outlined many of these issues in what they term "second-generation" AIDS economic research.

Business Costs

The costs of HIV/AIDS to business are different from the societal costs defined in the second section of this chapter. The major difference is that only a portion of the direct and indirect societal costs of the illness is borne by business. Businesses also may incur certain costs that are not traditionally measured from the societal perspective.

The HIV/AIDS business costs that are most directly measurable have been termed "illness-based employment costs" (Farnham 1994; Farnham and Gorsky 1994). Illness-based employment costs are the incremental costs to a firm of having an employee who is HIV-positive. These include changes in (1) health insurance; (2) short-and long-term disability insurance; (3) life insurance; (4) recruiting, hiring, and training costs; and (5) pension plans (a cost saving or an offset to the other costs).

A firm's health insurance costs are influenced by (1) the number of persons with HIV infection or AIDS who are employed, (2) the costs of treating HIV infection and AIDS, (3) the nature and extent of the health benefits provided to different types of employees, (4) the degree of experience rating of the plans, (5) the extent to which employees with HIV/AIDS report medical claims to their insurer, and (6) the reactions of insurers to the epidemic–that is, the use of HIV testing or the decision to exclude certain groups in the underwriting process. Medical providers, such as hospitals, may engage in cost shifting to maximize their reimbursement from different employer insurance plans and to cover the cost of uncompensated care. This can result in differential health insurance costs to large and small businesses.

Disability insurance costs are affected by the work history of persons with AIDS and the amount of income replacement for long-term disability policies for different types of employees. Life insurance costs are influenced by the amount of death benefits provided and by the degree of experience rating. Recruiting, hiring, and training costs depend upon the average cost of these activities and the average duration of employment for different types of employees. Pension plan offsets (cost savings) to the firm depend upon the amount of income replaced, the number of years for the average pension, the probability of an employee being vested, and the probability of an employee surviving to collect a pension (Farnham and Gorsky 1994).

The *societal* indirect costs of the epidemic (section II of figure 3.1), or the lost value of market and nonmarket output, are *not* out-of-pocket expenses incurred by employers. Assuming that employees can be replaced, the illness-based employment costs are the major costs to employers of a worker with HIV or AIDS.

The size of both business and societal costs is the result of the interplay of a variety of factors. For example, the illnesses of older employees are likely to be more costly for employers given the higher salaries and accrued benefits of these employees. However, the deaths of older employees will result in larger pension plan savings to employers, given both the larger benefits accrued by these employees and the shorter time period until receiving them. The costs of illnesses of young employees will be large from a societal perspective, given the number of years over which lost future earnings will be calculated.

Health Care Providers

The impact of HIV/AIDS on the providers of health care services is another significant perspective for policy analysis. Concern has been expressed over the financial impact of HIV infection on public and private hospitals. Andrulis et al. (1987, 1989, 1992) have provided a number of insights on these issues based on the results of three surveys.

Andrulis et al. (1987) argue that the nation's major teaching hospitals and large city public institutions bear a disproportionate burden of care for AIDS patients and that Medicaid programs have greatly assisted these hospitals in providing care to these individuals. Public hospitals in this survey, conducted in 1985, accounted for 61 percent of the AIDS patients versus 35 percent for private hospitals and 4 percent for Veterans Administration facilities (Andrulis et al. 1987, 1344).

A 1987 survey of 276 hospitals treating at least one AIDS patient showed a continuing concentration of patients in certain hospitals. Ten percent of the hospitals treated 58 percent of the patients, and 4 percent of the hospitals treated 32 percent of the patients (Andrulis et al. 1989, 785). Public hospitals had a significantly higher percentage of AIDS patients whose payer source was Medicaid or who paid out of pocket. This increasing concentration of care means that "inner-city hospitals where AIDS patients are concentrated may find their ability to provide health services in general severely compromised. Moreover, it may become more difficult to draw broader political and community support for increased resources from areas and providers not influenced by the epidemic" (Andrulis et al. 1989, 793).

In a more recent survey, Andrulis et al. (1992) note that measuring only the utilization of services by persons with AIDS, as defined by the CDC, will significantly understate the total burden of HIV on hospitals. In this study they compare the use of inpatient hospital services by HIV-infected individuals without diagnosed AIDS with the population of AIDS patients in the same hospitals. The authors found that for every 100 AIDS hospital admissions there were another 53 admissions for HIV-infected individuals without diagnosed AIDS. The proportion of admissions for "other-HIV" patients not covered by some form of public or private health insurance was significantly higher than for the AIDS group (Andrulis et al. 1992, 2484).

This outcome may have resulted from a higher proportion of drug users in the other-HIV group or from variation in eligibility requirements among state Medicaid programs. The lack of third-party payment may place more financial pressures on public hospitals and make private hospitals less likely to treat HIV-infected patients before a diagnosis of AIDS. The authors note, "the substantial resources it takes to meet the demand for care, the crowding that is occurring in many inner-city hospitals, and the shortfalls in HIV-related revenues may require hospitals to place a limit on the number of HIV-related cases they can accept" (Andrulis et al. 1992, 2486).

The Federal Government

It is clear from the discussion of the impact of HIV/AIDS on hospitals that the federal Medicaid program plays a major role in financing the costs of the epidemic. Medicaid is actually a combined federal-state program where states receive grants from the federal government to pay for acute and long-term care for low-income households. Eligibility criteria and the generosity and mix of benefits vary tremendously among the states, which establish these criteria (Aaron 1991, 63–65). This program is not to be confused with Medi*care*, the federal government program that provides access to acute care services for the elderly and disabled.

It has been estimated that Medicaid covered 40 percent of the persons with AIDS, including 90 percent of the children with AIDS, in 1990 (cited in Davis et al. 1991). Important policy questions center on the financial impact of HIV/AIDS on the Medicaid program and on how well the program covers services needed by persons with HIV and AIDS.

Baily et al. (1990) list the following major issues regarding HIV/AIDS and Medicaid:

1. "Many impoverished HIV-infected persons have difficulty establishing Medicaid eligibility" (100).
2. "Those who do qualify for Medicaid often have difficulty obtaining the services they need" (101).
3. "Medicaid often does not reimburse for the full cost of care received by AIDS patients, even for covered services" (102).
4. "The geographic concentration of the epidemic and the variability in State Medicaid programs produce an uneven distribution of the financial burden of HIV-related care across State and local governments and health care providers" (102).
5. "As the epidemic continues, Medicaid's share of HIV-related expenditures is likely to increase relative to the shares of other private and public payers" (102).

Many of these problems arise from the discretion given to the states in establishing the eligibility and benefits for Medicaid. Pascal et al. (1989) have ranked the states in terms of both measures of ease of access to their Medicaid systems (the ratio of the Medicaid population to the poverty population, income eligibility cutoffs, and automatic eligibility of persons with AIDS for the medically needy program) and the extent of coverage and reimbursement of services. The latter ranking includes measures of coverage for AZT, hospice services, and nursing home services. These rankings can be used to analyze the relationships between private and public sources of funding of medical treatment for persons with HIV/AIDS, such as whether they are complements or substitutes, and how well the Medicaid program meets the needs of these individuals in the various states.

Green and Arno (1990) have documented the increase in Medicaid financing ("medicaidization") of AIDS cases for New York City, San Francisco, and Los Angeles for the period 1983 to 1987. "All three cities," they reported, "experienced marked increases in the proportion of AIDS-related hospitalizations financed by Medicaid and precipitous declines in the private insurance share during the study years" (Green and Arno 1990, 1263). The percent of AIDS hospitalizations increased from 40 to 53 percent in New York City, from 19 to 30 percent in San Francisco, and from 10 to 28 percent in Los Angeles. The authors also found that AIDS patients were more likely to be admitted via an emergency room and in a public hospital than were privately insured patients (Green and Arno 1990, 1264).

In a series of studies, Fanning et al. (1991), Ellwood et al. (1991), and Andrews et al. (1991) have examined the impact of HIV infection on the Medicaid programs of New York State and California, the two states with the largest AIDS caseloads. The contrasts between the two states support the concept of a dual epidemic in New York—one that is male, homosexual, higher-income, and less dependent upon Medicaid and the other, which is poor, drug-related, female, and Medicaid-dependent (Fanning et al. 1991, 1034). The states also differed in total expenditures and in utilization of both inpatient and outpatient services. Lifetime Medicaid expenditures averaged $30,000 in New York and only $20,000 in California. More inpatient services and fewer outpatient services were utilized in New York than in California (Andrews et al. 1991, 1055).

Policy Implications

Defining and measuring the economic costs of HIV/AIDS are complex tasks given the diverse nature of the epidemic and the variety of epidemiologic and economic factors influencing the estimates. Moreover, cost estimates are undertaken for different purposes. Policymakers need to make certain that the cost figures they use are relevant for the questions they want answered.

Societal Cost Estimates

Aggregate societal cost-of-illness estimates are most useful for making cost comparisons across diseases and for showing the total impact on society of various illnesses. The methodology developed by Rice and her associates facilitates these comparisons, although many of these studies now need to be updated to incorporate recent epidemiologic data. For example, the cost-of-illness study by Rice, Hodgson, and Kopstein (1985) uses 1980 data. Although prices can be updated in a straightforward manner, it is much more difficult to adjust for changes in the technology of treating illnesses over time. It was noted in the second section that the estimates of the direct and indirect costs of AIDS by Scitovsky and Rice (1987) are also outdated for the same reasons. The calculation of both direct and indirect costs for a range of illnesses shows whether the impact on society of the illness is manifested in direct medical expenses or lost productivity from premature disability and death.

Lifetime societal medical cost-of-illness estimates detail the expenditures that will be incurred over the course of an illness for an individual. Although these estimates are well developed for HIV/AIDS (Hellinger 1991, 1992, 1993), there are few comparable figures for other diseases. Thus, at present, it is very difficult to place the lifetime HIV/AIDS cost estimates in context with other illnesses because most of the estimates for other illnesses are by either annual costs or costs per episode of illness.

Economic Analysis of HIV/AIDS Prevention Programs

Lifetime cost-of-illness estimates form the basis for the economic analysis of disease prevention and treatment programs. However, these estimates must be used in cost-effective or cost-benefit studies to evaluate how additional or incremental expenditures on different prevention or treatment interventions will affect the course of a disease. "Only if we could instantly and costlessly rid ourselves of the disease and all its consequences would estimates from cost-of-illness studies represent society's savings" (Sindelar 1991, 33–34).

For example, in their cost-benefit analysis of publicly funded HIV counseling, testing, referral, and partner notification services (CTRPN), Holtgrave et al. (1993) used Hellinger's (1991) estimates of the lifetime cost of a person with AIDS as one of the measures of the monetary benefits of an infection prevented. They also chose the more conservative human capital approach, as compared with the willingness-to-pay approach discussed in the second section, to value the lives saved by HIV CTRPN. These monetary benefits were then compared with CTRPN direct program costs and ancillary costs of other programs essential to the operation of the CTRPN program.

The cost-of-illness estimates used in these studies have to be adjusted to reflect the fact that, on average, preventing an HIV infection now would result in *not* incurring a diagnosis of AIDS 10 to 12 years in the future. Guinan, Farnham, and Holtgrave (1994) have analyzed how the time pattern of these costs, combined with assumptions about knowledge of an individual's infection and time spent in various stages of HIV disease, can be used to develop a standard estimate of the medical cost savings of a case of HIV infection prevented. This is accomplished by calculating the present value of these costs using an appropriate discount rate (Drummond et al. 1987).

The method developed by Guinan, Farnham, and Holtgrave (1994) defines component values of the medical cost savings. This enables both researchers and policymakers to analyze how sensitive the cost estimates are to changes in the values of the underlying parameters and to incorporate new data in the model when they become available. Comparable epidemiologic assumptions and present value calculations need to be included in the economic evaluation of prevention activities for other diseases to develop resource allocation strategies across a broader range of health interventions.

Alternative Perspectives

Undertaking an economic analysis from a perspective other than that of society as a whole can provide insights on how various individuals or groups will react to an illness or epidemic. For example, the response of business firms to the HIV epidemic will be influenced by the perceived costs of the illness to them. If the costs are perceived as low, firms may tend to ignore the problem. If the costs are perceived as extremely high, firms may attempt to dismiss or avoid hiring employees they fear are at risk for HIV infection. However, given recent court cases and antidiscrimination legislation such as the Americans with Disabilities Act of 1990, the latter strategy may result in legal action against the firm.

Accurate knowledge about the impacts of HIV/AIDS on employers can help firms put costs in perspective, develop more rational approaches to managing the effects of the disease among their employees, and retain productive and skilled HIV-infected employees as long as their health permits. Estimates of these costs can also be used in the economic evaluation of workplace education and prevention strategies and other public policies.

Cost estimates from the perspective of health care providers and government programs financing medical services can show the expected impact on government budgets and whether particular providers are likely to be severely burdened by a given illness. Thus, although the overall economic impact of HIV/AIDS on society is not likely to be disproportionate compared to other illnesses (Bloom and Carliner 1988), the impact on public hospitals, particularly teaching hospitals in urban areas, is very great (Andrulis et al. 1987, 1989, 1992). The magnitude of this impact on service providers will be influenced by government financing programs such as Medicaid. Thus, any analysis of the economic costs of HIV/AIDS from the perspective of one of the participants in the system invariably has implications for other participants and their share of the costs.

Future Research Issues

The extensive research on the lifetime costs of HIV/AIDS has highlighted the new methodologies needed to improve these estimates. Hellinger's (1993) estimates are based on the ACSUS, which follows a sample of individuals in various stages of HIV infection over time to gather data on both the course of the disease and changes in cost and financing factors. This approach helps to overcome many of the weaknesses of earlier research, which often measured only the costs of a single provider or ignored out-of-pocket expenses and costs not covered by insurance. The differences in results between this study and Hellinger's previous research (1991, 1992) illustrate how changes in both the course of an illness and in the methodology for analyzing it influence research results needed for public policy decisions.

The distinction between illness costs and charges discussed in the second section should also be mentioned again in closing. In estimating the lifetime costs of HIV and AIDS, Hellinger (1993, 474) uses the term *cost* but defines this to mean "total charges for services". Many studies in the health services literature do not make a clear distinction between these two terms. While the costs of various provider services are needed for the economic evaluation of both treatment and prevention activities, data on provider charges are much more readily available than data on the actual opportunity costs of providing the services. Moreover, given the cost shifting that most hospitals undertake, there is often little relationship between patient charges and the actual costs of providing the medical services.

Finkler (1982) and Drummond et al. (1987) outline methods for estimating the true economic costs of providing services. Although these methods are generally more complex than simply using charge data, the implications of this issue for the correct estimation of the economic *costs* of illness and of prevention programs need to be explored in greater detail.

References

Aaron, H. J. 1991. *Serious and Unstable Condition. Financing America's Health Care.* Washington, D.C.: The Brookings Institution.

Anderson, J. E., A. M. Hardy, K. Cahill, and S. Aral, 1992. "HIV Antibody Testing and Posttest Counseling in the United States: Data from the 1989 National Health Interview Survey." *American Journal of Public Health* 82 (November): 1533–35.

Andrews, R. M., M. A. Keyes, T. R. Fanning, and K. W. Kizer, 1991. "Lifetime Medicaid Service Utilization and Expenditures for AIDS in New York and California." *Journal of Acquired Immune Deficiency Syndrome*, 4 (October): 1046–58.

Andrulis, D. P., V. S. Beers, J. D. Bentley, and L. S. Gage. 1987. "The Provision and Financing of Medical Care for AIDS Patients in U.S. Public and Private Teaching Hospitals." *Journal of the American Medical Association* 258 (September 11): 1343–46.

Andrulis, D. P., V. B. Weslowski, and L. S. Gage. 1989. "The 1987 U.S. Hospital AIDS Survey." *Journal of the American Medical Association* 262 (August 11): 784–94.

Andrulis, D. P., V. B. Weslowski, E. Hintz, and A. W. Spolarich. 1992. "Comparisons of Hospital Care for Patients with AIDS and Other HIV-Related Conditions." *Journal of the American Medical Association* 267 (May 13): 2482–86.

Arno, P. S., D. Shenson, N. F. Siegel, P. Franks, and P. R. Lee. 1989. "Economic and Policy Implications of Early Intervention in HIV Disease." *Journal of the American Medical Association* 262 (September 15): 1493–98.

Baily, M.A., L. Bilheimer, J. Wooldridge, K. Langwell, and W. Greenberg. 1990.

"Economic Consequences for Medicaid of Human Immunodeficiency Virus Infection." *Health Care Financing Review* Annual Supplement (December): 97–108.

Bloom, D. E., and G. Carliner. 1988. "The Economic Impact of AIDS in the United States." *Science* 239 (February 5): 604–10.

Bloom, D. E., and S. Glied. 1989. "The Evolution of AIDS Economic Research." *Health Policy* 11: 187–96.

Brookmeyer, R. 1991. "Reconstruction and Future Trends of the AIDS Epidemic." *Science* 253: 37–42.

Centers for Disease Control and Prevention (CDC). 1990. "HIV Prevalence Estimates and AIDS Case Projections for the United States: Report Based upon a Workshop." *Morbidity and Mortality Weekly Report* 39 (No. RR-16, November 30), 5–7.

——. 1993a. "Update: Mortality Attributable to HIV Infection among Persons Aged 25–44 Years—United States, 1991 and 1992." *Morbidity and Mortality Weekly Report* 42 (November 19): 869–72.

——. 1993b. *HIV/AIDS Surveillance Report* (February): 1–23.

——. 1993c. *HIV/AIDS Surveillance Report* (July): 6–7.

Cooper, B. S., and D. P. Rice. 1976. The Economic Cost of Illness Revisited. *Social Security Bulletin* 39 (February): 21–36.

Davis, K., R. Bialek, C. Beyrer, P. Chaulk, P. Cowley, J. Harlow, and R. Chu. 1991. *Financing Health Care for Persons with HIV Disease: Policy Options.* Baltimore: Johns Hopkins School of Public Health.

Drummond, M. F., G. L. Stoddart, and G. W. Torrance. 1987. *Methods for the Economic Evaluation of Health Care Programmes.* Oxford: Oxford University Press.

Ellwood, M. R., T. R. Fanning, and S. Dodds. 1991. "Medicaid Eligibility Patterns for Persons with AIDS in California and New York, 1982–1987." *Journal of Acquired Immune Deficiency Syndromes* 4 (October): 1036–45.

Fanning, T. R., L. E. Cosler, P. Gallagher, J. Chirarella, and E. M. Howell. 1991. "The Epidemiology of AIDS in the New York and California Medicaid programs." *Journal of Acquired Immune Deficiency Syndromes* 4 (October): 1025–35.

Farnham, P. G. 1994. Defining and Measuring the Costs of the HIV Epidemic to Business Firms. *Public Health Reports.* 109 (May-June): 311–318.

Farnham, P. G., and R. D. Gorsky. 1994. "Costs to Business for an HIV-Infected Worker." *Inquiry* 31 (Spring): 76–88.

Finkler, S. A. 1982. "The Distinction Between Cost and Charges." *Annals of Internal Medicine* 96: 102–9.

Fisher, A., L. G. Chestnut, and D. M. Violette. 1989. "The Value of Reducing Risks of Death: A Note on New Evidence." *Journal of Policy Analysis and Management* 8 (Winter): 88–100.

Green, J. and P. S. Arno. 1990. "The Medicaidization of AIDS." *Journal of the American Medical Association* 264 (September 12): 1261–66.

Guinan, M. E., P. G. Farnham, and D. R. Holtgrave. 1994. "Estimating the Value of Preventing a Human Immunodeficiency Virus Infection." *American Journal of Preventive Medicine* 10: 1–4.

Hellinger, F. J. 1990. "Updated Forecasts of the Costs of Medical Care for Persons with AIDS, 1989–93." *Public Health Reports* 105 (January-February): 1–12.

———. 1991. "Forecasting the Medical Care Costs of the HIV Epidemic: 1991–1994." *Inquiry* 28 (Fall): 213–25.

———. 1992. "Forecasts of the Costs of Medical Care for Persons with HIV: 1992–1995." *Inquiry* 29 (Fall): 356–65.

———. 1993. "The Lifetime Cost of Treating a Person with HIV." *Journal of the American Medical Association* 270 (July 28): 474–78.

Hodgson, T. A. and M. R. Meiners, 1982. "Cost-of-Illness Methodology: A Guide to Current Practices and Procedures." *The Milbank Quarterly* 60 (Summer): 429–62.

Holtgrave, D. R., R. O. Valdiserri, A. R. Gerber, and A. R. Hinman. 1993. "Human Immunodeficiency Virus Counseling, Testing, Referral, and Partner Notification Services: A Cost-Benefit Analysis." *Archives of Internal Medicine* 153 (May 24): 1225–30.

Hyman, D. N. 1993. *Public Finance. A Contemporary Application of Theory to Policy* 4th ed. New York: The Dryden Press.

Landefeld, J. S,. and E. P. Seskin. 1982. "The Economic Value of Life: Linking Theory to Practice." *American Journal of Public Health* 72 (June): 555–66.

Office of the Surgeon General. 1993. Surgeon General's report to the American public on HIV infection and AIDS. Washington, D.C.: U.S. Government Printing Office.

Pascal, A. 1989. "Conceptual Issues in Assessing the Economic Effects of the HIV Epidemic." *Health Policy* 11 (April): 105–13.

Pascal, A., M. Cvitanic, C. Bennett, M. Gorman, and C. A. Serrato. 1989. "State Policies and the Financing of Acquired Immunodeficiency Syndrome Care." *Health Care Financing Review* 11 (Fall): 91–104.

Rice, D. P. 1966. "Estimating the Cost of Illness." *Health Economics Series No. 6*, PHS Pub. No. 947–6. Washington, D.C.: U.S. Government Printing Office.

Rice, D. P., T. A. Hodgson, and A. N. Kopstein. 1985. "The Economic Costs of Illness: A Replication and Update." *Health Care Financing Review* 7 (Fall): 61–80.

Scitovsky, A. A. 1988. "The Economic Impact of AIDS in the United States." *Health Affairs* 7 (Fall): 32–45.

———. 1989. "Studying the Cost of HIV-Related Illnesses: Reflections on a Moving Target." *The Milbank Quarterly* 67: 318–44.

Scitovsky, A. A., and D. P. Rice. 1987. "Estimates of the Direct and Indirect Costs of Acquired Immunodeficiency Syndrome in the United States, 1985, 1986, and 1991." *Public Health Reports* 102 (January-February): 5–17.

Sindelar, J. L. 1991. Economic cost of illicit drug studies: critique and research agenda. In *Economic Costs, Cost-Effectiveness, Financing, and Community-Based Drug Treatment*, Research Monograph #113. Edited by W. S. Cartwright and J. M. Kaple. Rockville, MD: National Institute on Drug Abuse. Pages 33–45.

Sisk, J. E. 1987. "The Costs of AIDS: A Review of the Estimates." *Health Affairs* 6 (Summer): 5–21.

Glossary

AIDS versus HIV: *AIDS*, or acquired immunodeficiency syndrome, is a disease in which the body's immune system breaks down. The immune system fights off infections and certain other diseases. Because the system fails, a person with AIDS develops a variety of life-threatening illnesses including *Pneumocystis carinii pneumonia* and Kaposi's sarcoma.

HIV, or human immunodeficiency virus, is the virus that causes AIDS. Because the median time from HIV infection to date of diagnosed AIDS is 10 years, infected persons may not know they are infected and can appear completely healthy. A person who is infected can infect others, even if no symptoms are present. The two main methods for transmitting HIV infection are (1) having unprotected sexual intercourse with an infected person and (2) sharing drug needles or syringes with an infected person.

Costs versus Charges for Services: The charges or fees that appear on the bills of health care providers such as hospitals often do not reflect the true cost of providing those services. Hospitals engage in *cost shifting*, in which they charge different individuals or groups fees higher or lower than the actual costs of providing the services to maximize reimbursements from various third-party payers and to provide care for those who are not insured and are unable to pay.

Direct versus Indirect Illness Costs: *Direct costs* are the value of the resources used in diagnosing, treating, and preventing illnesses. They are composed of (1) *personal medical costs* associated with the provision of medical services such as hospital and physician visits, outpatient services, home care, drugs, and other therapies to individuals and (2) *nonpersonal costs* generated by research, screening programs, health education, and support services.

Indirect costs are a valuation of both the market and nonmarket output lost to society due to premature death and disability from the illness. They are usually measured as the foregone earnings of affected individuals, derived either from labor market data or imputed (estimated) for nonmarket activity.

Medicaid versus Medicare: Medicaid is a combined federal-state government program that pays for acute and long-term care for low-income households. Medicare is the federal government program that provides access to acute care services for the elderly and disabled.

Monetary versus Nonmonetary Costs: Monetary costs are those costs that can be explicitly valued in dollar terms. Nonmonetary costs incorporate real effects of an illness that may be impossible to measure in dollar terms.

Opportunity Costs: Opportunity costs measure the value of resources used in a particular activity such as treating an illness. They are usually measured from a *societal* or *social* perspective, showing the overall impact on society. This may involve imputing or measuring costs, such as the value of time, which are often not measured in a bookkeeping or accounting sense. When costs are measured from the perspective of individuals or groups, the *incidence* or *distributional impact* of the costs is being measured.

Part 2

Labor Market Issues

4

The Economic Effects of Mandated Job Accommodation for People with Disabilities

Carolyn L. Weaver

Introduction

Most people are concerned about people with disabilities and would like them to be treated fairly. But upon whom should the cost of fair treatment fall, and what is it that constitutes fair treatment? This is an area, like rationing of lifesaving medical technology or licensing of child-care providers, where the emotional response for many people is immediate and very strong. Of course, people will say that people with disabilities should be protected from discrimination.

The essay by Carolyn Weaver is provocative because it goes against the grain of the responses many people would make. She examines the incentives created by different approaches to the treatment of people with disabilities on the job. The Americans with Disabilities Act mandates "job accommodation"—although what this means exactly has yet to be decided. Generally, it is the courts that will decide since the act itself is written so vaguely that many interpretations are possible.

Different incentive structures call forth different behaviors. Under various regimes for the treatment of people with disabilities in different countries and at different times, the numbers of people claiming disabilities has fluctuated rather markedly. Should this be the concern of economists? First, it should be pointed out that Weaver does not claim that the basic problem is cheating. The basic problem is that "job accommodation," as that term is ultimately defined by case law, may not be an efficient solution. The problem is that the costs to society of job accommodation may outweigh the benefits to society of job accommodation. There is a separate but important question about the incidence of these costs–that is, the identities of the beneficiaries and losers in the scheme of job accommodation.

Another intriguing possibility is that the employment prospects of some people with disabilities may be hurt by the Americans with Disabilities Act. The analysis here is very similar to the analysis economists would use in discussing the effects of a minimum wage or similar regulation. Enforcement is never complete and firms may be able to "choose" a more preferred over a less preferred person with a disability. The cost of job accommodation, according to this argument, will be built into the cost of using labor in general, with the effect that there will be a tendency to use less labor because its effective cost has increased.

Many would argue that the employment status of people with a disability does not fall into the category of a "classical" market failure. It is simply that some people are less fortunate than others, and a more transparent scheme of compensation, say, direct government disability payments, will be more efficient.

The Americans with Disabilities Act is likely to come increasingly to public attention in the next few years. Few know its requirements, but businesses are already wary. Experts on "ergonomics"–the science of human-machine interface–can be found in large corporations. One of their primary tasks are to protect the corporation from liability under the Americans with Disabilities Act.

Advances in medicine, science, and technology, together with changes in the labor market itself, have opened new opportunities in the workplace for people with disabilities.[1] People with severe physical impairments, such as blindness or quadriplegia, who once had little hope of competing in the job market are gaining college educations and moving into professional jobs. People with mental retardation or certain forms of severe mental illness are finding their way into entry-level jobs in the service sector. And workers afflicted with once-debilitating diseases or injuries are returning to work.

Despite these advances, total employment among people with disabilities remains relatively low. According to aggregate statistics (which must be interpreted carefully because of the problems associated with the self-reporting of health limitations), less than half of working-aged people with disabilities are in the labor force. Among those who do work, part-time work is more prevalent and hourly wages are lower than among nondisabled workers.

Table 4.1 presents data from the Current Population Survey, compiled by the U.S. Bureau of the Census, on the employment and earnings of working-aged men with disabilities. In these data, a person is considered

TABLE 4.1   Work Experience and Mean Earnings of Men by Work Disability Status
and Age, 1987

		AGE				
	Total	16-24	25-34	35-44	45-54	55-64
Status						
Disabled						
Total number (in thousands)	6,071	671	1,247	1,308	1,190	2,285
Percent						
Worked	41.8	51.9	54.3	46.6	43.6	28.3
Year-round	17.1	10.2	23.5	20.4	23.5	10.5
Nondisabled						
Total number (in thousands)	69,063	15,691	19,659	15,528	10,285	7,900
Percent						
Worked	92.1	79.7	96.8	98.1	97.5	85.8
Year-round	65.2	26.6	74.3	81.2	82.7	65.3
Earnings						
Mean earnings, all employed men (in dollars)						
Disabled	15,497	6,463	14,102	18,388	20,385	15,187
Nondisabled	24,095	7,581	22,362	31,082	33,775	28,899
Ratio of disabled to nondisabled	0.643	0.823	0.631	0.592	0.604	0.526
Mean earnings, year-round employed (in dollars)						
Disabled	24,200	N/A	22,249	27,524	26,618	22,601
Nondisabled	29,994	14,985	25,637	34,223	36,681	33,116
Ratio of disabled to nondisabled	0.807	N/A	0.868	0.804	0.726	0.683

Sources: U.S. Bureau of the Census (1989) and Oi (1991).

to have a work disability if he or she is reported (by him- or herself or another adult in the household) to have a health problem or disability that prevents work or that limits the kind or amount of work he or she can do.[2] According to the data, 41.8 percent of men with disabilities so measured reported working in 1987, compared to 92.1 percent of nondisabled men, with the proportion as low as 28.3 percent among older men (those aged 55 to 64) with disabilities. Whereas close to two-thirds (65.2 percent) of nondisabled men reported working year-round, the ratio was less than one in five (17.1 percent) for men with disabilities. Mean earnings for men with disabilities were roughly 64 percent of those for nondisabled men, although among year-round workers the ratio was 81 percent. As University of Rochester economist Walter Oi (1991, 31) summarizes the data, the employment record of people with disabilities is "dismal."

With the enactment in 1990 of the Americans with Disabilities Act (ADA), the federal government made a major commitment to promoting the employment of people with disabilities.[3] Hailed by its proponents as landmark legislation that will improve the lives of 43 million Americans, the ADA is a comprehensive civil rights measure that bans discrimination in employment, public accommodations, public services, transportation, and telecommunications.

The focus of this chapter is the employment title of the ADA. As will be argued, the employment title has a key flaw that will limit its effectiveness and create potentially serious economic inefficiencies: in addition to banning employment discrimination, the law imposes on employers a duty to accommodate the mental or physical limitations of people with disabilities. This distorts a basic civil rights measure into a mandated benefits program for people with disabilities. While some people with disabilities will surely gain, perhaps markedly so, in terms of higher wages and better job opportunities, many others, particularly those who are low-skilled, with more severe disabilities, or seeking entry-level positions, will experience modest (if any) gains and could well find their job opportunities restricted. The potential clearly exists for the gains to people with disabilities to be outweighed by the economic costs imposed on society as a whole.

The Economic Meaning of Discrimination

To analyze the likely costs and benefits of the ADA, it is useful to begin with a simple model of the economics of discrimination. Based on the competitive theory of discrimination developed in the seminal research of University of Chicago economist Gary Becker (1971), economic discrimination means failing to hire, retain, promote, or compensate identical people on equal terms, where *identical* means making the same net contribution to the firm's output or profits. For example, some employers may be repelled by people with severe deformities, fearful of noncontagious diseases, or ill-informed about the intellectual capabilities or social skills of people with physical impairments. To have an adverse effect on wages and employment, such aversions must be manifest in employers' willingness to incur some cost to avoid people with disabilities. Absent discrimination, employers would be driven by competition to compensate workers such that the value of an additional hour worked equaled the cost of that additional hour.[4]

To see how economic discrimination affects wages and employment, consider a firm that discriminates against people who are black. From an economic perspective, this means that the firm is unwilling to hire blacks at the same wage (or total compensation) as equally productive whites, or, stated another way, it demands fewer blacks than whites at any particular wage. The reduced demand for blacks among firms that discriminate reduces the relative wages of blacks. Interestingly, however, it also creates an economic opportunity for nondiscriminators: firms that do not discriminate can hire these equally productive workers and produce the same output at lower economic cost. Lost profits is the price an economic discriminator pays to indulge his or her preference for discrimination.

The imposition of a simple antidiscrimination law (of the "equal-pay-for-equal-work" sort) would implicitly tax this preference for discrimination, increasing the demand for minority workers and raising their wages (Landis 1968). For the economy as a whole, such a law need not result in any productivity losses since it would merely induce a substitution of one type of worker for another equally qualified type.[5]

The ADA goes well beyond an equal-pay-for-equal-work requirement, however. Rather than amend existing civil rights statutes to include people with disabilities, Congress created a new civil rights law that on its face requires unequal treatment of equals. In particular, it bars employment discrimination against people who are (1) "disabled" (that is, have a physical or mental impairment that "substantially limits one or more of the major life activities," have a record of such an impairment, or are regarded as having such an impairment) and (2) able to perform the "essential functions" of the job *with or without reasonable accommodation*.[6] The remedies and procedures of the Civil Rights Act of 1964 apply.

Apart from creating a broad and potentially ambiguous class of people considered disabled, the ADA includes in the protected class people who, in an economic sense, are not as productive or who do not make the same contribution to the profitability of the firm as nondisabled people with the same qualifications. These are the people who can perform only the essential functions of the job and who can do so only with accommodation. At the same time, the ADA expands the concept of discrimination to include employers who fail to hire these lesser-qualified/higher-cost individuals or who fail to make costly accommodations.[7] While promoting the employment of this much broader group may be a highly valued social goal, the antidiscrimination, reasonable accommodation approach is a costly and inefficient way of attempting to achieve it.

What Is "Reasonable Accommodation"?

Under the ADA, employers are required to make whatever accommodations to the job or workplace are necessary to permit a "qualified individual with a disability" to perform the "essential functions" of the job. In general terms, this means, for example, making offices or work sites readily accessible and usable, restructuring jobs or modifying work schedules, acquiring or modifying equipment, and modifying examinations and training materials. Companies are excused from making accommodations that would impose an "undue hardship" on their operations, taking into account the size and financial resources of their business.[8]

Sounds reasonable enough, but what will it mean in practice? Regulations issued by the U.S. Equal Employment Opportunity Commission (EEOC), which became effective on July 26, 1992, together with congressional reports on the legislation, reveal that the employer's obligations will be interpreted expansively. Accommodations include the following: modifying hours or responsibilities to reduce workload and stress for someone with, say, a heart condition or mental disorder; providing additional unpaid leave for someone requiring treatment; hiring a proofreader (or using another employee) to assist someone with a disorder affecting accuracy; providing an interpreter for someone who is deaf or a mechanical page-turner for someone with no hands or with limited physical dexterity; or making structural changes in the workplace for someone with a mobility impairment—whatever may be necessary, in other words, provided the accommodation does not impose an undue hardship on the business. The larger and more profitable the business, the more costly will be the accommodations that are likely to be found "reasonable."

The reasonable accommodation provision thus amounts to a requirement that employers incur costs in hiring members of the protected class, whether in the form of direct expenses for accommodations, indirect expenses associated with management time, or foregone output. Employers must incur these costs, moreover, without weighing the expected benefits in terms of increased sales or output.[9] This is not to suggest that firms should be permitted to make judgments as to the desirability of hiring people with disabilities who can produce on equal terms with nondisabled people; this would be barred under the simplest antidiscrimination law. The issue is the net cost of accommodation and who should properly finance it.

Balancing Expected Benefits and Expected Costs

If scarce resources are to be put to their highest-valued uses, firms must be in a position to evaluate expected benefits and expected costs, which determine the expected returns to an outlay, and to make decisions accordingly. In unregulated, competitive markets, firms cannot incur the expense of an accommodation (or pension plan or on-the-job-training program) unless they expect to recoup enough extra output or sales in the future to make the investment worthwhile; if labor is mobile, workers will not incur the cost unless they expect to recoup it through either improved employment opportunities or increased wages later. If both the worker and employer expect positive returns on an investment, the employer will offer it, the employee will accept it, and both will be made better off.[10] It is the flexibility of wages and other components of the compensation package that allows the interests of employees and employers to be aligned to generate these positive market outcomes.[11]

Wheelchair ramps for people with mobility impairments, job coaches for people with mental retardation, interpreters for people who are deaf no less than pensions, on-the-job-training, and day care will be provided in private markets if they can be structured as part of a mutually beneficial, productivity-enhancing arrangement between the worker and the employer. For example, an employer may well furnish and bear a substantial portion of the cost of a wheelchair ramp and other physical accommodations for an employee if in doing so accessibility is enhanced for customers and future employees. However, the cost of an interpreter, who provides quite specific benefits to a worker who is deaf, is likely to be borne largely by that worker (in the form of reduced wages), and the interpreter is likely to be offered by the employer only if the worker judges the expense to be worth incurring. The size or profitability of the firm–the criterion to be used in assessing whether an accommodation must be made–bears no necessary relationship to the efficient business decision to invest in recruiting, screening, hiring, training, and in other ways accommodating different individuals. The key is the relationship between expected costs and expected benefits, which determines expected returns.[12]

Certainly there are exceptions to these generalizations. Some firms undoubtedly fail, because of discrimination, to provide accommodations that would be cost-beneficial, and other firms, out of benevolence, surely offer accommodations that are not apparently cost-beneficial. However, the mere presence or absence of accommodations provides no immediate indication of economic discrimination, where this term is taken to mean an aversion to or avoidance of people with disabilities that is unrelated to productivity and manifest in hiring and pay decisions.

By directly regulating the terms of employment contracts with people with disabilities–banning certain arrangements and dictating others–the ADA will tend to increase the cost of hiring people with disabilities and thus distort business decisions. The law mandates accommodation but generally precludes adjustments in wages or other compensation. It mandates a level of accommodation without regard to expected benefits, and it does so for economic discriminators and nondiscriminators alike. The ADA is not, therefore, structured to economize on the resources needed to achieve wage and employment gains for people with disabilities. The law will impose economic inefficiencies and, as discussed later, a potentially undesirable redistribution of income.

Empirical Studies on the Cost of Accommodation

Congress enacted the ADA without any rigorous analysis of its costs and benefits. However, one small-scale study of the costs of accommodation was widely cited by proponents of the legislation to suggest that accommodations would be very inexpensive. Conducted in 1982 by Berkeley Planning Associates, this study reported that half of the cases of accommodation involved no costs; another 30 percent involved costs under $500; and less than 5 percent involved costs over $5,000 (Berkeley Planning Associates 1982).

Unfortunately, the scope and design of this study seriously limit its value for purposes of drawing inferences about the aggregate cost of the ADA requirement. Apart from being quite dated, the study relied on survey data gleaned from just 367 responding companies–federal contractors already subject to a reasonable accommodation requirement under Section 504 of the 1973 Rehabilitation Act. Moreover, the results were biased, tending to understate the cost of accommodation for contractors and noncontractors alike. The cost data reported in this study generally included out-of-pocket costs only, excluding, for example, the cost of management time and the time of engineers as well as the costs associated with added supervision and training for the workers with disabilities (Collignon 1986; Rosen 1991). In some cases, even the cost of construction materials was ignored. Moreover, the study did not assess which of these costs would have been incurred in the absence of the law–due to voluntary accommodations–or how costs would be affected by hiring additional workers with disabilities. (One would expect the marginal cost of accommodation to rise as workers with more severe disabilities are drawn into the labor market by the enactment and enforcement of the ADA.) Finally, the study did not assess the indirect costs of accommodation, such as reductions in the availability of programs that boost productivity. (One would expect firms to cut back on other forms of compensation, such as on-the-job training for unskilled workers or job counseling and medical treatment for employees who have just become disabled.) As University of Chicago professor Sherwin Rosen (1991, 23) has noted, the figures reported in this study should be considered "a liberal lower bound" on accommodation costs.

Of course, even if it were demonstrated that most accommodations were inexpensive, with costs properly measured, the efficiency or inefficiency of the law would turn on the question of how costs were distributed across firms and whether the benefits were commensurate. As indicated earlier, the costs a firm must incur depend not on the benefits likely to result but on who seeks employment with what kinds of disabilities and accommodation needs and how the cost of providing accommodation stacks up under the undue hardship test. This is hardly a recipe for an efficient allocation of costs.

Beyond that, there is virtually no empirical research on the extent of discrimination against people with disabilities or on the benefits expected to result from eliminating discrimination or mandating accommodation. In fact, the one study cited by federal regulators as containing empirical estimates of these benefits concluded, "given the state of existing knowledge, there is no basis for anything more than an informed guess" (EEOC 1991a, 8584; O'Neill 1976, 5). The problem discussed in the next section, is that disability is not a concrete, observable characteristic that is conducive to careful measurement. Moreover, the potential earnings of people with disabilities–particularly those who do not work and may never have worked–cannot be known.

Uncertainty of the Legal Standard

Apart from the inefficiencies stemming from the reasonable accommodation mandate, there will be inefficiencies stemming from the uncertainty of the legal standard (Weaver 1991a). Under the law and regulations, there are no guidelines for employers that delineate the essential versus unessential functions of different jobs, the types of accommodations that are appropriate for different disabilities or jobs, or even the range and severity of impairments covered by the ADA. For all but the most severely impaired workers or those with obvious physical or mental impairments, the question of who is disabled, and thus who may file a claim of civil rights violation, will be unclear.[13] (Recall that under the ADA, individuals need not even be presently disabled or limited in their work ability to enjoy the full protections of the act.) Moreover, the determination of what accommodations are necessary or appropriate, and whether the individual with these accommodations can perform the essential functions of the job, must be made before medical evidence can be gathered or inquiries can be made as to the nature or severity of the individual's impairment. Uncertainties will abound as employers attempt to assess, on a case-by-case basis, their duty to accommodate, taking into account the limitations of particular individuals, the nature of particular jobs, and the financial and other circumstances of their businesses.

These uncertainties will be compounded by practical questions about what constitutes discrimination, questions that do not arise in other civil rights cases. For example, is it legal to hire one person with a disability over another if the former requires less costly accommodation? Is it legal to hire an individual (with or without a disability) who can perform all aspects of a job over a person with a disability who can perform only the essential aspects? Is it legal to reduce wages if accommodations include reduced workloads or reduced quotas for speed or accuracy?

Firms will respond to these uncertainties in different ways. Some will overcomply; some will undercomply. Under reasonable assumptions, too much accommodation–that is, accommodation that costs society more than it is benefited–will result (Calfee and Craswell 1984).

The Costs and Benefits

Evidently, the reasonable accommodation requirement will increase the cost of hiring people with disabilities, and this, in turn, will tend to discourage their employment. If, therefore, the ADA is to have its hoped-for effects, it will have to be aggressively enforced, meaning that aggrieved individuals will have to press their claims and the EEOC will have to redirect its limited resources away from complaints involving other minorities toward those involving people with disabilities. With aggressive enforcement, the employment and wages of many workers with disabilities will surely rise. Paradoxically though, the extent of these gains is likely to be in direct proportion to the costs (the economic inefficiencies) the courts are willing to impose on the private sector. As the courts decide just who is covered and just what is "reasonable," they have the capacity to fundamentally alter the costs and benefits of the law.

With these caveats, the following generalizations can be made:

1. In the case of the many people who need no accommodation in the jobs they hold or seek, the reasonable accommodation provision should impose no inefficiencies. (This group comprises people who, for example, have had cancer that is in remission or who have a hearing impairment that is corrected with a hearing aid.) In addition, the equal pay and equal employment opportunity elements should serve to root out true economic discrimination. The primary inefficiencies will result from a substitution away from individuals who can perform all aspects of their jobs toward individuals who cannot and a general increase in the cost of laying off workers with disabilities. People who already have jobs will benefit at the expense of those who do not.

2. Many other people need relatively inexpensive accommodations, some of which would have been provided privately through agreements with employers. To the extent accommodation agreements would have been reached voluntarily–in which case they would tend to reflect an efficient level of accommodation in conjunction with wages and other

compensation–the law will generally force firms to increase wages or quite possibly invest too much in accommodation, or both. In firms that are economic discriminators, the law will likely increase the wages and employment of people with disabilities; because of the absence of any weighing of benefits and costs, however, these adjustments could be either inadequate or excessive.

3. Still others covered by the law will require very costly accommodations and, as stated before, in at least some of these cases, firms will be required to spend too much on accommodation, wages, or both. As in the case of people needing lower-cost accommodations, the test of "too much" is not the cost of the accommodation or even the cost in relation to profits; it is the cost in relation to expected benefits. If expected costs exceed expected benefits, the resources devoted to alternative uses–whether plant and equipment, research and development, other private investments, or hiring and accommodating other workers with disabilities–would have yielded a higher return. And the cost to society in terms of resources foregone exceeds the gains to the affected people with disabilities.

In short, the equal pay and equal employment provisions of the ADA, to the extent they are actively enforced, should serve to root out economic discrimination and thus increase the employment and wages of people with disabilities. The reasonable accommodation provision, however, will make some people with disabilities more costly to hire and generally reduce the flexibility of employment contracts, thereby undermining the opportunities of some workers and creating distortions in the labor market (Weaver 1991b; Rosen 1991).

The reasonable accommodation requirement amounts to a mandated benefits program for people with disabilities–an off-budget spending program that will increase labor costs, inhibit job formation, and, quite possibly, produce an undesirable distribution of gainers and losers. Income and wealth will tend to be transferred from consumers generally (through higher product prices), "nondisabled" substitute workers (through a decreased demand for their services), and shareholders of affected firms toward a segment of the disabled population–largely the higher skilled, and among them, the ones who already have jobs. Opportunities for some people with disabilities, particularly those who are unskilled and severely impaired–whose opportunities are already restricted by the minimum wage–will be further restricted (Burkhauser 1992).

The differential impacts of the ADA on people with disabilities are not likely to be limited to those based solely on skill level. Consider, for example, the person with a degenerative disease, such as Parkinson's disease, or a disease with episodic symptoms, such as certain forms of mental illness; the person requiring costly accommodation; or even the person who is not disabled but is at increased risk of disability (for example, an older worker).

Firms contemplating hiring these people–in contrast to, say, a midcareer worker with a stable medical condition (perhaps a veteran with limited use of the legs and requiring little or no accommodation)–face relatively greater exposure to legal liability or a legal liability that is relatively more difficult to assess. This liability translates into a potential cost of employment that is in addition to any direct cost of accommodation.

Or consider the person with mental retardation who is part of a community-based program attempting to arrange employment for a team of young adults with mental retardation. Such programs typically offer job coaches to monitor and ensure performance. The employer contemplating hiring this team now has to be wary of the obligations to continue employment, to finance the job coaches, or to take on other responsibilities if the team's performance does not live up to expectations. Risks that previously were borne by the workers and the employment program are shifted to the employer. And certain mutually beneficial arrangements between the workers and employer (whether more training or counseling and less accommodation, more accommodation and less wages or other benefits, or less compensation for a job!) are simply illegal. While it may seem only reasonable to try to shield people from these adjustments, this protection (when mandated on employers) comes at a cost: the employment of some people with disabilities will suffer.

Based on economic theory, we can conclude that the ADA will increase the employment and wages of some people with disabilities, perhaps quite substantially. Higher-skilled workers with less-disabling impairments and, among them the ones who already have jobs, are likely to benefit as employers attempt to meet the spirit of the ADA in a least-cost manner. But for many others, particularly low-skilled, severely impaired people, the gains are likely to be modest at best and may well be negative. The potential clearly exists for the gains to people with disabilities to be outweighed by economic costs for society as a whole.

The Inherent Limits of the Civil Rights Approach

What few proponents acknowledged during the debate over the ADA will become evident as the law is implemented in the 1990s: the civil rights/reasonable accommodation approach is not only costly but inherently limited in its ability to help people with disabilities. There are, after all, many people who are too severely impaired to work given their age and education and many others who have impairments of such severity that, given the state of our knowledge and technology, they are not well suited for competitive employment. For them, the ADA amounts to an entitlement to something they cannot use. Still others have impairments of such severity that, given the availability of Social Security Disability Insurance (DI), Supplemental Security Income (SSI), and Medicare and Medicaid–and the work disincentives embedded in these programs–they are simply not in the market for a job. (Over 3 million people with disabilities receive DI cash payments, which are conditional on nonwork, and almost none of these people return to work.)[14] For them, the ADA amounts to an entitlement to something they will not use–at least not until the value of work relative to income support is altered sufficiently. It is just not known how large the remaining group is–those who are currently employed or could reasonably expect to become employed and whose wages and employment opportunities can be improved by the ADA.

Even with strict enforcement and broad acceptance of the goals of the ADA, moreover, earnings gaps are likely to prevail because the ADA does nothing to improve the skills that people with disabilities bring to the labor market. To appreciate the powerful role of education alone, Burkhauser (1990) reported that in 1987 the ratio of earnings of men with disabilities to the earnings of men without disabilities was 30 percent for men who did not finish high school, rising to 64 percent for men with a high school degree and to 72 percent for men with at least some college. Family incomes of men with disabilities who had high school degrees stood at an impressive 91 percent of family incomes of similarly situated nondisabled men. Evidently, the earnings gap between people with and without disabilities varies markedly by level of educational attainment (Burkhauser, Haveman, and Wolfe 1993).

The Unique Nature of Disability

A central flaw in the ADA, drawing as it does on the civil rights model, is its failure to reckon with the unique nature of disability (Weaver 1986, 1991a; Oi 1991; Oi and Andrews 1991). Unlike race, the minority classification that gave rise to the 1964 Civil Rights Act, the condition of disability itself–the underlying physical or mental impairment–generally places a limitation on work ability; it tends to reduce productivity on the job or limit the jobs that individuals are capable of performing.

In addition, unlike race, disability is a complex and changing phenomenon. An individual may be born with a disability or become disabled. The condition may deteriorate or improve, disappear or reappear, or lead to death. It may have an impact on work ability now and not later or later but not now, but the impact on work is rarely all-or-none.

And, unlike race, disability is inherently a condition affected by individual choice. For many people, though certainly not all, there is a choice about whether or not to work and how much to work. All of us know someone who has overcome a very severe disability to work, either because of financial necessity or personal wherewithal, and most of us know someone who does not work despite circumstances that would permit it. There are people everywhere in between these two extremes who decide at some point during the course of or following their illness or injury whether or not to work and, if so, whether to work part- or full-time.

There are also choices about occupation (coal miner, construction worker, or clerk; professor or pilot), lifestyle (smoking, drinking, drug use, or skydiving), education, training, rehabilitation, insurance coverage, and quality and timing of medical care. All of these choices affect the probability and severity of impairment and the probability, extent, and rate of recovery. Many of these same choices, together with motivation and family, community, and public support, influence how disabling an impairment will be in the labor market.

Incentives, Work, and Disability

That disability is not a concrete, black-or-white medical condition unaffected by individual choice has two important implications for government policy. First, incentives matter. Poorly designed government programs can increase the proportion of the population reporting impairments and work disabilities and increase the economic costs of disability. Second, accurately assessing who is disabled in terms of work ability and to what degree is an elusive goal at best.

As Leonard notes (1986, 64):

> The crux of the matter is that disability is not simply a medically defined condition, but depends rather on an array of psychological, sociological, and economic factors. A person who perceives himself or herself as disabled may thereby become disabled. A person who is perceived by others as disabled may thereby be disabled. A person who finds greater economic returns to disability than to work may not struggle so hard to work. This need not be a question of fraud or dissembling, but merely of adapting to the given incentives.

Disability, in other words, is an "elusive and elastic" state (Oi 1991, 31).

Tables 4.2 and 4.3, which report data on the number of people receiving government disability transfer payments in various countries, are illuminating in this regard. The four countries included in these tables, the Netherlands, the United States, Sweden, and Germany, have pursued quite different policies for people with disabilities. Social policy in Germany and Sweden, in contrast to social policy in the Netherlands and the United States, has focused more on keeping people with disabilities at work than on providing income support for those who do not work.[15]

TABLE 4.2   Number of Disability Transfer Recipients, 1970 – 1989 (in thousands)

	1970	1975	1980	1985	1989	Growth in 1970s Percent	Growth in 1980s Percent
The Netherlands							
Full disability pensions	186	322	565	632	706		
Partial disability pensions	44	57	108	130	177		
Total	230	379	673	762	883	193	31
United States							
Disability insurance	1,394	2,489	2,859	2,656	2,999		
Supplemental security income	870	1,723	1,777	1,942	2,210		
Total	2,264	4,212	4,635	4,598	5,209	105	12
Sweden							
Total	188	289	293	323	361	56	23
Germany							
Full disability pensions	812	980	1,237	1,563	1,256		
Partial disability pensions	387	255	182	142	114		
Early retirement for handicapped		17	76	258	255		
Total	1,199	1,252	1,495	1,963	1,625	25	9

Source: Aarts, Burkhauser, and de Jong (1992).

Referring to table 4.2, in the United States, for example, the number of people receiving DI or SSI payments was nearly 2.3 million in 1970, rising to 4.6 million in 1980 (an increase of 105 percent) and again to 5.2 million in 1989. In the Netherlands, the number of disability recipients jumped a whopping 193 percent in the 1970s and by close to one-third in the 1980s. West Germany and Sweden, by contrast, experienced much slower (but still healthy) growth in the benefit rolls over the period. Table 4.3, which indexes the number of disability recipients by the number of active participants in the labor force, reveals the same basic trends–rapid growth in the 1970s and substantially slower growth in the 1980s, with wide variations in the incidence of disability across all four countries. Whereas in 1989, 139 people in the Netherlands received disability payments per thousand workers–fully 13.9 percent–the figure stood at 7.8 percent in Sweden and 4.3 percent in the United States.

One needn't be a physician, scientist, or epidemiologist to know that these data cannot be taken as a measure of the actual incidence of severe health-related problems. High unemployment, on the one hand, coupled

TABLE 4.3   Number of Disability Transfer Recipients Per Thousand–Labor Force Participants, Ages 15-64, 1970–1989

	Number per Thousand					Growth in 1970s (Percent)	Growth in 1980s (Percent)
	1970	1975	1980	1985	1989		
Netherlands	49	77	126	130	139	157	10
United States	27	42	41	51	43	52	5
Sweden	49	67	68	74	78	39	15
West Germany	51	54	59	72	55	16	−7

Source: Aarts, Burkhauser, and de Jong (1992).

with generous and rising disability benefits (particularly in the Netherlands
and the United States) on the other, led large numbers of workers to
withdraw from the labor market in the 1970s. Generally improved economic
conditions, tighter eligibility, and in some cases, reductions in expected
disability payments moderated these trends in the 1980s. As the authors of
this cross-national study conclude, "the root cause of the increasing
incidence of disability over the past two decades has more to do with policy
medicine these countries provided their health-impaired workers than with
any change in the underlying health of their citizens" (Aarts, Burkhauser,
and de Jong 1992, 3).

The data presented here suggest a link between the generosity of
government programs and the incidence of disability–and thus of the
element of choice and the role of incentives–but they do not constitute
empirical evidence on the matter. Isolating the work incentive effects of
government policy requires empirical techniques that attempt to hold
constant other causal factors, such as the unemployment rate. It also requires
creativity in the selection of data. Among other problems, there is the crucial
issue of arriving at a measure of health or disability.[16] For example, some
studies use survey data on self-reported health or activity limitations, while
others use data on mortality to infer health status in earlier periods
(Haveman, Wolfe, and Huang 1989).

A considerable amount of such empirical research has been conducted
in the United States, by economists Donald Parsons (1980, 1982), Jonathan
Leonard (1979), and John Bound (1989, 1990), among others, on the
relationship between the DI program and the labor force participation of
older men. This research supports the contention that increases in DI
benefits, holding everything else the same, have had a large and significant
effect on reducing labor supply. While each study reports somewhat
different results, the range of estimates suggests that at least one-half of the

marked decline in the labor force participation of older men in the 1960s and 1970s was due to DI.[17]

Policymakers seeking more effective programs for people with disabilities at lower economic cost must come to grips with the incentives inherent in government policy. Neither the extent of disability nor the aggregate cost of disability can be minimized if federal policy continues to ignore the unique and complex nature of disability and the interplay between disability, incentives, and individual choice. Policymakers will be confronted with this reality in the years ahead as the ADA is implemented and its high cost and limited effectiveness are revealed.

Conclusions ~~in provimenth~~

Promoting the employment of people with disabilities requires expanding the number of such people willing and able to work; improving the information and understanding employers have about their skills, capabilities, and potential; and enhancing–not undermining–employers' incentives to hire them. Public policy should foster an environment in which people with disabilities bring strong skills to the workplace and employers have the incentive to develop creative new ways of incorporating them into their workforces. Incentive-based approaches to reform hold real promise for promoting the employment of people with disabilities at lower economic costs than mandated benefit-type programs.

Notes

1. This paper draws on Weaver (1991b, 1992).

2. Other criteria (less commonly cited) include having not worked in the past year because of illness or disability; having ever left a job or retired for health reasons; not working because of a long-term physical or mental illness or disability that prevents any kind of work; and receiving Social Security Disability Insurance or Supplemental Security Income based on a disability. U.S. Bureau of the Census (1989).

One of the problems with survey data, as noted by Oi and Andrews (1991, 2), is that "the line separating the disabled from the nondisabled is fuzzy depending on the activity and environment. An inability to reach or to lift could be a seriously disabling condition for a lobster fisherman but only a nuisance for a dispatcher. In a survey, the latter may not even admit to having a work limitation." Survey responses also reflect the extent to which disability is viewed as a "legitimate" reason for being out of the labor force, and views on this may change over time.

3. Americans with Disabilities Act of 1990, 42 U.S. Code 12101 (July 26, 1990).

4. In addition, when there are fixed costs of employment, such as those associated

with certain types of accommodations, the worker's total product will equal or exceed his total cost (Rosen 1991).

5. Inefficiencies would stem from compliance costs, such as those associated with modifying application and hiring procedures, or from employers' costs for defending themselves against erroneous claims of discrimination (which would also increase the cost of laying off less productive workers).

6. Major life activities are "basic activities that the average person in the general population can perform with little or no difficulty" such as walking, talking, seeing, breathing, sitting, reaching, learning, and working. Equal Employment Opportunity Commission (1991b, 35741).

7. This follows directly from the law, which defines a qualified person with a disability as "one who, with or without reasonable accommodation, can perform the essential functions of the employment position," and defines discrimination to include not making accommodations to the physical or mental limitations of a qualified person (other than accommodations that would impose an "undue hardship," meaning "a significant difficulty or expense").

This construction of the law has led analysts Oi and Andrews (1991, 15) to conclude that employers will be "discouraged from searching for the most highly qualified applicant" and will be encouraged instead to pursue a "satisficing policy." In their words, "the efficiency losses from a satisficing hiring policy might be small if the variance in performance across individuals is small. If, however, the variance is large, as it is perceived to be when filling a highly skilled position, an obligation to take the first qualified applicant could entail a substantial opportunity cost."

8. Other factors to be considered include the type of business, the composition of the workforce, and the cost and nature of the accommodation.

9. Congress explicitly rejected an amendment that would have related accommodation costs to the value of the job, as measured by the compensation paid. Under the amendment, accommodation costs for an individual would have been capped at 10 percent of the individual's salary. See Equal Employment Opportunity Commission (1991b, 35730).

10. *Positive returns* refers to a return that is at least as good as could be earned on alternative investments; employees and employers are better off in an *ex ante* sense.

11. Minimum wage laws limit the adjustments that can be made in the wage component of the compensation package, thereby reducing the likelihood of accommodation (and thus of employment) for unskilled workers with disabilities.

12. According to Rosen (1991, 26), "there is no inherent reason to expect that labor markets free of government intervention will fail to provide job accommodations in normal job situations. . . . [A]ccommodation would occur precisely in those situations where it should occur–where its benefits exceed its costs. The worker would not be accommodated where accommodation is inefficient."

13. As acknowledged by the Equal Employment Opportunity Commission, neither the law nor the regulations "attempt a laundry list of impairments that are disabilities. The determination of whether an individual has a disability is not necessarily based on the name or diagnosis of the impairment the person has, but rather on the effect of that impairment on the life of the individual. . . . The

determination. . . . must be made on a case by case basis." Equal Employment Opportunity Commission (1991b, 35741). For more on the subjectivity inherent in, or the uncertainties surrounding, deciding who has a disability, see Weaver (1986, 1991a).

14. DI is the federal government's largest cash program for people with disabilities. To be eligible for DI, a worker must be unable to perform any substantial gainful activity anywhere in the national economy. Benefits are payable after a five-month waiting period; after two years on the benefit rolls, disabled workers are eligible for Medicare. Individuals who work (even with severe disabilities) are generally not eligible for benefits. In recent years, just 1 percent to 2 percent (or less) of beneficiaries have returned to work annually; the vast majority remains on the benefit rolls for life. For more on the program, see Social Security Administration (1993) and Weaver (1992).

15. In these countries, programs or policies emphasizing work have included rehabilitation, government-provided jobs, job quotas, and government subsidies for hiring people with disabilities. See Aarts, Burkhauser, and de Jong (1992).

16. Also, individual's expected incomes in *and* out of the labor force, theoretically important to the labor supply decision, are unobservable. See Leonard (1986).

17. For summaries of this literature, see Leonard (1986), Oi and Andrews (1991), and Bound (1990). See also Parsons (1991).

References

Aarts, L., R. V. Burkhauser, and P. de Jong 1992. *A cautionary tale of European disability policies: Lessons for the United States.* Syracuse, NY: Metropolitan Studies Program, The Maxwell School, Syracuse University, ISSN 1061–1843 (February).

Americans with Disabilities Act. 1990. 42 U.S. Code, sec. 12101, 26 July. 1990.

Becker, Gary S. 1971. *The economics of discrimination.* 2d ed. Chicago: University of Chicago Press.

Berkeley Planning Associates. 1982. *A Study of Accommodations Provided to Handicapped Employees by Federal Contractors: Final Report. 2* vols. Prepared under contract no. J-9–E-1–0009 to the Office of the Assistant Secretary for Employment Standards, U.S. Department of Labor. Berkeley, CA: Berkeley Planning Associates.

Bound, J. 1989. "The Health and Earnings of Rejected Disability Insurance Applicants." *American Economic Review* 79: 482–503.

———. 1990. "Disability Transfers and the Labor Force Attachment of Older Men: Evidence from the Historical Record." *National Bureau of Economic Research Working Paper No. 3437* (September).

Burkhauser, R. V. 1990. "Morality on the Cheap: The Americans with Disabilities Act." *Regulation* (summer): 47–56.

———. 1992: "Beyond Stereotypes: Public Policy and the Doubly Disabled." *The American Enterprise* 3: 60–69.

Burkhauser, R. V., R. H. Haveman, and B. L. Wolfe. Forthcoming. "How People with Disabilities Fare when Public Policies Change." *Journal of Policy Analysis and Management.*

Calfee, J. E., and R. Craswell. 1984. "Some Effects of Uncertainty on Compliance and Legal Standards." *Virginia Law Review* 70: 965–1003.

Collignon, F. C. 1986. "The Role of Reasonable Accommodation in Employing Disabled Persons in Private Industry." In *Disability and the Labor Market: Economic Problems, Policies, and Programs*. Edited by Monroe Berkowitz and M. Anne Hill. Ithaca, NY: ILR Press, 196–241.

Equal Employment Opportunity Commission. 1991a. "Equal Employment Opportunity for Individuals with Disabilities: Notice of Proposed Rulemaking." 29 CFR Part 1630, *Federal Register* 56 (28 February 1991): 8578–603.

——. 1991b. "Equal Employment Oportunity for Individuals with Disabilities: Final Rule." 29 CFR Part 1630, *Federal Register* 56 (26 July 1991): 35726–56.

Haveman, R. H., B. L. Wolfe, and F. M. Huang. 1989. "Disability Status as an Unobservable: Estimates from a Structural Model." *National Bureau of Economic Research Working Paper, No. 2831* (January).

Landis, W. M. 1968. "The Economics of Fair Employment Laws." *Journal of Political Economy* 76; 507–45.

Leonard, J. S. 1979. "The Social Security Program and Labor Force Participation." *National Bureau of Economic Research Working Paper, No. 392* (August 1).

——. 1986. "Labor Supply Incentives and Disincentives for Disabled Persons." In *Disability and the Labor Market: Economic Problems, Policies, and Programs*. Edited by M. Berkowitz and M. A. Hill. Ithaca, NY: ILR Press, 64–94.

O'Neill, D. M. 1976. *Discrimination Against Handicapped Persons: The Costs, Benefits, and Inflationary Impact of Implementing Section 504 of the Rehabilitation Act of 1973 Covering Recipients of HEW Financial Assistance*. Arlington, VA: Public Research Institute (18 February 1976).

Oi, W. Y. 1991. "The Workfare-Welfare Dilemma." In *Disability and Work: Incentives, Rights, and Opportunities*. Edited by C. L. Weaver. Washington, D.C.: The AEI Press, 31–45.

Oi, W. Y. and E. S. Andrews. 1991. *The ADA in a Labor Market for People with Disabilities*. Unpublished manuscript (3 January 1991).

Parsons, D. O. 1980. "The Decline in Male Labor Force Participation." *Journal of Political Economy* 88 (February): 117–34.

——. 1982. "The Male Labor Force Participation Decision: Health, Reported Health, and Economic Incentives". *Economica* 49 (February): 81–91.

——. 1991. "The Health and Earnings of Rejected Disability Insurance Applicants: Comment." *American Economic Review* 81 (December): 1419–26.

Rosen, S. 1991. "Disability Accommodation and the Labor Market." In *Disability and Work: Incentives, Rights, and Opportunities*. Edited by C. L. Weaver. Washington, D.C.: The AEI Press, 18–30.

Social Security Administration. 1993: *Social Security Bulletin: Annual Statistical Supplement, 1993*. Washington, D.C.: U.S. Government Printing Office.

U.S. Bureau of the Census. 1989. *Labor Force Status and Other Characteristics of Persons with a Work Disability: 1981–1988*. Current Population Reports, Series P-23, No. 160. Washington, D.C.: U.S. Government Printing Office.

Weaver, C. L. 1986. "Social Security Disability Policy in the 1980s and Beyond." In *Disability and the Labor Market: Economic Problems, Policies, and Programs*. Edited by M. Berkowitz and M. A. Hill. Ithaca, NY: ILR Press, 29–63.

———. 1990. "The ADA: Another Mandated Benefits Program?" *The American Enterprise* 1: 81–84.

———. 1991a. "Disabilities act Cripples Through Ambiguity." *The Wall Street Journal* (31 January 1991), A15.

———. 1991b. "Incentives Versus Controls in Federal Disability Policy." In *Disability and Work: Incentives, Rights, and Opportunities*. Edited by C. L. Weaver. Washington, D.C.: The AEI Press, 3–17.

———. 1992. "Reassessing Federal Disability Insurance." *The Public Interest* 106; 108–21.

5

Black–White Wage and Employment Differentials: The Spatial Mismatch Hypothesis

David L. Sjoquist

Introduction

It may come as a surprise to some to learn that black–white wage and employment differentials have been increasing *in recent decades, the very same decades during which blacks made undoubted gains in social acceptance. Blacks had always earned and been employed less than whites. That was a familiar fact for the two decades following World War II. But since the mid-1950s, remarkable events have occurred on the social and legal front. The Supreme Court struck down* de jure *racial segregation of schools in its decision in* Brown *v.* Board of Education *in 1954. The Civil Rights Act of 1964 was passed, and implemented; it was also strengthened by amendments in 1972. While racial divisions persist, they are* supposed *to be diminishing. The issue of racial wage and employment differentials seems to be a problem of a previous generation.*

Some may appreciate that this is not the actual record, but few probably are aware that that is not the statistical record, at least as concerns wage and employment differences between blacks and whites. In this chapter, David Sjoquist examines the spatial mismatch hypothesis, and its younger cousin, the skills mismatch hypothesis, as an explanation for the increasing racial differential. The spatial mismatch hypothesis was formulated more than 25 years ago to explain these differences. This hypothesis holds that the underlying factors accounting for the increase in wage and employment differentials are the changing structure of the economy and the persistent barriers to adjustment that prevent blacks from attaining the wage and employment levels of whites.

What does the spatial mismatch hypothesis say? It relies on a central fact of urban life in the United States. Since the end of World War II, both population *and* jobs *have been suburbanized. The fastest growing areas are suburban areas. As a corollary, central cities have experienced exactly the opposite effects. All is well, or at least all is not so bad, if everyone can adjust to these changes. But blacks may face more constraints. Since blacks, at least initially, are more predominantly located in central cities, they need to commute to the new suburban jobs. But they have fewer means for commuting–blacks have lower incomes and lower rates of automobile ownership. Public transportation to the new suburban jobs is less available–for technical and perhaps also for other reasons.*

One can think about the spatial mismatch hypothesis on two levels. First, from the point of view of positive economics, is it true? Can we test the validity of the spatial mismatch hypothesis? Sjoquist reviews the literature, which is mixed on this question, and also calls upon his own work to address this issue. Second, we can approach the spatial mismatch hypothesis from the normative or policy perspective. What should be done? The spatial mismatch hypothesis carries with it a specific set of policy recommendations, which Sjoquist develops in detail in this chapter.

One of the most perplexing and unsettling economic issues in the United States is the large and growing disparity between blacks and whites in wage levels and employment rates, a pattern that is especially evident among less-skilled workers. The United States has had decades of affirmative action legislation, made efforts to improve the economic performance of lower-skilled workers a priority, and experienced nearly a decade of continuous albeit slow growth of the national economy. It is thus troubling that blacks have yet to reach equality with whites and are now doing worse when compared to previous decades.

The average earnings of black males have declined relative to whites since 1975. Likewise, the percentage of black males who are employed has fallen. Bound and Freeman (1992) explored differences in wages and employment rates for young black and white males (defined as those with less than 10 years of work experience) over the period 1973–1989. Controlling for the amount of education and experience, they found that the wage rate for young black males reached approximately 94 percent of the wage rate for young white males in 1975. From that time, the black wage rate began to fall, and by 1989 the ratio of the wage rate of young black males relative to whites had fallen to about 83 percent.

Bound and Freeman also investigated the changes in the employment rate for these two racial groups. They found that after controlling for the level of education and experience, the employment rate for young black males relative to young white males has fallen since 1973. For example, for young black males with five years of experience and a high school degree, the employment rate was 84 percent in 1973 and 74 percent in 1989. For the equivalent group of young white males, the employment rate was 93 percent in 1973 and 89 percent in 1989. The difference was 9 percentage points in 1973 but widened to 15 percentage points in 1989 (Bound and Freeman, 207.)

What is the cause of this deterioration in the position of blacks relative to whites? Many hypotheses have been offered to explain this observed pattern in wage and employment rates. In this chapter, however, we focus on one of the many possible explanations: namely, the spatial mismatch hypothesis. We also briefly explore a related hypothesis known as the skills mismatch hypothesis. This chapter explores these two hypotheses, their theoretical underpinnings, the empirical evidence, and the policy implications.

The spatial mismatch hypothesis says that the cause of the black–white disparity in employment outcomes is the shift in jobs, especially blue-collar jobs, from the central city to the suburbs and beyond. It is argued that as job opportunities for lower-skilled workers move to the suburbs, central city residents are less able to find employment and those who do receive lower wages. Furthermore, it is argued that housing discrimination prevents minorities from moving to the suburbs. Since blacks are more likely to reside in the central city than are whites, in part because of housing discrimination, they bear the brunt of the burden that results from the migration of jobs to the suburbs.

The skills mismatch hypothesis is related to the spatial mismatch hypothesis and is based on changes that have occurred in the structure of employment in the U.S. economy. The forces that have led to this transformation include changes in the technology of production, increased foreign competition, and the increase in offshore production of many products. The skills mismatch hypothesis contends that as a result of these changes jobs that were disproportionately held by blacks have disappeared faster than jobs disproportionately held by whites. In addition, the jobs that are being created require a different and usually higher set of skills than the skills possessed by many of the blacks who have been displaced. As a result, blacks relative to whites are less able to find employment and must accept lower wages; wages and employment rates for blacks have thus declined relative to these whites. This transformation of the composition of jobs is especially evident in central cities where over the past several decades there has been a shift from blue-collar, lower-skilled jobs to white-collar, information-processing jobs requiring higher skills.

These two hypotheses have recently received increased attention in the discussion of the rise of the urban underclass. The urban underclass refers to the growing concentration of residents within large central cities who endure long periods of poverty and exhibit forms of deviant behavior such as dropping out of school, criminal activity, teenage pregnancies, and the like. Wilson (1987) has argued that the rise in the level of concentrated poverty, especially among blacks, within large central cities in the United States is in part the result of the inability of low-skilled minority workers to find employment. Wilson argues that the movement from the city to the suburbs of jobs that are desirable for low-skilled workers and the higher skill requirements of jobs that have located in central cities have significantly reduced the ability of low-skill central city workers to obtain meaningful work.

We should note at the outset that not everyone accepts the spatial mismatch hypothesis. And even those who do accept the hypothesis do not necessarily believe that it is the only explanation. Opponents argue, first, that while there has been a movement of jobs from the city to the suburbs, it does not necessarily follow that this explains the decline in the wages or employment of low-skilled workers. There are many possible explanations for the decline in employment and wages. The rise in welfare program benefits has reduced work incentives, engaging in crime has become a profitable alternative to work, and the increase in white female labor force participation has displaced minorities from jobs they might otherwise have had. Second, the empirical evidence on the spatial mismatch hypothesis is mixed; some studies find evidence that supports the hypothesis while others do not.

Understanding the cause of the relatively lower employment rate and wage levels for blacks is necessary in order to design appropriate policy. For example, if the spatial mismatch hypothesis is correct, then one policy that should be considered is a transit program that improves the spatial access to suburban jobs. If the hypothesis is not true, then such transit programs may not be needed.

This chapter proceeds as follows. In the second section the theoretical foundations for the spatial and skills mismatch hypotheses are explored. In the third section, the initial research on the hypothesis is presented, and more recent research is discussed in the fourth section. Policies for addressing the problem are then discussed in the last section.

Theoretical Underpinnings

Spatial Mismatch

To illustrate the theory behind the spatial mismatch hypothesis, we will use a simple supply-and-demand model. In particular, the spatial mismatch hypothesis is explained, using some simplifications, within the context of a two-sector general equilibrium model. In the model, the two sectors refer to the two geographic labor markets represented by the central city and the suburbs. *General equilibrium* refers to the concept that the two sectors or markets are interconnected so that changes in one market affect the other market. Thus, until supply equals demand in both markets and no firm or individual in one jurisdiction is able to do better by relocating to the other jurisdiction, an equilibrium does not exist.

Equilibrium with No Commuting—We start with the first labor market, which we take to be the central city. Suppose, for purposes of the argument, that all workers are equally productive and that all jobs are identical. Further, assume, temporarily, that there is no commuting or migration of jobs or workers into or out of the central city. In other words, we consider the central city to be a closed market for labor. Within the central city, we can represent the labor market by a simple supply-and-demand graph. The equilibrium wage and the equilibrium quantity of labor are determined where the supply curve and the demand curve intersect.

Figure 5.1, graph A, represents the central city labor market. The supply of labor, denoted S_c, is upward sloping, suggesting that at a higher wage, more individuals are willing to work or to work longer hours. The downward-sloping demand, denoted D_c, reflects the willingness of businesses to hire more workers or have workers work more hours as wages decrease. Equilibrium occurs at a wage of w_c and a quantity of labor L_c.

Consider now the suburban labor market, represented as graph B in figure 5.1. Like the central city, the suburban labor market has a supply and demand for labor, denoted S_s and D_s, respectively. This determines the equilibrium wage as w_s and the equilibrium quantity of labor as L_s.

Suppose that the population is the same in both markets so that the supply curves are identical. However, as illustrated in figure 5.1, the demand for labor is greater in the suburbs than in the city. Given that the two supply curves are the same, it follows that the wage in the suburbs w_s is higher than the wage in the city w_c. Furthermore, since the population is the same in the two jurisdictions, and $L_c < L_s$, it follows that the percentage of the population employed is higher in the suburbs than in the central city; that is, the employment rate in the city is lower than in the suburbs. With the possibility of migration or movement of workers or firms between the two jurisdictions ruled out, figure 5.1 represents an equilibrium in both markets and thus a general equilibrium.

Equilibrium with Commuting—Now relax the assumption that the two labor markets are closed, and instead allow workers to commute between the two jurisdictions. For the time being, continue to assume that individuals and firms cannot change residences. With the higher wage rate and more plentiful job opportunities in the suburbs, individuals living in the city can be expected to seek employment in the suburbs. City residents who are employed will seek jobs in the suburbs because the wage rate is higher in

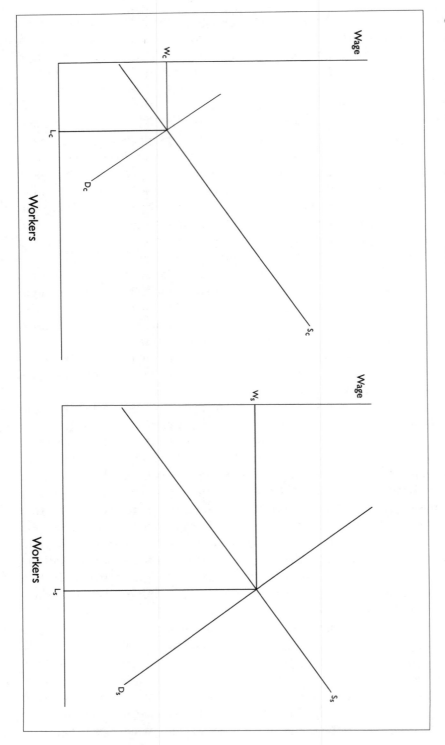

Figure 5.1   Two Labor Markets, No Commuting.

the suburbs. In addition, some of the city residents without jobs–that is, those who are willing to work at a wage of w_s but not at a wage of w_c, will also seek suburban jobs.

The willingness of city residents to seek employment in the suburbs causes an outward shift in S_s, the supply of workers to the suburban labor market and an equal but inward shift in S_c, the city labor supply. These shifts in supply will result in a decrease in the suburban wage and an increase in the central city wage. It will also increase the number of central city residents who are employed and reduce the number of suburbanites who are employed. This is illustrated in figure 5.2. Lines S_{c0}, S_{s0}, D_{c0}, and D_{s0} represent the original supply-and-demand curves from figure 5.1. Lines S_{c1} and S_{s1} represent the supply curves after city residents commute to the suburbs. (Note that there is no change in the demand for labor in either market.)

Central city residents who obtain jobs in the suburbs will have to commute farther to their jobs. (For simplicity we assume that there is no commuting if one works in the jurisdiction in which one lives.) Since commuting to the suburbs involves time and money, central city residents will not seek jobs in the suburbs if the suburban wage is too low. Thus, in order for the city resident to be willing to incur the cost of commuting, the wage in the suburbs must exceed the wage in the central city by the cost of commuting. The farther away the job, the longer the commute, and thus the greater the cost of commuting.

Suppose the cost of commuting from the city to the suburbs, denoted C, is the same for all city residents and is fixed. For a city resident who is willing to work in the city at a wage of no less than w_c, the wage in the suburb must be at least equal to $w_c + C$ before that individual is willing to take a job in the suburbs. Thus, the number of central city residents commuting to the suburbs will expand until the difference between the wages in the two labor markets just equals the cost of commuting. Thus, in an equilibrium in which some city residents work in the suburbs, w_{1s} must equal $w_{c1} + C^2$. Thus the wage, net of commuting cost, is lower for city residents than for suburban residents. In figure 5.2 $w_{c1} = w_{s1} - C$, so it is an equilibrium. In figure 5.2, lines S_{c1} and S_{s1} are drawn under the assumption that $w_c = w_s - C$.

As seen in figure 5.2, there has been an increase in the number of city residents who are employed and a decrease in the number of suburban residents who are employed. The numbers of city and suburban residents who were originally employed are given by L_{c0} and L_{s0}, respectively. The numbers of workers employed in the city and suburbs are now L_{c1} and L_{s1}, respectively. L_{c1} is also the number of city residents who now work in the city, while L_{s1}' is the number of suburban residents who now work in the suburbs. The number of city residents who work in the suburbs is given by

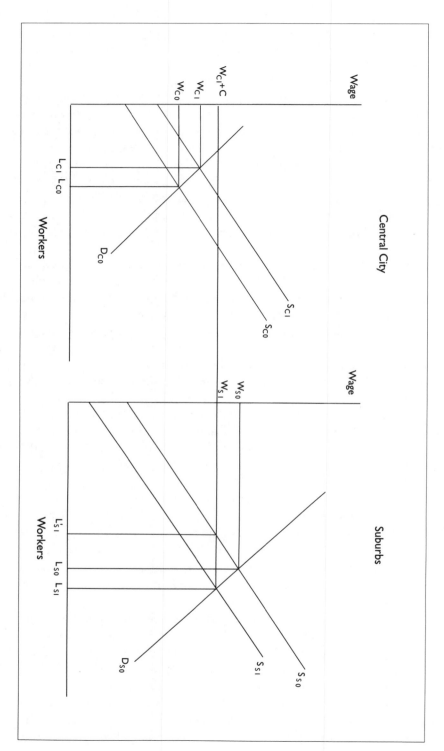

Figure 5.2 Equilibrium with Commuting.

$L_{s1}-L'_{s1}$, which is greater than $L_{c0}-L_{c1}$. Thus, the number of city residents who work increases as a result of commuting. However, the employment rate for city residents is less than for suburban residents since the wage rate, net of commuting cost, is less for city residents than for suburban residents.

Increase in Number of Jobs in Suburbs—Figure 5.3 illustrates what would happen if for some reason the number of firms in the suburbs increased while decreasing in the city. Figure 5.3 includes the equilibrium established in figure 5.2. Thus, the lines given by D_{c0} and D_{s0} represent the original demand curves (from figure 5.1), while lines S_{c1} and S_{s1} represent the supply curves from figure 5.2. The initial equilibrium is represented by the equilibrium wages w_{s1} and w_{c1} and the equilibrium quantities of labor by L_{c1} and L_{s1}. The suburbanization of firms results in a decrease in the demand for workers in the city and an increase in demand in the suburbs. Lines D_{c1} and D_{s1} represent the new demand curves. With no additional commuting, the new equilibrium will be given by the equilibrium wages w_{s2} and w_{c2} and equilibrium quantities of labor by L_{c2} and L_{s2}. The shift in firms to the suburbs results in a decrease in the number of city residents who are employed and a decrease in the wage received by city residents who work in the city–but also an increase in the wage of city residents who work in the suburbs. The number of city residents who no longer work as a result of the suburbanization of firms equals $L_{c1}-L_{c2}$.

Of course, as a result of the suburbanization of firms, additional city residents will now commute to the suburbs. As before, allowing additional commuting increases the supply of labor in the suburbs and reduces it in the city. If the cost of commuting is the same as before the suburbanization of firms, then commuting will offset completely the effect of the suburbanization of firms, wages will be unchanged, and the same number of city residents will be employed. However, as firms suburbanize, they are likely to locate farther and farther from the central city, and therefore the cost of commuting to these newly suburbanized jobs will be higher. If this is true, then the effect of the suburbanization of jobs and additional commuting will be to reduce employment of central city workers.

Equilibrium Allowing Change of Location—Suppose now we also allow firms, as well as individuals, to move between jurisdictions. Given sufficient time, we expect that suburban firms will move to the city in response to the lower wages and that those city residents who work in the suburbs will move to the suburbs in order to avoid the commuting costs. If relocation costs are zero, then the result of this migration of firms and individuals is for the wage rates and the likelihood of getting a job to be equalized across the two labor markets–that is, $w_c = w_s$ and $L_c = L_s$ and therefore central city residents will be at no disadvantage vis-à-vis suburban residents.

Labor Market Imperfections—The foregoing analysis assumes perfectly functioning labor markets, including perfect information about jobs and

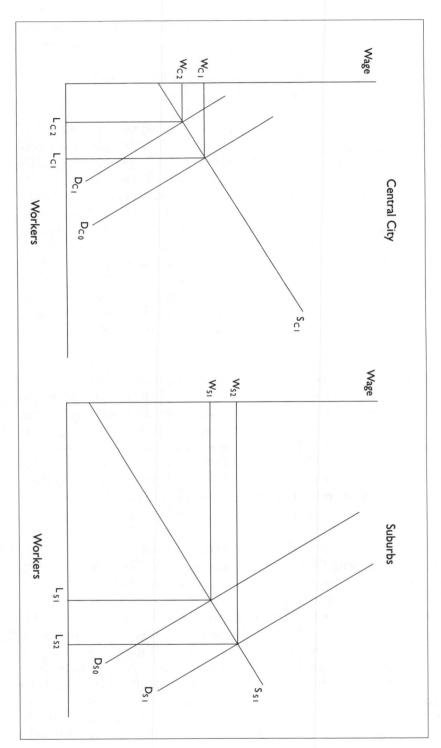

Figure 5.3   Shift of Firms from City to Suburbs.

wage rates. It also assumes no real or perceived differences in workers, jobs, or location and that in the long run individuals and firms are free to locate wherever they desire. But if these assumptions do not hold, then the equilibrium in which wage rates and employment rates are equal will not necessarily occur. This is the conclusion of the spatial mismatch hypothesis, which suggests that wages and employment rates will be lower for city than for suburban residents. Thus, for the spatial mismatch hypothesis to hold, the labor market or the housing market must not function perfectly or the long-run equilibrium must take a very long time to be achieved.

There are several imperfections that might exist that would prevent the attainment of the equilibrium described here. First, workers differ in their abilities. If some central city residents have very low skills and if there is a legal minimum wage that exceeds what firms are willing to pay these low-skilled workers, then these workers may not find employment either in the city or the suburbs. Second, information regarding wages and the availability of job openings may be, and no doubt is, imperfect. For example, many jobs are filled through word of mouth, which makes obtaining information about job openings very difficult. Third, for some workers commuting to the suburbs might be very expensive or perhaps even an impossibility because of an absence of public transit. Fourth, discrimination in the housing market or suburban zoning (motivated by whatever reason) may preclude residents of the central city from moving to the suburbs. The existence of these conditions will prevent the labor markets from reaching the long-run equilibrium in which the employment rates and wages are the same for city and suburban residents.

Employer Discrimination—Another potential source of imperfection in the functioning of the labor market is employer discrimination against certain types of individuals. Let us assume that firms located in the suburbs discriminate against black workers. In particular, suppose that suburban employers are less willing to hire black workers than white workers. We can interpret this to mean that for equally qualified black and white workers, the employer is willing to pay the white worker a higher wage or alternatively will hire the black worker only if the worker is willing to accept a lower wage than the white worker.

There are several possible reasons why discrimination by employers may be more prevalent in the suburbs. First, employers who do not want to hire black workers may decide to locate in areas where there are mainly white workers. Since few blacks live in the suburbs, firms that discriminate against blacks will locate in the suburbs. Likewise, these firms are not likely to move to the city in response to lower wage rates there. Second, discrimination may be caused by customer and employee pressure on the employer. Perhaps white customers prefer to shop in stores that do not employ black workers. Since suburban stores will have more white than black customers, these stores will tend to hire white workers rather than black workers. Similarly, if white employees resist the hiring of black employees, then businesses with mainly white workers may feel pressured to avoid hiring black workers. Firms with large white staffs are more likely to be found in the suburbs since firms tend to draw their workforce from individuals who live nearby.

To incorporate suburban employer discrimination into the analysis, we have to construct a new suburban supply of black workers and white workers. (This analysis follows the work of Gary S. Becker [1971].) For simplicity, we assume that employers in the central city do not discriminate and that suburban employers are willing to hire black workers only if the wage paid to black workers is less than the wage paid to white workers.[3] In particular, assume that the difference in the wages equals a fixed amount, represented by d, and referred to as the discrimination premium. Under this assumption, suburban employers consider the white wage as the cost of hiring a white worker but the cost of hiring a black worker as being equal to the wage paid to black workers plus the discrimination premium. We further assume that the total numbers of whites and blacks are the same and that the supply curves of blacks and whites are the same–that is, that at any given wage the number of blacks who are willing to work is the same as the number of whites.

The first step is to construct the market supply curve of labor in the city and suburbs. Initially assume that no commuting takes place. The supply curve in the city is simply the sum of the supply curves for whites and blacks living in the city. To construct the suburban labor supply we determine for each value of w_{sw} the suburban wage paid to white workers, the number of white workers supplied at that wage, and the number of black workers supplied at that wage less d. For example, in Figure 5.4, L'_{sw} (L''_{sw}) in graph A is the number of white workers who are willing to work at the wage W'_{sw} (W''_{sw}), and L'_{sb} (L''_{sb}) in graph B is the number of black workers who are willing to work at the wage $W'_{sw} - d$ $(W''_{sw} - d)$. The sum of L'_{sw} (L''_{sw}) and L'_{sb} (L''_{sb}) equals L'_s (L''_s), which is presented as S_s in graph C of figure 5.4. We also show the supply of labor in the suburbs if there was no discrimination, denoted as S'_s.

In figure 5.5, we incorporate in graph B the suburban supply of labor curve from graph C of figure 5.4. Figure 5.5 illustrates the two labor markets, still assuming no commuting. In the city, since employers do not discriminate, equilibrium occurs where D_c intersects S_c. The demand for workers in the suburbs, D_s, represents the number of workers that the employers will hire given the wage paid to white workers is W_{sw} and the wage paid to blacks is $W_{sb} = W_{sw} - d$. The intersection of S_s and D_s in figure 5.5 determines for the suburban labor market the total number of workers hired, L''_s, and the wage paid to white workers, W''_{sw}. Black workers are paid W''_{sb}. These

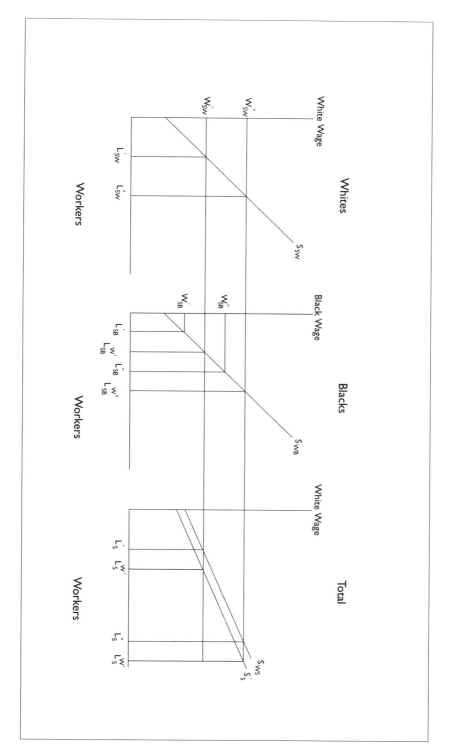

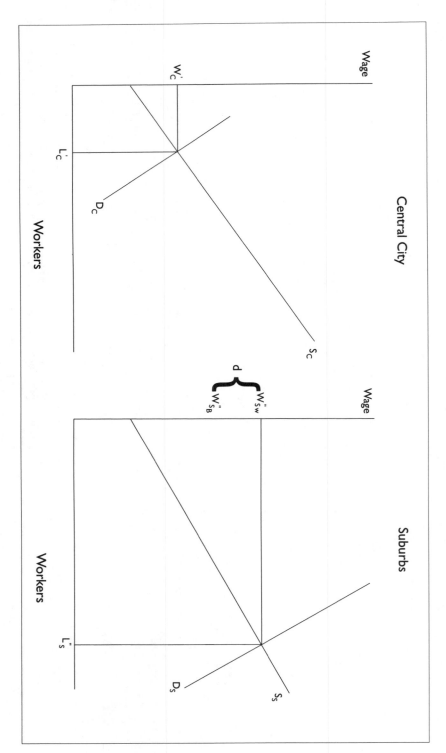

Figure 5.5   Equilibrium with Employer Discrimination, No Commuting.

wages are the same as W''_{sw} and W''_{sb} from figure 5.4. Thus, from figure 5.4 we see that the number of white workers hired equals L''_{sw} and the number of black workers hired equals L''_{sb}. Note that the number of white and black workers hired equals the number of white and black workers who are willing to work at the equilibrium wages, W''_{sw} and W''_{sb}.

In figure 5.5, the equilibrium wages in the two markets are not equal. Thus, there is an incentive for individuals to commute or move and for employers to move. We assume, however, that individuals and employers do not move and thus consider only commuting. If workers are free to commute, then in equilibrium the wage rate for black workers, net of any commuting cost, will have to be the same in the two markets. The same condition must hold for white workers.

As constructed, in figure 5.5 the wage rate for blacks is higher in the suburbs than in the city. Thus, blacks from the city will choose to commute to work in the suburbs, thereby reducing the wage in the suburbs and increasing it in the city. Since the wage paid to whites in the city is the same as that paid to blacks (recall that we assumed that city employers do not discriminate) and is lower than what whites can get in the suburbs, white city residents will also commute to the suburbs. Furthermore, because of discrimination, black workers will earn less than white workers, and the percentage of blacks who work will be less than that for whites. These conclusions follow since in equilibrium the wage in the city must equal the wage for blacks in the suburbs, net of the commuting cost, which is less than the wage for whites in the suburbs.

If we assume that all central city whites commute to the suburbs, then it follows that central city blacks will commute as long as the suburban wage for whites, less the discrimination premium and the cost of commuting, is greater than the wage in the central city. Thus, equilibrium will be the same as in figure 5.3 except that the difference in the two wage rates will equal the sum of the commuting cost as well as the discrimination premium. The number of whites hired will be greater than the number of blacks since blacks receive a lower wage than whites. Since the white population equals the black population, it also follows that the employment rate for blacks is less than that for whites.

Skills Mismatch

The skills mismatch can be addressed in a framework similar to that used for the analysis of spatial mismatch. Rather than two spatially separated markets, consider the markets for two different skill levels. (The analysis also applies to any two types of skills that require an investment in training or retraining to switch between.) For this discussion assume that there are high-skill jobs and low-skill jobs. Because it is costly to acquire a higher skill (or to retrain), the wage for the high-skill worker in equilibrium will be greater than the wage of the low-skill workers. If the wage rate for high-skill workers increases relative to low-skill workers, then it will pay for a low-skill worker to invest in human capital and become a high-skill worker. An equilibrium of the supply and demand for the two types of labor is equivalent to that illustrated in figure 5.2. Instead of city and suburb, the two markets are low- and high-skill workers, and instead of commuting cost, it is the cost of obtaining the higher skill. The difference in the wage between the high- and low-skill worker is just small enough so that no low-skill worker finds it to his or her advantage to invest in becoming a high-skill worker.

Now suppose that the demand for low-skill workers falls and the demand for high-skill workers increases. Such a shift could occur, for example, if a change in technology makes it advantageous to replace low-skill workers with high-skill workers in the production process. The result of the shift will be an increase in the wage for high-skill workers and a reduction in the wage for low-skill workers.

To the extent that blacks are more likely to possess the skill for which demand falls, they will bear the greater burden of the shift in demand for specific skills. If that is correct, then wages for blacks will fall, as will the employment rate. Only after retraining or the acquisition of additional skills will the wage and employment rate increase.

This change in the relative wages provides an incentive for individuals to acquire additional skills, increasing the supply of high-skill workers and reducing the supply of low-skill workers. Over a sufficiently long period of time, the number of high-skill workers relative to the number of low-skill workers will increase as more individuals invest more heavily in human capital. In the long run, the result of this adjustment will be to bring the difference in the wages back to their initial levels. However, it is likely that this adjustment will occur only after a long period of time. To increase the supply of high-skill workers requires either that existing low-skill workers acquire additional skills or that new entrants into the labor force possess higher levels of training. Either process requires time. Thus, the short-run equilibrium in which high-skill workers receive a wage premium may exist for a protracted period of time.

A similar effect can occur if there are shifts in the supply of the two types of labor. For example, suppose it becomes more expensive to acquire additional skills or the quality of education or training obtained by certain groups of individuals, say blacks, declines. Although it will require substantial time for such changes to be reflected in the supply of certain skills, the effect of such shifts will be an increase in the supply of low-skill workers and a decrease in the number of high-skill workers. The wage difference will widen, with the wage for the low-skill worker falling relative to the high-skill worker.

The change in relative wages will provide incentives for firms to shift production techniques and adopt production processes that rely more heavily on lower-skill workers. The result of the shift in the production process will be to reduce the wage difference, although the difference will still be larger than before the change in the skill mix of the labor force. But again, such a response on the part of firms may require substantial time, and thus the wage and employment differential may exist for a long period of time.

Initial Research on Spatial Mismatch

The spatial mismatch hypothesis was first addressed by John F. Kain in 1968. Kain (1968) was concerned with the low employment rate of central city blacks, particularly those blacks with lower skill levels. He argued that there was a spatial mismatch in urban areas, with jobs for low-skill workers being increasingly concentrated in the suburbs but with low-skill black labor residing in the central city. What he observed was essentially the situation presented in figure 5.1. But Kain further argued that housing discrimination prevented blacks from locating in the suburbs and hence taking advantage of the better job opportunities. Kain did not prove, or even investigate the possibility, that housing discrimination existed. But he did observe that housing patterns of blacks suggested racial housing segregation.

Kain developed and tested three hypotheses:

- Residential segregation affects the geographic distribution of black employment. In order to avoid commuting costs, individuals are likely to work close to their place of residence. If blacks are segregated within certain areas of the city, it then follows that we would expect them to work near those areas. This situation is implicit in figure 5.2.

- Kain also argued that residential segregation increases black unemployment. Kain argued that employers are more prone to hire blacks if the percentage of blacks within the area surrounding the firm is high. In other words, the demand for black workers depends upon the percentage of blacks in the area. Since blacks are segregated, suburban firms are less willing to hire blacks than if blacks were housed more uniformly across the metropolitan area. The model presented earlier, incorporating employer discrimination, suggests that fewer blacks will be employed as a result of discrimination by suburban employers.

- Kain further noted that since World War II there has been a pattern of suburbanization of employment. He argued that this suburbanization, combined with residential segregation and the difficulties of finding and obtaining jobs distant from one's residence, has hindered the employment of blacks. Within the structure of our model, the suburbanization of jobs is associated with a shift to the right in the demand for labor in the suburbs and a shift to the left in the city's demand for labor. Housing discrimination prevents blacks from moving to the suburbs, and hence the labor market does not achieve either the short-run equilibrium illustrated in figure 5.2 or the long-run equilibrium in which the wage rate and the employment rate are the same in both labor markets.

In essence Kain argued that the shift of jobs from the city to the suburbs, and the corresponding housing discrimination in the suburbs and difficulties associated with job access, results in blacks being less able to find employment and firms being less willing to hire black workers. Thus, there was both a demand side and a supply side argument to Kain's hypothesis.

On the demand side, Kain argued that suburban employers were less willing to hire black workers than were city employers. Because suburban firms had primarily white customers or white employees, there was pressure on employers not to hire black workers. This pressure stemmed from the fear that white customers and employees would object to the firm hiring black workers. On the other hand, if the area surrounding the firm had a large concentration of blacks, then the firm would feel pressure to hire blacks. However, housing segregation meant that blacks did not live near the site of suburban jobs.

On the supply side, Kain argued that even if suburban employers were willing to hire blacks, the spatial separation between black residents and job opportunities would reduce information that blacks have about job openings. This lack of information would reduce the number of jobs that blacks obtained in areas that are distant from their residences. Furthermore, even if a black could locate and obtain a suburban job, the longer commuting time would discourage blacks from taking suburban jobs.

To investigate these hypotheses, Kain employed data from Detroit and Chicago. Each city was divided into workplace zones that represented small geographic areas within each city. He used these data to estimate the following regression equation separately for each city:

$$E = \alpha + \beta R = \gamma D, \tag{5.1}$$

where

E is the percentage of employment in the workplace zone held by blacks.

R is the percentage of residents in the workplace zone who are black.

> D is the distance between the center of the workplace zone
> and the major black ghetto.
>
> α, β, and γ are parameters to be estimated.

From the hypotheses, we expect E and R to be positively related; that is, the estimated value of β is expected to be positive. The hypothesis is that with more blacks living in the zone, more of the jobs within that zone will be held by blacks. Kain found, as expected, a positive (and statistically significant) value for β.

Likewise, the farther away an employment zone is from the bulk of black residences–that is, the greater the value of D–the less likely it is that a black will be employed in that zone. In the model presented in figure 5.2, we assumed that C was constant, but clearly living farther away increases the commuting costs and hence reduces the likelihood of employment. Kain found that γ was negative; that is, the greater the distance between an employment zone and the black ghetto, the lower the percentage of blacks employed in that zone.

More Recent Evidence

Kain's research was conducted over 25 years ago, and so it is appropriate to ask whether there has been any change during the intervening period that renders the idea of spatial mismatch irrelevant. Economic theory suggests that over time, barring any barriers to mobility, employers and workers will relocate, and the resulting new equilibrium will eliminate any effect of the initial spatial mismatch. But we need to look at what has happened to the location of jobs and workers.

It is very well documented that jobs have suburbanized. It is not true that employers have literally moved to the suburbs although that does happen. Instead, through the natural birth and death process of firms, employment within the central cities of most large metropolitan areas has declined, while increasing in the suburbs. During recessions, firms go out of business with little difference between the business death rates in the city and the suburbs. During expansions, however, new firms are more likely to be created in the suburbs than the city. Furthermore, as firms expand, they are more likely to expand in the suburbs to obtain the additional space they need.

The suburbanization of employment is the result of several forces. The change in the technology of production and transportation has meant that manufacturing firms need large, inexpensive tracts of land, tracts that are found outside the central city. Improvements in communication technology have reduced the need for firms to be located in close proximity to one another, and thus there has been a decentralization of many industries. Also, many firms avoid central cities because of the higher tax rates and such problems as crime and traffic congestion.

Table 5.1 shows the central city share of unskilled employment for several large metropolitan areas in 1970 and 1980 and the percentage change during that period. Notice that the central city share of jobs, including less-skilled jobs, decreased during that decade. While not presented in table 5.1, there has also been a change in the industrial composition of jobs within the central city. In the immediate post–World War II period, manufacturing was located in the central cities. During the past several decades, cities have lost manufacturing jobs to the suburbs and beyond. In addition, many of the retail and wholesaling jobs have also disappeared from the central cities as middle-class families have moved to the suburbs. In place of these jobs, central cities now house high-skill, information-processing types of jobs along with low-skill, low-wage service jobs. Thus, the supply of blue-collar jobs and low- to moderate-skill jobs has expanded in the suburbs relative to the city.

But as the jobs have left the central city, so have the residents. Table 5.1 also shows the central city share and change in the share of unskilled workers. Notice that in nearly all of these metropolitan areas there has been a decrease in the central city share of these workers. Most of these cities have also experienced an absolute loss in the number of workers, not just a loss of share.

This pattern is consistent with the model presented earlier. As jobs

TABLE 5.1   Changes in Jobs and Workers

MSA	Percentage of MSA Unskilled Jobs in Central City		Percentage Change	Percentage of MSA Unskilled Workers in Central City		Percentage Change
	1970	1980		1970	1980	
New York	74.3	64.0	−13.9	72.0	62.2	−13.60
Chicago	54.8	45.3	−17.3	58.1	46.9	−19.30
Los Angeles	45.2	45.2	0.0	41.5	40.4	− 0.03
Philadelphia	50.0	40.7	−18.6	48.5	36.6	−24.50
Detroit	38.8	27.4	−29.4	45.4	29.1	−35.90
San Francisco	38.1	34.3	−10.0	28.5	22.3	−21.80
Washington, D.C.	48.0	41.0	−14.6	46.1	26.4	−42.70
Dallas	53.0	47.3	−10.8	57.9	33.1	−42.80
Houston	76.5	73.7	− 3.7	54.4	59.4	9.20
Boston	38.8	34.3	−11.6	28.5	23.5	−17.50

Source: Census of Population

become more plentiful in the suburbs, workers follow. (We do not want to imply that the only reason that city residents left the city is to find employment. It is clear that other forces such as urban problems like crime, taxes, and school quality have also been at play.) The loss of central city population has been largely a white phenomenon, although more recently blacks have spilled out of the city, locating in areas along the edge of the city.

The data in table 5.1 suggest that workers are not trapped in the central city. However, it is not clear from table 5.1 whether the shifts in workers have been sufficient to offset the suburbanization of jobs. Thus, we need to look at other evidence. There are at least three ways of empirically exploring the spatial mismatch hypothesis. First, we could relate the employment rate and wage rate in the central city to the degree of job suburbanization. The hypothesis suggests that the greater the degree of suburbanization, the lower the employment and wage rates will be, particularly for lower-skilled minority workers. A second approach is to see whether lower-skilled minority workers who work or live in the suburbs have better labor market outcomes. Finally, we can investigate whether the level of access to jobs is related to the likelihood of having a job. We will consider a few of the studies that have used each of these approaches.

The Effects of Suburbanization

Our model suggests that if jobs shift to the suburbs faster than workers, employment rates and wages in the central city will fall. An early study along these lines was conducted by Mooney (1969). He used 1960 Census of Population data from 25 metropolitan areas to explore, via regression analysis, the relationship between the black male employment rate within the high poverty rate areas of each metropolitan area and the metropolitan-wide unemployment rate. The relationship between these rates would provide a measure of aggregate demand for workers and various measures of the centrality of blue-collar jobs within the metropolitan area. He found that the more centralized the location of jobs, the higher the employment rate within the black community. However, he also found that the effect of the unemployment rate was greater than the effect of the location of jobs. He thus concluded that macroeconomic policy designed to tighten labor markets offered the best chance for improving the employment and income conditions of blacks. He found that a 1 percentage point increase in the unemployment rate within the metropolitan area led to a 2.9 percentage point decrease in the employment rate for black males living in high poverty rate areas within the central city. On the other hand, a 1 percentage point increase in the proportion of jobs located in the suburbs led to a 0.19 percentage point decline in the employment rate for the same group of black males.

Farley (1987) updated Mooney's research using 1980 census data and obtained results that support Mooney's finding. In particular, Farley found that central city black unemployment relative to the white unemployment rate was higher the more suburbanized were the blue-collar jobs. Leonard (1987) also considered the effect of suburbanization of jobs and found that, in Los Angeles and Chicago, as jobs moved farther away from the central city over time, the typical black employed in blue-collar jobs worked closer to the central city.

The work of Moody focused on employment rates and used aggregate data, for which it is not possible to control for individual differences such as education, marital status, gender, and the like. Ihlanfeldt and Sjoquist (1989) investigated the effect of job suburbanization on earnings using individual (micro) data. They found, for a large sample of metropolitan areas, that wages of central city residents were lower the greater the decentralization of jobs, suggesting that the decentralization of population has not kept up with the decentralization of employment opportunities. They related the level of earnings, less commuting cost, for individual central city lower-skilled workers to the degree of suburbanization of low-skill employment opportunities. Data on individual heads of household were obtained from the Panel Study of Income Dynamics (PSID).[4] Regression equations were estimated in which the dependent variable was the earnings of the head of the household less an estimated cost of commuting. Several independent variables were used to control for the characteristics of individuals that may affect earnings–for example, age and education. Another set of variables were included to control for differences between the metropolitan area in which each of these individuals resided. These variables included the unemployment rate and the percentage of the population that is black. The variable of most interest was the suburbanization of employment, which was measured as the percentage of low-skill jobs located in the suburbs. Separate regressions were run by race and gender.

The authors found that suburbanization of jobs has had a negative effect on earnings of male central city workers regardless of race. For males, a one standard deviation change in the percentage of low-skill jobs housed in the suburbs would result in a $1,000 change in annual earnings. The effect for females was smaller.

The Effect of Working in the Suburbs

Another approach to investigating whether spatial mismatch is still an issue is to determine whether wages for blacks who work in the suburbs are higher than for those of equal skill who work in the central city. If suburban job opportunities are in fact better, as claimed by the mismatch hypothesis, then we would expect to find that those blacks who do find employment in the suburbs will have higher earnings. Note that this approach does not address the likelihood of finding employment either in the city or the suburbs; it considers only those blacks with jobs. There are several studies that have approached the issue this way but with mixed results.

Danziger and Weinstein (1976) found, after controlling for differences in characteristics such as education and age, that blacks who lived in the city and worked in the suburbs earned 11 percent more than blacks who lived in the city and worked in the city. The reason for the higher earnings was that suburban workers worked in occupations and industries that were better paying. Thus, if blacks working in the city retained their same occupation and industry when they worked in the suburbs, there would be no advantage for a black to work in the suburbs. But if working in the suburbs means changing occupation and industry, then being employed in the suburbs will be beneficial. Similar findings were obtained by Straszheim (1980), who studied blacks in the San Francisco area. He found that blacks without any college education earned approximately 10 percent more by working in the suburbs than in the city.

Ihlanfeldt (1988) found a similar effect in the Atlanta area–namely, that blacks earned more in the suburbs. Ihlanfeldt controlled for occupation, so that the effect on wages was not the result of differences in occupations between the city and suburbs. However, in another study using data from Philadelphia, Detroit, and Boston, Ihlanfeldt (forthcoming b) did not find any spatial difference in wages for black workers. Ihlanfeldt (1992a) studied the wages for fast-food restaurants in Atlanta and found that starting wages are significantly higher in the suburbs than in the city.

The Effect of Living in the Suburbs

Another way of investigating the effect of central city location on blacks is to compare the earnings of blacks who live in the city with comparable blacks who live in the suburbs. Studies that were conducted shortly after Kain published his work found that blacks living in the suburbs did not do any better than blacks living in the city. Some of the more recent studies, however, find that a suburban residential location does benefit blacks. Kasarda (1989) found, for example, that among less-educated blacks, the employment rate for blacks living in the suburbs was slightly higher than for those living in the central city. Price and Mills (1985) studied the differences in earnings among 25-to-59-year-olds who work full-time. They found that blacks who live in the suburbs earned 6 percent more than central city residents, controlling for both education and occupation. Jencks and Mayer (1990) made similar comparisons for each of three years, 1959, 1969, and 1979. For the first two years, they found no significant difference between central city and suburban residents in earnings. However, for 1979 they did find a significant difference for blacks who did not attend college.

Comparative studies of city and suburban residents is, however, hindered by the possibility that the researcher cannot control for differences in the two groups. In other words, blacks who live in the suburbs may be different than blacks who live in the city in some important but unmeasured way. Rosenbaum and Popkin (1991) studied a group of individuals who were essentially randomly selected for location in either the suburbs or the central city. The project, known as the Gautreaux program, was a housing relocation program in Chicago for low-income black families. The program offered neither employment counseling nor anything similar, and thus any results should have been due to location and not other factors. The authors found that a suburban relocation led to increased employment but no difference in wages after controlling for other factors. The blacks who relocated to the suburbs moved to middle-class neighborhoods, and thus the positive effect on employment could be due to better access to employment opportunities or to a demonstration effect from being among middle-class families.[5]

The Effect of Job Access

A central assumption of the spatial mismatch hypothesis is that access to jobs affects the employment rate. While Kain found support for that assumption, it is possible that changes in transportation may have eliminated any effect. There have been many studies that have investigated this aspect of Kain's hypothesis (these studies have been reviewed by Holzer 1991, Ihlanfeldt 1992b, and Kain 1992), but here we focus on a few key studies.

Many of these studies have focused on youth, and there are two reasons for doing so. First, if any group is to be affected by spatial mismatch it should be youth because they should be more sensitive to the length of commute than adults. Second, the residential location of a youth is not as likely to be affected by whether or not the youth has a job. The latter is an important issue. Suppose that an individual who obtains a new job moves closer to the place of employment. If this happens, we would find that people with a job live close to their job. This would lead us to believe, falsely, that living close to a place of work increases the probability of having a job.

One of the first studies of the effect of job access on youth employment was conducted by Ellwood (1986) using Chicago as the basis of the study. Ellwood investigated the relationship between the employment rate within census tracts of 16-to-21-year-old, out-of-school youths and various measures of job access, controlling for other factors including the percentage of the census tract population that was black. Regardless of how he measured job access, Ellwood found that job access was of only minor importance.

In contrast to Ellwood, Ihlanfeldt, and Sjoquist (1990) found large and significant effects of job access on youth. Using data from the 1980 Census of Population, they studied the employment of individual youths living in Philadelphia, Chicago, and Los Angeles in 1980. They measured the degree of spatial mismatch, or job access, by the average commuting time of lower-skilled workers from each youth's neighborhood. The greater the commuting time, controlling for the means of transportation, the greater the distance from the place of residence to the jobs that a youth might take. Variables were included to control for differences in the characteristics of the youths–namely, age, education, gender–and in family background–such as income and marital status. The dependent variable in the regression equations was whether the youth had a job. Separate regressions were run by race, age group, and school enrollment status.

The regression results suggest that the greater the commuting time, the lower the likelihood that a youth was employed. The effect was substantial; in Philadelphia, for example, a one standard deviation increase in commuting time (2.2 minutes for whites and 3.7 minutes for blacks) reduced the probability of having a job by 3.8 to 5.1 percentage points for whites and 4.0 to 6.3 percentage points for blacks, depending upon the age and gender group. The results of Ihlanfeldt and Sjoquist's research suggest that perhaps 50 percent of the large difference in the employment rates of black and white youth can be accounted for by the difference in access to employment opportunities.[6]

These and other studies of the effect of job access have been recently reviewed by Holzer (1991). He concludes that "it seems fair to say, therefore, that the preponderance of evidence from data of the last decade shows that spatial mismatch has a significant effect on black employment" (118).

Policies to Address Spatial Mismatch

If the market adjustments have not been sufficient to eliminate the effects of any spatial mismatch, what policies might be adopted to overcome the spatial separation of low-skill workers and employment opportunities? There are two general approaches to this problem: get the workers to the jobs, or get the jobs to the workers. A more general approach is to increase the skill level of low-skill workers; however, since this option does not address directly the spatial issue, we will not consider it further.

Getting People to the Jobs

Getting people to the jobs involves either improving transportation systems or changing the residence of blacks. Access can also be increased by reducing barriers such as lack of labor market information and employer discrimination. We consider each in turn.

Improving Transit—Automobile ownership among low-income households is low. Thus, one obvious approach to improving the access of central city workers to suburban jobs is to reorient mass transit from a focus on getting suburbanites into the central business district to a focus on getting central city residents to suburban jobs. However, suburban jobs are usually widely dispersed and thus not easily served by fixed bus routes. Efficient operation of large buses relies on economies of scale; there must be a large number of customers to justify the operation of a full schedule on a given route. Operating buses to serve a few central city workers who may work at several different firms and who work different hours is very expensive.

Buses are also a very slow mode of transportation, so that trips to the distant suburbs from the central city of even modest-sized metropolitan areas can take well over an hour. Rapid transit would be faster but such routes are fixed, and either changing them or adding sufficient new lines to serve the widely dispersed job sites would be prohibitively expensive. Thus, except for very large suburban employers or for areas of high employment density, public transit is not likely to be a feasible solution.

Instead of changing mass transit, a system of minivans that serves specific groups of businesses has been suggested. Several experiments with such forms of transit have been attempted, but they have generally not been a big success. However, large suburban businesses that have been unable to hire sufficient numbers of low-skill workers, and thus have had to pay high wages, have been able to develop systems to transport workers from the end of rail or bus lines.

Evaluations of earlier transit programs found that the provision of special reverse-commuting bus transportation options did not affect the employment rates among low-skilled central city residents. But as was noted earlier, the extent of suburbanization has increased, and hence the newer transportation programs may have an effect. However, little analysis has been conducted on these recent programs (see Hughes 1989).

Integrating the Suburban Housing Market—A second way of increasing the access to jobs for central city blacks is to eliminate racial discrimination in housing. Although there has been a reduction in the level of racial housing segregation, evidence suggests that racial discrimination has not been eliminated. While blacks have moved to the suburbs, this has generally meant moving to areas just outside the central city and adjacent to existing black communities in the city.

But even if outright housing discrimination is eliminated, low-income households face other barriers. For example, many suburban areas engage in a practice called fiscal zoning. These communities adopt zoning and building codes that require large minimum lots and expensive housing. Or the government restricts the number of rental units and adopts policies that require large apartments. This practice prevents lower-income households, and hence lower-skilled workers, from obtaining housing in these areas (see Pogodzinski 1991).

The lower availability of certain services in the suburbs results in many low-income, low-skilled individuals being trapped in the city. Public housing is not widely available in the suburbs, and the limited availability of public transit in the suburbs is a serious limitation.

To open up the suburbs to low-income households will require a change in national housing policy from a supply-based approach (that is, the construction of low-income or public housing, usually in the central city) to a demand-based approach under which individuals are given housing vouchers and are free to rent anywhere they choose. Second, it will require making public transit more readily available in the suburbs.

In advocating a policy in which blacks move to the suburbs, there is an assumption that the effect will be positive. There are two offsetting effects that result from such desegregation. If, as Kain found, employers are less likely to hire blacks when the percentage of residents who are black living in the surrounding community is lower, then desegregating the residences of blacks will lower the black employment rate. On the other hand, moving blacks closer to employment opportunities will increase the ability of blacks to obtain employment. Thus, whether desegregation will increase or decrease the employment of blacks is an empirical question and depends upon the relative magnitudes of the two effects.

Using the results of his regression analysis, Kain estimated the potential increase in employment if, instead of blacks being concentrated within the ghetto, the percentage of blacks in each workplace zone was the same. He found that desegregating the black population would substantially increase black employment.

Kain's result, however, has been criticized. Offner and Saks (1971) conducted an analysis similar to Kain's but used a different form for the regression equation. Their results imply that if the black population is decentralized, the percentage of the black population employed will decrease. Thus, Offner and Saks argue that a policy that moves blacks to the suburbs, and hence results in less concentration of blacks, is undesirable.

Another way of looking at this question is to observe whether blacks who live in more desegregated communities do better. Masters (1974, 1975) investigated the relationship between the ratio of non-white to white income and the degree of racial segregation within the metropolitan area. He found no evidence of a significant relationship between the two variables and thus no evidence that desegregation has any effect on earnings of blacks. Masters did use data for earnings in 1959 and 1969, which limits the applicability of the results to current conditions.

In a more recent paper, Cain and Finnie (1990) investigated the effects of several demand-side variables on hours of work by young black men aged 16 to 21, including the degree of racial segregation within the community. They found that the more segregated the community in which the black youth lives, the lower the number of hours the youth works, a result that is counter to the result obtained by Kain (1968, 1990). Cain and Finnie argue that segregated neighborhoods curtail the number of hours because the level of income in black communities is generally low and because businesses are less likely to locate there.

Improving Job Information—Improving the ability of central city workers to commute to suburban jobs assumes that they can obtain jobs in the suburbs. But for central city workers to obtain jobs in the suburbs, individuals must first be able to find and apply for job openings. To do this involves both obtaining information concerning jobs to apply for and obtaining a job offer once it is applied for.

Without access to an automobile, searching for a job in the suburbs is difficult. Low-skill individuals make significant use of direct application to firms in their search for jobs, with many individuals making in-person inquiries without knowing whether the firm has an opening. To rely on mass transit to get from one suburban firm to another is very time-consuming. Thus, the lack of automobile ownership among low-income households severely limits their ability to search in suburban labor markets.

While many low-skill workers apply for jobs without knowledge of their availability, others do attempt to obtain information about job openings. Newspaper want ads, state employment agencies, and private employment agencies are three common methods for obtaining information. However, many employers do not advertise their job openings. It is reported that many openings for less-skilled jobs are filled through referrals from those already working for the firm. Thus, unless you are a relative or friend of a current employee, it is difficult to learn about a job opening, especially among small- to midsize firms.

Job Discrimination—Knowing about jobs and having the ability to commute to them is of no help unless you receive an offer from an employer. There is evidence, however, that suburban employers discriminate against minority workers, as was suggested in the model presented earlier.

We can distinguish between two types of employee discrimination. The first is straight out bigotry; some white employers simply dislike minorities and refuse to have them in their workforce. The second type of discrimination is referred to as statistical discrimination, which can be explained as follows. Suppose there are two classes of individuals, A and B, and that, on average, workers in group B are not as productive or as skilled as those in group A. When an individual comes into a firm for an interview, the employer is not able to determine the actual ability of the individual. The employer can reduce to some extent the uncertainty about the skills and attitudes of an individual but cannot eliminate all of the uncertainty. Some information can only be obtained by observing the individual at work, and of course that can only happen if the individual is hired.

Some employers, however, may have developed expectations about the behavior of individuals who belong to a particular group based on some characteristic such as race, age, gender, religion, and so on. This expectation may be derived from their own experiences with other members of this group, from the experiences of other employers they have talked to, or from unfounded perceptions about members of the group. Suppose that the employers know, or simply believe, that on *average* members of group B are not as productive as members of group A. They also know or believe that some members of group B are more productive than some members of group A. Without direct observations of the applicant, these employers rely on the percentages and assume that because the individual is a member of group B there is higher probability that this individual is not a hard worker. Thus, the employers are less inclined to hire a member of group B.

Many employers have negative opinions about members of racial minorities. They also associate being in the central city with being members of a lower class and with having a poor education. Kirschenman and Neckerman (1991), for example, conducted 185 interviews with employers in the Chicago area in order to get at the attitudes toward and perceptions of racial groups. They concluded that "Most [employers] associated negative images with inner-city workers, and particularly with black men. 'Black' and 'inner-city' were inextricably linked, and both were linked with 'lower-class' " (231).

Additional evidence was obtained by Turner, Fix, and Struyk (1991). They sent pairs of black and white individuals with similar backgrounds to interview for job openings. The researchers found that the black member of the team was less likely to get an interview and, if given an interview, was less likely to be made an offer.

Bringing Jobs to the Workers

Rather than focusing on getting central city minorities to suburban jobs, an alternative policy is to redevelop the central city. What are the prospects of improving access by redeveloping the central city ghettos? The evidence is not encouraging. The expansion of black businesses is limited by shortages of purchasing power in the community, adequate financial capital, and entrepreneurs. Bates and Bradford (1979) found, for example, that efforts to force the expansion of the minority-owned businesses simply led to an increase in the failure rate among the businesses. In many cities community development corporations (CDCs) have been established to assist the development of minority businesses. While there are success stories, CDC businesses have generally not proved to be very profitable.

A newer approach to inner city development is the urban enterprise zone (UEZ). UEZs are designated areas within the city that satisfy certain conditions, usually with respect to poverty levels or unemployment rates. Businesses located within the zone, or that in some cases move into the zone, enjoy certain benefits that might include lower property tax rates, less regulations, or credits for hiring local residents. While no national enterprise zone program has been enacted, several states have such programs. Although promising on paper, the research that has evaluated such programs finds limited effects. For example, in a study of four enterprise zones in Maryland, the U.S. General Accounting Office (1988) found that while there were some increases in growth within the zones, the businesses largely responsible for the growth said that it was not the enterprise zones that were responsible.

Summary

The growing inequality between whites and blacks in terms of earnings and employment rates is a serious national issue. The spatial mismatch hypothesis is one of several possible explanations for this phenomenon. There is also empirical evidence that job suburbanization has an effect on the labor market outcomes of low-skilled blacks.

Knowing the cause or causes of the divergence between white and black workers is important for designing appropriate policy. If policymakers do not know the cause, then the policies that are proposed may not effectively address the problem. If the spatial mismatch hypothesis is a major factor, there are several obvious directions that policy alternatives might go. However, the evidence that these approaches will work or will be successful is not encouraging. Evidently, finding a solution to the problem will depend upon further research and exploration.

Notes

1. The employment rate is the ratio of employed workers to the population.

2. If in figure 5.1, the difference in the two wage rates is less than the commuting cost, then no city resident will commute to the suburb.

3. Employers cannot legally hire black and white workers into similar positions and pay the black workers less. However, the employers can accomplish the same thing by requiring higher skill levels for black workers than for white workers for the same position. While this is also illegal, the likelihood of the firm being detected is low.

4. The PSID is an ongoing annual survey of a large sample of households from throughout the United States. As the title suggests, the survey focuses on income and its determinants.

5. Wilson (1988) has argued that the lack of middle-class role models in those areas of the central city that have high rates of poverty leads to aberrant behavior patterns, including weaker attachment to the labor market.

6. In other research, Ihlanfeldt and Sjoquist (1991) investigated the effect of job access across a large sample of metropolitan areas. They again found that access had an important effect on the employment rates of youth. In a subsequent study, Ihlanfeldt (1992b) found additional support for the importance of job access in explaining black youth employment rates, and obtained similar results for Hispanic youth (Ihlanfeldt, forthcoming).

References

Bates, T., and W. Bradford. 1979. *Financing Black Economic Development*. New York: Academic Press.

Becker, G. S. 1971. *The Economics of Discrimination*. 2d ed. Chicago: University of Chicago Press.

Bound, J., and R. B. Freeman. 1992. "What Went Wrong? The Erosion of Relative Earnings and Employment among Young Black Men in the 1980s." *Quarterly Journal of Economics* 107 (1): 201–32.

Cain, G. G., and R. E. Finnie. 1990. "The Black-White Difference in Youth Employment: Evidence for Demand-Side Factor." *Journal of Labor Economics* 8 (1, Pt. 2): 5364–95.

Danziger, S., and M. Weinstein. 1976. "Employment Location and Wage Rates of Poverty-Area Residents." *Journal of Urban Economics* 3: 127–45.

Ellwood, D. T. 1986. The spatial mismatch hypothesis: Are there teenager jobs missing in the ghetto? In *The Black Youth Employment Crisis*. Edited by R. B. Freeman and H. J. Holzer, pp. 147–87. Chicago: University of Chicago Press.

Farley, J. E. 1987. "Disproportionate Black and Hispanic Unemployment in U. S. Metropolitan Areas." *American Journal of Economics and Sociology* 46: 129–50.

Holzer, H. J. 1991. "The Spatial Mismatch Hypothesis: What Has the Evidence Shown?" *Urban Studies* 28 (1): 105–22.

Hughes, M. A. 1989. *Fighting Poverty in the Cities: Transportation Programs as Bridges to Opportunity*. Washington, D.C.: National League of Cities.

Ihlanfeldt, K. R. Forthcoming a. "Intra-urban Job Accessibility and Hispanic Youth Employment Rates." *Journal of Urban Economics*.

——. Forthcoming b. "Intra-urban Wage Gradients: Evidence by Race, Gender, Occupational Class, and Sector." *Journal of Urban Economics*.

——. 1992a. *Housing Segregation and the Wages and Commutes of Urban Blacks: The Case of Atlanta Fast-Food Restaurant Workers*. Research Paper Series No. 30. Atlanta, GA: Policy Research Center, Georgia State University.

——. 1992b. *Job Accessibility and the Employment and School Enrollment of Teenagers*. Kalamazoo, MI: W. E. Upjohn Institute for Employment Research.

——. 1988. "Intra-metropolitan Variations in Earnings and Labor Market Discrimination: An Economic Analysis of the Atlanta Labor Market." *Southern Economic Journal* 55: 123–40.

Ihlanfeldt, K. R., and D. L. Sjoquist. 1991. "The Effect of Job Access on Black and White Youth Employment: A Cross-sectional Analysis." *Urban Studies* 28: 255–65.

———. 1990. "Job Accessibility and Racial Differences in Youth Employment Rates." *American Economic Review* 80: 267–76.

———. 1989. "The Impact of Job Decentralization of the Economic Welfare of Central City Blacks." *Journal of Urban Economics* 26: 110–30.

Jencks, C., and S. E. Mayer. 1990. "Residential Segregation, Job Proximity, and Black Job Opportunities." In *Inner-City Poverty in the United States*. Edited by L. E. Lynn Jr. and M. M. McGreary, 187–222. Washington, D.C.: National Academy Press.

Kain, J. F. 1968. "Housing Segregation, Negro Employment, and Metropolitan Decentralization." *The Quarterly Journal of Economics* 82: 175–97

———. 1992. "The Spatial Mismatch Hypothesis: Three Decades Later." *Housing Policy Debate* 3 (2): 371–460.

Kasarda, J. D. 1989. "Urban Industrial Transition and the Underclass." *Annals of the American Academy of Political and Social Science* 501 (January): 26–47.

Kirschenman, J., and K. M. Neckerman. 1991. " 'We'd Love to Hire Them, but . . .'. The Meaning of Race for Employees." In *The Urban Underclass*. Edited by C. Jencks and P. E. Peterson. Washington, D.C.: The Brookings Institution.

Leonard, J. S. 1987. "The Interaction of Residential Segregation and Employment Discrimination." *Journal of Urban Economics* 21: 323–46.

Masters, S. H. 1974. "A Note on John Kain's Housing Segregation, Negro Employment and Metropolitan Decentralization." *The Quarterly Journal of Economics* 88: 505–19.

———. 1975. *Black-White Income Differentials: Empirical Studies and Policy Implications*. New York: Academic Press.

Mooney, J. D. 1969. "Housing Segregation, Negro Employment, and Metropolitan Decentralization: An Alternative Perspective." *The Quarterly Journal of Economics* 83 (2): 299–311

Offner, P., and D. H. Saks. 1971. "A Note on John Kain's Housing Segregation, Negro Employment, and Metropolitan Decentralization." *The Quarterly Journal of Economics* 85 (1): 147–60.

Pogodzinski, J. M. 1991. "The Effects of Fiscal and Exclusionary Zoning on Housing Location: A Critical Review." *Journal of Housing Research* 2 (2): 145–60.

Price, R., and E. Mills. 1985. "Race and Residence in Earnings Determination." *Journal of Urban Economics* 18: 350–63.

Rosenbaum, J. E., and S. J. Popkin. 1991. "Employment and Earnings of Low-Income Blacks Who Move to Middle-Class Suburbs." In *The Urban Underclass*. Edited by C. Jencks and P. E. Peterson. Washington, D.C.: The Brookings Institution.

Straszheim, M. 1980. "Discrimination and the Spatial Characteristics of the Urban Labor Market for Black Workers." *Journal of Urban Economics* 7: 119–40.

Turner, M., M. Fix, and R. J. Struyk. 1991. *Opportunities Denied, Opportunities Diminished: Racial Discrimination in Hiring*. Washington, D.C.: U.S. Department of Housing and Urban Development.

U.S. General Accounting Office. 1988. *Enterprise Zones, Lessons from the Maryland Experience*. Washington, D.C.: U.S. Government Printing Office.

Wilson, W. J. 1987. *The Truly Disadvantaged*. Chicago: University of Chicago Press.

Part 3

Housing, Public Finance, and Infrastructure

6

A Public Choice Perspective on Zoning and Growth Controls: NIMBYism, the Tiebout Mechanism, and Local Democracy

J. M. Pogodzinski

Introduction

Among the factors usually cited for continuing racial segregation in housing are local zoning ordinances. Some requirements, like large lot sizes, may have the effect, and some say the purpose, of excluding low-income people or members of some ethnic or racial groups. Furthermore, such restrictive local regulations may increase housing prices all around.

This last is the point emphasized in a recent report by a presidential Advisory Commission on Regulatory Barriers to Affordable Housing. The commission made several recommendations, among them that some of the decision-making authority over land-use questions be removed from the local to the state level.

Zoning is a governmental intervention in the market, and so economists usually ask about the market failure that justifies such an intervention. On the other hand, from what we might term the public choice perspective, the alleged market failure may simply be a rationale for government intervention pursued for other and less worthy reasons. The problem with such government intervention is that it may lead to government failure–the misallocation of resources due to government intervention.

The Advisory Commission and its supporters argue strongly that local zoning regulations and growth controls have adverse impacts on housing

145

prices. However, the commission's analysis is incomplete and flawed. The analysis (implicitly) views the effects of zoning as a supply-side phenomenon, whereas zoning affects both the demand curve and the supply curve. This chapter develops a straightforward model to discuss these demand and supply effects and to deduce their welfare implications. The model involves utility functions, and a numerical example is developed that allows one to trace through the welfare effects of policy changes.

An important strand of work that dovetails with some of the Advisory Commission's concerns is William Fischel's work on regulatory takings. Fischel compares the legal environment in California with that in other states and concludes that California is less hospitable to developers than other states. (A chapter of his manuscript is entitled "California's War on Developers.") Fischel also compares housing prices in California with housing prices in the rest of the United States—and concludes that factors other than the different legal environments cannot explain the much greater increase in California housing prices compared with the rest of the United States.

From a policy perspective, some of the commission's recommendations are troubling because while they may have the intended impact on zoning regulations and prices, they may also have unintended consequences. The main category of possible unintended consequences is in the area of local public finance. If local jurisdictions can no longer use zoning for exclusionary purposes, but current residents retain authority over taxes and local expenditures, how will their decisions in these areas be affected by reduced authority over zoning?

In a recent report called "Not in My Back Yard": Removing Barriers to Affordable Housing (hereafter the "NIMBY Report"), a presidential advisory commission identified land–use zoning and growth controls along with other local barriers as significant factors in the increase in housing prices and the reduction in affordable housing in the 1980s.[1] According to the commission's report as much as 25 to 30 percent of the price of housing is due to excessive regulations, principally local regulations like building codes, zoning ordinances, and various kinds of growth controls. I will argue in this chapter that the commission's figure of an effect as large as 25 to 30 percent is problematical. The NIMBY Report asserts that this is the effect of excessive regulations, but that term is never defined (although the report offers several examples).

One of the most commonly heard criticisms of zoning by developers is that the process of obtaining approvals is very long and uncertain. Approvals for some projects take years, and numerous unexpected hurdles need to be overcome. Local zoning authorities have broad discretion in the administration of zoning laws. The Advisory Commission recommended a number of procedural changes in the way zoning is administered. Probably the most far-reaching of these recommendations was that states should enact legislation that establishes time limits on building code, zoning, and other approvals and reviews and that states should establish a legal presumption of approval. It would be incumbent upon the local regulatory agency to "clearly demonstrate why the regulatory rejection was appropriate and in the public interest" (NIMBY Report, Recommendation 7–5, 14).

The thrust of the commission's recommendations is that the decision about local land use should be removed as far as possible from the local jurisdiction. The commission's greatest hope is that the federal government will establish a system of rewards and punishments for states and localities that would in turn encourage removal of various regulations the commission views as barriers to affordable housing. Although the commission considered all types of local barriers to housing affordability, I will focus principally on residential zoning and to a lesser extent on growth controls.

In this chapter, I take exception to two aspects of the commission's report. First, the NIMBY Report relies on an implicit economic model of zoning that, while quite plausible, is incomplete in a way that affects the welfare evaluation of conclusions arising from the model. Second, the commission's policy recommendations, while they would almost undoubtedly have some of the desirable effects the commission intends, are unlikely to be enacted for a reason related to the commission's incomplete zoning model. I advance a proposal that would not share this defect. Furthermore, the commission's recommendations might have unintended adverse effects, which I discuss in the last section of this chapter.

The issue of appropriate land-use regulations is important for several reasons. The potential adverse effect of local regulations on the supply of housing is large. Overly stringent regulations may increase economic and racial segregation, contribute to lower real incomes for poor people, and lower overall productivity. Moreover, these apparently are continuing problems. The commission noted that in the preceding 24 years no fewer than 10 federally sponsored commissions, studies, or task forces had addressed the issue of local barriers.

The Legal Background

Most zoning ordinances in the United States are based on a model statute dating from the 1920s (O'Sullivan 1993, 314). Consequently, although zoning is a state matter usually administered by local governmental units, zoning regulations are similar in form and content across much of the United States,

The division of land uses is based on the triad: residential, commercial, and industrial.

The legal basis for zoning is the *police power* of the state–that is, the right of the state to regulate matters associated with the health, safety, and welfare of its citizens. The same police power is, for example, the justification for the state requiring immunizations for children attending schools. In the case of zoning and other issues, the states delegate their authority to lower levels of government–for example, municipalities who act as agents of the state.

The constitutionality of zoning as an application of the police power has long been recognized by the courts. The U.S. Supreme Court recognized the constitutionality of basic zoning in the case *Village of Euclid* v. *Ambler Realty Co.* (1926). It is interesting to note, however, that the lower court in the same case raised issues that later critics of zoning have dwelt on. That court recognized that the application of the police power might impose costs upon nonresidents and indeed might provide a pretext for parochial or narrowly self-interested behavior.[2]

In the case of zoning, the principal constraint on the state's power is the question of whether the zoning constitutes a *taking*. The U.S. Constitution provides that private property cannot be "taken" without just compensation. The question then is what constitutes the taking of private property. Clearly, as the courts have long recognized, the zoning of a property affects its value, and an adverse zoning of the property may result in a clear and measurable diminution of the value of land. To take a realistic example, in the East Bay area of San Francisco, land zoned residential is very valuable. In Livermore, an East Bay community about 35 miles from San Francisco, the city government has decided to preserve a significant amount of land exclusively for viticulture. (The people of towns in the Livermore Valley sometimes style the area as the "second Napa Valley.") Acreage presently devoted to growing grapes is worth several times more if zoned residential.

The courts have ruled, however, that merely to have the value of property reduced does not constitute a taking. In order for a zoning decision to constitute a taking, virtually all the value of the land would have to be destroyed; that is, the land would have to have virtually no value in its zoned state relative to an alternative zoning. This standard is rarely met in practice. Land 35 miles from San Francisco may be worth a great deal if single-family homes can be located on it, but growing grapes on such land is an alternative use that has some value and enough value so that zoning the land for viticulture does not constitute a taking.

While the broad rule of takings is the one just described, the takings issue as concerns zoning and growth controls is played out in state courts, and state court rulings differ on the treatment of property rights in this area. Below I will examine a claim by Fischel (1993) that rulings of the California Supreme Court on zoning-related property rights issues significantly increased housing prices in California compared with the rest of the United States.

The Economic Background

Zoning is a government regulation of the use of private property. Such government regulation is usually justified by economists on the presumption that there is a *market failure*. A market failure is a circumstance in which the private market will fail to achieve an efficient allocation of resources. By "efficient" I mean *Pareto-efficient*; that is, an allocation is efficient if there is no other feasible allocation such that at least one person is made better off while all others are no worse off. A number of circumstances may lead to market failure for example, increasing returns to scale in production or indivisibilities (see Layard and Walters 1978, 22–26), but here I focus on two possible causes of market failure: externalities and monopoly power. The basic cause of the market failures I will discuss and of the appropriate responses to them relate to how incentives are structured in the different circumstances I will consider.

An externality or external effect is a circumstance in which one economic actor's actions affect another economic actor's outcomes in a fashion that is not reflected in the market. Consider the classic (Coase 1960) example of smokestack emissions from a steel mill affecting the costs of a laundry.[3] With no government regulation of any kind, the steel mill does not have an incentive to take account of the costs it imposes on the laundry and also on society. Therefore, typically, too much steel will be produced and consequently too many resources will be devoted to keeping clothes clean. The price of steel is too low and does not reflect the *social* cost of producing steel.

Several solutions to this externality problem may be considered. The government might directly regulate the steel industry, either specifying the quantity of steel to be produced or establishing a tax rule so that the steel producer, pursuing maximization of profit, produces the desired quantity. Either of these solutions would require the government to know the costs of production of the steel producer and the cost of the damages to the laundry and also to have some motivation for pursuing the optimal objective. The solutions differ in a subtle fashion. Direct government stipulation of the amount of output provides no flexibility in the response of the firm, whereas the imposition of the appropriate tax rule allows the steel mill to adjust its output or pollution level as market conditions change. The tax rule method operates through the price system–it consists of an adjustment of the price to reflect the social cost.

In the situation just described, there is an implicit assignment of property rights. Now consider making an explicit assignment of "property rights in air quality," and assume there are no transactions or bargaining costs. If the assignment of such a property right to clean air was made to the laundry, then the steel mill would be liable for damage to the laundry. In contrast, the right to damage the air to a certain extent (a pollution right) might be assigned to the steel mill. The onus is then on the laundry to "bribe" the steel mill to reduce its output to the socially desired level (or one that will be more profitable, net of bribe, for the laundry, which in this case amounts to the same thing). It can be shown that either of these approaches will lead to an efficient allocation of resources. This result is known as *Coase's Theorem* (see Mueller 1989, 28–35). Thus, on efficiency grounds, there is nothing to choose between placing the onus on the steel mill or on the laundry. As a practical matter, such liability rules operate *ex post* as opposed to government regulations, which operate *ex ante*.

Finally, suppose the steel mill and the laundry were to merge, that is, to have a single owner. This owner would be interested in maximizing the joint profits of the steel mill and the laundry and consequently would choose the socially optimal output for the steel mill since that is also the joint profits maximizing output. This outcome arises because, as with the property rights assignment, the tax, or the regulation, the *externality has been internalized*.

Zoning Externalities

Several kinds of externalities are associated with land use. When one use of adjacent or nearby land conflicts with another use, these uses are referred to as *incompatible*. A classic example is the slaughterhouse located next to a residence. The smell and noise of the slaughtering operation constitute a negative externality on the residents next door. The entire array of solutions mentioned earlier are available to address this problem, but in practice the only solution usually employed is zoning–that is, segregating the incompatible uses in different areas. This is *use–zoning* in which land is zoned into one of the three broad categories of use (residential, commercial, and industrial).

Use-categories may be more or less refined. Within the residential use-category, zoning regulations will specify some areas for single-family dwellings (SFDs) and some areas for multifamily dwellings (MFDs) such as apartment buildings. In addition to use-zoning, there is, within a use-category, another level of zoning that we might call *characteristics-zoning*.[4] For example, within the SFD use-category, zoning regulations may specify several features, like, the minimum lot size, the maximum height of a structure, the maximum coverage of the lot by structures, the minimum setback of the structure from the lot line, the minimum side yard, and the minimum backyard. Frequently these requirements are overlapping, making some requirements redundant–for example, for a lot meeting the minimum lot size, the minimum setbacks may make the maximum coverage requirement redundant. Thus, some zoning requirements might be binding while others are nonbinding. Fischel (1992, 172–73) has argued that this feature of zoning has led to misinterpretation of some statistical results to show that zoning does not affect house prices since the "wrong" aspect of zoning was the focus of the analysis. Such overlapping zoning requirements may severely reduce the latitude builders have in designing structures that can be constructed on such lots (see Colwell and Scheu 1989 and Cannaday and Colwell 1990).

What kinds of externalities are supposed to be controlled by characteristics-zoning? Several might be proffered. Requiring large minimum lot sizes is a way of decreasing density, and reduced density is thought to be more healthful and also to reduce traffic congestion.[5] Greater minimum side yards and backyards may provide residents of SFDs with greater privacy. The other regulations may be thought to contribute to the ambience of the neighborhood, which affects one's enjoyment of one's house.

Economic Analysis of Residential Zoning

My analysis of residential zoning is divided broadly into two parts: an analysis of the effects of residential zoning and an analysis of the determinants of residential zoning. I will argue later that the two parts cannot be considered separately in an empirical analysis, but it is convenient for purposes of exposition to consider them separately for now, especially since a great deal of the literature has considered them separately.

There are two main effects of residential zoning that have been analyzed in the literature: the effect of zoning on housing prices and the effect of zoning on household location. Most empirical analyses of residential zoning have focused on the first of these effects. To study the effects of zoning I will employ a simple supply-and-demand model of the housing market (adapted from Pogodzinski and Sass 1990). This model abstracts from numerous important features of actual housing markets, principally the idea that housing is a *heterogeneous* good. The model is static and therefore best interpreted as a long-run model.

The Effects of Zoning on Prices

Consider the supply of and demand for housing in a given local jurisdiction that is part of a metropolitan area consisting of several such jurisdictions in which demanders and suppliers might operate. The demand and supply in the given jurisdiction are depicted as D_H and S_H, respectively, in figure 6.1. The demand for housing in this jurisdiction depends on variables with which demand is usually associated–namely, the price of housing in the jurisdiction (the own-price), the prices of substitutes and complements, and income. For reasons I will discuss later, it may also depend on the zoning in this jurisdiction as well as zoning in neighboring jurisdictions.

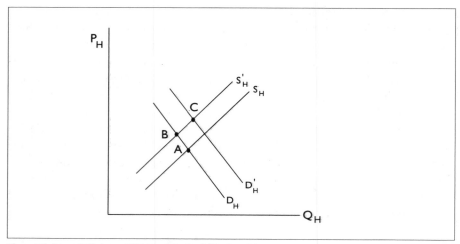

Figure 6.1   Effects of Zoning in the Housing Market.

Likewise, the supply of housing in this jurisdiction depends on own-price; on input prices, like the price of land in the jurisdiction; and on the technology used to produce housing. Different technologies may be used in different jurisdictions since the various jurisdictions may follow different building codes. The price of land in each jurisdiction depends in part on the supply of such land, which depends on a number of factors, including the use-zoning decision of the jurisdiction.

Zoning also influences the supply of housing since characteristics-zoning can force the choice of a particular combination of inputs to produce housing. To see this, consider the production isoquants represented in figure 6.2. This figure assumes that the homogeneous good "housing" is produced from "land" and "housing capital."[6] Suppose that we can represent minimum lot-size zoning and related zoning constraints such as maximum height, minimum setbacks, and maximum lot coverage as a requirement that the amount of housing capital associated with land cannot be more than a specified ratio, $K/L = \alpha$.[7] The zoning requirement forces a deviation from the otherwise-optimal input combination decision (represented by the expansion path denoted β in figure 6.2), and means that for each level of "housing" produced, costs are greater with zoning than without.

Depending on the nature of the model (whether long-run or short-run), it can be argued that zoning affects the supply of housing (see Henderson 1985, Buttler 1981, and Pogodzinski and Sass 1991). It is possible, for example, that as a consequence of zoning, as modeled here, *marginal costs* increase. Hence, the supply curve of housing (in figure 6.1) shifts to the left as increasingly stringent zoning is imposed (changes in the parameter α in figure 6.2). Thus, the supply curve of housing is affected in two ways by

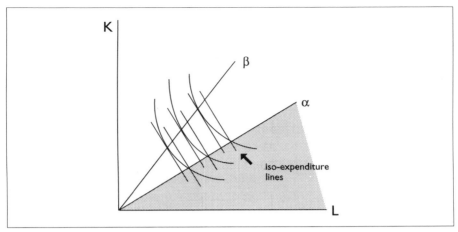

Figure 6.2   Effects of Zoning on Input Use.

zoning. Characteristics-zoning alters the permissible input combination, which may affect marginal costs, and use-zoning affects the price of land available for housing, which is an input price and hence affects the supply of housing. More stringent zoning of either kind can be expected to reduce the supply of housing. This is illustrated in figure 6.1 by a shift in the supply curve to S_H' and a change from the initial equilibrium at A to the new equilibrium at B.

This is the main effect of zoning from the Advisory Commission's point of view and the only effect accounted for by the commission when evaluating the policy implications of zoning. From the commission's perspective, zoning raises the price of housing because it reduces the *supply* of housing and thereby also reduces the *quantity* of housing. The welfare analysis is straightforward. The intent of the commission's recommendations is to have the supply curve shift in the other direction as zoning restrictions are eased.

Broad Statistical Evidence on the Price Effect

The commission has presented evidence in support of its case against zoning, and additional evidence has been presented in congressional hearings and in a special issue of *Housing Policy Debate* devoted to the NIMBY Report.[8] The evidence in the NIMBY Report itself can be briefly summarized as follows. The NIMBY Report bases its case on aggregate statistics such as the National Association of Realtors (NAR) Homeownership Affordability Index. The NAR National Affordability Index and its regional disaggregation are presented in figures 6.3A and 6.3B, respectively (reproduced from the commission's exhibit 1.1). A value of 100 on the NAR

Affordability Index means that a household of median income has 100 percent of the income needed to qualify to purchase a median-priced existing house.[9] The changes in the National Affordability Index illustrated in figure 6.3A are interpreted in the NIMBY Report to reflect mostly macroeconomic factors (the recession of the early 1980s), whereas the regional distribution of the affordability indices in figure 6.3B is taken as evidence of the influence of zoning and growth controls. The NIMBY Report states: "The regional values for the NAR index in December 1990 range from 82 in the West, where regulatory barriers are widely regarded as particularly strong, to 144 in the Midwest. The regional patterns are made up of numerous local diverse housing markets, populations and housing regulations. *Because housing regulations are local it is not surprising that affordability varies substantially within regions.* In the West, for example, the NAR affordability indices range from 43 in Los Angeles to 119 in Denver" (NIMBY Report, 1–2, emphasis added).

The commission considers California to be one of the principal states where stringent zoning and growth controls have increased housing prices most dramatically.[10] The special status of California is suggested by the disaggregated NAR Affordability Index since by its size California dominates the data for the West. The special status of California is also suggested by the disaggregation of the regional NAR Affordability Index. Los Angeles (a California city) is remarkably unaffordable, even by the standards of the West.

This focus on California as a special case is taken up in two works by Fischel, one of which is part of a commentary on the commission's report in *Housing Policy Debate*. Fischel (1991) compares the increase in housing prices in California to the increase in housing prices in the rest of the United States. The ratio of California prices to the rest of U.S. prices was 1.27 in 1960, 1.35 in 1970, and 1.79 in 1980. Fischel then examined whether this differential price change can be ascribed to differences in a variety of factors, such as population growth, land and water scarcity, and income. Although California differs from the rest of the United States along several of these dimensions, Fischel judges the differences along these dimensions not to be sufficient to account for the changes in prices in the decade 1970–1980, and he therefore concludes that growth controls may account for a significant portion of the increase in California housing prices.

The California Supreme Court and Regulatory Takings

A more comprehensive development along the same lines is contained in Fischel (1993). The claim here is that a series of decisions by the California Supreme Court in the late 1960s and early 1970s (the most famous being its 1972 *Friends of Mammoth* decision) resulted in a dramatic run-up of housing prices. Recall that the takings issue as concerns zoning is played out in state

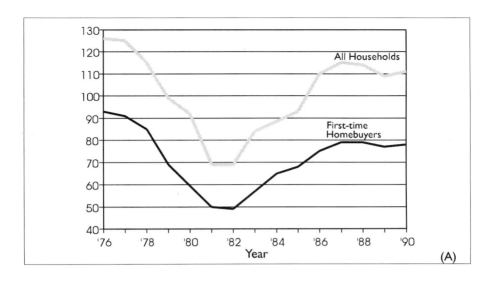

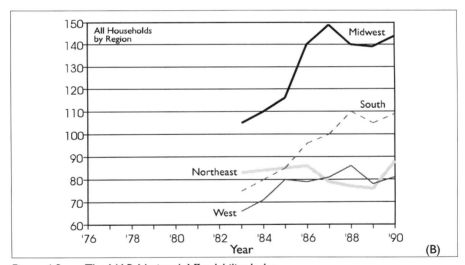

Figure 6.3   The NAR National Affordability Index.
Source: National Association of Realtors

courts. In what he refers to as "California's War on Developers," Fischel cites the following examples as evidence of the California Supreme Court's antideveloper bias. Other state courts were more balanced (see Fischel 1993, 14–15).

Damages. "The Court made a point of steering the discussion of remedies away from damages, to the great relief of municipal officials who would be under considerable voter pressure if they had to raise taxes to pay for regulatory takings or the higher municipal insurance premiums" (Fischel 1993, 11);

Vested rights. In most states, developers who had begun work on a project acquired a "vested right" to complete it. "In a series of decisions," Fischel writes, "the California vested rights doctrine was narrowed nearly out of existence" (Fischel 1993, 11);

Due process. This requirement, which had historically been part of the protection of property rights, was turned against development interests (Fischel 1993, 11);

Attorney fees. The California court subsidized antideveloper parties by awarding payment of attorney's fees to antidevelopment forces, despite a U.S. Supreme Court policy rejecting such awards (Fischel 1993, 12);

Annexation. The California court made annexations, a prodevelopment device, more difficult (Fischel 1993, 12);

Environmental impact. The *Friends of Mammoth* decision made environmental impact statements and requirements mandatory for *private* development projects of moderate to large size (Fischel 1993, 32–34).

Fischel (1993, chapter 6, 1) explicitly argues that state-level aggregates are more appropriate for evaluating the effect of such differential statewide regulatory takings decisions than local level data. Both works by Fischel consider a catalog of factors that might have caused a greater increase in house prices in California than elsewhere. The list includes:

1   Growth rate of California population versus growth of population elsewhere;
2   Growth of construction costs in California versus growth of construction cost elsewhere;
3   Growth of personal income in California versus growth of personal income elsewhere;
4   Quality of life in California versus quality of life elsewhere;
5   Potential land and water scarcity in California versus similar factors elsewhere;
6   Other California-specific factors, like Proposition 13.

Each of these factors is rejected in turn as a full explanation for the run-up of housing prices. Fischel points out, for example, that although California grew in population faster than that of the United States as a whole in the 1970s, its rate of growth in that decade was the *lowest* it had been since California joined the Union. Hence, reasons Fischel, growth cannot account fully for the run-up of housing prices. Similarly, personal income growth is rejected as a complete explanation for the growth of California housing prices. In 1960, California median family incomes were 20 percent higher than the U.S. average, but by 1980 they were only 2 percent higher (Fischel

1993, 22). Likewise, all the other reasons are rejected as full explanations for the increase in housing prices.

Fischel makes a powerful case that growth controls are related to the increase in housing prices in California and marshals a variety of evidence that growth controls have had an adverse effect. There are three cautions I would make concerning Fischel's claim. First, although part of the analysis is statistical in the sense that statistics are referred to, it does not employ regression analysis, which I will argue is the appropriate technique here. The problem with Fischel's statistical analysis, and the problem that regression analysis is designed to address, is that each of the factors he mentions affects housing prices simultaneously. It is not possible, simply by putting variation in other factors out of mind, to deduce the influence of a given factor on housing prices. It is not possible, for example, simply by looking at the record of growth, to decide whether growth has affected housing prices or not, unless the other factors affecting housing prices are held constant. This is what is accomplished by regression analysis. It is a case of the sum of the parts explaining more of the whole than each appears to explain individually. (Here, admittedly, more sophisticated statistical analysis is hampered because a single state–California–is said to possess the special takings doctrine.)

Second, many of the same factors that cause housing prices to rise–for example, increases in population, increases in income, and scarcity of land and water–are the same factors that "cause" growth controls. If housing prices rise and there are growth controls, do they do so because of the growth controls, or because of the underlying factors, which are masked by the growth controls? Sophisticated statistical techniques are needed to distinguish such effects (see my discussion below of endogenous zoning).

Third, Fischel's analysis suffers from some of the same problems as the Advisory Commission's analysis–the implicit assumption that the effect of zoning is only on the supply side. Suppose we acknowledge, as seems almost undeniable, that zoning and growth controls increase housing prices. Is this because they decrease supply, which we may take to be undesirable, or is it because they increase demand, which we may take to be desirable (or at least more problematical)?

Regression Analysis of the Effects of Zoning on Prices

There has been a substantial amount of empirical work that relies on sophisticated regression analysis to attempt to determine what impact zoning has on the price of housing. Most of this work has involved the use of the *hedonic price equation* (or *hedonic model*) since the housing stock is heterogeneous. The hedonic model can be explained as follows. Consider a product like a house, H, which has N characteristics, where C_1 is the amount of the first characteristic (say, number of bedrooms), C_2 is the amount of the second characteristic (say, lot size), C_3 is the amount of the third characteristic (say, air conditioning), and so on. Some of these characteristics may be viewed as desirable by the consumer, others as undesirable. In the market, we observe that houses have many different prices. The price of a house depends on the characteristics it contains. Thus, the price, P_H, is a function of the characteristics $C_1, C_2, C_3, \ldots, C_N$. Suppose for convenience that we assume the price is a linear function of the characteristics, i.e.,

$$P_H = \gamma_0 + \gamma_1 C_1 + \gamma_2 C_2 + \gamma_3 C_3 + \ldots + \gamma_N C_N. \tag{6.1}$$

Thus we view the price of the house H to be decomposed into components associated with each of the characteristics. The terms $\gamma_n C_n$ appear as "price times quantity" terms in this decomposition, and the coefficients γ_n in expression (6.1) can be interpreted as *implicit prices* (that is, as prices on implicit or unobserved markets for characteristics). Preferred characteristics have positive implicit prices, while bad characteristics have negative coefficients. For example, numerous studies (one of the earliest was Oates 1969) have investigated the association between house prices in some jurisdiction and local taxes and public expenditures. Typically, such studies report, for example, a positive coefficient for public expenditures on education and a negative coefficient for taxes.

A typical approach to determining the impact of zoning on the price of housing would be to incorporate "zoning variables" in a hedonic price-of-housing equation. Estimates of the hedonic equation based upon various specifications (using a wide variety of functional forms of such equations for example, linear, polynomial, logarithmic), and incorporating a wide variety of additional variables (for example, various measures of public expenditures and taxes, neighborhood characteristics, and such housing characteristics as whether the house has a significant view) have been made in the literature. Furthermore, a great variety of data sets has been used to estimate the equations. Although theory has guided the development of the econometric study of zoning, the theory is not so specific as to suggest particular functional forms for the regression equation, and data limitations have been a feature of every study of zoning. On the one hand, with the wide variety of specifications and data sets, it would be surprising if these studies were to come to the same conclusion. On the other hand, if they did, our confidence in the conclusion would be reinforced since it would be robust across a wide variety of specifications and data sets.

The results of econometric analysis of zoning are mixed. Certainly, no strong conclusion of the sort offered by the Advisory Commission about the large effects of zoning regulations is supported by an examination of a broad cross section of the empirical literature. For example, Pogodzinski and Sass

(1991) evaluated 28 empirical studies of zoning and found that a number of the studies show *no* significant effect of zoning on housing prices at all. How can such a conclusion of no effect square with the theory developed here?

First, some of these studies are flawed. Some employ very poor data sets, others involve questionable specifications. Yet these factors alone do not account for all of the studies in which zoning does not appear to have any effect. A second explanation sometimes offered (see Mark and Goldberg 1981, 1986) is that zoning has no independent effect on the price but merely *follows the market*; that is, land is zoned for the use to which it would have been put in a non(governmentally) regulated market in any case. We may consider that this comes about in one of two ways. First, zoning authorities may be "market-responsive", that is, they either make original zoning as the market would have dictated or make rezonings (zoning variances) to meet market conditions. Second, we might interpret the result as *the market follows zoning*; that is, if nearby land is zoned for some noxious use–say, a slaughterhouse–over time residents would move away until an equilibrium is established in which land uses are segregated.

Private Zoning

How should we interpret the initial equilibrium at *A* in figure 6.1? Is this the equilibrium with no zoning? If there was no zoning, how would the market respond? The answer: by creating private zoning. This private zoning is called a *restrictive covenant*.[11] Imagine that a new subdivision is to be created in an area unregulated by any local government. Why would I be willing to buy a house in this subdivision if, after all, someone could put up a slaughterhouse next door? The private developer seeks to maximize profits on the sale of houses and would be willing to provide a *guarantee* to the buyer about the character of the neighborhood.

This raises the question: Why involve government at all? Why not leave all these questions of regulation of land use to the private market and allow a system of covenants to govern land use? The main issue involves the quality of the guarantee represented by governmentally imposed zoning versus the quality of the guarantee represented by a restrictive covenant. "Private zoning" of some form may be more prevalent than might at first be suspected. Some zoning that was initially private may have been adopted virtually unaltered as public zoning. Fischel (1994) discusses the example of Foster City, California, a municipality that was developed by T. Jack Foster, Sr. and his sons. The developer bought up a large tract of land and initially layed out the plan of the city including areas consisting exclusively of SFDs and areas consisting of mixed SFDs and MFDs. When Foster turned the development over to the local government, it adopted his zoning as the municipal zoning and, indeed, fought regional authorities who tried to change the original zoning plan. Fischel interprets Crone's (1983) statistical evidence as indicating that the original Foster zoning was efficient.

While Fischel's example of Foster City seems to illustrate the smooth operation of private zoning, it is problematical whether the process would work in a situation where there are many owners of nearby property. Reliance solely on restrictive covenants is based on the idea that externalities can be fully internalized. This is a question of incentives and whether individual incentives can always be harnessed to the social good. One major point to consider is the *hold-out problem*. Suppose all parcels within a certain subdivision have been brought under restrictive covenants except for one at the very center of the subdivision (and thus in a position to impose externalities on all the others). The owner of that parcel now demands exorbitant payments to have his parcel brought under the restrictive covenant. Nonetheless, restrictive covenants have been a viable alternative to zoning in some localities.

Zoning may be viewed as a cost-effective way to obtain a guarantee about land use and, therefore, as a mechanism for reducing uncertainty about some factors that affect house values. Since uncertainty about house values is reduced, demanders are willing to pay more for an otherwise equivalent house. We might expect, if this is a significant effect of zoning, that more stringent zoning might be perceived by demanders as representing a better guarantee than less-stringent zoning. (The specific belief would be that zoning variances are less likely to be granted for more stringently zoned areas than for less stringently zoned areas). The choice of zoning over restrictive covenants should depend on the costs of providing either kind of guarantee.

More Complex Effects of Zoning

Objections can be raised to the Advisory Commission's analysis of zoning and also to the evidence presented to support that analysis. I turn first to an evaluation of the theoretical framework and then examine empirical evidence on the effects of zoning on household location.

The analysis of the effects of zoning is more complex than the model that implicitly underlies the NIMBY Report. Consider the possible effects of zoning on the demand for housing. As mentioned earlier, the demand for housing in a given jurisdiction depends on the price of housing in that jurisdiction, that is, on the own-price and also on the prices of housing in neighboring jurisdictions–that is, on the prices of substitute housing. These prices, in turn, are affected by the pattern of zoning regulations in a metropolitan area, so demand for housing in a particular jurisdiction depends on zoning in that jurisdiction (directly) and also on zoning in neighboring jurisdictions (through the effect on prices mentioned before).

The market demand for housing in a given jurisdiction is the summation of the individual demands for housing in that jurisdiction. Thus, it is roughly comprised of two parts: the individual demand and the number of demanders. For simplicity, suppose there are only two classes of demanders: rich and poor. The rich differ from the poor because they have more money and also, we will suppose, because they have different preferences. These preferences may differ over several dimensions–for example, different preferences for public expenditures and taxes. Suppose also that the rich are intolerant of residing next door to the poor.[12] (In reality, the poor may also not like residing next door to the poor, but suppose the rich like this even less. The example developed below supposes that only the rich are sensitive to the other occupants of the jurisdiction.) The poor act like a negative externality in consumption.

Consider now the initial equilibrium at A in figure 6.1, and suppose that the jurisdiction in question imposes more stringent zoning. Suppose also that no other jurisdiction alters its zoning. The demand for housing in the jurisdiction in question is affected in two ways. Some demanders (the poor) may be "zoned out" (that is, prevented from residing in the jurisdiction solely because of the more stringent zoning law–an effect mentioned by the Advisory Commission). Thus, the number of demanders falls, and holding all other factors constant, demand declines. However, in our simple model, the attractiveness of the jurisdiction to the rich has increased, and therefore, rich people who reside outside the jurisdiction may be attracted to this jurisdiction, and each rich person's demand has also increased.[13] This is represented as an increase in the individual demand of rich people. Thus, more stringent zoning results in two effects on the demand for housing, which we may term the *mobility* (or *interjurisdictional*) *effect* and the *quantity effect*.

The mobility effect may increase or decrease demand, depending on the numbers of rich and poor people who are attracted to or repelled from the jurisdiction. It is based upon the *Tiebout mechanism* (see Tiebout 1956). The idea behind the Tiebout mechanism is that households "vote with their feet," seeking the most preferred jurisdiction from among available jurisdictions. The quantity effect - is unambiguous in direction. A reduction in the number of poor people in a particular jurisdiction leads to an increase in the demand for housing by each rich person who resides in the jurisdiction (and also on the part of the poor who remain if they share the same preferences). What is the net result of these effects? I will develop now an example that suggests that the effect is to shift the demand curve to the right, from D_H to D_H' establishing an equilibrium like C in figure 6.1.

What of the commission's welfare evaluation? The situation is now more complex. The price of housing is higher, but the effect of zoning on the quantity of housing is ambiguous. The effects of zoning on rich and on poor are also complicated. If the wealthy are in fact willing to pay more for housing if the poor are not nearby, they are made better off. (We may not want to endorse this kind of economic discrimination, but it is at least very difficult for plaintiffs to establish as a motivation.) What of the poor? Some at least have been zoned out. Where did they go? To the *next-best jurisdiction*. (Recall that we assumed the zoning in other jurisdictions did not change.) Their increased demand for housing there raises the price of housing until the (identical) poor people could achieve the same utility in the original jurisdiction as in the next-best jurisdiction, although the two groups of poor consumers would consume different bundles of goods.[14] Both sets of poor (those now residing in the original jurisdiction and those now residing in the next-best jurisdiction) are made worse off by the increase in the stringency of zoning. In order to make a welfare evaluation of this situation, we must ask whether the gains of the gainers are greater than the losses of the losers.

An Example

Consider the following example. There are two classes of consumers, rich and poor. Rich consumers have an income of $M = 200$, while poor consumers have an income of $M = 160$. Consumers of each type residing in the same jurisdiction are identical. Both types of consumers have utility functions defined on the amount of a generic consumption good, C, and the amount of housing, H, of the following form (where "ln" is the natural logarithm operator):

$$U(C, H) = ln(C) + \alpha ln(H). \qquad (6.2)$$

For poor consumers we assume that $\alpha_p = 1$ always. For the rich, α_r depends inversely (weakly) on the number of poor people who reside in the same jurisdiction as they do; that is, $\alpha_r(\Pi'') \geq \alpha_r(\Pi')$ if $\Pi' < \Pi''$, where Π is the number of poor people residing in a given jurisdiction. This formulation treats housing as a continuously divisible and homogeneous good for convenience of analysis.

Consumers maximize the utility (6.2) subject to

$$M = p_H H + p_c C, \qquad (6.3)$$

taking as given the numbers of poor and rich people in each jurisdiction. This yields demand curves for the consumption good and housing of the following forms:

$$C^* = M/([1 + \alpha]p_c) \qquad (6.4a)$$

$$H^* = \alpha M/([1 + \alpha]p_H).$$ (6.4b)

Assume that the initial distribution of consumers is as follows:

Jurisdiction 1: Number of rich = 100   Number of poor = 75
Jurisdiction 2: Number of rich = 0   Number of poor = 200

Suppose further that α_r (75) = 1 for the rich. And suppose that initially both jurisdictions have identical long-run supply curves of housing, given by: $Q_S^1 = Q_S^2 = 5p_H$.

Equilibrium requires that the housing markets in each of the jurisdictions clear, that is, $Q_D^j = Q_S^j$, and also that no consumer desires to move from the jurisdiction where he or she currently is located, in other words, $V_1^{rich} = V_2^{rich}$ if the rich reside in both jurisdictions and $V_1^{poor} = V_2^{poor}$ if the poor reside in both jurisdictions (where v denotes the *indirect utility*, that is, $V = U(C^*, H^*)$. (If one or the other group resides in only one jurisdiction, its utility there must be at least as large as its utility in the other jurisdiction.)

The initial distribution of consumers given here is an equilibrium, since identical prices are determined,[15] and no individual from either group can increase his or her utility by moving to the other jurisdiction. This equilibrium has the following features:

Jurisdiction 1: p_H = 56.57, H_{rich}^* = 1.77, C_{rich}^* = 100 v_1^{rich} = 5.17, H_{poor}^* = 1.41, C_{poor}^* = 80, v_1^{rich} = 4.73, aggregate housing consumption = 282.84

Jurisdiction 2: pH = 56.57, H_{poor}^* = 1.41, C_{poor}^* = 80, v_1^{poor} = 4.73, aggregate housing consumption = 282.84

This equilibrium is illustrated in figure 6.4 as *A*.

Suppose now the rich, who are politically dominant in jurisdiction 1, impose more stringent zoning. They do so out of a desire to raise their own utility. Recall that α depends inversely on the number of poor with whom the rich reside. The same consumption bundle $(\tilde{C}, \tilde{H})$ will generate more utility for a rich person, if it is consumed in a jurisdiction where fewer of the poor are present. By imposing zoning of the sort that could increase long-run marginal costs of producing housing, the rich can make it advantageous for the poor to live in the other jurisdiction. Of course, higher housing costs (interpreted in this context as an increase in the user-cost of housing) impact adversely on the rich as well. So the payoff from reducing the number of poor persons in the jurisdiction must be large enough relative to the increase in required housing price to force the poor to move away. The formulation assumes (for convenience only) that the poor suffer no disutility from residing with other poor people–they are indifferent as to the household type with whom they share a jurisdiction. The effect on the supply of housing is represented by a shift of the housing supply curve, that is, the new housing supply curve is of the form $Q_S^1 = \beta p_H$, where β must be some number less than 5 for a reduction in supply.

Three effects occur simultaneously when the poor move from jurisdiction 1 in response to a shift in the long-run supply curve brought about by zoning. First, their in-migration to jurisdiction 2 raises the housing price there. Second, the reduced number of poor people in jurisdiction 1 increases the value of α for the rich, changing the rich peoples' demand for housing. Third, the utility realized in the final equilibrium, is determined for the new value of α for the rich. We suppose that $\alpha_r(0) = 5$.

We assume that the rich impose zoning just stringent enough to keep the poor from desiring to reside in jurisdiction 1.[16] Thus, in the new equilibrium the rich will reside exclusively in jurisdiction 1 and the poor exclusively in jurisdiction 2, but the housing prices in each jurisdiction will be higher. In jurisdiction 1 this will be for two reasons. The supply of housing will be reduced because of the zoning-induced change in the long-run marginal cost of producing housing and also because demand has increased since the rich, in the absence of the poor, desire more housing. In jurisdiction 2 the price of housing will be higher because of the in-migration of poor people from jurisdiction 1.

The new equilibrium can be summarized as follows:

Jurisdiction 1: Number of rich = 100, number of poor = 0, $\alpha_r(0) = 5$, $\beta = 3.79$, $p_H = 66.33$, $H_{rich}^* = 2.51$, $C_{rich}^* = 33.33$, $V_1^{rich} = 8.11$, aggregate housing consumption = 251.26

Jurisdiction 2: $p_H = 66.33$, $H_{poor}^* = 1.21$, $C_{poor}^* = 80$, $V_2^{poor} = 4.57$, aggregate housing consumption = 331.66

This equilibrium is illustrated in figure 6.4 as *B*.

To compensate each poor person for the monetary loss associated with the new equilibrium requires $1.08 or, in the aggregate, about $297.79. To compensate the rich, if we were to recreate the *status quo ante*, would require $4.35 or about $434.54 in the aggregate.[17]

The situation is different, however, if our initial assumptions differ. Suppose the initial distribution had been:

Jurisdiction 1: Number of rich = 50   Number of poor = 137.5

Jurisdiction 2: Number of rich = 50   Number of poor = 137.5

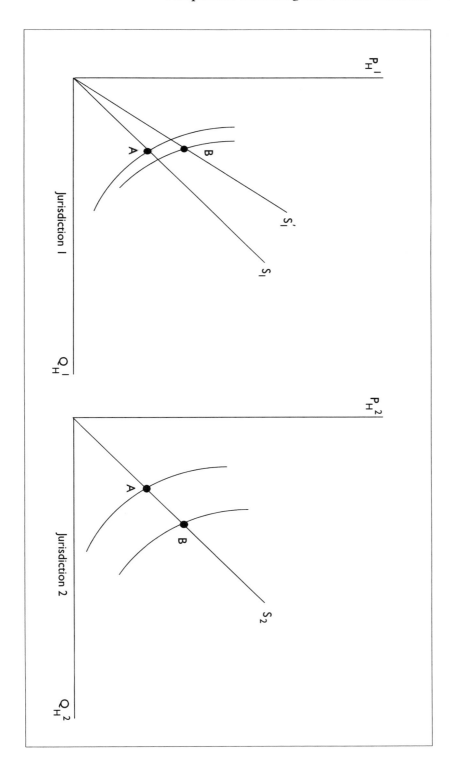

Figure 6.4   Interjurisdictional Effects of Zoning.

And suppose that $\alpha_r(137.5) = \alpha_r(75) = 1.$[18] Then the equilibrium would be just the one we have exhibited at A. However, from this new initial situation, the rich are not politically dominant in either jurisdiction.

There are several lessons from the example. First, zoning can enhance efficiency. This is so in the example because the poor act like a negative externality upon the rich. By segregating the poor from the rich, this externality is minimized. The poor lose, but the losses of the poor are less than the gains of the rich. So, although the politics of local jurisdictional voting would not support such an outcome in the case of an equal distribution of rich and poor between the two jurisdictions, the rich should in that case form a coalition-of-the-whole and bribe the poor to move to a single jurisdiction separate from themselves.

On the other hand, we have not counted any social costs associated with the segregation of society into income groups. It is not the burden of this paper to argue whether there are such costs or whether they are large. Rather, given the right of jurisdictions to impose zoning as in the example, then inducing the rich voluntarily to accept some poor among them will require compensation. Under zoning, the only cost of excluding the poor is the increased user-cost of housing, which in our example the rich are willing to bear to be rid of the poor. If they were offered a bounty for accepting poor people, or if they were given a quota of poor to accept and offered the possibility of increasing or decreasing the quota–based upon purchases or sales of "quota" amounts in a market–the solution would be different. At a sufficiently high price, the rich would be induced to accept some poor people among them because it would increase their income. The situation is analogous to the sale of "pollution licenses." (Rubin, Seneca, and Stotsky [1990] developed a model of New Jersey's Fair Housing Act and cite evidence to suggest that municipalities trade off among various options for meeting target levels of low-income housing, as suggested above.)

Zoning and Household Location

The most significant social effect of zoning is probably its impact on household location, but that is also the least-analyzed aspect of zoning, both from a theoretical and an empirical point of view.[19] In the Tiebout mechanism described above, households move in search of their most preferred jurisdiction. It would seem that an appropriate empirical specification would have as the dependent (left-hand) variable a measure of the number or proportion of, say, poor people in a jurisdiction and, on the right-hand side, various variables, including zoning variables, which are hypothesized to explain this proportion. I term such models *demographic* models.

An early and suggestive study was conducted by Branfman, Cohen, and Trubek (1973). They sought to explain the clustering of the poor as a function of variables representing fiscal incentives. These include the property tax burden, municipal property tax dependence, local school burden, and the presence of an educational equalization formula, race, housing availability, and zoning fragmentation. They measured clustering as an index based on deviation of the proportion of the poor in each municipality from an equal distribution of the poor across all municipalities in the metropolitan area. The zoning fragmentation variable is the number of zoning authorities per million persons. Branfman, Cohen, and Trubek conjectured that a larger number of small local authorities would more nearly reflect the interests of voters of relatively uniform interests and hence increase the degree of clustering.[20]

Branfman, Cohen, and Trubek obtained positive and significant coefficients on all variables except their fiscal incentive variables (all but one of which is insignificant). Although Branfman, Cohen, and Trubek treat the zoning fragmentation variable as the only zoning variable, housing availability is based upon the affordable housing stock, which might also be considered zoning-determined.

Shlay and Rossi (1981) examined the impact of zoning on a number of variables including variables representing the distribution of households across jurisdictions. They estimate separate regressions for the city and the suburbs. In their most important regression from our point of view, the dependent variable, is the number of non-whites in the census tract in 1970; the explanatory variables include the number of non-whites in the census tract in 1960, three zoning variables (an index of exclusionary zoning, the percentage of the tract zoned for business, and the percentage of the tract zoned for manufacturing), the change in tract population from 1960 to 1970, and the tract area. Of these variables, the number of non-whites in 1960 is positive and significant in both the city and the suburban regressions, the three zoning variables are insignificant, changes in tract population are positive and significant in the city but not significant in the suburban regression, and tract area is also positive and significant in the city but not the suburban regression.

There is no real theoretical framework to the model of Shlay and Rossi. One might give a justification after the fact for the appearance of some of these variables. The lagged dependent variable might represent the attraction of like to like. Ethnic enclaves form and are sustained because they provide some advantage to members of the enclave. The positive and significant coefficient on the lagged dependent variable might be taken to be a measure of the strength of this kind of "agglomeration economy."[21] On the other hand, it is also true that there is an inertia to moving, that is, it is costly and so the demographic composition of census tracts is likely to change only slowly. Thus, the interpretation of the coefficient on the lagged dependent variable is adulterated.

The Shlay and Rossi model is ad hoc. The relative paucity of variables is notable, but if we consider variables that plausibly determine the number of non-whites in a local jurisdiction, surely we must include employment opportunities as an explanatory variable. The spatial mismatch hypothesis (see Sjoquist, chapter 5 of this volume) suggests this is an important explanatory variable, which is missing from Shlay and Rossi's specification.

Zoning as Politically Determined

A growing literature has addressed the question: Where does zoning come from? Ostensibly zoning is imposed to mitigate the effects of an externality. Implicit in this formulation is the notion that local governments act to maximize social welfare and that they have the information needed to accomplish the task. A variety of alternative motivations have been imputed to local governmental authorities in making zoning decisions, some of which have been suggested by the preceding discussion. Local authorities may act so as to reduce the fiscal burden of *current* residents. They might do this by discouraging, through zoning regulations, the migration to the local jurisdiction of households (principally the poor) that are likely to consume more in publicly provided goods than they contribute in taxes. This has been termed *fiscal zoning*. Poor people can be discouraged from residing in a jurisdiction if housing is expensive there relative to other jurisdictions, and some zoning arrangements–for example, large minimum lot sizes–can make housing more expensive. Or local zoning authorities may pursue the objective of excluding some racial or ethnic minority (apart from the group's wealth). This has been referred to as *exclusionary zoning*. The focus on current residents is critical. Local zoning authorities are political bodies, responsible to the local electorate. Current residents have a vote; *potential* residents do not. The crux of the Advisory Commission's recommendations to remove the zoning decision from the lowest political unit (the municipality) to a higher one (the state) is to reduce the influence of current residents and thereby to empower potential residents.

While this discussion suggests that zoning may be pursued for distinct purposes, it should be emphasized that zoning is the product of one mind.[22] Another way of saying this is that the zoning decision is part of an optimal solution that contains other elements–for example, local fiscal variables. Several studies attempt to identify which of several distinct motivations may predominate in the zoning decision, whereas a more holistic approach may be more appropriate.

In the theory developed above, zoning was treated as *exogenous*–that is, determined outside of the economic model. I turn now to the question of the determinants of zoning and the associated question of treating zoning as *endogenous*–that is, determined within the economic model.

The Monopoly-Zoning Hypothesis

The literature on the determinants of zoning has evolved from less specific to more specific theories. The earliest contributions are associated with the *monopoly-zoning hypothesis*. The concept was first developed by White (1975) and further elaborated by Hamilton (1978) and Fischel (1980). How do jurisdictions have the wherewithal to engage in such practices as fiscal or exclusionary zoning? If there were so many local jurisdictions that an alternative to living in any particular jurisdiction was easily found, such practices as fiscal or exclusionary zoning would not occur. It is only because local jurisdictions have a degree of market power or monopoly power that they can successfully engage in such practices. It is true furthermore that the greater the extent of this monopoly power, the more likely jurisdictions are to engage in fiscal or exclusionary zoning. The core of the monopoly-zoning hypothesis, then, is that there should be a positive correlation between a measure of the monopoly power of a local jurisdiction and the restrictiveness of its zoning, holding constant other factors.

The key question in this literature centers on the appropriate measures of the monopoly power of a local jurisdiction. Two measures of market power have appeared in the literature: measures of jurisdictional growth and concentration measures. The latter are roughly based on the *concentration ratio* familiar from industrial organization.[23] (A third variable, a measure of the number of zoning variances granted, is mentioned in passing in some of the literature.) A concentration measure is a measure of the strength of competitor jurisdictions. The greater this number, the less is the presumed market power of the jurisdiction. Similarly, jurisdictions that face no pressure to expand should not be counted as market-powerful. However, using recent actual growth may confound the study since the actual growth may reflect effectively applied countergrowth measures, including zoning.

The most recent contribution to the literature on the monopoly-zoning hypothesis is a study by Rose (1989). Rose estimated regressions of the form

$$ln(P) = \alpha + \beta ln(N) + \gamma ln(\hat{N}) + \delta ln(Y) + \mu ln(L) + \eta ln(C) + epsilon, \qquad (6.5)$$

where P is the price of vacant land in an urban area, N is the population of the area $\hat{N}$ is the population growth from 1970 to 1980, Y is the per capita income for the MSA (metropolitan statistical area) in which the urban area is located, L is the total land available within a specified distance of the center of the urban area, and C is a zoning concentration measure.[24]

Rose estimated nine variants of the regression equation (6.5), corresponding to three different measures of concentration on three different data sets for the price data. His results provide moderate support for the monopoly-zoning hypothesis; all nine coefficients on the concentration measure (η in expression (6.5)) are negative as predicted, but only four of the nine are significant at the 10 percent level, and only one at the 5 percent level.[25] However, it seems difficult to accept that some other jurisdiction-specific factors–for example, the quality of schools and local fiscal variables–would not be capitalized into (or reflected in) land prices and these are not included in Rose's specification.

Explicitly Political Theories

Davis (1963) was the first to outline what might be termed a political theory of zoning based upon majority voting. Davis compared the interests of developers, renters, and owner-occupiers in the zoning decision. He argued that renters and developers prefer "proper" or "correct" zoning, which he defines as zoning that eliminates external diseconomies but does not create any external economies, albeit for different reasons. Developers are interested in capturing for themselves the maximum gains and are, according to Davis, in a position to capture the gains from eliminating external diseconomies but not from creating external economies. Renters prefer the so-called proper zoning because more stringent zoning would result in higher rents, and it has been revealed that higher-quality neighborhoods with higher rent are not preferred by renters to their present neighborhoods.

Davis's theory is very suggestive of an approach to developing an empirically estimable theory of the political determinants of zoning. Such a theory would look for the determinants of zoning in the features that are important in identifying the interests of the median or representative voter. In suburban areas and in many cities, the median voter is likely to be a homeowner, and hence homeowner interests are likely to be politically dominant.[26]

Rolleston (1987) studied the determinants of both use and characteristics zoning as a two-stage process. She first constructed an index of residential zoning restrictiveness. In the index related to minimum lot size, this is based on a weighted average of minimum lot sizes. Minimum lot sizes within a jurisdiction can be ranked from greater to lesser restrictiveness: $L_1, L_2, \ldots, L_n$. A weighting function associates with each lot size a weight, $w(\ )$, satisfying the condition $w(L_g) > w(L_h)$ if minimum lot size g is more restrictive than minimum lot size h. For example, Rolleston assigned the following weights to various residential lot sizes: less than $\frac{1}{4}$ acre = 20, $\frac{1}{4}$ to $\frac{1}{2}$ acre = 40, $\frac{1}{2}$ to 1 acre = 60, 1 to 3 acres = 80, and 3 or more acres = 100.

This weighting scheme is used to construct an index of residential zoning restrictiveness, employing the following formula:

$$\text{RRI}_j = (\sum_{k=1}^{n} w(\text{L}_k)L_{kj})/L_j ,$$
(6.6)

where RRI_j denotes the residential restrictiveness index of jurisdiction j, L_{kj} is the total acres in jurisdiction j zoned category k restrictiveness, and Lj is the total acres zoned residential in jurisdiction j. Analogously, Rolleston defined a Business Restrictiveness Index for jurisdiction j.

Rolleston sought to examine the influence of a variety of variables on the RRI_j, including the percentage of the jurisdiction that is residential, the magnitude of the business tax base, population density, a measure of the fiscal status of the jurisdiction, and a measure of the proportion of minorities in the jurisdiction.[27] The results of Rolleston's estimation yield significant coefficients on both fiscal and exclusionary variables but not on externality variables. She concludes, "The results show that communities with smaller minority populations relative to surrounding communities . . . tend to practice more restrictive zoning, supporting the exclusionary hypothesis."[28]

Pogodzinski and Sass (forthcoming) extend the analysis of endogenous zoning in a number of ways. The work of Rolleston was based upon a political theory, but the theoretical development was incomplete. While zoning is determined in the local political process, so are other variables, notably local expenditures and taxes–variables, which in one form or another, appear as explanatory variables in Rolleston's analysis. Furthermore, some of the right-hand side variables in her analysis are arguably determined by zoning. For example, while zoning might be influenced by fiscal conditions, fiscal conditions might be influenced by zoning. Failure to account for the two-way causality could mean that the estimates of Rolleston suffer from *simultaneous equations bias.* To overcome these and related problems in the estimation of endogenous zoning equations, Pogodzinski and Sass specify a system in which both zoning and local fiscal variables are determined in the political arena. This political arena is dominated by the "representative voter," and demographic, topographical, and other features of the local jurisdiction are used to describe this voter and the choices he or she faces.

One result of this study is to examine the influence of a variable like median income on the choice of tax rate and minimum lot zoning. Generally, holding other factors constant, higher median income is correlated with lower tax rates and also with higher minimum lot sizes. This suggests a trade-off between tax base and tax rate in financing public expenditure. Tax revenues TR (from a property tax) are equal to the tax rate t multiplied by the tax base TB. The tax base is the value of (residential) property and consists of the per-unit value of housing times the quantity of housing, i.e.,

$$\text{TB} = P_H \times Q_H. \tag{6.7}$$

Both of the terms on the right-hand side of the tax base expression are influenced by zoning decisions–use-zoning influences the quantity of housing in a local jurisdiction, and all types of zoning influence the price of housing. Suppose that a jurisdiction pursues a relatively restrictive zoning policy and allows development mostly of large, expensive houses. Then potentially such a policy can act to increase both P_H and Q_H. Then, to finance a given level of public expenditure or to collect a given level of tax revenue, it is possible to lower the tax rate.

Indeed, we might imagine that different communities and different individuals might have preferences over how a given level of public expenditure is to be financed, some preferring higher tax bases and lower tax rates, others preferring lower tax bases and higher tax rates. The reason to prefer the higher tax rate is that if the tax base is too large, the entry price to the jurisdiction might be too much to afford. This consideration would apply to poorer people. The wealthy on the other hand would typically prefer the opposite. They can afford the entry price and in any case the increases in tax base represent themselves as capital gains to owner-occupiers, who are more likely to be rich. We might associate higher median incomes with a greater propensity to be a "suburban Republican." Indeed, we might define a "suburban Republican" as someone who prefers to finance the given level of public expenditure by policies that increase the tax base and reduce the tax rate. These results suggest that zoning is part of the entire decision about financing local public expenditures and that representative voters trade off between aspects of zoning and local fiscal variables.

Interactions of Zoning with Local Public Finance

Consideration of the Tiebout mechanism with a finite number of jurisdictions and heterogeneous population raises the following question about incentives. Suppose each local jurisdiction produces a publicly provided good (like education), and suppose that the publicly provided good is financed by an income tax.[29] To gain access to the public good, one need only reside in the jurisdiction, and access can be gained by owning any amount of housing. Now suppose initially that rich people predominate in some jurisdiction and finance a high level of educational expenditures. Others are attracted by the high level of educational expenditures–specifically, poor people enter the jurisdiction, buy a very small amount of housing to gain access, and effectively ride free on the high level of education financed mainly by the rich. If the rich cannot create some barrier to this free riding, they might seek another jurisdiction where their financing of the local, publicly provided good will not be diluted by the poor, and a game of musical jurisdictions begins.

This issue was first raised by Hamilton (1978) and discussed by Fischel (1980) (see also Fischel 1992). The basic issue concerns the stability of a Tiebout equilibrium. Hamilton asserted that zoning is a mechanism to prevent the free riding of the poor on expenditures financed by the wealthy; that is, it is a means of making the tax system efficient. The efficiency arises because each individual pays more nearly the marginal cost he or she imposes on the system. Without zoning, at an equilibrium with substantial free riding on the part of the poor, the rich will be willing to finance a lower (and suboptimal) level of local public expenditure. This suggests that if zoning is not allowed to perform the exclusionary role it does here, other, and perhaps worse, effects such as reducing the level of local public expenditures, might result.

Consider now the effect of removing the decision about zoning from the local level to a higher level as recommended by the Advisory Commission. We need to make several assumptions before we can say what the results might be. Suppose that the effect of removing local control of zoning is to make all local jurisdictions more accessible–that is, to relax zoning restrictions across the board. Suppose also that local jurisdictions retain control of significant aspects of their own expenditures; that is, school expenditures, police expenditures, and the like continue to be locally determined. And finally, suppose that the dominant group in a given jurisdiction does not change.

There are potential effects on both the level and the composition of local public expenditures. As to the composition of public expenditures, the politically dominant rich people might alter the public consumption profile to reflect their increased concern about crime, and away from public school expenditures, which are attractive to the poor and for which the rich can find a suitable substitute. Altogether, the denial of the ability to exclude the poor might lead to a reduction in the level of public expenditure as the wealthy seek private and exclusive substitutes for the publicly provided goods.

There is a solution to this problem along the lines of that suggested by the Advisory Commission–namely, to mandate centrally the level and composition of public expenditures. But it would be undesirable to remove *all* local decision-making authority. These potential effects would be mitigated if the costs of accommodating the poor were compensated in some way. This might be done by the following kind of scheme. Within a metropolitan area, each municipality is assigned a target amount of low-income housing that it is to accommodate. These target amounts can then be traded at whatever price the market will bear among the local jurisdictions in the metropolitan area. In this way, the target number of people is accommodated in the metropolitan area in such a fashion that municipalities where the poor can be accommodated at lower cost have more of the poor and also have increased revenues. This approach can be expected to reduce horizontal inequities when compared with the current system. Compared with a system that mandates a given level of low-income housing or reduction in barriers, the comparison would have to include such factors as costs of enforcement and costs associated with changes in the level and composition of public expenditures.

I am grateful to William A. Fischel, David Saurman, and David L. Sjoquist for detailed comments. Any errors are my responsibility.

Notes

1. Advisory Commission on Regulatory Barriers to Affordable Housing, "*Not in My Back Yard*": *Removing Barriers to Affordable Housing* [NIMBY Report], Report to President Bush and Secretary Kemp, Washington, D.C., 1991.

2. The trial court in the *Euclid* case wrote, referring to zoning: "In the last analysis, the result to be accomplished is to classify the population and to segregate them according to their income or situation in life. The true reason why some people live in a mansion and others in a shack . . . is primarily economic. It is a matter of income and wealth. . . ." *Village of Euclid* v. *Ambler Realty Co.*, 297 F. 307, 316 (1924), overturned by U.S. Supreme Court, *Village of Euclid* v. *Ambler Realty Co.*, 272 United States 365 (1926), cited in King (1978, 461).

3. This is an example of a *negative* externality (also called an *external diseconomy*), that is, a situation in which one actor is imposing a cost upon another actor. There are also examples of *positive* externalities (or *external economies*). The same type of economic problem arises with external economies – not enough (rather than too much) of some good or service may be produced. We focus on external diseconomies because these are the ones usually associated with zoning. This example is of an externality in production, but we can also define externalities in consumption, that is, externalities that act through an effect on the utility function of a household rather than through an effect on the profit function of a firm.

4. See Pogodzinski and Sass (1991b). We might also call these "capital/land ratio limits" since they are frequently modeled this way (see the discussion below and figure 6.2).

5. Whether minimum lot-size zoning reduces congestion is problematical, as the Advisory Commission recognized (NIMBY Report, 2–4). For a given increase in population, minimum lot-size zoning forces the size of the urban area to expand, increasing the length of commutes in the aggregate.

6. The analysis underlying this figure is static rather than dynamic, so some

latitude must be made in interpreting the figure. Suppose that housing services in each period are produced by using the services of land and the services of housing capital. The prices referred to here are the rental rates for these services, although most SFDs are purchased outright, in which case the rental rates for these inputs are reflected in the purchase price.

7. This is a reasonable interpretation of how the minimum lot-size requirement operates in conjunction with other zoning requirements in practice. The permissible combinations of K and L are indicated by the shaded region of figure 6.2. Strictly speaking, a particular minimum lot-size requirement would be represented as a vertical line in figure 6.2.

8. Committee on Banking, Finance, and Urban Affairs, *Report by the Advisory Commission on Regulatory Barriers to Affordable Housing (Joint Hearings)*, Serial No. 102–57, Washington, D.C.: U.S. Government Printing Office, 1991; *Housing Policy Debate*, Volume 2, Issue 4, 1991.

9. That is, the median household income is just that income needed to qualify to obtain a standard mortgage for the median-priced house.

10. For example, the Advisory Commission names three California cities and Detroit as having particularly acute affordability problems for poor renters. The problems in Detroit are not blamed on regulatory barriers (NIMBY Report, 1–5).

11. Restrictive covenants are private agreements in perpetuity usually about the use of land. These agreements usually cover mundane topics such as the property can only be used for residential purposes, but in the past some restrictive covenants have included provisions that the property could not be sold to blacks or Jews. These latter provisions have been held to be not enforceable by a court since they are contrary to public policy.

12. I have represented this intolerance as pure "discrimination" – not justified on any other rational basis, like the tax burden such poor people might represent to the local jurisdiction or the likely higher crime rates (see O'Sullivan 1993, 687–94). It is of course possible to give such alternative interpretations, but it is not necessary for the result. Likewise, one might suppose that rich people's aversion to the poor is based upon their higher income–that is, that "it is all income elasticity." That interpretation may also be reasonable but, again, not necessary for the result.

13. Each rich person is willing to consume more housing the fewer poor people there are in the jurisdiction, other factors held constant. Do rich people actually move to larger houses as the number of poor people declines? They may do so in some long-run sense. The fewer the number of poor people in the neighborhood, the more confidence I have in the investment value of a house, and therefore the larger the house I am willing to invest in. (I make a choice of investing in housing over investing in, say, bonds.)

14. The analysis is similar to that met in two parts of microeconomics. When discussing income and substitution effects of a price change, we say a given consumer has the same *real* income at two different consumption bundles if both consumption bundles lie on the same indifference curve. When discussing the long-run equilibrium of the perfectly competitive firm, we say that entry to the industry stops when economic profits go to zero. Here, entry by the poor to the

next-best jurisdiction stops when the price of housing there has risen so as to equalize their real income between the two jurisdictions.

15. Based on the assumptions given above, $Q_D^1 = \{[(100)(200)]/2p_H\}+\{[(75)(160)]/2p_H\}$ and $Q_D^2 = \{[(200)(160)]/2p_H\}$. Thus, $Q_D^1 = Q_D^2$. The market clearing condition $Q_D^j = Q_S^j = 5p_H$ can be solved for $(p_H)^2 = 3{,}200$, or $p_H = 56.56854249$. We take the generic consumption good as the *numeraire*, so $p_C = 1$.

16. This amount is determined by first determining the housing price in jurisdiction 2, assuming all of the poor reside there. Market-clearing in jurisdiction 1 will require (*) $\beta p_H = (100)\{\alpha M/[(1+\alpha)p_H]\}$. If the poor are to remain in jurisdiction 2, p_H^1 must be at least as large as p_H^2, and we can then solve expression (*) for β.

17. The compensations are computed by determining the difference in indirect utility. With α constant and assuming that the newly determined prices prevail in jurisdiction 2, the difference in indirect utility is given by $\Delta V = (1 + \alpha)\ln(M)$, with $\alpha_p = 1$ for the poor. For the rich, α_r changes, but if the *status quo ante* were to be established, $\alpha_r(75) = 1$, so the same formula, $\Delta V = (2)\ln(M)$, is employed.

18. This is the assumption that past some threshold level of externality, the rich are made no worse off by additional poor people residing in the same jurisdiction.

19. This material is based upon Pogodzinski (1991).

20. This is contrary to what one would expect based upon the monopoly-zoning hypothesis discussed later.

21. An agglomeration economy is a spatial economy of scale. Agglomeration economies are the basis for urban economics (see O'Sullivan 1993, chapter 2).

22. I am grateful to William Fischel for emphasizing this point to me.

23. See, for example, Nicholson (1985, 468–70).

24. The symbol "ln" preceding *P* and the right-hand variables stands for *natural logarithm*. This is a useful mathematical function that allows nonlinear equations to be estimated using linear regression techniques. Suppose we believe that the true relationship between *P* and the variables on the right-hand side of (6.5) is given by $P = \alpha N^\beta \hat{N}^\gamma Y^\delta L^\mu C^\eta$. This certainly is a nonlinear function. However, we can "linearize" it by using two facts about natural logarithms. First, $\ln(xy) = \ln(x) + \ln(y)$. Second, $\ln(x^\alpha) = \alpha\ln(x)$. Moreover, the coefficients in this formulation have the interpretation of *elasticities*–that is, they express the effect of a percentage change in one variable upon a percentage change in another variable. The coefficient β in expression (6.5), for example, is the *population elasticity of vacant land price*–that is, the percentage by which vacant land price will change for, say, a 1 percent change in the population of the area. The remaining coefficients in expression 6.5 have analogous interpretations.

25. The regression equation is estimated by finding the best-fitting straight line that fits all of the observations. Typically, no straight line fits all the observations exactly, and the fit of the straight line differs also along different dimensions or variables. Coefficients of regression equations are called statistically significant if, accounting for this variability along the dimension of the particular variable, the mean value of the coefficient differs sufficiently from zero so that there is great confidence that the true value is different from zero. Statistical significance is a matter of degree–it depends on how much confidence I wish to have that the true value differs from zero. If I am willing to accept 90 percent confidence that the true value differs from zero, then I am willing to accept a 10 percent significance level. If I am

willing to accept only a 95 percent confidence level, then I am willing to accept only a 5 percent significance level. A coefficient of a regression equation that is *insignificant* is indistinguishable from zero at the agreed-upon confidence level.

26. In addition to the papers cited below there is an important series of papers by McMillen and McDonald (1989; 1990; 1991a,b,c).

27. Rolleston's equation explaining the residential restrictiveness index appears as part of a system of equations. See Pogodzinski (1991) for details.

28. Rolleston (1987, 17).

29. It is necessary to assume that the publicly provided good is an "impure" local public good that is, a public good subject to crowding.

Bibliography

Advisory Commission on Regulatory Barriers to Affordable Housing. *"Not in My Back Yard": Removing Barriers to Affordable Housing." Report to President Bush and Secretary Kemp, Washington, D.C., 1991.*

Branfman, E. J., B. Cohen, and D. M. Trubek. "Measuring the Invisible Wall: Land Use Controls and the Residential Pattern of the Poor." *Yale Law Journal* 82, 3, (January 1973): 483–508.

Buttler, Hans-Jurg. "Equilibrium of a Residential City, Attributes of Housing and Land-Use Zoning." *Urban Studies* 18 (February 1981): 23–39.

Cannaday, R. E., and P. F. Colwell. "Optimization of Subdivision Development." *The Journal of Real Estate Finance and Economics* 3 (June 1990): 195–206.

Coase, R. H. "The Problem of Social Cost." *Journal of Law and Economics* 3 (October 1960): 1–44.

Colwell, P. F., and T. F. Scheu. "Optimal Lot Size and Configuration." *Journal of Urban Economics* 26 (March 1989): 90–109.

Committee on Banking, Finance and Urban Affairs. *Report by the Advisory Commission on Regulatory Barriers to Affordable Housing (Joint Hearings).* Serial No. 102–57. Washington, D.C.: U.S. Government Printing Office, 1991.

Crone, T. M. "Elements of an Economic Justification for Municipal Zoning." *Journal of Urban Economics* 14 (1983): 184–205.

Davis, O. A. "Economic Elements in Municipal Zoning Decisions." *Land Economics* 39 (1963): 375–86.

Fischel, W. "Zoning and the Exercise of Monopoly Power: A Reevaluation," *Journal of Urban Economics* 8 (1980): 283–93.

———. "Comment." *Housing Policy Debate* 2, 4 (1991): 1139–60.

———. "Property Taxation and the Tiebout Model: Evidence for the Benefit View from Zoning and Voting." *Journal of Economic Literature* 30 (1992): 171–77.

———. *Regulatory Takings and Local Self-Governance: Economic and Political Alternatives to Constitutional Adjudication.* Book manuscript. 10 (December 1993).

———. "Zoning, Nonconvexities and T. Jack Foster's City." *Journal of Urban Economics* 35 (1994).

Hamilton, B. "Zoning and the Exercise of Monopoly Power." *Journal of Urban Economics* 5 (1978): 116–30.

Henderson, J. V. "The Impact of Zoning Policies which Regulate Housing Quality." *Journal of Urban Economics* 18 (November 1985): 302–12.

King, P. E. "Exclusionary Zoning and Open Housing: A Brief Judicial History" *The Geographical Review* 68, 4 (October 1978): 459–69.

Layard, P. R. G., and A. A. Walters. *Microeconomic Theory*. New York: McGraw-Hill, 1978.

Mark, J. H., and M. A. Goldberg. "Land Use Controls: The Case of Zoning in the Vancouver Area." *AREUEA Journal* 9 (1981): 418–35.

——. "A Study of the Impacts of Zoning on Housing Values over Time." *Journal of Urban Economics* 20 (1986): 257–73.

McMillen, D., and J. McDonald. "Selectivity Bias in Urban Land Value Functions." *Land Economics* 65 (1989): 341–51.

——. "A Two-Limit Tobit Model of Suburban Land-Use Zoning." *Land Economics* 66 (1990): 272–82.

——. "Urban Land Value Functions with Endogenous Zoning." *Journal of Urban Economics* 29 (1991a): 14–27.

——. "A Simultaneous Equations Model of Zoning and Land Values." *Regional Science and Urban Economics* 21 (1991b): 55–72.

——. "A Markov Model of Zoning Change." *Journal of Urban Economics* 30 (1991c): 257–70.

Mueller, D. C. *Public Choice II*. Cambridge: Cambridge University Press, 1989.

Nicholson, W.. *Microeconomic Theory*. New York: Dryden Press, 1985.

Oates, W.. "The Effects of Property Taxes and Local Public Spending on Property Values: An Empirical Study of Tax Capitalization and the Tiebout Hypothesis." *Journal of Political Economy* 77 (November/December 1969) 957–71.

O'Sullivan, A.. *Urban Economics*. 2d ed. Irwin, 1993.

Pogodzinski, J. M. "The Effects of Fiscal and Exclusionary Zoning on Household Location: A Critical Review." *Journal of Housing Research* 2, 2 (1991): 145–60.

Pogodzinski, J. M., and T. R. Sass. "The Economic Theory of Zoning: A Critical Review." *Land Economics* 66, 3 (August 1990): 294–314.

——. "Measuring the Effects of Municipal Zoning Regulations: A Survey." *Urban Studies* 28, 4 (1991a): 597–621.

——. "Zoning and Hedonic Housing Price Models." *Journal of Housing Economics* 1 (1991b): 271–92.

——. "The Theory and Estimation of Endogenous Zoning." *Regional Science and Urban Economics*. Forthcoming.

Rolleston, B. S. "Determinants of Restrictive Suburban Zoning: An Empirical Analysis." *Journal of Urban Economics* 21, 1 (January 1987): 1–21.

Rose, L. A. "Urban Land Supply: Natural and Contrived Restrictions." *Journal of Urban Economics* 25, 3 (May 1989): 325–45.

Rubin, J., J. Seneca, and J. Stotsky. "Affordable Housing and Municipal Choice." *Land Economics* 66 (1990): 325–40.

Shlay, A. B., and P. H. Rossi. "Keeping Up the Neighborhood: Estimating Net Effects of Zoning." *American Sociological Review* 46, 6 (December 1981): 703–19.

Sjoquist, D. L. "Black-White Wage and Employment Differentials: The Spatial

Mismatch Hypothesis." In *Readings in Public Policy*. Edited by J. M. Pogodzinski. Cambridge, MA: Blackwell, forthcoming.

Tiebout, C.. "A Pure Theory of Local Public Finance." *Journal of Political Economy* 64, 5 (October 1956): 416–24.

White, M. J. "Fiscal Zoning in Fragmented Metropolitan Areas." In *Fiscal Zoning and Land Use Controls*. Edited by E. S. Mills and W. E. Oates. Lexington, MA: Heath-Lexington, 1975.

Glossary

Characteristics-zoning: The stipulation of requirements about the relation of structures to land and other inputs within a use-category.

Coase's Theorem: The statement that different assignments of property rights result in equally efficient allocations of resources.

Concentration Ratio: A ratio of the output of the top n firms in an industry to the total industry output.

Efficient: See *Pareto-efficient*.

Endogenous: Internal to the model.

Exclusionary zoning: Term applied to the concept that local jurisdictions select zoning ordinances so as to attract or repel households of a particular racial or ethnic group.

Exogenous: External to the model.

Externalities: A circumstance in which one economic actor's actions affect another economic actor's outcomes in a fashion not captured by the market.

Fiscal Zoning: Term applied to the concept that local jurisdictions select zoning ordinances so as to attract households that will contribute more in tax revenue than they consume in publicly provided services.

Hedonic Price Equation (or Model): An econometric method that decomposes the price of a heterogeneous good into the value of its characteristics.

Heterogeneous Good: A good with several features or qualities.

Implicit Prices: The prices of characteristics on implicit or unobserved markets as determined by an application of a hedonic price equation.

Indirect Utility: The realized utility–that is, the value of the utility function evaluated at the optimal consumption bundle.

Market Failure: A circumstance in which the private market, left to its own devices, does not achieve an efficient allocation of resources.

Market Power: A circumstance in which an economic actor has strategic influence over the price.

Mobility (or Interjurisdictional) Effect: The effect of zoning regulations in attracting or repelling households to a particular jurisdiction.

Monopoly-Zoning Hypothesis: The idea that the "market power" of a jurisdiction in establishing zoning is determined by the strength of competition with nearby jurisdictions.

Next-Best Jurisdiction: That jurisdiction or municipality that is the next best to the jurisdiction of current residence.

Pareto-Efficient: An allocation of resources is Pareto-efficient if there is no other feasible allocation such that at least one person is better off while all others are no worse off.

Police Power: The legal basis for state action to protect the health and welfare of citizens.

Quantity Effect: The effect of zoning regulations on the quantity of housing services demanded by any particular income–taste class of households.

Regulatory Taking: The appropriation of private property indirectly, via a regulation like zoning.

Restrictive Covenant: A private agreement usually about the use of land, which limits the uses to which the land can be put and which binds not only the present owner but also all future owners.

Simultaneous Equations Bias: The bias introduced in econometric estimates by failing to account for the simultaneous nature of some processes–for example, that the equilibrium price and equilibrium quantity are simultaneously determined by supply and demand–meaning that such methods as ordinary least squares regression are inappropriate.

Taking: The appropriation of private property.

Tiebout Mechanism: The mechanism named for Charles Tiebout that contemplates that households will "vote with their feet" and choose their jurisdiction of residents based upon self-interested considerations.

Use-Zoning: The segregation of land into different use-categories.

Zoning Follows the Market: The idea that zoning authorities are guided mainly by market considerations in determining initial zoning or rezonings.

7

Secondary Mortgage Markets, Efficiency and Market Failure

Ellen P. Roche

Introduction

How can "value" be created or enhanced? The right and ability to resell *something may contribute to its value. Consider automobiles. We may participate either as buyers or sellers in the used car market. Although we would not usually think along these lines, the fact that I can resell my automobile contributes to its value. If such sales were restricted or eliminated, I would be less willing to buy an automobile in the first place and willing to pay less for it if I did buy it since I would be stuck with whatever I purchased.*

Resales of such objects as automobiles come easily to mind, but resales of financial instruments may not. There are three main points developed in Ellen Roche's chapter on secondary mortgage markets. First, she describes the instruments *of the mortgage market. Second, she describes the* institutions *(and their regulation) of the mortgage market. Third, she analyzes the* efficiency *of the mortgage market.*

The instruments of the mortgage market include not only mortgages but also instruments that can be constructed from mortgages. A central fact to consider here has an analogue in computer design: how more reliable machines can be constructed from less reliable components. In the secondary mortgage market, mortgages are bundled in a particular fashion, and the bundles are sold to investors. In a sense these bundles are more valuable than the sum of their parts.

There are a variety of institutions in the mortgage market, but particular attention is paid to GSEs–government-sponsored enterprises. Examples include Fannie Mae (the Federal National Mortgage Association) and Freddie Mac (the Federal Home Loan Mortgage Corporation). Roche's chapter ad-

dresses two sorts of issues involving these institutions. First, what do they do?
Second, why is there a need for government sponsorship of such institutions?
   The efficiency analysis of the mortgage market is based upon the analysis
of the distribution of various kinds of risk. Mortgage markets are regulated.
What effects have such regulations had, and what issues still need the
attention of regulators?

Secondary mortgage markets are the nexus between international capital
markets and U.S. government support for housing. On the one hand,
secondary mortgage markets are part of a complex network of markets that
contribute to the efficiency of U.S. and world capital markets. On the other
hand, secondary mortgage market institutions, one part of secondary
mortgage markets, are part of U.S. housing policy charged with providing
liquidity to the housing market. Through the use of sophisticated financial
instruments, the secondary mortgage market provides a mechanism for
investing international capital at competitive rates of return in U.S. owner-
occupied and multifamily rental housing. This mechanism is then used as
an instrument of government policy to provide financing for low- and
moderate-income housing.

   In this chapter, secondary mortgage markets will be described and
analyzed for the contribution they make to the financial sector and the
housing market. The particular role of secondary mortgage market institutions will be discussed along with their public mission to serve low-,
moderate-, and middle-income home buyers. This chapter will also discuss
the efficiency considerations for government support of the secondary
mortgage market.

Secondary Mortgage Markets in Context

Secondary mortgage markets exist to match the needs of people who want
to borrow money for housing with the needs of people who want to invest
money in housing. The secondary mortgage market provides a mechanism
for the borrower to receive the money for the housing and for the investor
to receive an adequate return. This function is one of a general class of
activities that can be described as financial intermediation–the matching of
financial needs. In the past, financial institutions met the needs of borrowers
and investors by investing deposits in housing. However, financial deregulation made it difficult to invest short-term liabilities in long-term assets.

   Secondary mortgage markets are merely one type of secondary market
that exists in the United States today. A secondary market can be distinguished from a primary market because a primary market exchange must

precede a secondary market exchange. Some examples will make this distinction clearer. To raise capital, a corporation can sell stock to investors through an initial public offering of the stock. This is a primary market–the sale of a finished product to a purchaser. If the investor decides to sell the stock, the sale will typically occur between two investors (or their representatives) on a stock exchange, such as the New York Stock Exchange. Most of the trades are secondary in the sense that no new shares of stock are involved. The stock being traded was initially acquired through an initial public offering (the primary market) but in the stock exchange (the secondary market) is merely traded among investors. Although no new stock is produced, the stock exchange and other secondary markets support the primary market by providing information about the price of traded items and by adding to the value of the items traded in primary market by providing liquidity–that is, the ability to sell the asset when desired. Secondary markets occur in nonfinancial markets and are common when the assets being sold retain value over time. For example, purchasing a new automobile from a dealer occurs in the primary market for automobiles, but purchasing a used automobile from the current owner occurs in the secondary market for automobiles. To see that the secondary market adds value to the primary market, observe that advertising for new automobiles claims that the car being promoted retains its value longer than competing automobiles. This value is established through the secondary market.

Beyond the secondary market is another market that I will refer to as the *tertiary market* where products sold in the secondary market are sold in a different form. This market uses the mortgages sold in the secondary market to create new financial products such as pass-though securities, also known as mortgage-backed securities (MBS). These securities may also be combined and split in different ways to produce interest-only or principal-only securities. Again, such a tertiary market can exist only if the primary and secondary markets exist, and it supports the value of the exchanges in the primary and secondary markets, although no new products are sold.

In describing and analyzing secondary mortgage markets, it is important to distinguish several different markets that support and depend on the secondary mortgage market. The secondary mortgage market does not exist in a vacuum. It is only one of a series of markets that provide the home buyer with the funds to purchase a house. While secondary mortgage markets exist in other countries, they operate differently.

Conceptually, markets exist as a transaction between a buyer and a seller. The housing market, then, consists of the transactions between buyers and sellers of housing. When a house is purchased without borrowing–that is, with 100 percent equity–there is no involvement with the mortgage market. However, since housing is a high-cost durable good that provides a flow of services over time, housing is often purchased using debt obtained through the primary mortgage market.

The Primary Mortgage Market Today

The primary mortgage market (the primary market) consists of transactions in which people buy (borrow) and sell (lend) money to purchase housing. The amount purchased is the size of the mortgage, and the price is the interest rate and related fees. A mortgage is a financial instrument that involves the exchange of the loan amount for the promise of repayment of the principal and interest and the right to seize the collateral if the repayment does not occur according to the terms of the mortgage contract. The interest rate is the sum of the risk-free rate plus adjustments for risk. Collateral is the asset pledged to secure the loan, and in the case of a mortgage, the collateral is the property.

Mortgage Instruments—The terms of the mortgage contract can vary along several dimensions. In general, mortgages can be described as fixed-rate mortgages (FRMs) and adjustable-rate mortgages (ARMs). The classic FRM requires monthly payments of principal and interest over 30 years. The interest rate is fixed at origination–that is, when the loan terms are finalized and are based on prevailing market rates. Given the term of the loan, the mortgage amount, and the interest rate, monthly payments are calculated as those equal payments that will result in a discounted present value equal to the mortgage amount.[1]

The monthly payment is level over the life of the mortgage, but the interest payment portion of the monthly payment falls (and the principal payment portion increases) reflecting the decrease in the outstanding balance of the mortgage (see figure 7.1).

An ARM could have monthly payments over 30 years, but the interest rate applied to the outstanding balance of the mortgage is adjusted to reflect market interest rates. The number and type of adjustments are endless. For example, a one-year ARM has payments that adjust every year, and the interest rate is adjusted according to changes in the rate on the one-year U.S. Treasury bond. At each adjustment date, the schedule of payments required to pay off the mortgage by the original term is recalculated and a new mortgage payment is derived. Some ARMs limit changes in the interest rate to 2 percent per year and 6 percent over the term of the mortgage (see figure 7.2).

In other countries, variable-rate mortgages are more common: in the United Kingdom the mortgage institutions (known as building societies) increase mortgage interest rates in response to market changes at their own discretion, and the size of the increases is limited only by competition. In Mexico, a dual-indexed mortgage is very popular due to the high inflation rates that have occurred in that country. Every year the originating banks

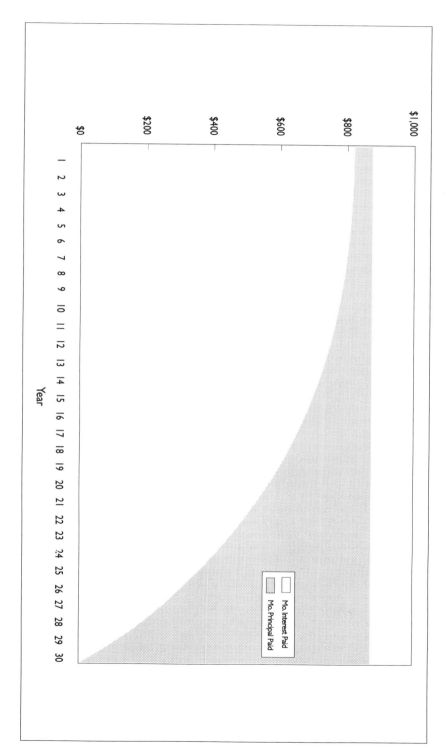

Figure 7.1   Interest and Principal on Fixed-Rate Mortgage ($100,000 Initial Unpaid Balance, 10% Rate, 30 Years).

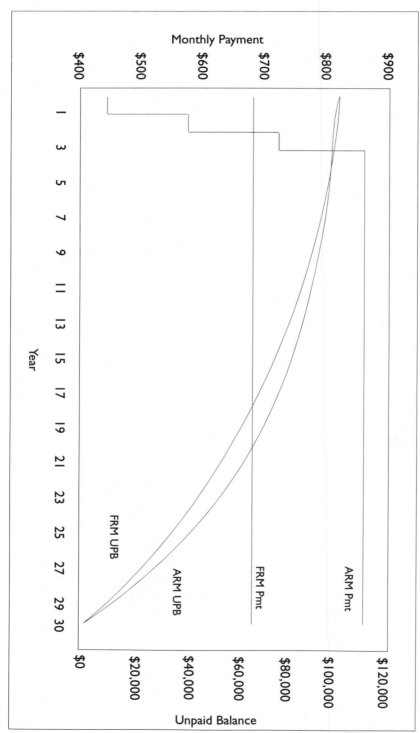

Figure 7.2   Monthly Payment and Unpaid Balance (Adjustable-Rate Mortgage (2%/6% caps) vs. Fixed-Rate Mortgage).
Note: Mortgage rates rise permanently by 8% at outset of year 3, affecting ARM only.

use a current interest rate index to recalculate the outstanding balance of the mortgage to limit the interest rate risk of the lenders. The payments are adjusted according to a wage index to preserve affordability. If inflation is much higher than wage growth, it may be difficult for the borrower to pay off the entire mortgage balance and thus many of these mortgages are insured by the government. These few examples give a brief introduction to the full range of mortgage products available.

Significance—Some statistics will provide a sense of the size of this market:

- In 1992, 64 percent of U.S. households owned their own homes (Joint Center for Housing Studies, 27).

- According to the 1989 American Housing Survey, 87 percent of all first-time home buyers bought their homes with a mortgage.

- In 1992, $800 billion in single-family mortgages were originated, and at the end of the year there was $2.9 trillion in mortgage debt outstanding. This represented 23.4 percent of total domestic nonfinancial debt outstanding at the end of 1992.

In addition to size, it is important to understand the significance of housing finance for the housing market. There are several major benefits of mortgages:

1. Debt financing of the purchase of a residence
2. Reduction of liquidity constraints
3. Leverage of assets
4. Increased liquidity of assets

First, mortgages allow debt financing of the purchase of a residence. If debt financing were not available, all housing purchases would require 100 percent equity financing–that is, all-cash purchases. As a durable good, a house can be expected to provide a flow of housing services for 30 years or more. With 100 percent equity financing, payment is required for these services in advance. However, debt financing allows payments over time and increases the congruence between the flow of services and the payment for these services.

Second, most potential buyers do not have the full purchase price of a house in cash and thus are "liquidity-constrained": they do not, that is, have the cash to purchase the asset today but could pay over time for the flow of housing services received over time. The buyer may represent a stream of labor income over 30 years, and the present value of this income stream would be sufficient to purchase the house. However, the financial markets are incomplete because there is no market that permits potential home buyers to obtain a long-term loan against their future earnings without some other guarantee or collateral.

What is it that causes this incompleteness in markets? Incomplete markets occur when it is impossible to purchase something regardless of the price. Markets may be incomplete for many reasons, but a common characteristic of these markets is asymmetric information, that is, the buyer and the seller have different information, and it is difficult to credibly reveal this information. In the case of a loan, for example, two borrowers each promise to work hard for 30 years to pay off what is owed. One of the borrowers really means it, but the other borrower is planning to take the money, spend it on a vacation, and then live off society for the rest his or her life. There is no way for the good borrower to be distinguished from the bad borrower in a way that will convince the lender that he or she is going to make the payments. In addition, once the loan is made, given the elimination of debtors' prisons and slavery, there is no way to compensate the lender if the borrower does not make the payments. Finally, once the good borrower receives the loan, what is the incentive to make the payments, given the weak enforcement powers available to the lender? There is a moral hazard because the incentive structure does not encourage the borrower to make payments. There may also be incomplete markets due to regulation of financial institutions. The market may be completed by unregulated entities–known as loan sharks–who are willing to accept the higher risk because they charge a higher interest rate and establish different remedies for the nonpayment of the loan. Because of these problems, there is no market that permits individuals to obtain a long-term loan against their future earnings at any price: there is an incomplete market for lifetime earnings.

One way people have obtained loans is to promise that the lender can take something (collateral) if the borrower does not make the payments. Contract law allows the lender to take possession of any promised collateral, and this mitigates several problems associated with incomplete financial markets.

Good borrowers thus reveal themselves because they are the ones who are willing to provide valuable collateral in order to get the loan. Bad borrowers would not make this promise, knowing that they have no intention of repaying the loan. In addition, the borrower is encouraged to make the payments, once the loan is made, for the same reason: to guarantee the return of the valuable collateral. The reduced risk associated with collateral loans is also subject to fewer regulatory barriers. Collateral loans seem perfect, but it should be recalled that collateral loans imply that you are lending to people who already have assets. People still cannot borrow against their lifetime earnings.

When home buyers obtain a mortgage to purchase a residence, the collateral is the combination of the cash down payment and the house. The lender is allowed to take the property and keep the down payment and any other payment made if the borrower does not make all the mortgage payments in a timely manner. Although the ability to make the mortgage payments is a function of lifetime earnings, the collateral makes the mortgage possible by providing a partial solution to what would otherwise be an incomplete market. Indeed, the availability of mortgages is primarily responsible for making housing affordable for large numbers of people. As an illustration, in a recent report by the Bureau of the Census on affordability, the issue is defined completely in terms of the type of mortgage selected; the report states that "The most prominent single reason owners could not afford a house was because their income was not sufficient to qualify for the necessary mortgage" (Savage and Fronczek 1993, ix).

Third, mortgages release a portion of the value of the land to be employed in the economy in exchange for access to collateral. For example, you may purchase a house valued at $250,000. You may live in the house, or you may rent it to others. Without a mortgage, you would have to sell the property to release the value for a different purpose. However, if you purchased the house with $50,000 equity and a $200,000 mortgage, then the $200,000 could be invested elsewhere. Assuming the return on the investment is greater than the rate of return to the house, then the total return on the $250,000 is higher because of the ability to release the value of the property through the mortgage.

The collateral guarantees the mortgage because mortgage contracts in the United States allow the lender to take the collateral property if the mortgage is not paid. Thus, the ability to seize the collateral changes the property rights: the borrower must make the payments to get the collateral back rather than the lender suing to get the loan repaid.

The ability to take the property is governed by state law and varies somewhat from state to state. But in general, the easier it is for the lender to seize the property for nonpayment of the mortgage, the easier it is to obtain a mortgage that approaches the full value of the property (see figure 7.3). The greater the percentage of a property's full value that may be borrowed, the less equity or savings is required to purchase a house. In the United States today, the typical home buyer can borrow up to 90 percent of a property's value. Without the existence of a primary market, low- and moderate-income households who are liquidity-constrained could not purchase housing: they would rent or purchase land and build a structure over time as income was earned.

This principle is even more important in the purchase of multifamily rental dwellings because of the higher cost of the buildings. Without the ability to fund the purchase with debt, it would be difficult to organize the construction of these dwellings, which are so important for low- and moderate-income households.

Figure 7.3   Collateral and Equity.

In countries that do not have well-developed financial markets, the purchase of housing is restricted to those who are have low liquidity constraints–typically the upper-income groups who can finance with large amounts of equity. Others rent or save their money to purchase the land and then build a structure over time as money becomes available. This approach is common for large segments of the population in developing countries and also occurs in more developed countries such as Turkey where population growth and urbanization have overwhelmed the ability of both the financial and physical infrastructure. The U.S. primary mortgage market uses debt to allow liquidity-constrained, lower-income households to pay for housing over time as they receive the service.

Fourth, the mortgage is a financial asset that can be exchanged in a market just like other real assets such as property. This feature can be used to increase the liquidity or the funds available to the primary mortgage market. The mortgage can be sold for cash that can in turn be lent for the purchase of another home or for other purposes. When the mortgage is exchanged for cash or another security, the transaction is taking place in the secondary mortgage market.

The long-term mortgage allows the transfer of three types of risk from the borrower to lender: the risk of default, the funding or interest rate risk, and the prepayment risk. The default risk is the probability that the borrower will not repay all of the principal and interest due on the mortgage. Although the lender has access to the collateral, the lender often sustains losses if there is a default. Thus the lender accepts some risk. The funding or interest rate risk is the risk that market interest rates will rise above the mortgage rate and the current cost of funding the mortgage will be greater than the yield on the mortgage. If the mortgage has been funded with short-term debt, then the lender will be losing money. Similarly, the prepayment risk is the possibility that when interest rates decline, the borrower will pay the mortgage in full by borrowing money at a lower interest rate. The lender then must reinvest the money in a lower-yielding investment. In exchange for accepting these risks, the lender charges a premium for each risk component that is added to the risk-free interest rate. Thus mortgage interest rates are typically greater than the interest rate on a comparable maturity U.S. Treasury bond, which is a proxy for the risk-free rate. The trading of mortgages can be used to allocate the risks associated with a mortgage to the entity that bears the risk at the lowest cost.

The secondary mortgage market can facilitate the allocation of risk as well as provide liquidity to the primary mortgage market. In the next section, secondary mortgage markets will be described and analyzed in more detail.

The Secondary Mortgage Market Today

The secondary mortgage market is the exchange of mortgages, sometimes called *whole mortgages*, for cash or financial instruments where mortgage originators (the original mortgage issuers) are the sellers and other financial institutions are the buyers. The market is secondary in the sense that the products exchanged (mortgages) are created in the primary market and are being resold in a market that is one level removed. Although secondary mortgage markets have become known for their innovative financial instruments, the strict definition of a secondary mortgage market is simply a market in which mortgages are traded.

Primary mortgage market liquidity is increased when a mortgage is exchanged for cash that is then available to lend to someone else. The goals of the exchange are to reduce the risk of the originator and to increase the liquidity or the funds available to the primary mortgage market. When originators trade mortgages for cash from investors, these trades encourage mortgage lending.

Trading individual mortgages entails high transaction costs due to high information costs. In addition to the specifics of the loan amount, interest rate, term, frequency of payment, amortization schedule, and other aspects of the individual transaction, the mortgage represents underlying institutional arrangements involving:

- property rights
- property registration

- property appraisal
- underwriting rules
- documentation

When individual loans are traded, the transaction costs are high because some of the underlying information is complex and specific to each mortgage and some of the underlying information is institutional and specific to the state, the appraisal firm, the lender, or others. To reduce the information costs associated with trading mortgages and thus create liquidity and facilitate allocating the risk, standards were developed for many aspects of a mortgage. Standardization of property rights is the most basic and crucial because it leads to the standardization of access to collateral.

Once a standard is established, mortgages meeting that standard are traded faster and with lower transactions costs due to the information efficiencies. These efficiencies can reduce the cost of mortgage finance for those who meet the standard. Standardization of mortgage information has resulted in the treatment of individual mortgages as essentially identical to each other. Certifying that they meet the standard allows many loans to be traded as a homogeneous group rather than as a series of unique investments.

These groups of mortgages are then used to create other financial instruments, including the pass-through securities or mortgage-backed securities (MBS).[2] Another set of standards was developed for MBSs that allows these new securities to be traded with low transactions costs. This low-cost trading increases the number and range of investors for the mortgage market because these investors can quickly buy and sell their mortgage investments in response to changing market prices. Reducing the transactions costs also allows improved allocation of risk to the investor who can bear the risk at the lowest cost. Through the development of MBS, the investor base has expanded to include commercial banks, insurance companies, pension funds, and foreign representatives of these groups.

Before secondary mortgage markets, investors consisted of those who deposited their savings in depository institutions, such as banks and savings and loans. Now, through the creation of pass-through securities and other derivatives, the housing market can attract investors from around the world and from all sectors of the economy. For example, pass-through securities provide monthly payments of interest and principal, and prepayments are realized as repayments of principal. To introduce Japanese investors to the prepayment characteristics of MBSs, a mutual fund invested in MBSs and then made semiannual payments, like a bond, and the principal prepayments were spread over the portfolio to smooth the cash flow. Real Estate Mortgage Investment Conduits (REMICs) and Collateralized Mortgage Obligations (CMOs) allow the principal and interest payments from a pool of

MBSs to be distributed over time in almost any pattern to meet the needs of the investors.

Activities—The mortgages purchased by Fannie Mae and Freddie Mac may be used to create MBS or other mortgage securities that are sold to investors. In addition, Fannie Mae and Freddie Mac also invest directly in mortgages by holding mortgages in their portfolios and funding them with debt.

The MBS represents a pool of mortgages for which the issuer, either Fannie Mae or Freddie Mac, guarantees the timely payment of principal and interest to the investor in return for an insurance premium referred to as a guarantee fee. Unlike Government National Mortgage Association (GNMA) securities, these securities do not carry the full faith and credit of the U.S. government. Under this arrangement, Fannie Mae and Freddie Mac retain the risk of default for the mortgages in the pool and sell the interest rate risk and the prepayment risk. Investors accept the interest rate risk, which is similar to that of a bond, and the prepayment risk, which is unique to mortgages, and then are rewarded by the possibility of earning a yield that is greater than that of a comparable maturity U.S. Treasury bond. For mortgages retained in portfolio, Fannie Mae and Freddie Mac retain the prepayment and the interest rate risk as well as the default risk, and thus are the investor as well as the provider of credit enhancement.

Fannie Mae and Freddie Mac have a fiduciary responsibility to earn a competitive rate of return for their shareholders within the broader goal of attracting capital to the mortgage market. Thus they attempt to maximize their profitability in the secondary mortgage market activities they pursue, subject to the constraints imposed by their charters and their regulators. Increasing profits and market share have raised public policy concerns. Since 1990, net income at Freddie Mac has risen an average of 24 percent, and 1993 net earnings were $786 million. Over the same time period, Fannie Mae's net income rose an average of 16 percent, and 1993 net income was $1.87 billion. It has been estimated that almost half of all mortgages originated are bought by these two secondary mortgage market institutions.

Fannie Mae and Freddie Mac are restricted in the types of mortgages they may purchase. All the loans must have at least a 20 percent down payment or credit enhancement to limit the loss exposure in case of default. For 1993, the largest single-family mortgage that could be purchased by Fannie Mae and Freddie Mac was $202,450. The limit increases as housing prices increase. Conventional loans that follow the underwriting guidelines of Fannie Mae and Freddie Mac and that meet the loan-limit test are referred to as conforming loans.

Conventional loans that do not meet the standards of Fannie Mae and Freddie Mac are referred to as nonconforming. If the mortgages do not meet the loan-limit restrictions, they are described as jumbo mortgages. There are private sector secondary market institutions that pool nonconforming mortgages for resale as pass-through securities to investors. Some of these are primary market institutions such as commercial banks, and some are private sector, nondepository financial institutions. Regulatory actions that have limited the use of credit enhancement have restricted the growth of this segment of the market. The secondary mortgage market is often considered to center on the activities of Fannie Mae and Freddie Mac.

Public Purpose—In addition to Fannie Mae and Freddie Mac, secondary mortgage market institutions include private sector institutions that create securities with jumbo and nonconforming mortgages and GNMA. However, the public purpose mission is unique to Fannie Mae and Freddie Mac. Since 1968, Fannie Mae has been required to achieve the dual mission of financial returns and serving the public purpose. Although it may appear that these goals are mutually inconsistent, in 1992 new legislation was passed that required Fannie Mae and Freddie Mac to increase their commitment to low-income households and to increase their capital levels and regulatory costs, thus strengthening the commitment to the public purpose and yet increasing their financial strength.[3] Fannie Mae and Freddie Mac will now be required to achieve several goals:

1. In 1993 and 1994, 30 percent of the total number of dwelling units financed had to be low- and moderate-income housing,
2. In 1993, Fannie Mae and Freddie Mac had to purchase 28 percent (30 percent in 1994) of the total number of dwelling units financed for housing located in central cities.
3. During the transition period in 1993 and 1994, for Fannie Mae and Freddie Macs purchases of mortgages on housing for low- and very low-income families had to be more than $2 billion in excess of the 1992 purchases.

In addition, Fannie Mae and Freddie Mac are covered by the Home Mortgage Disclosure Act that requires reports on the distribution of mortgage purchases by several protected classes, such as race, income, and gender.

The History and Development of the Secondary Mortgage Market

Context—The secondary mortgage market was conceived when the U.S. financial system was threatened with collapse and the financial infrastructure was a mere skeleton of the system we know today. The Depression threw the economy into a crisis that affected all productive sectors including the financial and mortgage markets.

In the 1920s and 1930s, the number, size, and variety of institutions and financial services were very limited. When the liquidity of these institutions evaporated during the Depression, the transfer of funds from savers to borrowers and investors was suspended. As a result, borrowing for mortgages and other investments across the full spectrum of the economy stopped. Because of this, the U.S. government created a number of financial and other institutions to increase the liquidity of the financial markets and assist capital market transactions, thus assisting the economic recovery.

Mortgage Markets—Prior to the stock market crash in 1929, homes were purchased with mortgages in which the payments were calculated based on a 20-year amortization schedule with, however, a balloon payment required after five or ten years. Lenders were unable to accept the risk of financing a long-term mortgage because they had mostly short-term liabilities–checking and savings accounts. To remain solvent in case depositors withdrew their money, short terms were necessary. When these loans required refinancing during the Depression, many were unable to do so due to low liquidity in the banking system. These homeowners lost their homes. In addition, the unique characteristics of each mortgage prevented the trading of large volumes of mortgages in a secondary market such as was available to stocks and bonds.

To facilitate the exchange of funds between borrowers and lenders, the government created several specialized housing finance institutions to increase liquidity to the primary mortgage market and thus increase mortgage lending. These institutions were supported by the establishment of a larger set of financial institutions whose purpose was to support capital market transactions in all sectors of the economy.[4] One of the specialized housing institutions was the Federal National Mortgage Association. Fannie Mae, as it has come to be known, was created in 1938 as an agency of the federal government to provide liquidity to the U.S. mortgage markets by purchasing mortgages from originators, thus operating in and supporting the secondary mortgage market. From 1938 to 1968, government appropriations were used for mortgage purposes. Beginning in 1956, Fannie Mae also issued debt to support its operations. A secondary market is one of several arrangements that increases liquidity to the primary market. Others include depository-based funding, advances to primary market lenders, and direct access to the capital market. Depository institutions, such as savings and loans, use checking and savings deposits to finance mortgages. Advances to primary market originators are loans from specialized financial institutions that use mortgages held in the portfolio of the institution as collateral. Direct access to the capital market occurs when primary market institutions sell debt, equity, or other securities without using other institutions for financial intermediation. Some large primary market players in the United States are able to use this mechanism without also utilizing the secondary mortgage market.

Before the development of a secondary mortgage market, the United States had a large number and variety of financial institutions that served the housing sector. This was so because the housing finance sector was segmented from the rest of the capital in the U.S. economy, and funding for housing in one region was segmented from savings in other regions. These institutions include both depositories such as savings and loans (S&Ls) and commercial banks as well as nondepositories like mortgage banks. S&Ls and savings banks collected savings from residents of the community and then provided financing for houses, small businesses, and later automobiles. However, there were few mechanisms for savings institutions from one region of the country to provide housing finance for a house in another region of the country. Commercial banks were the financial intermediaries for corporations. The financial regulation of these institutions was separate and tailored to their role in the U.S. economy at the time the regulation developed. As the roles of these institutions changed over time, so has the regulation.

The secondary mortgage market allowed the introduction of the 30-year, fixed-rate, and fixed-payment mortgage, and most of these new mortgages carried government mortgage insurance. Mortgage credit began to flow again because the default risk was reallocated to the government through both the secondary mortgage market and the government mortgage insurance program. Due to its national coverage, the secondary mortgage market was able to address the geographic segmentation of the market. Money from savers in one region could be directed to borrowers in those areas of the country that had a higher capital need. This is described as intermediation of capital across geographic regions. This system operated quietly through the 1960s following the great peacetime expansion of the U.S. economy.

In 1968, the organization was split into the GNMA, a government agency, and Fannie Mae, a privately capitalized corporation with a congressional charter that restricted the business to mortgages. With the establishment of GNMA, now part of the U.S. Department of Housing and Urban Development (HUD), the secondary mortgage market was split along regulatory lines. GNMA purchased only mortgages whose default risk is insured by government programs (Federal Housing Administration [FHA] and the Department of Veterans Affairs [VA]). The FHA provides mortgage insurance to home buyers with small down payments in exchange for a premium. The VA provides more generous terms to former members of the armed services. GNMA creates pools of these mortgages for sale to investors in the form of pass-through securities. GNMA MBSs are government securities and carry the same full faith and credit guarantee that U.S. Treasury bonds do. Thus, in the case of a failure to pay, the holders of GNMA MBSs also would become creditors of the U.S. government and would have call on the receipts of the government to pay them. FHA- and VA-insured mortgages are referred to as government mortgages in contrast to all other mortgages, which are referred to as conventional mortgages.

Fannie Mae could continue to purchase government-insured loans but was also granted permission in 1968 to purchase conventional mortgages. Mortgage banks were the primary source of mortgages because these banks do not invest in mortgages; that is, they do not have a mortgage portfolio as was the case with most S&Ls at that time. A mortgage bank does not accept deposits, and its primary business is the origination and servicing of mortgages. Commercial banks and credit unions were not originating a large volume of mortgages in 1968, but Fannie Mae could purchase a mortgage from any originator. S&Ls received special treatment in 1972 when the Federal Home Loan Mortgage Corporation (Freddie Mac) was chartered to create pass-through securities. The issuance of the first pass-through security opened the door to the broader capital markets. Freddie Mac was directed by the Federal Home Loan Bank Board, a regulatory agency that also had jurisdiction over S&Ls. Freddie Mac stock could only be held by S&Ls, and they were Freddie Mac's primary customers.

The inflation of the late 1970s and early 1980s brought turmoil to the S&L industry as interest rates were decontrolled for everyone except S&Ls, thus destroying their depositor base as savers sought higher interest rates elsewhere. When there was a loss of deposits during the bank runs of the Depression, S&Ls stopped lending. However, in the 1980s, when they were deprived of their traditional means of funding loans held in portfolio, the S&Ls sold an increasing share of originations to the secondary market. There was no interruption in the supply of funds to the mortgage market. The higher levels of purchases overwhelmed the capacity of the secondary market agencies to absorb mortgages into their portfolios. There was an explosion in the volume of pass-through securities as the needs of investors for higher yields was matched by the demand for the secondary mortgage market agencies to purchase increasing volumes of mortgages.

Recent Developments—In 1989, the Financial Institutions Recovery, Reform, and Enforcement Act (FIRREA) changed Freddie Mac's structure and charter to be identical to Fannie Mae's. Their charters define their missions: to provide liquidity to low-, moderate-, and middle-income households. Their stock is publicly traded, and they are exempt from some securities registration requirements and state and local income taxes. There are 18 members of the board of directors of which 5 are appointed by the president of the United States and 13 are elected by their shareholders. GNMA, Fannie Mae, and Freddie Mac are referred to as the secondary mortgage market agencies. GNMA is a government agency. Fannie Mae and Freddie Mac are also referred to as government-sponsored enterprises (GSEs) along with several other institutions, such as the Student Loan Marketing Association (Sallie Mae) and the Federal Home Loan Banks.

Financial safety and soundness are regulated by the Office of Federal Housing Enterprise Oversight, an independent agency. The public purpose housing goals are also regulated by the secretary of HUD. The U.S. Department of Treasury has a role in approving the timing of Fannie Mae's bond sales to ensure the smooth functioning of the debt markets.

Impact—The secondary mortgage market has evolved over the 50 years since its first appearance into an important link between the housing market and the international capital markets. Through the creation of innovative financial instruments, those who seek financing for a house purchase can be assured that funds will be available throughout the country and throughout the economic cycle. In the next section, the economics of the mortgage market will be discussed in more detail.

The Economics of the Secondary Mortgage Market

Now that you understand the structure and history of the secondary mortgage market, it is time to discuss the underlying economic principles of this special market. The economic forces underlying the secondary mortgage market today are more compelling than in the 1930s when the market was organized.

The Economics of Information

Efficient capital markets require that prices reflect all available and relevant information. This criterion is weaker than the requirements for perfect capital markets.[5] However, efficient capital markets imply that intermediaries will be cost minimizers and receive only a fair rate of return, that asset prices reflect all available information, and that investors will direct funds to investments with the highest rate of return. The standards of an efficient market may be difficult to achieve given that mortgage markets are characterized by uncertainty and asymmetric information.

All markets are characterized by the inability to predict the future, but this inability has a larger impact on the mortgage market than some others because of the long-term nature of the mortgages. For example, I do not know what the price of oranges will be next year when I purchase an orange to eat today, but knowing the future price would have little effect on my consumption decision. Not knowing the price of housing next year affects the mortgage contract because a fall in prices increases the risk of default. In addition, not knowing the interest rates next year makes it difficult to predict the return on a mortgage investment. Unexpected changes can result in losses to the homeowner, the servicer, the insurer, and the investor.

Generally, moral hazard occurs when the cost to the lender is affected by the actions of the borrower and the lender has incomplete information.

In the mortage market, moral hazard can be described as the possibility that a borrower promises to repay the mortgage but does not plan to fulfill the contract. It is impossible for the lender to learn this information, as the borrower has no incentive to reveal these plans. For example, if housing prices decline, the borrower may maximize his or her wealth by defaulting on the mortgage and purchasing another house.

If the lenders could perfectly predict which borrowers would default and prepay as well as the future course of house prices and interest rates, then only good borrowers and good properties would get mortgages and bad borrowers and bad properties would not. Thus there would be no default costs and no investment losses, and the cost of the borrower could be reduced to the time-value of money. Due to uncertainty and asymmetric information, however, the lender cannot know which borrowers will default, which will prepay, and which will pay the entire term of the contract. Thus, the lenders raise the cost of borrowing to include a premium for the risk of default and prepayment.

To minimize the risk of loss associated with these information problems, the lenders, investors, and insurers collect information about the borrower, the property, and the economy as a proxy for the perfect information. This information is qualitative and quantitative as well as expensive to collect and verify, which further increases the cost of borrowing.

Before the secondary mortgage market developed, mortgages were originated and traded as individual investments, and the uncertainty and information problems resulted in high-risk premiums. For some loans, less information was required by originators because the risks were borne by the federal government: the default risk was insured by the FHA mutual insurance program, and the interest rate and prepayment risk could be reallocated to the federal government through its purchase of long-term mortgages by Fannie Mae.

Over time, less information was required for all loans because standards were developed for mortgages that could be insured and purchased. The most important and least understood economic benefits of the secondary mortgage market are the information efficiencies that have developed through standardization in the primary and secondary mortgage markets. Standardization enables the processing of large numbers of mortgages very quickly and at low cost per loan because the individual components of a mortgage (for example, the appraisal, the terms, and so on) conform to the standard and can be communicated in code. These standards were the beginning of commoditization of mortgages in which one mortgage is essentially identical to the next. The standardization and commoditization of the mortgage market are vital to the functioning of today's mortgage market.

Risk Allocation

As described earlier, imperfect information results in uncertainty and risk in the mortgage contract. For a traditional 30-year fixed-rate mortgage the lender has the default, prepayment, and interest rate risk. These risk components can be reallocated to the borrower and to other mortgage market participants through changes in the mortgage contract and through secondary market transactions.

Changing the mortgage contract changes the exposure to uncertainty and thus the risk allocation. For example, a mortgage contract with an adjustable interest rate transfers some of the interest rate risk from the lender to the borrower because the lender now has an asset that moves with the market, but the borrower has the risk of higher mortgage payments if interest rates rise. The prepayment risk is reduced with this mortgage. If there is mortgage insurance or other credit enhancement, the default risk is shared between the lender and the insurer.

Secondary market transactions reallocate mortgage risk through the sale of the mortgage or its components. When a mortgage is sold to the secondary mortgage market, the lender sells most of the default and prepayment risk and all of the interest rate risk. (The lender sells or retains the servicing rights, which have a small amount of prepayment and default risk–if the mortgage is terminated, there will be no servicing fees.) If the mortgage is held in portfolio, the secondary mortgage market agency retains all the risk. However, if the mortgage is used to create a pass-through security, then the interest rate and prepayment risk and a small portion of the default risk is passed to the MBS investor. (Although the investor does not suffer losses from the foreclosure, default will appear as a prepayment.)

The information problems discussed here are echoed in the process of risk allocation. When borrowers can select a mortage contract from a broad menu of contracts available, the contract may reveal the expected length of stay in the house or sensitivity to interest rate changes and thus ameliorate some information asymmetries. The prepayment risk and interest rate risk that result from uncertainty concerning future interest rates are the prime determinants of the variation in MBS prices. There is one additional risk factor that is part of the secondary market transaction: institutional default risk. The investor is promised principal and interest payments and must rely on the servicer or intermediary to transmit these payments in a timely manner.

The reallocation of risk provided by the secondary market has provided investors with the opportunity to invest in mortgages and the housing finance market with access to capital from sectors outside of savings in depository institutions. Through issues of equity, debt, and MBSs, the secondary mortgage market attracts investors from every segment of the U.S. economy and abroad.

With efficient capital markets where prices reflect all available information, then the risks and returns of mortgage investing can be estimated and fairly priced. This allows the trading of mortgages and derivatives until the marginal rate of return is equated for all participants. Thus, the secondary market facilitates the increased allocative efficiency.

Market Structure and Competition

The description and analysis of a market begin with a definition of the product. The secondary mortgage market agencies operate in several different product markets: the market for credit enhancement of pass-through securities and other mortgage derivatives and the market for mortgage investments. In addition, there are many segments of these two general markets.

Fannie Mae has one direct competitor–Freddie Mac–that has a charter identical to Fannie Mae's. However, there are other institutions that compete for some segments of its business. For example, Fannie Mae competes with GNMA for FHA and VA loans. However, given GNMA's pricing advantage, most FHA and VA business is given to GNMA. In addition, Fannie Mae competes with private sector institutions for all conforming mortgages (those with loan amounts below the conforming limit). As home prices rise, Fannie Mae will be able to purchase mortgages with higher loan amounts. Thus, Fannie Mae competes with secondary mortgage institutions that purchase and create securities using jumbo mortgages. In addition, although some of the mortgages below the conforming limit do not currently meet Fannie Mae's underwriting requirements, there are pressures to purchase more of these mortgages. Fannie Mae therefore competes with institutions that purchase or create securities with conforming mortgages.

The market is often described as a duopoly consisting of Fannie Mae and Freddie Mac. The two GSEs have special privileges in the secondary market that make it difficult for others to compete directly. Specifically, Fannie Mae and Freddie Mac can issue debt at interest rates lower than that of triple-A corporations and without institutional risk. In addition, they are exempt from some regulations of the U.S. Securities and Exchange Commission (SEC). Although the Fannie Mae and Freddie Mac securities are not guaranteed by the U.S. government, they are government-sponsored enterprises that dominate the secondary mortgage market. If these institutions were to experience losses, many investors believe the U.S. government would support the institutions to preserve stability in the mortgage market.

However, rather than a duopoly, the more accurate description is that of contestable markets. Although the secondary mortgage market might appear to have a small number of players, in truth the market is very competitive. The mortgage market has changed dramatically over the last 10 years, and financial engineering promotes constant change in both the primary and secondary markets. In addition, there is increasing attention being focused on the low- and moderate-income segment of the mortgage market. These changes provide the opportunity for private sector firms to develop niche markets where the importance of information economies and risk allocation is less important. These firms have the technology and experience to exploit any aspect of the market not covered by the GSEs or any pricing that cannot be supported in the private sector.

In exchange for some of the advantages the secondary market receives, the charter is restricted to investment in residential mortgages. Fannie Mae and Freddie Mac have to balance their fiduciary responsibilities and their public purpose mission to the government.

Macroeconomic Impact

The housing industry continues to be an important component of the economy. Macroeconomic effects are revealed mostly through the role of housing in the business cycle. However, the cyclical nature of housing is less pronounced today than it was in the 1930s. Given that most housing construction and purchase are debt financed, the demand for housing is a function of interest rates. Before the decontrol of interest rates offered by depository institutions, when market rates rose, the demand would decrease and the construction and purchase of housing would slow. High interest rates limited investment in housing and production began to fall, creating a recession that brought lower interest rates and gave home buyers the incentive and ability to participate in the market. Thus, it was understood that housing through the purchase of homes often led the economy out of recessions with additional impact on related sectors such as construction, employment, and home furnishings.

With the increased liquidity in the housing finance market, funds continue to be available even when market interest rates are high. Thus, the pent-up demand that characterized earlier recessions has been weakened in modern recessions, and the role of housing in leading the economy out of recession is diminished. The continuous availability of funds has also reduced some uncertainty in the market and lowered costs. Increased access to housing finance has contributed to the improvement in housing conditions over the last 50 years, and housing continues to provide one of the most important contributions to wealth for homeowners in the United States.

Because the secondary mortgage market has facilitated the trading of mortgages, any investor can achieve a geographically diverse portfolio that has a lower default risk than a geographically specialized portfolio. As regional recessions have racked the U.S. economy and local financial institutions have suffered the consequences, the value of a national institution that can diversify these geographic risks has never been more clear. With interstate branching, geographic intermediation can be carried out by many financial institutions. The decline of some of the original justifications has led to suggestions that the secondary mortgage market institutions be privatized or have their markets restricted.

The secondary mortgage market succeeded in lowering the cost of borrowing by (1) reducing the transaction costs related to funding the mortgage, (2) improving the risk allocation, and (3) contributing to the maintenance of the supply of housing finance during the periods of high interest rates and regulatory change that resulted in restructuring of the primary mortgage market.

What Do Secondary Mortgage Markets Contribute to Society?

Secondary mortgage markets have been shown to reduce mortgage interest rates, encourage financial innovation, increase the allocative and operational efficiency of the capital markets, and provide financing for low-, moderate-, and middle-income households that the U.S. government has been unable to serve.

Interest Rates

Research has been undertaken to analyze the impact of the secondary mortgage market institutions on interest rates. Hendershott and Shilling (1989, 102) hypothesized that interest rates on mortgages eligible for purchase or securitization by the secondary mortgage market agencies are lower than those that are above the conforming loan limit. After controlling for geographic region, mortgage instrument, type of originator, and loan-to-value ratios, the authors measured the difference in the contract interest rate and the effective loan rate (including points and fees) between eligible and ineligible loans. They concluded: "expanded agency securitization of conventional FRMs has significantly lowered the rates on both conforming loans and loans somewhat above the conforming limit . . . by 30 and 15 basis points respectively" (112). This has an impact on individual homeowners through lower interest rates for mortgages and thus more affordable housing. Lower interest rates would raise homeownership and the quantity of housing demanded by owners: "the expected increase in demand is closer to 1%" (114).

Sirmans and Benjamin (1990) also analyzed the relationship between mortgage rates and interest rates in the secondary mortgage market by comparing mortgages eligible for securitization and those above the conforming loan limit. They found that securitization reduces interest rates to borrowers by 40 to 50 basis points on a 30-year fixed rate mortgage (198).

These efficiencies extend beyond the impact on interest rates to the borrowers whose loan is purchased by a secondary mortgage market agency. The methodology of the Hendershott and Shilling paper construes the impact of the secondary mortgage market somewhat narrowly because it only considers the impact of the agencies on the loans it is likely to purchase, not the impact of the secondary mortgage market on the markets for housing and housing finance.

The information efficiencies developed by the secondary mortgage market agencies are now commonly used in the jumbo market to take advantage of the benefits of standardization developed by the agencies for conforming loans.

Financial Innovation

The secondary mortgage market has been at the cutting edge of financial engineering in its effort to increase operational efficiency and reduce the cost of mortgage finance to borrowers. The development of sophisticated financial instruments such as REMICs and CMOs is due in large part to the commitment of the secondary mortgage market to creating a market for these instruments. These instruments allow investment in 30-year FRMs without requiring a 30-year investment. Investors may choose short-, intermediate-, or long-term investments and may also choose the proportion of interest payments and principal payments to receive. This and other innovative financial instruments have encouraged investment in the mortgage market from all sectors of the economy.

Allocative and Operational Efficiency

When housing finance investment was limited to those investing in depository institutions, other investors could not benefit from the returns on mortgage investing. By expanding the investment base, the secondary mortgage market increases the ability of investors to equate the marginal rate of return on investments across the economy rather than just a restricted portion of it. The demands of this broad base of investors for pricing information ensure that the prices reflect all available information and that the risks and returns of mortgage investing are fairly priced–this increases allocative efficiency.

Increased operational efficiency is a function of competition in the market. Although it is often said that the market is a duopoly supported by government subsidy, the market is very dynamic, and there are opportunities for entrants in many areas of the market. In addition to the competition from the other secondary mortgage market agencies, the contestable nature of the secondary mortgage market provides the competitive pressure that increases operational efficiency.

Financing Low- and Moderate-Income Housing

The secondary mortgage market has brought tremendous benefits to renter and owner households that meet the standards established for middle-income and middle-class homeowners. Those who do not conform to this model may not directly benefit from the efficiency of a standardized market. This is the dark side of standardization: diversity is difficult to accommodate. Nonstandard credit history, self-employment, or financial support from an ethnic or cultural group affiliation are by definition not part of the standardized, volume-oriented secondary mortgage market. These mortgage applications are likely to come from minority groups or lower-income households who have had less interaction with formal financial institutions because of discrimination, restricted access, or lack of financial sophistication.

These households might be considered the responsibility of the U.S. government under its mandate to provide a decent home and a suitable living environment for all Americans. However, the reality of the budget deficit and the realization that the government is limited in its ability to provide for the diverse and ever-changing needs of the population has resulted in pressure on the private sector, especially GSEs, to become instruments of the government. As depository institutions are charged with lending in urban areas through the Community Reinvestment Act and are persuaded to serve the diverse populations through reporting under the Home Mortgage Disclosure Act, so too must the secondary mortgage market make its contribution. By requiring the secondary mortgage market agencies to do more, Congress and HUD are acknowledging the success and value of the secondary mortgage market.

These institutions have a dual mission: first, they are required to obtain adequate financial return for their shareholders and increase the capital available for housing in the United States. Second, they are required to address the housing finance needs of low-income households. It is easy to view these two goals as conflicting because it might be said that mortgage financing for low-income housholds is not as profitable as the middle-income standardized business. However, any market that requires a product or service can be profitable. Special programs have been developed, and attempts are being made to remove the middle-class bias from the underwriting guidelines so that more households can benefit from the efficiencies created by the secondary mortgage market.

Conclusion: Why GSEs Are Needed in the Secondary Mortgage Market

The housing finance and capital markets have changed substantially since the first secondary mortgage market agency was created. Recently, questions have been raised about the need for continued government support of secondary mortgage markets. Specifically, some critics look at the size of these agencies and are concerned that the government is exposed to large contingent liabilities; if the agencies defaulted on their bonds, the government would have to pay off the investors. From the opposite perspective, the charge is made that high profit levels are inappropriate and that profits should be limited or returned to the U.S. Treasury. However, these arguments misunderstand the contribution and nature of GSEs.

Government Support

Government support of the secondary mortgage markets is crystallized in the agencies Fannie Mae, Freddie Mac, and GNMA. As described earlier, Fannie Mae and Freddie Mac have an advantage over private sector secondary mortgage market intermediaries in raising debt and also with respect to some securities regulations. However, the secondary mortgage market is also supported by the government through the web of protection for financial institutions provided by deposit insurance, the Federal Reserve Banks, and the Federal Home Loan Banks.

The variety and depth of U.S. government support of the secondary mortgage markets are justified in several ways:

- The private market has failed to provide long-term FRMs.
- Housing is an important component of the economy.
- Homeownership results in externalities that contribute to the social fabric of society.
- Well-developed and stable financial institutions contribute to the growth of the economy.

The secondary mortgage market support began in 1938 and was enhanced in 1968 and 1972 but did not become an important feature of the housing finance markets until the financial crisis of the 1980s. As the secondary mortgage market for nonconforming loans has developed, the secondary mortgage market could have emerged without government support, but it would probably not have achieved the universal coverage and therefore the efficiencies that have been achieved by the secondary market today.

Now that it is established, it might appear that the secondary mortgage market could be sustained without the continued support of the GSEs. This has led to calls to privatize Fannie Mae and Freddie Mac by eliminating the benefits they currently receive from their government sponsorship. The government could remove the exemption from SEC regulations, and the MBSs, REMICs, and CMOs would continue to be issued with perhaps a small increase in price to account for this new cost. The government could also remove the $2.25 billion line of credit that the agencies have with the U.S. Treasury.

The Fannie Mae and Freddie Mac portfolios combined are worth over $250 billion. The agencies purchase over 50 percent of all mortgage originations in any one year, and their presence in the market allowed for the continuous supply of mortgage finance during the crisis faced by depository institutions in the 1980s. If Fannie Mae or Freddie Mac required this credit, it is likely that the U.S. financial markets would be facing a crisis larger than a temporary capital shortage by two financial intermediaries. The markets would probably continue to perceive Fannie Mae and Freddie Mac securities as having the implicit guarantee of the U.S. government because of the vital role the agencies play in the mortgage finance and capital markets rather than because of the specific wording of their charter. Thus, the difference in debt cost would not likely be significant, and the motivation for reducing the contigent liability of the government would not be justified. In addition, Congress and HUD would be more effective using moral suasion with a GSE to provide additional housing finance for low-income households than they would be with a private sector financial intermediary.

Impact of the Secondary Mortgage Market

The impact of the secondary mortgage market on the U.S. financial system cannot be measured merely by looking at the secondary mortgage market institutions, and the importance of the secondary mortgage market institutions cannot be evaluated only by an economic analysis of the changes in the mortgage interest rate. The entire financial system and the provision of government support for housing have been realigned through the influence of the secondary mortgage market institutions.

It may be that these arrangements allow too much profit. Although the level of profit may seem large, the rate of return on equity is competitive with other comparable institutions. Fannie Mae and Freddie Mac bring efficiency to the secondary mortgage market by reducing information costs and increasing the investment vehicles. Standardization and the maintenance of this standardization could not be achieved by a marginal player. For example, the Federal Housing Administration (FHA) does not set the standard. Fannie Mae or Freddie Mac alone could not set the standard. It is only through the GSE arrangement that these organizations have created the public good called commoditization of mortgages that has resulted in lower costs and increased consumer choice across the country.

In addition, this benefit is being created for housing–a good that many consider a basic right or at least one of the most important components of the American Dream. Housing is an investment that represents a large portion of the net wealth of many households. The housing market has important implications for the economy. The government and the private sector working separately have been unable to provide a sufficient quantity of housing to provide decent shelter for all who need it. The GSEs have reduced the cost of housing finance across the market and are working to extend their markets to include mortgages with nontraditional characteristics.

Since GNMA was created in 1968 and Fannie Mae was organized as a GSE, there has been a tension between the requirement to attract capital from the private sector and the advantages that are associated with agency status. Fannie Mae and Freddie Mac are subject to the discipline of the market and face the market for the acquisition of mortgages in a competitive stance. Although there are only two GSEs in the secondary mortgage market, the market is contestable, and inefficient behavior would result in lower profits and decreased market share. In addition, the GSEs are subject to the discipline of the political system through Congress's ability to revise their charter and HUD's to develop regulations. This arrangement ensures that these agencies serve their dual mission in the housing finance market. To eliminate either side of this equation could produce a government agency unresponsive to changes in the dynamic housing finance market or a private sector institution with no obligation to serve the lower-income segments of the market. The combination of public and private components serves the housing finance markets well at little cost to the government.

Notes

1. For example, for a 30-year FRM with an interest rate of 10 percent, the payment will be $877.57.

Initial principal: $P_0 = \$100,000$
Number of payments: $n = 360$
Interest rate: $i = .10/12 = .008333$ / month
Payment: PMT $= (P_0 * i) / (1 - (1 + i)^{-n})$
$= (100,000 * .008333) / (1 - (1 + .008333)^{-360})$
$= \$877.54$
Interest payment in period i for periods $i = 1, 2, 3, \ldots 360$
$\text{INT}_i = (P_{i-1} * i)$
$\text{INT}_1 = (P_{1-1} * .008333) = 100,000 * .008333$

$$\text{INT}_1 \quad = \$833.33$$

Principal payment in period i for periods i = 1, 2, 3, . . . 360

$$\text{PRN}_i \quad = \text{PMT}-\text{INT}_i$$
$$\text{PRN}_1 \quad = 877.54-833.33 = \$44.21$$

Principal balance remaining at the end of period i for periods i = 1, 2, 3, . . . 360

$$P_i \quad = P_{i-1}-\text{PRN}_i$$
$$P_1 \quad = P_0- \text{PRN}_1 = 100,000 - 44.21$$
$$P_1 \quad = \$99,955.79$$

2. The term *pass-through* is used to distinguish the source of the collateral for the securities. A general obligation bond may draw on the general revenues of the issuer to make payments to the bond purchasers. Investors in a pass-through security have access to the cash flow of the collateral allocated to that individual security. For MBSs, a pool of mortgages serves as collateral and any and all mortgage payments are passed through to the investor. However, the investor has no call on the general obligations of the issuer.

3. The Federal Housing Enterprises Financial Safety and Soundness Act of 1992 was enacted as Title XIII of the Housing and Community Development Act of 1992, Public Law 102–550, approved October 28, 1992, 106 Stat. 3672.

4. Other important U.S. financial and regulatory institutions that continue to play roles in the housing finance system were also created as responses to the Depression-era financial crisis: for example, deposit insurance and the regulatory structure of depository institutions.

5. Perfect capital markets require that (1) there are no transactions costs or regulations and all assets are divisible and liquid, (2) there is perfect competition in the product and securities markets, (3) information is costless and uniformly disseminated, and (4) all individuals are rational and maximize utility.

References

Federal Home Loan Mortgage Corporation. 1984. *The Secondary Market in Residential Mortgages.* Washington, D.C.: FHLMC (December).

Hendershott, P. H., and J. D. Shilling. 1989. "The Impact of the Agencies on Conventional Fixed-Rate Mortgage Yields." *Journal of Real Estate Finance and Economics* 2: 101–115.

Joint Center for Housing Studies of Harvard University. 1993. *The State of the Nation's Housing, 1993.* Cambridge, MA: JCHS.

Kuhn, R. L.. 1990. *Mortgage and Asset Securitization.* Homewood, IL: Richard D. Irwin, Inc.

Layard, P. R. G., and A. A. Walters. 1978. *Microeconomic Theory.* New York: McGraw-Hill, Inc.

Person, K. J. 1987. *Introduction to Mortgages and Mortgage-Backed Securities.* New York: Salomon Brothers Inc. (September).

Salomon Brothers Inc. 1984. *Housing Finance in a Deregulated Environment.* New York: Salomon Brothers (September).

Savage, H. A., and P. J. Fronczek. 1993. *Who Can Afford to Buy a House in 1991?* U.S. Bureau of the Census, Current Housing Reports, H121/93–3. Washington, D.C.: U.S. Government Printing Office.

Sirmans, C. F., and J. D. Benjamin. 1990. "Pricing Fixed-Rate Mortgages: Some Empirical Evidence." *Journal of Financial Services Research* 4: 191–203.

Glossary

Adjustable-Rate Mortgage (ARM): A mortgage characterized by interest rates and monthly payments that are adjusted at regular intervals based on changes in a specified index. Also called a variable-rate mortgage.

Appraisal: A written evaluation of a property that includes an estimate of the market value.

Balloon Mortgage: A mortgage in which the principal and interest payments are amortized over a longer period than the actual term of the mortgage; as a result, the borrower must pay off the outstanding balance with a lump-sum payment at the end of the mortgage term or refinance the mortgage.

Basis Points (BP): One basis point is 1/100th of 1 percent; 1 bp = 0.01 percent.

Capital Markets: Markets (including informal markets as well as organized markets and exchanges) where short- and long-term loanable funds in the form of mortgages, stock, and bonds are bought and sold.

Collateral: The asset used as a security for a loan to demonstrate good faith and to provide some remedy to the lender in case of default. In the case of a mortgage, the collateral is the property.

Commoditization: The process by which a single good becomes essentially identical to the next.

Conventional Mortgage: All mortgages that have private mortgage insurance or no mortgage insurance. Mortgages are either conventional mortgages or government mortgages.

Default Risk: The possibility that the borrower will not pay the outstanding balance of the loan either monthly as scheduled or in a lump-sum payment.

Dual-Indexed Mortgage (DIM): A mortgage that has two indices: one for the interest and one for the payment. The interest rate charged on the outstanding balance is tied to the lender's cost of funds, and the monthly payment is tied to some measure of household income. Any divergence between the two indices that results in unpaid interest is compensated by lengthening the term of the mortgage.

Equity/Equity Financing: The amount of cash or the size of the down payment plus the appreciation of the property; the residual value of the property beyond the mortgage.

Fixed-Rate Mortgage (FRM): A mortgage for which the interest rate does not vary over the term of the mortgage. This mortgage is generally characterized by fixed payments.

Government-Insured Mortgages (FHA, VA): Mortgages for which the default risk is guaranteed by the Federal Housing Administration (FHA) or the Department of Veterans Affairs (VA). Also referred to as government mortgages.

Government-Sponsored Enterprises (GSEs): An organization that combines aspects of a private sector organization and a government agency. For example, Fannie Mae has a government charter that provides it with a public mission to serve low-, moderate-, and middle-income households but is capitalized by stock that is publicly traded on the New York Stock Exchange.

Guarantee Fee: The insurance premium paid to a financial intermediary in exchange for the transfer of the default risk.

Incomplete Markets: Incomplete markets occur when it is impossible to purchase a product at any price; there is no supply curve, no matter how high a price is offered. The financial markets are incomplete because there is no market that permits potential home buyers to obtain a long-term loan against their future earnings without some other guarantee or collateral.

Interest Rate Risk: The possibility that an asset will change in value when market interest rates change; mortgage investments fall in value when interest rates increase.

Jumbo Mortgage: A mortgage with a loan amount that is above the GSE loan limit.

Liquid: Readily converted into cash: liquid assets.

Liquidity-Constrained: Purchasers do not have the cash to purchase the asset today but could pay over time for the flow of services received over time.

Loan-to-Value Ratio: The percentage of a property's value (the sales price or appraised value, whichever is lower) that a lender is willing to finance.

Mortgage: A pledge of property as security for a debt; collectively, the security instrument, the note, the title evidence, and all other documents and paper that evidence debt.

Mortgage-Backed Security (MBS): An investment issued by Fannie Mae representing an interest in a pool of mortgages. Payments on the underlying mortgages are passed through each month from the servicer of the mortgage to the security holder.

Mortgage Origination/Originators: Individuals or financial institutions that accept loan applications and arrange for a new mortgage to be issued. This process involves marketing, interviewing applicants to obtain information for the application, acquiring the documents necessary for underwriting the borrower and the property, negotiating with the applicant, and setting the price and terms of the mortgage.

Nonconforming Mortgage: A mortgage that does not meet the underwriting guidelines of the GSEs.

Participation Certificates (PC): A pass-through security issued by Freddie Mac. Payments on the underlying mortgages are passed through each month from the servicer of the mortgage to the security holder.

Pass-through Security: The generic name for MBSs and PCs or any other security in which the investor has an interest in an asset and the payments on the underlying assets are transferred from the institution that collects the payments to the investor.

Prepayment: Any amount paid to reduce the principal of a loan before the due date.

Prepayment Risk: The loss that could occur if the mortgage balance is repaid partially or fully when current mortgage rates are below the contract rate on the mortgages.

Primary Market (general): The sale of a finished product to a purchaser.

Primary Mortgage Market: The sale of money (lending) to a purchaser (borrower).

Property Registration: The recording of property ownership and any loans that use the property as collateral.

Secondary Market (general): The sale and purchase of products that were produced and sold originally in a primary market; markets where no new goods are produced but used goods are traded; secondary markets are common for assets that retain value over time such as houses, automobiles, and mortgages.

Secondary Mortgage Market: The buying and selling of existing mortgages or MBSs.

Securitization: The process of converting mortgages into MBSs.

Servicing: The tasks a lender performs to protect the mortgage investment, including collecting the monthly payments, managing the escrow accounts, dealing with delinquencies, and overseeing foreclosures and payoffs.

Swap: The exchange of loans for MBSs rather than cash.

Underwriting: The analysis of risk, the determination of the appropriate loan amount, and the setting of the interest rate and other terms and conditions based on a judgment of both the borrower's creditworthiness and the value of the real property that will secure the loan.

8

Infrastructure and the Economy

Charles R. Hulten
Robert M. Schwab

Introduction

In this chapter, Hulten and Schwab critically examine a proposition that many may consider obvious, namely that increased public infrastructure spending, for example on roads, bridges, and the like, will result in increased economic growth. Hulten and Schwab, along with other economists, are unconvinced that additional infrastructure spending will have the desired positive effects. Hulten and Schwab examine three kinds of evidence in the infrastructure debate: econometric studies, cost-benefit studies, and engineering needs studies.

Infrastructure spending has declined markedly since 1968, but the debate is about the interpretation of the decline rather than the fact of the decline. In examining aggregate econometric studies bearing upon the infrastructure debate, one of the key issues is whether spurious correlation is causing some researchers to obtain a large and positive effect of public infrastructure upon economic growth. Spurious correlation is the correlation of two genuinely unrelated variables with a third (unrepresented) variable. For example, in economic time series, many variables that we suppose are unrelated follow similar time paths because they are affected by the same underlying processes. By introducing a correction for this (by considering changes over time) Hulten and Schwab obtain no significant effect of public infrastructure upon growth.

The authors also examine regional (disaggregated) studies. Here, the record is mixed. Early studies concluded that infrastructure investment had accounted for the faster growth of the Sun Belt. But later work took account of "fixed effects"; that is, the possibility that states differ from one another for reasons that do not vary over time (for example, that Iowa is very cold in the winter while parts of California have a wonderful climate year round).

213

*Accounting for these effects caused the association of public capital invest-
ment and state economic perfomance to vanish.*

*Hulten and Schwab introduce their own framework for the analysis of the
public infrastructure debate–the multifactor productivity (MFP). Roughly
speaking, the growth of MFP equals the growth of private output that is not
accounted for by private input and therefore is an indirect way to capture
the productivity contribution of public infrastructure. They also examine
international studies.*

*The main economic lessons are that such "obvious" propositions as that
public infrastructure has a significant impact on economic growth must be
subjected to rigorous testing. Unexpected statistical results, like the insignifi-
cance of public infrastructure in explaining productivity should not be
dismissed simply as a statistical anomoly. Economic forces operate sometimes
in contrary fashion to what we might expect. The point is especially important
when we contemplate investment in the "information superhighway." What
is the appropriate role of government in this investment?*

The debate over infrastructure policy has been long and sometimes
acrimonious. A number of reports, including *America in Ruins* (Choate and
Walter 1981) and *Fragile Foundations* (National Council on Public Works
Improvement 1988), have argued that a massive new commitment to public
investment is imperative.[1] Those who favor increased spending see sharp
declines in infrastructure spending in the 1970s as a key cause of U.S.
economic problems over the last two decades and a major reason the United
States has struggled in international markets. Thus proponents of additional
spending see the infrastructure issue as something far more than simply
sparing commuters the irritation of potholes and traffic jams. Instead, they
see infrastructure as one of the most important determinants of the
performance of the private economy. Some have proposed additional
spending of up to $200 billion per year.

Others, including ourselves, are unconvinced. While infrastructure problems certainly exist–congestion is a serious problem in some urban areas
and some bridges are in need of repair–critics argue that these problems
are often the result of poorly designed programs and policies or part of the
natural life cycle of infrastructure facilities. Opponents of greater spending
often see the slowdown in infrastructure spending in the 1970s and 1980s
as little more than the expected pattern given the near completion of the
Interstate Highway System and the end of the baby boom. In this alternative
view, the link between the private economy and additional government
infrastructure investment at this point is weak, at best. These critics would

thus conclude that, given federal budget deficits of more than $300 billion and pressing needs including medical care and environmental quality, public infrastructure investment should be a given a low priority.

Our goal in this chapter is to present an overview of some of the key issues in this debate. Three types of evidence have been put forward regarding the impact of infrastructure on the economy. Econometric studies look at the relationship between some measure of economic activity, infrastructure, and other plausible exogenous variables. Most of the studies in this group start with the abstract assumption that aggregate output (for example, real gross domestic product [GDP]) is systematically related to private inputs and public capital via an aggregate production function. Some estimate this production function directly; others estimate the economic dual of the production function, that is, the cost function. The focus of these studies has either been on the aggregate U.S. economy over time (why, for example, did the United States grow so much faster prior to 1974 than after?), regions (why did the Sun Belt grow faster than the Snow Belt?), and international comparisons (why has the Japanese economy performed so much better than the U.S. economy?). The second type of evidence comes from cost-benefit studies. Cost-benefit studies are an attempt to systematically quantify all of the social benefits and social costs associated with a specific infrastructure project. These studies are often prospective in their orientation (that is, they look ahead at proposed projects), though some are retrospective (that is, they look back at projects that have already been completed). The third source of evidence is drawn from engineering needs studies. These studies estimate the cost of reaching some specific performance objectives. Needs studies thus might, for example, estimate the cost of improving pavement quality or reducing congestion to certain levels on all roads.

In this chapter, we examine all three sources of evidence. The remainder of the chapter has the following organization: In the following section, we review past trends in infrastructure investment and investment needs studies. We then look at some of the econometric evidence on the link between public infrastructure investment and economic performance in the third section. We turn to cost-benefit studies in the fourth section and offer several policy recommendations and a brief summary and conclusions in the final two sections of the chapter.[2]

Past Trends in Investment

At first blush calculating spending on infrastructure might seem straightforward, but it turns out this question can lead to some confusion. Some analysts include spending by all levels of government, but some focus on only state and local government spending. Some include only investment (for example, the cost of building a new road), while others include other types of spending on infrastructure (for example, the cost of maintaining a road) as well. Moreover, some include all types of public capital, while others use a more restrictive definition that includes only "core infrastructure," which is often defined as highways, mass transit, rail, aviation, water transportation, water resources, water supply, and waste water treatment. Certain types of infrastructure are privately owned in some countries and publicly owned in others. It is thus important to be careful to understand the way infrastructure spending has been defined when comparing spending across time, regions, or countries.

Almost regardless of the definition we choose, however, both sides of the infrastructure debate would agree that infrastructure spending, measured as a share of GDP, fell sharply in the late 1960s and early 1970s. Figures 8.1 and 8.2 focus on capital expenditures by state and local government.[3] They show that public investment rose more or less continuously from around 2 percent of GDP in the early- and mid-1950s to 3 percent of GDP in 1968. Spending declined dramatically after 1968, falling to just over 1.5 percent of GDP in the early 1980s. As a consequence, the state and local capital stock grew roughly 1 percent per year in the late 1970s and early 1980s as compared to roughly 5 percent per year during most of the late 1950s and 1960s.

The *interpretation* of these trends, however, has been a subject of great debate. Proinvestment advocates have argued that the failure to invest in public capital was the result of shortsighted government policies that allowed the country's infrastructure to deteriorate sharply. There is evidence, for example, that pavement quality fell during the 1970s and that congestion increased during the 1980s. Some of this evidence comes from engineering needs studies. For example, a recent study by the Federal Highway Administration (FHWA) estimated that $46.2 billion was needed in 1992 just to keep highway and bridge performance at 1991 levels, but that only $35.9 billion was actually spent (U.S. Department of Transportation, 1993). In the same study, FHWA estimated that the cost to maintain 1991 performance and condition will average $51.6 billion per year over the next 20 years, and that the cost to improve capacity by 40 percent and eliminate the backlog of highway deficiencies will average $67.3 billion.

Critics are unpersuaded by these arguments. A decline in the share of GDP devoted to public capital formation cannot be taken *a priori* as compelling evidence of inadequate spending. In a dynamic economy, spending priorities are always changing. Defense spending, for example, fell from 9.5 percent of GDP in 1962 to 5.2 percent in 1992 and will almost certainly fall much further in the future. Sensible people might well debate whether defense cuts have been too large or too small, but few would argue

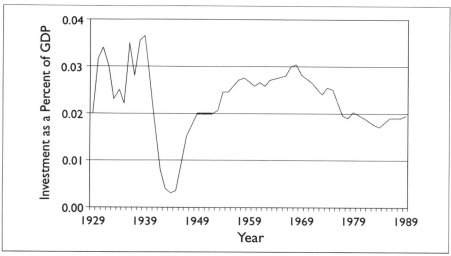

Figure 8.1   Investment in State and Local Capital. Source: Bureau of Economic Analysis.

that we should devote 9.5 percent of our productive capacity to defense simply because we did so in the past. The breakup of the former Soviet Union and the demise of communism throughout Eastern Europe have changed our defense needs dramatically. On the other side of the coin, no one would sensibly argue that we now spend too much on AIDS research because we spent nothing on such research 10 years ago.

While events as dramatic as the end of the Cold War occur only rarely, it is true that the need for infrastructure spending has changed significantly since the 1950s and 1960s when infrastructure spending peaked. During that period, major portions of the Interstate Highway System were completed, and thousands of schools were built to meet the needs of the baby boom. Once those schools were built and the interstate system was nearly complete, it is not surprising that spending declined. To accept peak spending as the norm is to frame the problem in a way that implies that anything less than peak spending is inadequate. Such a norm would commit the country to a continuous and endless program of building, regardless of need or voter preferences.

As for growing congestion, the U.S. Department of Transportation (1992) found that *average* travel time to work for the nation as a whole hardly changed between 1980 and 1990–21.7 versus 22.4 minutes. Of course, the additional 42 seconds is not spread evenly across the population of commuters, and congestion is a major problem in some areas such as Los Angeles. But while many would regard an extra 42 seconds in travel time to work as a nuisance, it is difficult to see that it could be the heart of a "crisis." This statistic is a useful reminder that the overall extent of the

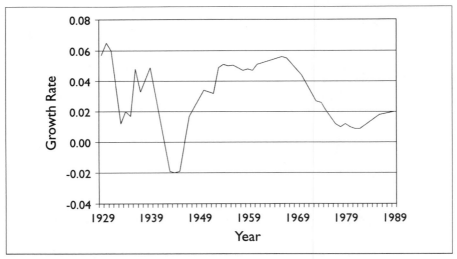

Figure 8.2   Growth Rate of State and Local Capital. Source: Bureau of Economic Analysis.

congestion problem is far less dramatic than the worst-case examples imply. Yet it is precisely these worst cases that get much of the attention in the press and in the policy debate.

Finally, the evidence from FHWA needs assessment studies must be interpreted with care. These studies are based on the amount of investment needed to maintain or improve average vehicle performance over the highway system. While they provide a framework for assessing the extent and location of possible spending needs, the FHWA warns that "The investment analysis results should not be represented as either preferred or optimal investment strategies. They represent investment and performance benchmarks to support further policy and budget analysis" (U.S. Department of Transportation, 1993, 175). In other words, taxpayers may conclude that, they have more pressing needs for some of the $51.6 billion required to maintain vehicle performance at past levels. This conclusion should not be very surprising. People are generally unwilling to spend the money that would be necessary to maintain their car or house in perfect working order and are equally unwilling to spend enough to avoid some degree of congestion and deterioration.[4]

Infrastructure Investment and Economic Performance

Most of the debate over infrastructure policy has focused on the link between infrastructure spending and economic performance. In a series of papers and articles, Aschauer (1989, 1991) argued that the decline in infrastructure investment was a key factor in the poor performance of the U.S. economy over the last two decades. His work, for example, implies that slower infrastructure investment could explain as much as 57 percent of the productivity slowdown in the 1970s and 1980s. Moreover, he finds the rate of return to infrastructure to be very high–around 70 percent in the following year, according to Robert Reich–and that the gain in output from an additional dollar spent on public capital is two to five times as large as the gain from an additional dollar spent on private capital (Aschauer 1991).

Aschauer's work stimulated a huge volume of literature. While some of the recent research in this area supports Aschauer's results (Canning and Fay 1993; Munnell 1990a; Fernald 1992), others have reached rather different conclusions. Aaron (1990), Hulten (1990), Schultze (1990), Jorgenson (1991), and Tatom (1991) have all argued that, for a variety of reasons, it is hard to put much faith in the results from aggregate time series studies. Why have these studies reached such different conclusions? It turns out that the time series evidence on this point is very fragile. In Hulten and Schwab (1992), we found that with slightly different statistical approaches, the same data could lead us to conclude that additional investment in infrastructure could have a dramatic impact on the private economy or virtually no impact. In his often cited 1989 paper, Aschauer modeled the *level* of aggregate output as a function of the *levels* of public capital, private capital, labor, time (as a proxy for technical change), and capacity utilization (to control for the effects of the business cycle). When we estimated models of this type, our results were very similar to his. We then argued that in time series work, there is always the danger of spurious correlation since many variables follow the same time trend. Economists who work with time series data often try to deal with this problem by recasting their analysis in terms of whether the *changes* in one variable can explain *changes* in a second variable (that is, they "detrend" the data). When we looked at the effects of changes in public capital on changes in private output, the impact of public capital vanished.[5]

Spurious correlation is a particular danger when we look at the relationship between economic performance and infrastructure. The problem is nearly unavoidable given the pattern of economic growth in the United States. The economy enjoyed a long period of strong economic growth beginning after World War II and continuing through the early 1970s but did not fare well in the next two decades. Thus almost every variable that fell sharply in the late 1960s or early 1970s is a plausible explanation of economic growth. Tables 8.1 and 8.2 suggest that infrastructure spending certainly meets this test. Not surprisingly, given these trends, Aschauer and others conclude that slower spending caused many of our economic problems of the last two decades. But of course other variables followed essentially the same pattern. Average SAT scores, for example, fell 90 points

Table 8.1   Average Annual Growth Rate of Public Capital

	NE	MA	ENC	WAC	SA	ESC	WSC	M	P	Total	Snow Belt	Sun Belt
	Region [1]											
All Public Capital												
1970–78	2.72	2.94	1.89	2.66	3.86	2.50	2.65	3.04	1.45	2.55	2.49	2.61
1978–86	0.05	–0.19	0.10	0.81	1.84	0.58	2.28	3.15	0.68	0.86	0.11	1.58
1970–86	1.39	1.38	0.99	1.74	2.85	1.54	2.47	3.10	1.06	1.70	1.30	2.09
Highways												
1970–78	0.68	1.68	1.33	1.76	3.10	1.99	1.71	2.00	1.27	1.76	1.46	2.06
1978–86	–0.43	–0.39	–0.09	0.56	0.99	0.84	1.35	1.51	–0.29	0.38	–0.08	0.81
1970–86	0.13	0.65	0.62	1.16	2.05	1.42	1.53	1.76	0.49	1.07	0.69	1.43
Water and Sewer												
1970–78	4.95	4.74	1.74	2.59	4.25	3.28	2.63	2.60	2.76	3.18	3.19	3.18
1978–86	2.23	1.74	1.99	2.03	3.18	1.62	3.47	4.77	1.60	2.34	1.93	2.74
1970–86	3.59	3.24	1.87	2.31	3.71	2.45	3.05	3.69	2.18	2.76	2.56	2.96
Other Public Capital												
1970–78	4.05	3.35	2.53	3.93	4.55	2.88	3.83	4.57	1.19	3.10	3.22	2.96
1978–86	–0.26	–0.60	–0.47	0.71	2.21	–0.06	2.83	4.36	1.01	0.79	–0.33	1.90
1970–86	1.90	1.37	1.03	2.32	3.38	1.41	3.33	4.46	1.10	1.94	1.45	2.43

1. NE = New England, MA = Middle Atlantic, ENC = East North Central, WAC = West North Central, SA = South Atlantic, ESC = East South Central, WSC = West South Central, M = Mountain, P = Pacific

between 1963 and 1980 and have remained roughly flat since. It might thus be as sensible to attribute the economic problems of the 1970s and 1980s as much to an education gap as to an infrastructure gap.

When economists are faced with the possibility of spurious correlation (and, in truth, spurious correlation is almost always a concern since it is always difficult to separate causation from correlation), they typically look for other evidence to support their case. Thus, for example, if infrastructure spending were truly a cause of slow growth, we should expect to find a significant slowdown in industries such as manufacturing that are very dependent on infrastructure but little change in other industries such as services and finance, insurance, and real estate. But in fact the exact opposite is true; the productivity slowdown in manufacturing has been very mild. The growth rate of GDP per hour of work in manufacturing was roughly the same in the 1973–87 period as it was during 1948–73. In contrast, in the private sector as a whole, GDP per hour grew at a rate only about one-third of the pre-1973 rate. Thus it is difficult to dismiss the charge of spurious correlation based on this evidence.

There is, in addition, an important issue of the direction of causality. It is

Table 8.2   Source of Growth in U.S. Manufacturing by Region, Average Growth Rate (Percentage Growth)

Growth Rate	NE	MA	ENC	WAC	SA	ESC	WSC	M	P	Total	Snow Belt	Sun Belt
Real Value Added												
1951–65	2.60	2.67	3.13	4.46	5.15	5.82	5.28	5.71	3.46	3.75	3.02	5.39
1965–73	2.46	2.12	3.27	5.29	5.46	6.14	6.26	7.49	5.22	4.01	3.01	5.73
1973–78	.069	–1.42	–0.04	1.50	0.86	1.17	5.23	2.28	1.88	0.74	–0.21	2.12
1978–86	3.85	1.27	0.69	2.95	4.76	2.43	1.94	6.03	3.53	2.44	1.53	3.60
1951–86	2.58	1.64	2.15	3.88	4.51	4.45	4.73	5.80	4.45	3.08	2.22	4.59
Capital[2]												
1951–65	0.39	0.52	0.72	1.06	1.29	1.63	1.74	1.58	1.31	0.87	0.63	1.42
1965–73	0.91	0.48	0.79	3.04	1.69	3.06	3.02	3.65	1.45	1.36	0.92	2.19
1973–78	0.48	0.40	0.69	0.26	1.26	1.20	3.36	1.12	1.49	0.99	0.53	1.71
1978–86	0.57	0.21	0.10	0.65	0.98	0.32	0.96	0.67	0.97	0.49	0.23	0.87
1951–86	0.56	0.42	0.59	1.30	1.30	1.60	2.09	1.78	1.29	0.91	0.59	1.51
Labor[2]												
1951–65	0.12	0.23	0.35	0.97	1.73	1.92	1.62	2.63	2.29	0.87	0.34	1.96
1965–73	–0.42	-0.46	0.44	1.19	1.70	1.93	2.18	2.76	1.13	0.75	0.11	1.74
1973–78	0.56	–1.31	–0.37	1.02	0.38	0.35	1.88	1.84	0.30	0.13	–0.38	0.76
1978–86	–0.15	–1.66	–2.12	–0.55	0.38	–0.55	0.41	2.14	1.68	–0.57	–1.51	0.54
1951–86	0.00	–0.58	0.30	0.68	1.22	1.13	1.32	2.44	1.60	0.41	–0.24	1.41
Multifactor Productivity												
1951–65	2.09	1.92	2.05	2.43	2.13	2.26	1.92	1.50	1.87	2.01	2.05	2.01
1965–73	1.97	2.11	2.04	1.06	2.07	1.15	1.05	1.09	2.64	1.90	1.99	1.80
1973–78	–0.34	–0.52	0.37	0.22	–0.78	–0.38	–0.01	–0.68	0.09	–0.38	–0.36	–0.35
1978–86	3.43	2.72	2.71	2.85	3.39	2.66	1.39	3.22	0.87	2.52	2.80	2.19
1951–86	2.02	1.80	1.85	1.90	1.99	1.72	1.32	1.49	1.56	1.76	1.87	1.66

1. NE = New England, MA = Middle Atlantic, ENC = East North Central, WAC = West North Central, SA = South Atlantic, ESC = East South Central, WSC = West South Central, M = Mountain, P = Pacific.
2. Weighted by each factor's share of value added.

not difficult to see that infrastructure can cause growth. It is, after all, impossible to imagine an advanced economy without roads and airports, electricity and telecommunications, and so on. Similarly, a new airport could significantly increase the growth of a region, and the Erie Canal, transcontinental railroad, and the Interstate Highway System almost certainly stimulated national growth. But it is also clear that growth can stimulate investment. Wealthy communities, for example, spend more for schools, streets, and parks because they can afford to do so; states that are growing quickly will build new roads to serve that growth. Infrastructure spending fell at the start of the Great Depression (see figure 8.1) because the country was too poor at the time to undertake significant government capital projects.

Thus the lines of causation that link growth and public investment are complex. It is perhaps best to think of infrastructure spending and growth as endogenous variables in a complex economic system. That is to say, public investment and growth are determined simultaneously, and thus it does not make much sense to interpret the observed correlation between infrastructure and economic performance as strong evidence in favor of causation.

Regional Studies

The problems with evidence based on aggregate data are sufficiently troubling that even one of the major advocates of additional infrastructure spending now agrees that "the critics are correct that the numbers emerging from the aggregate time series studies are not credible" (Munnell 1992, 195). Regional studies represent an attractive complement to macroeconomic studies since they offer a good opportunity to address the spurious correlation problem. To see this, let us compare studies of aggregate national growth to studies of state growth. As we argued above, the aggregate data in an important sense contain just two data points (strong growth until the early 1970s, weak growth thereafter), and thus it is difficult to separate the contribution of infrastructure to national growth from the effects of other important factors that followed a similar pattern nationally, such as education. A study of state growth, however, offers 50 opportunities to study the link between infrastructure and economic performance. For example, suppose that both state A and state B invested heavily in infrastructure and that student test scores fell sharply in A but not in B. If we find that both states grew rapidly, then we would have a strong piece of evidence that infrastructure is closely tied to growth; if, on the other hand, we find that B grew rapidly but A did not, then we would have evidence that the relationship between infrastructure and growth is spurious and that perhaps education is a key determinant of economic performance.[6]

Regional studies are particularly useful since public investment has followed very different patterns in different regions. Table 8.1 is drawn from Hulten and Schwab (1991) and sets forth estimates of the growth rates of regional public capital stocks during the 1970–1986 period. Over this entire period, the total public capital stock grew roughly 60 percent faster in the Sun Belt than in the Snow Belt.[7] Differences in the growth rates of roads and highways were particularly sharp. During 1978–1986, the stock of infrastructure essentially did not grow at all in the Northeast and Midwest but grew at an annual rate of about 1.6 percent in the South and West; differences were much smaller during 1970–1978.

Since the private economy grew much faster in the Sun Belt as compared to the Snow Belt, it would be reasonable to conjecture that regional differences in public investment spending might have caused at least part of the difference in regional growth. Some of the initial regional work, including Munnell (1990b) and Morrison and Schwartz (1991), did indeed come to this conclusion.

But other evidence was not so encouraging. Holtz-Eakin (1992); Garcia-Mila, McGuire, and Porter (1993); Evans and Karras (1991); and Eisner (1991) all found that infrastructure spending has little effect on regional economic performance. One of the important differences between these two sets of papers is a question of the appropriate way to think of the determinants of state growth. Holtz-Eakin (1992); Garcia-Mila, McGuire, and Porter (1993); Evans and Karras (1991); and Eisner (1991) all allow for the possibility of "fixed effects"; that is, that states differ from one another for reasons that do not vary (or at least do not vary a great deal) over time. Thus, for example, they allow for the possibility that Iowa is very cold in the winter, that parts of California have a wonderful climate virtually all year round, and that people will move to California to avoid Midwest winters. When these authors do not include fixed effects, their results are very similar to Munnell's, that is, they find that growth and infrastructure spending are closely related. When they include fixed effects, however, the relationship between state economic performance and public capital investment vanishes. It thus appears that Munnell's initial findings were quite misleading.

In Hulten and Schwab (1991), we looked closely at the manufacturing sector in different regions of the country. We used a somewhat different approach than did most of the literature in this field. In that paper, we initially calculated the growth rate of multifactor productivity (MFP) in each region. We have included as an appendix to this paper a "primer" on the calculation of MFP. Roughly speaking, the growth rate of MFP equals the growth of private output that cannot be explained by the growth of private inputs such as labor and private capital. The approach most people have taken (econometric estimation of regional cost or production functions) provides estimates of a wide range of parameters. For example, these studies allow researchers to look at the ease with which firms can substitute capital for labor, whether productivity growth has led firms to use more capital and less labor, and so on. The drawback to this approach is that while conceptually it seems straightforward to estimate a cost or production function econometrically, it turns out that for a wide range of reasons it is actually quite difficult in practice to do so.

Focusing on MFP raises a different set of issues. On the one hand it does not yield as much information as the econometric approach. But on the other hand as we explain in the appendix, it is straightforward both in practice and in theory to estimate MFP. Thus the two types of studies complement each other very nicely; the strength of one is the weakness of the other. If the two types of studies yield similar results about the infrastructure question, then we can have a fair amount of confidence that we have come to a sensible answer.

If those who argue that public capital is an important source of regional economic growth are correct, then we would expect to find that MFP grew faster in those regions that invested heavily in infrastructure. Our research, however, provides little support for this argument. Table 8.2 summarizes some of the results of our 1991 paper. Manufacturing output grew twice as fast in the Sun Belt as in the Snow Belt between 1951 and 1986. But we found that all of the difference in the growth of output was attributable to differences in the growth of capital and labor. We found virtually no differences in the growth rate of MFP; to the extent that we did find differences, in general, productivity grew slightly faster in the Snow Belt. Among the subperiods we studied, we found the largest differences in regional productivity growth during 1978–1986 when MFP grew 2.8 percent per year in the Midwest and Northeast but only 2.2 percent per year in the South and West. As we noted above, this was the period when the public capital stock grew significantly faster in the Sun Belt. In all, the evidence from our regional research suggests that the link between infrastructure investment and regional productivity growth is at best very weak.[8]

International Studies

There is a huge amount of literature that looks at the important question: Why do some countries grow so much faster than others? Levine and Renelt (1992) present a very extensive review of this research. Based on that review, they concluded that these studies shed very little light on the determinants of growth. In particular, they find no evidence that differences in infrastructure investment can explain international differences in economic performance.

Thus, the international evidence strongly suggests that inadequate infrastructure spending is not the source of U.S. competitive problems as some critics have argued. The great success of Japan's auto industry was not due to superior infrastructure capital. Nor were Detroit's problems due to a deteriorating American infrastructure. The infrastructure in Japan is, in fact, no better than in the United States and is probably worse. Recall, for example, that the Japanese hire people to stuff commuters onto trains at rush hour. Japanese auto producers were successful because they pioneered new production techniques such as quality circles and the just-in-time inventory system. Moreover, the decline in the U.S. steel industry was accelerated when the completion of one piece of infrastructure–the St.

Lawrence Seaway–allowed iron ore to be shipped to Japan, made into steel, and sold competitively on world markets.

Cost-Benefit Studies

Cost-benefit studies of proposed infrastructure projects rarely offer the same favorable picture of new public investments that econometric studies do. For example, the Congressional Budget Office (1988) surveyed a collection of cost-benefit studies that look prospectively at the returns available on future investments. They found a very mixed picture. The rate of return on expenditures to maintain highway pavement conditions was often very high, but the return on investments on new roads outside the most congested urban areas and to upgrade roads above minimum standards was typically very low.

There are a number of reasons why cost-benefit studies and econometric studies of the relationship between growth and public investment could come to very different conclusions. Perhaps, as we argued in the previous section of the paper, the econometric studies might be seriously flawed. Alternatively, perhaps the cost-benefit studies are seriously flawed. Aschauer (1991) and others have argued, for example, that cost-benefit studies are unlikely to recognize important "spillover" benefits. Thus, so this argument goes, while a cost-benefit study might capture the benefits from a particular project that accrue in the city or state in which the project is located, it would likely miss the benefits that accrue elsewhere. To understand this argument, consider a region that includes four cities: A, B, C, and D. Suppose we were considering building a road that would connect A and B. Suppose further that roads already exist that link A to C and B to D, but that there is no road from C to D. We might reasonably expect a cost-benefit study to capture the benefits that residents and businesses in A and B would receive from the new road. But even a very careful study might fail to realize that C and D also benefit from the new road since the residents of those cities would now be able to travel to all of the cities in the region. That is to say, some of the benefits of the new road extend beyond the area where the road would be built, and quite possibly a cost-benefit study would fail to capture these spillovers.

In the end, whether or not these spillovers are an important part of the debate is largely an empirical matter. Holtz-Eakin (1992) offers some interesting evidence on this point. He reasons as follows. If the spillover argument is correct, then we should expect to find that public capital has a larger impact on private output if we study groups of states, that is, regions, than if we study individual states. If we study individual states, then at best we will generate an estimate of the benefit to say Illinois of public investment in Illinois. But if we study regions, then we can generate an estimate of the benefit to Illinois and all of the other states in the Midwest from public investment in Illinois. He tests this hypothesis by estimating both regional and state aggregate production functions. He finds no evidence of any significant spillovers; infrastructure has almost no impact on the private economy in either his regional or state studies.

Alternatively, it is possible that neither the econometric studies nor the cost-benefit studies are seriously flawed but rather that public investment is subject to decreasing marginal returns. Most types of infrastructure come in the form of interlocking networks of investments. Thus, while initial investments might offer significant benefits, the returns to subsequent investments are much smaller, the returns to a third round smaller still, and so on. Even if we knew with certainty that the first investments in a network have a large payoff, we could not assume automatically that subsequent additions to the network would have the same payoff. Indeed, they probably would not. For example, while the construction of the Interstate Highway System had a major impact on the growth of American industry–particularly the regional distribution of economic activity–it is hard to imagine that a second interstate system would have nearly the same impact.

Finally, cost-benefit studies and econometric studies might yield very different views of the benefits from infrastructure spending because changes in the structure of the economy have substantially reduced the importance of transportation. Over time, the focus of economic activity has shifted away from the production of goods toward the production of services and information. Consider the following piece of evidence. In 1959, when the interstate highway program was still in its infancy, the service sector represented roughly one-third of the entire economy; today, that figure is over one-half. Given these changes, it would not be at all surprising that we "should" spend much less on transportation (as a proportion of total economic activity) than we did before; our ability to move bits and bytes is more important now than our ability to move cars and trucks. But if this is true, the prospective point of view of cost-benefit analysis is superior to the retrospective view of the econometric approach. The value of a new "information superhighway," for example, will not be discovered by studying the past return to road construction and extrapolating the results to the telecommunications industry.

Policy Issues

Infrastructure policy should be judged by far more than simply the number of dollars we spend on public capital. A strong case could be made that it would be possible to get far greater benefits from the infrastructure dollars we spend if we redesigned many of our infrastructure programs and spent our infrastructure dollars more wisely.

For example, far too little attention has been given to the efficient use, design, and management of infrastructure, and too much emphasis has been placed on new construction. This is nowhere more apparent than in the design of federal highway matching grants. In the early years of the interstate highway program, the main problem was to construct a large national network of high-speed roads. To achieve this goal, the federal government established a system of grants to states. Under these grants, a state would be required to pay only 10 percent of the cost of interstate highways, and the federal government would pay the remaining 90 percent.[9] Similarly, under the Urban Mass Transit Act (UMTA), the federal government paid a significant portion of the cost of acquiring new buses and constructing urban rail systems such as Washington D.C.'s Metro.

But under both programs, operating costs and maintenance and repair expenditures were originally ineligible for matching funds. It is not hard to see the sorts of incentives this provided state and local governments. Consider a state government that was about to spend $1 million on roads. If it spends that money to repair and maintain the existing roads, the federal government will not provide matching funds. But if it spends that $1 million on new roads, the government will match that spending with an additional maximum of $9 million. Thus, the state would receive $10 million of new roads by spending only $1 million of its own money. Similarly, it would make little sense for a state and local government to properly maintain its existing fleet of buses if the federal government would pay most of the cost of new buses but none of the cost of repairs and maintenance. Similarly, it is wiser for cities to install complicated and expensive automatic fare card systems than to hire people to sell fare cards if the federal government will pay most of the costs of constructing a rail system but will not pay for the operation of that system once it is completed. The situation has been corrected gradually, but it has left a legacy of poorly maintained mass transit systems, bridges, and roads in many areas.

Policymakers at all levels of government have not taken full advantage of a range of management and design decisions that could significantly increase the flow of infrastructure services without necessarily increasing the stock of infrastructure. Winston (1991), for example, argues persuasively that roads should be built much thicker and that road taxes should be based on axle weights in order to provide road users with the appropriate incentives. Others have suggested that computerized traffic signals could yield significant benefits. One recent study of Los Angeles estimated that computerized signals could reduce traffic delays by 30 percent in that city and reduce auto emissions by 13 percent.

Finally, Gramlich (1991) argues that a greater emphasis on pricing infrastructure properly must be a key element of our infrastructure policy. Currently, the pecuniary or monetary price of using most roads is zero. At a price of zero, the demand for any good will almost always greatly exceed supply; if, for some reason, we were to charge nothing for food, the result would almost certainly be chronic food shortages, just as we now seem to have chronic infrastructure shortages in some places. An alternative to spending more on new road construction would be to price the use of roads and other public capital efficiently (that is, to set the price equal to the costs that users impose on society, particularly the cost of increased congestion). This approach to efficient facility use becomes more attractive as the technology for collecting these user fees evolves.

It is not difficult to see the economic logic behind Gramlich's argument. Drivers who are considering using a road will balance the benefits they will receive against the costs they will incur. Thus, they will incorporate in their decision the value of their time, gasoline, wear and tear on their car, and so on. But they will ignore the costs they impose on others; in particular, they will ignore the congestion externality they cause. Put slightly differently, they will balance private benefits and private costs. Efficiency, however, involves a balancing of benefits and social costs, and social costs will exceed private costs by the amount of congestion a driver creates.[10] As a result, too many drivers will use a road, and congestion will be greater than is optimal.

One solution is to set a toll equal to the cost of congestion. We would expect drivers to include the toll as part of their cost when they are making a decision to use a road. But if the toll equals the externality, then a driver's private cost will equal social cost. As a consequence, the toll will lead to efficiency. A number of studies have used this theory to estimate the optimal toll. Keeler et al. (1975) found that for the San Francisco area, the optimal rush hour toll would be 11 cents to 32 cents (in 1992 dollars) per vehicle mile in the suburbs and 40 cents to $1.13 on central city freeways.

Summary and Conclusions

Our goal in this chapter has been to provide an overview of some of the important issues surrounding the debate over infrastructure policy. Several key conclusions emerge from this review. First, we find little evidence of a national infrastructure crisis. Second, the link between infrastructure and economic performance is very weak. Much of the research that followed Aschauer's work provides little support for the hypothesis that the slowdown in infrastructure spending caused the economy to perform poorly over the last 20 years. Third, many of our infrastructure problems can be traced to poor policy decisions rather than inadequate funding.

For example, transportation programs have focused on new construction at the expense of repairs and maintenance, and government has been slow to price infrastructure correctly, thus leading to inevitable congestion.

Almost certainly, the focus of the infrastructure debate will fall more and more heavily on new types of infrastructure such as the "information superhighway." These new projects should be evaluated on their own merits (and demerits). Estimates of the rates of return on past infrastructure programs are largely irrelevant to this assessment.

We thank the National Science Foundation for its support of this research and Michael Svilar and Andrew Kochera for their excellent work as our research assistants. We also thank Alicia Munnell for providing us with her data on public capital.

Appendix

The Measurement of Productivity Growth: A Primer

The sources-of-growth model is one of the dominant approaches to the analysis of economic growth. This model was developed by Solow (1957), Kendrick (1980), Denison (1979), and Jorgenson and Griliches (1967) and is the conceptual basis of our research on regional productivity growth (Hulten and Schwab 1984, 1991, 1993a). A simple version of the sources-of-growth model would begin with the assumption that aggregate output (defined as real value added) is systematically related to capital and labor via an aggregate production function. More formally, we can write the aggregate production function as

$$Q = AF(K, L) \tag{A.1}$$

where Q represents output, K is private capital, L is private labor, and A represents multifactor productivity (MFP), that is, technological change.

Output will grow because capital and labor grow and because these inputs are used more productively, that is, because K, L, and A grow; the object of the analysis is to determine how much of the observed growth of output should be attributed to these various sources of growth. The output elasticities of capital and labor play important roles in the sources-of-growth model. The output elasticity of a factor of production is defined as the percentage change in output that would result from a 1 percent change in that factor of production. Thus, if we call the output elasticities of capital and labor ε_K and ε_L, then

$$\varepsilon_K = \frac{\dfrac{\Delta Q}{Q}}{\dfrac{\Delta K}{K}} = \frac{\Delta Q}{\Delta K} \frac{K}{Q} \tag{A.2}$$

$$\varepsilon_L = \frac{\dfrac{\Delta Q}{Q}}{\dfrac{\Delta L}{L}} = \frac{\Delta Q}{\Delta L} \frac{L}{Q}$$

where Δ represents a change in a variable.

The analysis of growth would be straightforward if we knew the output elasticities of capital and labor. The following simple example should make this point clear. Suppose that we knew that ε_K equaled .25, ε_L equaled .75, K grew by 4 percent, L grew by 2 percent, and Q grew by 5 percent. The increase in capital would have caused output to grow by .25 x 4.0 = 1 percent; similarly, the increase in labor would have led to a .75 x 2.0 = 1.5 percent growth in output. It is clear from equation (A.1) that Q rises by 1 percent whenever A rises by 1 percent. Then, since Q actually grew by 5 percent in this example, A must have grown by 5.0–1.0–1.5 = 2.5 percent. More generally, if we knew the output elasticities of capital and labor, then we could always calculate the growth rate of A as a residual

$$\frac{\Delta A}{A} = \frac{\Delta Q}{Q} - \varepsilon_K \frac{\Delta K}{K} - \varepsilon_L \frac{\Delta L}{L} \qquad (A.3)$$

Unfortunately, ε_K and ε_L cannot be observed directly. But we can appeal to some basic microeconomic theory to develop estimates of these key parameters. In competitive markets, firms will continue to hire each factor of production until the value of the marginal product of that factor is equal to its price. Thus,

$$P_K = P_Q \frac{\Delta Q}{\Delta K} \qquad (A.4)$$

$$P_L = P_Q \frac{\Delta Q}{\Delta L}$$

where P_K, P_L, and P_Q are the prices of capital, labor, and output respectively. With a little manipulation of equation (A.4), it is easy to see that it implies

$$\frac{P_K K}{P_Q Q} = \frac{\Delta Q}{\Delta K} \frac{K}{Q} = \varepsilon_K \qquad (A.5)$$

$$\frac{P_L L}{P_Q Q} = \frac{\Delta Q}{\Delta L} \frac{L}{Q} = \varepsilon_L$$

The left side of the equation represents capital's and labor's share of the revenue from the sale of output. Equation (A.5) thus tells us that these shares equal the output elasticities of capital and labor. If we call these shares π_K and π_L, then we can write the growth equation in (A.3) as

$$\frac{\Delta A}{A} = \frac{\Delta Q}{Q} - \pi_k \frac{\Delta K}{K} - \pi_L \frac{\Delta L}{L} \tag{A.6}$$

Each term in (A.6), except the growth rate of the productivity index, can in principle be measured directly. Therefore, the growth of productivity can be estimated as a residual since all of the terms on the right side of (A.6) involve prices and quantities that can be observed directly. This yields the well-known "residual," "measure-of-our-ignorance," "total factor productivity," or "multifactor productivity."

Notes

1. We have used the terms "infrastructure" and "public capital" interchangeably. We recognize that there are some important differences between the two. Strictly speaking, the term public capital should be reserved for those investments that are owned by the public sector. Thus, it is easy to imagine infrastructure that in some cases is public capital and in some cases is not. Consider a toll road for example. Certainly, it is part of the nation's infrastructure. If it is owned by a state or local government, then it should be considered public capital; if it is privately owned (as some toll roads are) then it is not part of the public capital stock. This distinction is particularly important in international comparisons since some types of infrastructure such as telecommunications capital are privately owned in some countries but publicly owned in others.

2. In this paper we have looked only at some of the long-run policy issues in the infrastructure debate. Some have argued that additional infrastructure spending should play a key role in short-term economic policy. See Hulten and Schwab (1993b) for a discussion of this issue.

3. Figures 8.1 and 8.2 are based on data from the U.S. Bureau of Economic Analysis (BEA). The BEA includes the Interstate Highway System as part of the state and local capital stock.

4. It is also important to note that many of the worst problems are concentrated in a handful of states. For example, Sanders (1993) has shown that 40 percent of all bridges that have been classified as deficient are located in just six states. More than half of all bridges in New York State fall into this category as compared to 2 percent of Florida bridges and 6 percent of Oregon bridges. Sanders also shows that a similar pattern emerges in data on pavement quality.

5. Holtz-Eakin (1988) comes to the same conclusion.

6. Regional studies are certainly not free of all of the problems that plague aggregate studies. For example, it is just as important to be concerned about the line of causation (does higher infrastructure investment cause faster growth, or does faster growth cause higher investment?) in regional studies as it is in aggregate studies.

7. The Snow Belt includes the New England, Middle Atlantic, East North Central, and West North Central census divisions; the Sun Belt includes the South Atlantic, East South Central, West South Central, Mountain, and Pacific divisions.

8. Over a much longer period, however, regional per capita incomes (and thus presumably labor productivity) have converged. During the period that has received most of the attention in the infrastructure debate, however, there is little evidence of regional differences in productivity growth.

9. A second set of grants provided grants of 75 percent for other federally aided highways.

10. Of course, there may be factors other than congestion that would drive a wedge between marginal social cost and marginal private cost. Air pollution is a good example.

References

Aaron, H. J. "Comments on 'Why is Infrastructure Important?' " In *Is There a Shortfall in Public Capital Investment?* Edited by Alicia Munnell. Boston: Federal Reserve Bank of Boston, 1990.

Aschauer, D. A. "Is Public Expenditure Productive?" *Journal of Monetary Economics* 23 (1989).

——. *Public Investment and Private Sector Growth: The Economic Benefits of Reducing America's 'Third Deficit'.* Washington, D.C.: Economic Policy Institute, 1991.

Canning, D., and M. Fay. "The Effect of Infrastructure Networks on Economic Growth." Unpublished paper, Columbia University, January 1993.

Choate, P., and S. Walter. *America in Ruins: Beyond the Public Works Pork Barrel.* Washington, D.C.: Council of State Planning Agencies, 1981.

Congressional Budget Office. *New Directions for the Nation's Public Works.* Washington, D.C.: U.S. Government Printing Office, 1988.

Denison, E. F. *Accounting for Slower Economic Growth.* Washington, D.C.: The Brookings Institution, 1979.

Eisner, R.. "Infrastructure and Regional Economic Performance: Comment." *New England Economic Review* (September/October 1991).

Evans, P., and G. Karras. "Are Government Activities Productive? Evidence from a Panel of U.S. States." Unpublished paper, Ohio State University, 1991a.

Fernald, J. "How Productive is Infrastructure? Distinguishing Reality and Illusion with a Panel of U.S. Industries." Unpublished paper, Harvard University, 1992.

Garcia-Mila, T., T. McGuire, and R. H. Porter. "The Effect of Public Capital in State-Level Production Functions Reconsidered." University of Illinois Institute of Government and Public Affairs Working Paper No. 24, 1993.

Gramlich, E. M. "United States Infrastructure Needs: Let's Get the Prices Right." Paper presented at the American Enterprise Institute Conference on Infrastructure Needs and Policy Options for the 1990s, Washington, D.C., February 1991.

Holtz-Eakin, D., "Private Output, Government Capital, and the Infrastructure 'Crisis'." Columbia University Discussion Paper No. 394, 1988.

——. "Public Sector Capital and the Productivity Puzzle." National Bureau of Economic Research Working Paper No. 4144, 1992.

Hulten, C. R. "Discussion of 'Infrastructure and Regional Economic Performance.' " In *Is There a Shortfall in Public Capital Investment?* Edited by A. Munnell. Boston: Federal Reserve Bank of Boston, 1990.

Hulten, Charles, and Robert Schwab. "Regional Productivity Growth in U.S. Manufacturing: 1951–1978." *American Economic Review* 74 (1984).

——. "Public Capital Formation and the Growth of Regional Manufacturing Industries." *National Tax Journal* 44 (1991).

——. "Is There Too Little Public Capital in the U.S.?" Unpublished paper, University of Maryland, 1992.

——. "Joint Tests of Endogenous Growth and Technological Convergence: Regional U.S. Manufacturing Industries, 1970–1986." Unpublished paper, University of Maryland, 1993a.

——. "Infrastructure Spending: Where Do We Go from Here?" *National Tax Journal* 46 (1993b).

Jorgenson, D. W. "Fragile Statistical Foundations." *The Public's Capital* (Spring 1991).

Jorgenson, D. W., and Z. Griliches. "The Explanation of Productivity Change." *Review of Economic Studies* (July 1967).

Keeler, T., et al., *The Full Costs of Urban Transport.* Berkeley: Institute of Urban and Regional Development, 1975.

Kendrick, J. W. "Productivity Trends and the Recent Slowdown: Historical Perspective, Causal Factors, and Policy Options." In *Contemporary Economic Problems.* Edited by William Fellner. Washington, D.C.: American Enterprise Institute, 1980.

Levine, R., and D. Renelt. "A Sensitivity Analysis of Cross-Country Growth Regressions." *American Economic Review* (September 1992).

Morrison, C. J., and A. E. Schwartz. "State Infrastructure and Economic Performance." Unpublished paper, Tufts University, July 1991.

Munnell, A. H. "Why Has Productivity Growth Declined? Productivity and Public Investment." *New England Economic Review* (January/February 1990a).

——. "How Does Public Infrastructure Affect Regional Economic Performance?" *New England Economic Review* (September/October 1990b).

——. "Infrastructure Investment and Economic Growth." *Journal of Economic Perspectives* (fall 1992).

National Council on Public Works Improvement. *Fragile Foundations: A Report on America's Public Works.* Washington, D.C.: United States Government Printing Office, 1988.

Sanders, H. T. "What Infrastructure Crisis?" *The Public Interest* (winter 1993).

Schultze, C. E. "The Federal Budget and the Nation's Economic Health." In *Setting National Priorities: Policy for the Nineties.* Edited by H. Aaron. Washington, D.C.: The Brookings Institution, 1990.

Solow, R. M. "Technical Change and the Aggregate Production Function." *Review of Economics and Statistics* (August 1957).

Tatom, J. A. "Public Capital and Private Sector Performance." *Review* (May/June 1991).

United States Department of Transportation. *New Perspectives in Commuting.* Washington, D.C.: United States Government Printing Office, 1992.

———. *The Status of the Nation's Highways, Bridges, and Transit: Conditions and Performance*. Washington, D.C.: United States Government Printing Office, 1993.

Winston, C. "Efficient Transportation Infrastructure Policy." *Journal of Economic Perspectives* (Winter 1991).

Part 4

Youth Issues

9

Thinking about School Vouchers: Theory, Evidence, and Rhetoric

Joseph J. Cordes
Sheila Nataraj Kirby
Richard Buddin

Introduction

In this chapter, Joseph J. Cordes, Sheila Nataraj Kirby, and Richard Buddin discuss the issue of school vouchers. The central question addressed here concerns the appropriate scope for public intervention in the operation of private markets. This is a recurrent theme. We are accustomed to some kinds of interventions simply because they are familiar. For example, it seems natural for most Americans that local jurisdictions impose zoning restrictions since such zoning laws have been a feature of local American politics since the 1920s. Likewise, the idea that "public education" means "publicly produced education" is comfortably familiar.

Many economists have challenged such comfortable ideas about the locus of public decision making. In considering whether "public education" should be "publicly produced" one question economists focus on is whether education is a public good in the sense that economists use that term. A good is a pure public good if each individual's consumption of the good is exactly the same and if other peoples' consumption of the good does not diminish anyone's consumption of the good. A widely accepted example of such a pure public good is national defense. I am protected to exactly the same extent as everyone else by the "nuclear umbrella" and if additional people come in under the umbrella (for example, foreign visitors or immigrants) my level of protection is undiminished.

Education is different from this example of a pure public good. Indeed, some economists argue that most such local publicly provided goods (that is, goods traditionally financed by local government expenditures in the United States) are in fact private goods. If they are private goods, one economic rationale for government intervention in the market is undercut.

Education is often regarded as a "merit good," that is, a good that is good. Some people argue that education is "too important" to be left to the private market. Yet, even if we accept the idea that education should not be left to the private market, that does not imply that the present method of financing public education is the best. Defense is also an important matter, but tanks and aircraft, rather than being produced directly by the government, are produced by private firms acting as contractors to the government. It is certainly conceivable that the government could set up factories and hire workers directly to produce military equipment, but this is not the way the matter has largely been handled, even in war time. Tanks are produced by Chrysler Corporation for the U.S. government rather than by the U.S. government directly. In contrast, almost everywhere in the United States, education for most students is provided by people who are directly employed by units of local government. This chapter examines the alternatives to that arrangement.

The framework developed in the chapter is based upon indifference curves–a traditional tool of microeconomics. The analysis is both positive and normative. The main issues in the positive economic analysis concern how school choice will be affected by the introduction of school vouchers and whose school choice will be affected by the introduction of school vouchers. The main issue of the normative analysis is a judgment about the distribution of benefits and costs from a scheme of school vouchers.

In 1990, expenditures on elementary and high school education in the United States totaled approximately $230 billion or 4.2 percent of the gross domestic product (GDP). Of this total, almost 86 percent represented expenditures on public elementary and secondary education by local and state governments (U.S. Bureau of the Census 1993).

Presently, public support of elementary and secondary education in the United States has two noteworthy budgetary and institutional features. One is that public *finance* of elementary and secondary education is closely tied to public *provision* of education by government-run public school systems. The other is that access to public schools is closely linked to the family's place of residence.

These two attributes of American public education place some important limits on options faced by families with school-age children. Tying public finance to public provision of education effectively requires families to send their children to publicly run schools in order to receive the public subsidy for education. Within the public sector, choices are further limited by the extent to which families are required to send their children to schools within certain geographical boundaries.

In principle, there is no logical reason why public subsidies to education need to be provided in the manner described. Public subsidies for education could continue to be tied to attendance at public schools, but families could be given a wider range of choice among public schools. The public subsidy that is currently available only if a student attends public school could also be replaced in whole or in part by an education voucher that households could apply toward the cost of tuition in private as well as public schools.

While citizens and politicians alike generally agree that government has an important role to play in financing a significant portion of expenditures on elementary and secondary education, concerns about the performance of American public schools have sparked interest in expanding the range of publicly financed schooling options available to families with school-age children. Although as recently as the 1970s and 1980s, proposals to provide vouchers and tuition tax credits for education were soundly defeated in several legislatures, school choice is increasingly being hailed by many political and educational leaders and parents as an approach for reforming public education. A recent Associated Press poll revealed that 68 percent of respondents favored allowing parents to choose which schools their children attend.

Though many school choice proposals would allow families to choose among public but not private schools, serious proposals have also been made to provide school vouchers that could be used at both private and public schools. Such proposals have been at the center of recent political debates in California, Michigan, Georgia, and New Jersey and, less directly, in the 1993 gubernatorial race in Virginia.

Proponents of such voucher schemes argue that allowing families greater choice between private and public schools will improve the quality of education by encouraging competition among schools in providing educational services and will potentially reduce the overall costs of educating children. Skeptics counter that vouchers will not save money in the short run but rather will provide windfall gains at taxpayer expense to families with children already enrolled in private schools and in the long run will do little but further weaken already troubled public schools.

From the perspective of a public policy decision maker asked to evaluate the cost-effectiveness of educational vouchers, several questions arise:

1. What information is needed in order to make an informed decision, both about the feasibility and the desirability of introducing school vouchers?

2. How would vouchers work in theory, and what, if anything, is known about how they would work in practice?
3. What do we already know about the likely effects of vouchers, and what information is lacking?
4. How might the information needed to evaluate the effects of vouchers be acquired either before or after their adoption?

This chapter attempts to provide some answers to these questions. To set the stage, we first discuss where private school vouchers fit in the range of proposals for expanding school choice and the types of vouchers that have been proposed. We then briefly survey in the third section the arguments made for and against school vouchers. To provide a conceptual framework for analyzing the effects of vouchers, we review the economic model of school choice discussed in Pelzman (1973) and Sonstelie (1979, 1982) and use the model to analyze some effects of providing a voucher like that proposed in the recent ballot initiative in California. The fourth section of the chapter summarizes the relevant empirical evidence both on how families might respond to vouchers if they were provided and on how introducing vouchers might affect educational outcomes. The chapter concludes with a discussion of some implications for policy as well as for future research.

Educational Choice and Voucher Plans

School choice has become a fairly popular "buzzword" in debates about educational reform. In practice, however, the term can mean many different things. The concept of educational choice encompasses a variety of options and plans—at the school, district, and state levels. Although we are primarily concerned here with plans that allow choice between private and public schools through a voucher program, it might be helpful to briefly mention some of the other types of choice plans that have been implemented, most of which have focused on choice in *public* education. Following Young and Clinchy (1992), these plans can be classified as follows:

Alternative and Magnet Schools

Alternative schools—such as free schools, open schools, or schools without walls—are the oldest choice option in public education. Recently, such schools have tended to focus on at-risk students. Magnet schools were established in the 1970s as a less controversial response to integration than court-mandated busing. Some magnets offer specialized programs (such as performing arts or math and science), while others offer complete educational approaches. The purpose is to improve integration by appealing to a wide variety of students. Both alternative and magnet schools draw their students from the entire district.

"Second Chance" Options

Students at risk who are not doing well in the regular school system are offered the choice of attending public schools outside their assigned districts or private nonreligious schools or centers at the expense of the state. Several states including California, Colorado, Minnesota, Oregon, and Washington offer such "second chance" options.

Postsecondary Options

These types of plans allow high school students to attend postsecondary institutions and receive credit at both the high school and college level. The large majority of the states pay all tuition expenses, although in Utah the students share the cost while in Kansas they bear the full cost.

Intradistrict Plans

Such plans allow free choice among some or all of a district's schools; three states–Colorado, Ohio, and Washington–have implemented intradistrict choice within all districts. A newer model allows "controlled" choice, such as that found in some areas of Massachusetts, under which a school makes the final assignment based on space availability and integration guidelines.

Interdistrict Plans

In contrast to intradistrict plans that restrict choice to schools within the attendance zone or within a district, interdistrict plans allow free choice across some or all districts, provided the selected schools have space and maintain racial balance. In some cases, local districts are given the option of opting out of the plan or limiting the number of transfers. The receiving district or school makes the final assignment based on space availability and integration guidelines and is paid by the sending district and/or the state. Transportation costs are sometimes provided but more generally are the responsibility of the student. Arkansas, Iowa, Massachusetts, Minnesota, and Nebraska have implemented interdistrict plans, while other states will or are considering implementing such plans in the next few years.

Proposed and Actual Voucher Plans

All of the above programs for expanding school choice share the common feature of limiting school choice to publicly run schools. School vouchers differ from these proposals by allowing families to choose between private and public schools, as well as between different public schools.

Friedman Plan—Though the concept of school vouchers has been around since the time of Adam Smith, Milton Friedman (1955) played an important role in first raising and promoting the concept on the American scene. He proposed a uniform voucher that would be provided to parents. This voucher could then be used by families to defray the cost of tuition, with families allowed to pay "add-ons" to purchase a more costly education than that provided by the voucher for their child. Under Friedman's plan, each school would be required to meet minimal curriculum requirements with emphasis on instruction in basic skills and a common core of civic values. This would permit a wide variation among schools with respect to values and curriculum content. The schools would also have complete freedom in setting admissions policies.

Chubb and Moe Plan—In an influential book, Chubb and Moe (1990) recently set forth a radical and fairly specific voucher plan based in part on a proposal outlined by Coons and Sugarman (1978) several years earlier. This plan would do away with the current distinction between public and private schools; the state would set minimal criteria that define what constitutes a "public school"; any group or organization meeting these criteria would then be chartered as a public school with the right to receive money and enroll students. Schools would be compensated directly by the state for the students they enroll, with districts contributing predetermined amounts for each child based on an equalization approach so that, in poorer districts, the state share would be greater than in wealthier ones. Scholarships could be varied by educational needs within a district. No household would be allowed to increase the amount of the voucher through its own funds ("add-on") in order to "buy" more expensive education; however, "collective" add-ons would be permitted through a higher tax rate in the district.

Under this plan, each student would be free to attend any public school in the state and to the extent that tax revenues allow, transportation would be provided. The state would provide parents with information regarding the schools. Schools would be free to set their own tuition as well as admissions and dismissal policies subject only to nondiscrimination requirements. Each school would have sole authority to determine its governing structure, with no statewide tenure laws and minimal certification requirements. The state would not hold the schools accountable for student achievement or other quality dimensions of school performance. Instead, schools would be directly responsible to parents who would be free to choose and to leave the school if their expectations were not met.

While the Friedman and Chubb and Moe proposals offer general blueprints for how choice might be expanded to include private schools, neither has been put to a political test or put into practice. We conclude our survey of school choice plans by describing two voucher plans that have.

The Milwaukee Parental Choice Program—In the spring of 1990, the Milwaukee Parental Choice Program was initiated to provide poor families with an opportunity to send their children to private, nonsectarian schools in Milwaukee. The following material, taken from Witte, Bailey, and Thorn (1992), outlines the dimensions of the program.

TABLE 9.1   The Milwaukee Parental Choice Program

Family Qualifications:
   Students must come from households with income 1.75 times the poverty line or less.
   Students may not have been in private schools or in school districts other than the Milwaukee Public School District (MPS) in the prior year.
School Qualifications:
   Eligible schools must be private, nonsectarian schools with no religious affiliation or training.
   Schools cannot discriminate in selection based on race, religion, gender, prior achievement, or prior behavioral records. Schools were exempted by court ruling from the Education for All Handicapped Act.
   If classes are oversubscribed, selection is on a random basis.
   Choice students can only be 49 percent of the students in the school.
   Schools must meet at least one standard established for attendance, parental involvement, student achievement on standardized tests, or grade progress.
Program Specifications:
   Private schools receive the Milwaukee Public School per-member, state aid (estimated at $2,745 in 1992-93) in lieu of tuition.
   The total number of students in the Choice Program in any year is limited to 1 percent of the membership in the Milwaukee Public Schools (or an estimated 950 students in 1992–93).

The Milwaukee program is now in its third year and results from the first two years are available. Applications for and enrollments in the program have increased dramatically over time, from 341 in 1990 to 521 in 1991 and 613 in 1992. There are currently 11 schools participating, compared to the seven that participated in 1990–91 and the six in 1991–92.

The Milwaukee program is much more limited than a full-blown school voucher program in several aspects. It is restricted to poor families. While it gives families some choice between private and public schools, the range of choice is limited to include only certain kinds of private schools. Finally, payments are made to schools rather than to families, as would be the case under a true voucher.

Nonetheless, the Milwaukee program has received considerable attention both from proponents and opponents of private/public school choice. Later in the paper, we return to the Milwaukee Program to consider what lessons it offers regarding the possible effects of private/public school choice programs.

The California Ballot Initiative—Most recently, Californians went to the polls to consider Proposition 174: a ballot initiative that, if enacted, would have required that education vouchers be given to every California child enrolled in private or public elementary and secondary schools. The voucher proposal presented in Proposition 174 is relatively simple. It was written as a formal amendment to the California constitution that would entitle each K-12 student in the state to an education voucher that could be redeemed at public schools or at eligible private schools that enroll at least 25 students. The amount of this voucher was specified to be at least 50 percent of average state per-student expenditures for K-12 education in the previous year. The legislature could augment the size of the voucher for transportation costs or special needs. Had the proposal passed, it would have effectively made every California child enrolled in private and public elementary and secondary schools eligible to receive a tuition voucher equal to one-half of the current amount of state spending per pupil of $5,200, or $2,600.

To qualify for receipt of the voucher, a private school would have to meet two basic tests. First, a school could not discriminate based on race, ethnicity, color, or national origin. Schools were not precluded from restricting enrollment by gender, religion, or special needs, but other legal restrictions could apply in these circumstances. Second, private schools could not advocate unlawful behavior, teach hatred, or provide deliberately misleading information about the school. Public regulation of private schools was otherwise kept to a minimum level under the proposal on the belief that parents would make wise educational choices and monitor the performance of private schools.[1]

Though the proposal was soundly defeated, its supporters propose to submit a revised version again in the future. The central features of the California proposal are also likely to serve as models for voucher proposals elsewhere.

Pros and Cons of School Choice

Predictably, the California voucher proposal elicited strong reaction and questions from each side of the school choice debate. Some of these questions, at least in principle, can be resolved from empirical facts about the effects of school choice, but others cannot.

The Constitutional Question

One important issue that falls in the latter category is constitutional. Because the vast majority of nonpublic schools are religiously affiliated, a critical issue in the debate on private/public school choice is whether providing a voucher like that proposed in California would be constitutional.[2] In confronting this question when dealing with more targeted forms of state

aid to private education, the Supreme Court's task has centered on interpretation of two clauses of the First Amendment: the "establishment" clause
that forbids laws "respecting an establishment of religion" and the "free
exercise" clause that forbids laws "prohibiting the free exercise of religion."
The inherent tension between these two clauses has resulted in a doctrine
that often, in the words of Justice Byron White, "sacrifices clarity and
predictability for flexibility."[3]

Because our main purpose is to discuss how social science models and
data can contribute to the debate about vouchers, we will not take up this
important subject in detail. Suffice it to say that scholars who have, such as
Wells (1993), believe that the legal doctrine on church–state issues is moving
toward a lower wall of separation and that the First Amendment legal
arguments against voucher programs–provided these programs provide
money directly to parents and not to schools and include parents at both
public and nonpublic schools–may not carry as much weight as opponents
of voucher programs seem to believe. This suggests that vouchers may be
permissible on constitutional grounds, though opponents of vouchers are
likely to continue to raise arguments against vouchers based on alleged
denials of equal educational opportunities or on philosophical questions
about what such plans would mean to public schools in a democratic
society.

The Effects of Providing Vouchers

Unlike the constitutional question, most arguments advanced in favor of or
against vouchers are really statements about the presumed effects of
vouchers on both the provision and the outcomes of elementary and
secondary education. Witte (1992) has succinctly summarized the material
as follows:

Prochoice Arguments:
> Choice would require less bureaucracy and more school-level autonomy.
> Staff motivation, leadership, and morale would improve with educational choice.
> Parental involvement will be greater under choice.
> Schools will be more diverse, innovative, and flexible.
> As a result of the four preceding arguments, student achievement will increase under
> choice.
> Competition and market forces will reduce costs and increase efficiency under choice.

Antichoice Arguments:
> Selectivity of students will increase inequality between schools.
> Geographic distribution of students by race and class will produce inequitable choices
> and increase school segregation.
> Special needs of students with learning disabilities and handicaps will not be met as
> well under a choice system.

Accountability will be considerably reduced, and minimum standards will not be maintained under choice.

Information on schools will be costly, inadequate, and more readily available to families
of higher socioeconomic status.

The common school tradition will be lost as educational diversity increases.

As Witte points out, an important feature of these arguments is that they
are empirical or fact-based in nature. That is, they reflect what proponents
and opponents believe would happen if families were given a greater option
to choose between private and public schools through voucher programs
such as those proposed in the California ballot initiative. It is useful to briefly
examine some of these arguments in more detail.

Arguments for Private/Public School Choice—Critics of the current educational system argue that public schools are under substantial bureaucratic
pressures and beset with rules and regulations designed to impose common
higher-order values on a heterogeneous population of principals and
teachers (Chubb and Moe 1990). The incentives to bureaucratize the schools
are built into the system, given that this may be the only way to protect
policies in an uncertain political climate and the influence of unions in this
sector. The private school system, on the other hand, is built on "decentralization, competition, and choice" and because their main concern is to please
their clients, they have strong incentives to adopt effective school organizations that take full advantage of strong leadership, informal cooperation,
teacher professionalism, and innovation.[4] Under some plans, schools would
be granted a great deal of latitude in determining their own governing
structure. They may be run solely by teachers, a union, or a principal.
Schools would be given freedom and authority to set curriculum and staff
requirements and to set aside tenure laws. This would give the schools the
flexibility needed to put together well-functioning teams. Under such a
system, staff motivation and morale should improve considerably because
there will be a direct link between compensation and student achievement.

One argument in favor of vouchers is that they would make available a
wide range of educational options, giving all families a freedom of choice–
freedom that is currently limited to higher-income parents who can afford
the tuition and extra costs associated with private schools. Currently families
are assigned to public schools based on residence, and choice is severely
limited. Vouchers would reduce coercion and secure fundamental rights by
better matching education with the fundamental beliefs of parents.

Another rationale for school choice is the improvement in educational
outcomes that such a system would engender. Proponents point to research
by Coleman, Hoffer, and Kilgore (1982) that showed that students in Catholic
and other private schools have substantially higher achievement that those
in public schools, and discipline and student behavior were the primary

factors responsible for the greater success of private schools. Bryk and Lee (1993) also emphasize other factors that contribute to the success of Catholic schools: high expectations and rigorous academic curricula for all students, personal attention from teachers, and emphasis on shaping students' characters. A growing number of researchers agree that poor and minority students fare better in Catholic schools than do their counterparts in public schools. However, there are equally strong arguments raised by those against private/public school choice.

Arguments against Private/Public School Choice—Levin (1990) posits that there are two widely accepted social purposes of schooling: (1) providing a common set of values and knowledge that form the basis of a democratic society; and (2) requirement of equality in terms of access for all students regardless of color, race, or socioeconomic status. He argues that the market approach that relies on competition and diversity among schools will create an inherently "divisive system of education rather than one that converges on a common educational experience."[5] While some market advocates believe that it may be possible to protect against such balkanization and stratification through regulations, Levin points out that this is likely to make the whole system more cumbersome and costly and may not be constitutionally feasible. Indeed, this would undercut one of the strong arguments favoring private school choice.

The question of selectivity and stratification is one of the most debated issues in the area of private/public choice. Opponents of school choice believe that this will contribute to the further stratification of the school system: "The best prepared students from the most affluent and best-educated families will become increasingly concentrated in a limited number of elite schools, while the poorest students with the lowest levels of academic motivation and preparedness will be consigned to schools in the lowest strata."[6] Coleman (1992), however, points out that extensive stratification already exists in the current school system and the result of a voucher system would "not be to increase stratification: it would be to replace the current stratification by income and race by a stratification based on students' performance and behavior," although he admits that students' performance and behavior are correlated with income and race.[7]

Critics of vouchers point to the crucial role that information plays in making choice work and the difficulty in ensuring that all parents have adequate, equitable information regarding schools. The ability to collect and sort through information is likely to differ by socioeconomic class and this may further exacerbate stratification in schools. The related questions as to who will supply the information and who will ensure that this information will be accurate are also difficult to answer.

Witte (1992) provides a pithy summary: "Proponents of choice stress the primary value of liberty, a more equitable dispersion of that liberty, and pluralistic diversity. Opponents of choice stress equality, an integrated society, and common school traditions. Philosophers have been debating these value differences for thousands of years. It is no wonder that these arguments divide well-intentioned parents, education providers, and policy experts."[8]

As noted above, many of the claims and counterclaims about the effects of allowing private/public school choice are based on *predictions* about the likely effects of programs like the California ballot initiative. Broadly speaking, there are two different yet complementary ways of gauging the validity of such predictions. One is to see whether such predictions conform with predictions from reasonable models of how families and schools would behave if vouchers were to be provided. The other, more fact-based approach, is to see whether such predictions are consistent with observed behavior in situations that have certain important features in common with proposed voucher plans.

To assist the analyst in these endeavors, it is generally helpful to have a model of how private school vouchers affect family educational choices. One such model is discussed below.

The Economic Model of Private/Public School Choice

A first step in developing such a model is to examine how the current system affects household educational choices. The key feature of the current system that affects family educational choice is that parents can send their children to public schools, which are financed from taxes and hence available "free of charge," or to private schools, which do not receive a public subsidy. An important consequence of linking public support with public provision of education in this way is that families face significant financial incentives to enroll their children in public schools, even if they might otherwise prefer private schools. The main implications of influencing parental choice of schooling in this manner are illustrated in figures 9.1 through 9.4.

Figure 9.1 shows how providing a subsidy for attendance at public but not private schools affects the opportunities that are faced by a typical consumer of elementary and secondary education (assumed to be a family). In figure 9.1, line AD represents the family's income, after taxes, which can be spent on other consumption, Y, or on schooling, S. The family has the option of sending their child(ren) free of charge to a public school, where S_p defines the quantity of (quality-adjusted) schooling provided by the local public school system or of purchasing private schooling at a positive price.

Broadly speaking, the family faces the following alternatives. It can consume the quantity of schooling provided by the public system, in which case, all of the family's after-tax income is available to be spent on other

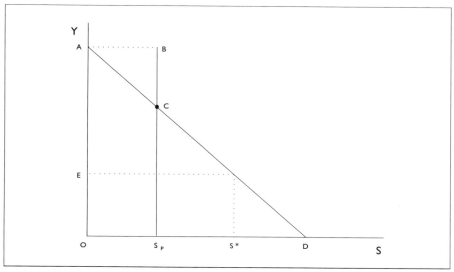

Figure 9.1   Schooling options (with fixed quantity subsidy Sp).

consumption Y. This choice is represented by point B in figure 9.1, where the family consumes S_p of schooling in the public system, and A units of other consumption. The family can also decide to forego the subsidy provided by free public schools and consume varying amounts of private schooling. In this case, however, schooling is consumed at the expense of private spending on other goods. For example, the decision to consume S^* units of private schooling means that the family forgoes consumption of AE units of other goods in order to pay private school tuition. Part of this amount, BC, is the public subsidy that the family gives up by not attending public schools.

Figures 9.2 through 9.4 show how different families respond to these options. Figure 9.2 shows how the presence of subsidized public schools affects the economic well-being and behavior of households whose tastes for education are such that they would choose to buy the same or less schooling in the private market that is provided by the public system. As may be seen, the existence of the subsidized public alternative either has no effect on the quantity of education consumed if public quantity S_p is the same as the desired quantity of private schooling or causes the household to consume more education if $S_p > S_o$. In both cases, the presence of free public schools raises the economic well-being of the household. In the case of the household with the indifference curves labeled b_1b_1 and b_2b_2, the option to attend free public schools is equivalent to increasing the household's cash income by the amount of the per-pupil cost of public schooling. In the case of the household with the indifference curves labeled a_1a_1 and

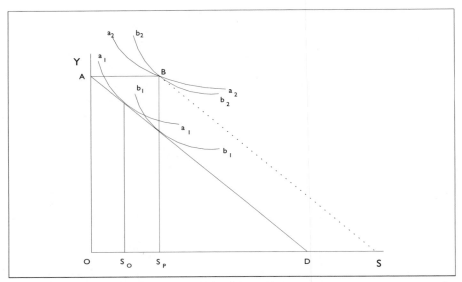

Figure 9.2   Consumer Choice: Households with Desired Quantity ≤ Sp Consume Sp.

a_2a_2, the option to attend free public schools is worth less to the household than the per-pupil cost because these households are compelled to consume more schooling than they would choose if they received an unrestricted cash grant equal in value to the public school subsidy.

Figures 9.3 and 9.4 show how public schooling affects the behavior of families who, in the absence of public schools, demand more education than is provided publicly. In figure 9.3, the family chooses public schooling even though it would prefer more schooling than is publicly provided. It does so because it values the public subsidy (more precisely, the added consumption of other goods made possible by that subsidy) more than it values the higher quantity of education that can be purchased privately. In figure 9.4, however, the family chooses private schooling despite the fact that it gives up the public subsidy to do so. That is, the choice depends on how the household trades off schooling versus other consumption.

Determinants of Private School Choice

The economic model of school choice implies that the decision to attend private instead of public schools will be sensitive to factors that affect the comparative benefits of private versus public schools and/or the comparative costs of these options. These factors depend on attributes of the family as well as on attributes of the public and private school choices.

Specifically, the economic model of school choice predicts that, holding public school quantity, tastes for education, and private school tuition constant, the likelihood of selecting private schools, as in figure 9.4,

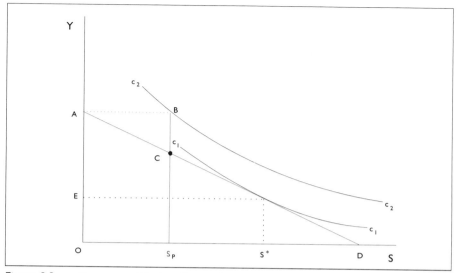

Figure 9.3   Consumer Choice: Some Households with Desired Quantity > Sp Consume Sp.

increases with family income because rising income widens the gap between the desired quantity of education, S* and the quantity that is publicly provided, S_p. The model also predicts that, holding family income, public school quantity, and private school tuition constant, the likelihood of selecting private schools will increase the more willing the family is to substitute education for other goods–for example, the greater its taste for education generally.

In addition, holding family income, tastes for education, and private school tuition constant, the model predicts that a family will be more likely to choose private schooling the larger is the (perceived) gap between public and private school quantity. Finally, holding family income, tastes for education, and the private/public quantity gap constant, the model predicts that a family will be more likely to choose private schooling the lower the tuition that is charged by private schools.

A Simple Model of Vouchers

The economic model of school choice summarized above provides a simple yet useful framework for analyzing how different types of families would respond to the introduction of a "California-style" voucher, such as that proposed in California Proposition 174.

Figure 9.5 corresponds to figure 9.1 and shows how a voucher that can be spent on up to *CV* of tuition changes the opportunities faced by families with school-age children. As in figure 9.1, line *AD* in figure 9.5 is family

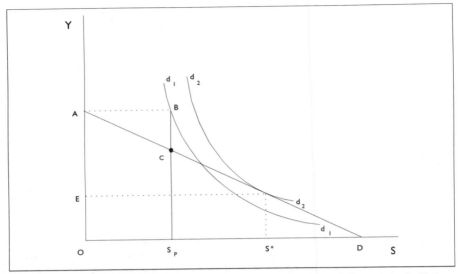

Figure 9.4   Consumer Choice: Some Households with Desired Quantity > Sp Shift to Private Schools.

income after taxes available for spending on education and all other goods (ignoring free public schools and vouchers), and S_p is the amount of public schooling that is available to households at no additional cost.

Consider first the case of public schooling. Under a voucher scheme, if a family sends its child(ren) to public school, two administrative arrangements are possible. One option would simply be to retain the status quo in public schools so that families would neither receive a voucher nor be charged for attending public schools. Alternatively, a family attending public schools could be charged an amount equal to the voucher, which would permit it to consume A units of other goods and S_p units of public schooling just as in figure 9.1, where no voucher is provided. If the voucher proposed under a California-style voucher were implemented in this manner, it would change the administrative mechanism by which attendance at public schools was subsidized but not the size of the subsidy. In the absence of the subsidy, parents would be able to consume S_p units of public schooling at no out-of-pocket cost. Under the proposed voucher, parents would have access to the same amount of public education, at a charge that would be exactly offset by the voucher. The voucher would simply substitute a portion of the direct subsidy provided to public schools, without augmenting that subsidy.

Unlike figure 9.1, however, if the family sends its child(ren) to a private school, it could use the voucher to offset up to CV ($2,600 in the case of Proposition 174) of the cost of private school tuition. This changes the family's opportunities in several ways. First, the voucher makes it possible

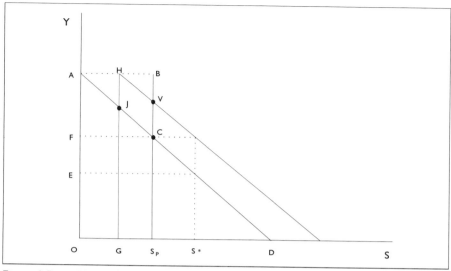

Figure 9.5   Effect of Introducing a California-Style Voucher

for the family to consume the quantity of private education that can be purchased with CV. This alternative is represented by OG units in figure 9.5. If the voucher is structured so that it can only be spent on tuition and cannot be used for other purposes, OG also defines the minimum amount of private education that the household could consume under the voucher program.

As in figure 9.3, the household can also consume more education privately than is provided in the public schools. With a voucher of CV, however, doing so requires the family to forego less consumption of other goods. For example, consuming S* units of private schooling requires the family to forego only AF units of other consumption, instead of AE units.

It is easily seen from figure 9.5 that replacing part of the direct public school subsidy with a voucher changes neither the behavior nor the economic well-being of households whose desired level of schooling in the absence of any subsidy is less than or equal to S_p. In the absence of the voucher, such families would choose public schools and consume A units of Y and S_p. This remains the economically rational choice after the voucher. This is true even in the case of families whose desired level of schooling absent subsidies is less than S_p. Though the voucher would, in principle, allow such families to consume A units of Y and $G < S_p$ units of schooling, it would also allow such families to consume the same amount of other goods (for example, A units), while consuming more education (for example, $S_p > G$) if they remained in public schools. Thus, enactment of voucher schemes as that embodied in Proposition 174 would have no

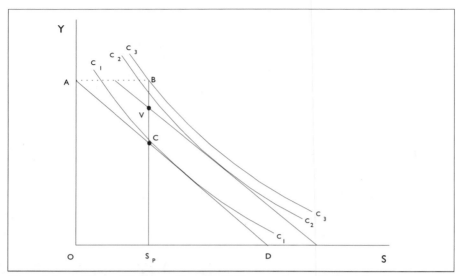

Figure 9.6   Effect of Voucher: Household Elects to Stay in Public School.

immediate effect on the amount of education consumed or the economic well-being of households whose desired amount of schooling was at or below that provided by their public school system.

Figures 9.6 and 9.7 show how providing a voucher affects families in public schools who have what might be termed a "latent demand" for private schooling. In these cases, providing a voucher would make private schooling more attractive than before because, in order to attend private school, a family would have to forgo only the *difference* between the public school subsidy BC and the voucher CV and not the entire subsidy as in figure 9.1 where there is no voucher. In figure 9.6, the family's best alternative is to remain in public school despite this change. In figure 9.7, however, the voucher provides enough incentive for the family to switch from public to private schools.

Figure 9.8 shows the effects of providing a voucher to families with children already in private schools. For these families, the voucher would be equivalent to an unrestricted cash grant equal in value to the voucher. In general, such households could be expected to respond to vouchers by purchasing more of all goods, including private education.

Predicted Effects of Vouchers on Latent Demanders

The number and the types of families depicted in figure 9.7 figured significantly in the policy debate about Proposition 174 and would play a similar role in debates about introducing vouchers elsewhere. This is so for several reasons. First, the fiscal effects of the California voucher proposal depended critically on the number of households who can be expected to

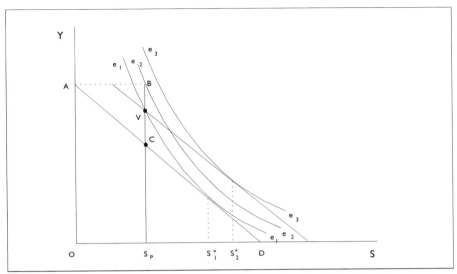

Figure 9.7   Effect of Voucher: Household Elects to Stay in Public School.

switch from public to private schools. The arithmetic was straightforward. Providing a voucher of $2,600 to each of the roughly 500,000 children currently enrolled in California private schools would have entailed an additional $1.3 billion in budgetary costs. At the same time, it was estimated that California would save $1,100 on each student enrolled in a public school who switched to a private school. Thus, for the proposed voucher to break even in budgetary terms, roughly 1 million students, out of some 5 million currently enrolled in California public schools, would have had to switch from public to private schools.

Second, as we have discussed above, the desired policy outcome of the voucher proposal depends on the (assumed) beneficial effects of competition between private and public schools for students. Families like those shown in figure 9.7 play a central role in this process because they comprise the "critical margin" at which such competition will take place.

Both the size and the character of this critical margin matter. While the economic model of school choice does not offer predictions about how many latent demanders will respond to a voucher, it provides some clues both about which families are most likely to switch, and why. These predictions largely parallel those about the determinants of private/public school choice in the absence of vouchers.

Reasons for Moving

Perhaps the most important prediction of the model for proponents of vouchers is that, holding income and tastes for education constant, the

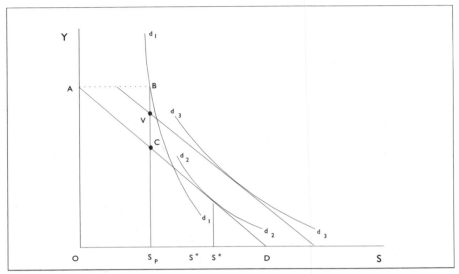

Figure 9.8   For Current Private School Parents, Voucher Acts as a Cash Subsidy.

likelihood of switching will increase as the (perceived) gap between the quantity of private versus public schooling widens. In this sense, public school systems will face stronger incentives to compete for students where the "need" for such competition is greatest.

Moreover, the model suggests that so long as parents care about "conventional" dimensions of educational quality, such as academic achievement, the concerns of voucher opponents that parents will use vouchers to acquire less education for their children in the private sector seem somewhat overstated. Thus, for example, while the California voucher proposal would, in principle, have allowed anyone to open a voucher-re-deeming private school with 25 or more students, it is hardly a foregone conclusion that such schools would have attracted latent demanders away from public schools.

Attributes of Movers

At the same time, the model also predicts that, holding private school tuition and public school quantity/quality constant, the likelihood of switching from public to private schools will vary positively with family income and family tastes for education. This implies that, at least initially, providing a California-style voucher may lower the average income of families remaining in public schools as well as the overall demand of those families for educational quantity/quality. This prediction of the economic model of school choice has mixed implications for the ultimate success of vouchers.

Effect of Price

Finally, the model predicts that latent demanders will be most likely to switch the higher is the ratio of the voucher CV to the implicit public school subsidy BC. This implies that the effects of vouchers will vary depending on local market conditions because this ratio depends on the cost of schooling. In other words, the effects of introducing vouchers may not be the same within a state.

Effects of Vouchers on Private School Families

Families with children already in private schools, like those shown in figure 9.8, also figured in the debate about Proposition 174, though for different reasons than did the latent demanders. Unlike latent demanders, such families do not provide the impetus for greater competition between public and private schools because they have already voted with their feet in selecting the latter. Thus, families with children already in private schools will not affect the outcomes of adopting a California-style voucher in the same way as families who are prompted to switch from public to private schools.

Indeed, because such families have chosen private schools, a California-style voucher would offer them a public subsidy for doing something they are already doing. In this sense, Proposition 174, like any similar voucher proposal, would confer "windfall gains" on families like those shown in figure 9.8.

The important policy question, however, is what to make of such windfalls. Critics of vouchers are concerned that vouchers will funnel tax dollars to subsidize consumption of private education by affluent families. Proponents of vouchers, however, counter that some families who select private schools do so in response to the government's failure to provide adequate schooling, for example, in central cities. Under this view the windfall gain received by these families simply allows them to share more equitably in a public benefit enjoyed by families whose children have access to high-quality public schools.

For these reasons, the socioeconomic profile of families with children already in private schools has a direct and important effect on the distributional incidence of voucher schemes like Proposition 174. The predictions of the economic model of school choice suggest that this profile will have elements that fit the priors of both voucher critics and voucher supporters. For example, the model predicts that, holding public school quality constant, higher income increases the likelihood of attending private schools, as claimed by voucher critics. At the same time, the model also predicts that families will have a greater incentive to choose private schools when public school quality is relatively poor. If lower public school quality is correlated with lower income, some lower-income families will have a strong incentive to choose private schools, as claimed by voucher supporters.

Evidence

What kinds of families will switch from public to private schools in response to vouchers? What attributes of public and private schools are likely to motivate the decision to switch? How many families can be expected to switch? As is suggested in the introduction, there is virtually no direct evidence bearing on these questions, and even indirect evidence is sparse. In addition, we present evidence on whether student achievement is higher in private versus public schools, an argument that underlies much of the debate on school choice. The evidence we find is inconclusive.

Types of Evidence

Broadly speaking, there are three types of evidence that could be brought to bear on the potential response to a voucher scheme like that proposed in California. Not surprisingly, each has its own limitations.

Experimental Data—Several experiments have been conducted, or are underway, to examine the effects of allowing school choice. Such experiments provide some clues about what prompts parents to switch schools but provide little information about the size or socioeconomic character of the response to a voucher proposal such as that embodied in Proposition 174. This is mainly because these experiments have been designed to assess the effects of school choice on the educational outcomes of those participating in the experiments.

Econometric Studies—Econometric studies of the determinants of private/public school choice under the current system (for example, in the absence of vouchers) are another source of evidence on the possible response to a voucher scheme such as Proposition 174. These studies fall into two categories: studies with aggregate data and studies with microlevel data. The former consist of a number of studies that attempt to predict private and public school enrollments either across school districts, counties, or census tracts; within states; or across states as a function of variables suggested by the economic model of private/public school choice (Sonstelie 1979 and 1982; Gemello and Osman 1984; Martinez-Vasquez and Seaman 1985; West and Palsson 1988; Hamilton and Macauley 1991; and Schmidt 1992). These studies are useful because they provide a check on the empirical validity of the economic model of school choice summarized above.

Yet, for several reasons, aggregate studies of private/public school enrollments are of limited value for gauging the initial response to voucher schemes. For example, the process of aggregating data into geographic units has generally made it possible to examine the effects of only a limited range of family characteristics on school choice. More generally, it is conceptually unclear how to make inferences from such aggregate data about how individual choices would be affected by a change in opportunities such as that resulting from introducing a voucher scheme. (For an excellent discussion of the limitations of aggregate studies, see Lankford and Wyckoff, 1992.)

Studies with microlevel data consist of a smaller number of studies that attempt to explain school choices made at the individual family level using micro data (Noell and Myers 1983; Kirby and Darling-Hammond 1988; Long and Toma 1988; and Lankford and Wyckoff 1992; and Buddin, Cordes, and Kirby 1993). As cogently argued by Lankford and Wyckoff (1992), in principle, such studies can be used to draw useful inferences about how changes in schooling opportunities will affect individual choices, which can then be consistently aggregated to estimate the aggregate effects of such changes.

In practice, however, such studies face their own data limitations. While micro data generally provide a rich array of information about individual family characteristics, they provide little or no information on the educational opportunities facing the individual family. Thus, researchers need to augment data on individual families as best they can with information on the characteristics of public and private schools among which individual families are presumed to choose. This is difficult to do mainly because of the limitations of data about private schools.

Qualitative Evidence—Lastly, evidence of a more qualitative sort about the possible effects of introducing vouchers can be gleaned from sources such as responses to surveys or observed responses to school choice programs in other countries. The usual caveats to the use of such data apply. Responses about what people say they might do in surveys may not track well with actual behavior and responses to school choice programs in other countries may reflect important institutional and cultural differences.

Main Findings

Despite the limitations of these various sources of evidence, it is nonetheless useful to briefly examine the picture they paint about possible responses to a voucher.

Who Will Switch?—Evidence on who switches comes from two sources—one, econometric studies based on cross-sectional data that analyze the characteristics of those parents choosing private schools and the Milwaukee experiment. There is strong, consistent econometric evidence that, other things equal, the probability of choosing private over public school increases with parental income and with parental education (which is assumed to be correlated with family tastes for education), as predicted by the economic model of school choice.

Results from the ongoing Milwaukee school choice experiment provide some additional evidence that higher levels of parental education increase the likelihood of choosing private over public school when given a choice. Choice parents, when compared to similar parents who are not in the program, appear to be more educated, to have somewhat higher educational expectations for their children, and to be more involved in their children's education. For more detail, see Witte, Bailey, and Thorn (1992).

Taken together, these results imply that families with higher parental incomes and/or education levels will be more responsive to the introduction of vouchers than will other families. This provides some empirical support for the above-stated conjecture that, initially, voucher schemes like the California proposal may lower the average income and the overall demand for educational quantity/quality among families remaining in public schools.

There is also evidence that residents of central cities are more likely to choose private schools. Lankford and Wyckoff (1992) report that the probability of attending a religious school increases by a factor of three for those living in central cities as compared to those living elsewhere in the Standard Metropolitan Statistical Area. Long and Toma (1988) also find that residence in central cities has a large positive effect on private schooling and speculate that this may be due to the greater crime and discipline problems that plague central city public schools.

Thus, while the estimated effects of income and education suggest that the windfall gains from introducing a voucher will tend to benefit higher-income and better-educated families, the evidence also provides support for the view that vouchers will benefit families who currently do not enjoy the same access to the good-quality, publicly subsidized public education enjoyed by other families because they reside in central cities.

Evidence on the attributes of schools that prompt families to choose private schools is also broadly consistent with the economic model of school choice, though it is more mixed than evidence on the effects of parental income and education. Econometric studies generally, though not uniformly, find that the probability of choosing private school rises as the "quantity/quality" of public schooling, as measured by variables such as test scores and per-pupil spending, declines. Responses to a 1983 household survey administered by the U.S. Department of Education, summarized in Lankford and Wyckoff (1992), also indicate that traditional dimensions of educational quality, such as staff, discipline, and academic standards, are considered to be "very important factors" in choice of school.

There is, however, also evidence that parents value attributes of schools that are not related to educational outcomes as conventionally defined. As noted by the Carnegie Foundation (1992), factors such as proximity to either home or work are frequently given as much or more prominence as academic considerations in surveys of parents who participate in choice programs limited to public schools that now exist in several states.

These latter findings should be interpreted with some care. It is possible that academic quality may matter less in choosing among alternative public schools because there is less variation in academic quality among public schools than between public and private schools. If so, the responses noted by the Carnegie Foundation need not indicate that differences in academic quantity/quality are not important in determining the response of parents to vouchers.

If, however, these findings are applicable to private/public school choice, they suggest that voucher proposals, such as Proposition 174, may prompt families to switch from public to private schools for reasons other than differences in academic quality. This would imply that the quantity/quality of education may not play as central a role in defining the "terms of competition" between public and private providers of education as voucher proponents would like.

How Many Families Will Switch?—Empirical evidence on how many families would switch from public to private schools if offered a voucher is quite limited. A principal reason is that school vouchers affect individual choices through their effect on the relative cost of public versus private schooling, and there is surprisingly little evidence on how these relative costs actually affect private/public school choice.

For example, among 14 econometric studies of school choice, six fail to include any variable for private school tuition as a determinant of private/public school choice, four find a negative and significant relationship between tuition and private enrollment as predicted by the economic model of school choice, one finds a negative and significant effect of tuition on nonparochial school enrollment and a positive (but insignificant) effect of parochial tuition on parochial enrollment, and three either fail to find a significant relationship between private school tuition and private school choice or find a positive relationship, contrary to theoretical expectations.

Among the studies that find a significant, negative relationship between private tuition and school choice, the range of estimates is wide. Kirby and Darling-Hammond (1988), Noell and Myers (1983), and Buddin, Cordes, and Kirby (1993) find that, although the effect of tuition on private school choice is negative and statistically significant, it is small. For example, the estimates obtained by Noell and Myers imply that cutting the cost of private schooling in half would increase the probability of attending private schools by at most 20 percent (for example, if the likelihood of attending private school was 0.2 before the change, cutting private school tuition by 50 percent would increase the likelihood to 0.22). Buddin, Cordes, and Kirby report an elasticity of −0.28 in private, elementary school enrollment with respect to tuition at nonreligious, private schools (that is, a 1 percent increase in private tuition is associated with a 0.28 percent decline in private enrollments).

Lankford and Wyckoff (1992), however, estimate that the probability of private school choice is quite sensitive to cost. In contrast to Noell and Myers, their estimates imply that cutting private school tuition by 50 percent would increase the likelihood of choosing private schools by between 45 and 160 percent (for example, if the likelihood of attending private school was 0.20 before the change, cutting private school tuition by 50 percent would increase the likelihood to between 0.29 and 0.52).

The Lankford and Wyckoff paper not only provides the main evidence that private school choice is likely to be sensitive to cost, but it also simulates how providing a voucher that reduced private school tuition to zero would affect the size and composition of religious school enrollment. The simulation implies that such a policy would double the proportion of students enrolled in private religious schools from 0.12 to 0.25.

A survey done by the Carnegie Foundation for the Advancement of Teaching in 1992 asked approximately 1,000 parents, "Is there some other school to which you would like to send your child? This school could be public or private, inside, or outside of your district, with your child's grade level." In response, 70 percent of parents said no, another 9 percent wished to transfer to a public school, and 19 percent of parents expressed a desire to transfer to private schools. However, because the desired schools were frequently rather far away (66 percent were 5 miles away or more), the availability of transportation was also important in determining whether such households would actually pursue these alternatives if given an opportunity. Eighty-three percent said they would be able to personally arrange to get their child to the alternative school at their expense, while 15 percent said they would be unable to do so.

Overall, then, neither the econometric nor the survey evidence provides much support for those who would argue that voucher schemes like Proposition 174 will provide budgetary savings (which, as we said earlier, would only occur if *over* 20 percent of families currently enrolled in public schools switched to private schools). One cannot, however, rule out the possibility that such schemes could be budget-neutral since this would require (for example, under Proposition 174) that "only" one-fifth of public school families switch to private schools. Though this response is greater than that which would be predicted by studies such as Kirby and Darling-Hammond (1988), Noell and Myers (1983), and Buddin, Cordes, and Kirby (1993), it is of the same order of magnitude as that simulated by Lankford and Wyckoff (1992) and of the same percentage as those expressing dissatisfaction with public schools in the Carnegie Foundation survey.

Student Achievement in Private versus Public Schools—Aside from how families react to school vouchers, we need to examine what increased competition between private and public schools and the likely transfer of large numbers of public school students would do to educational outcomes and the quality of education. Proponents believe that competition would force public schools to model themselves after more effective and efficient private schools and that, as a consequence, student achievement would be higher, pointing to the higher test scores of private school students. However, the evidence regarding the effectiveness of private schools appears somewhat mixed, suggesting that it is unclear exactly what the effect on educational outcomes is likely to be.

In a highly publicized study, Coleman, Koffer, and Kilgore (1981) used data from *High School and Beyond*, a federally funded study of 58,728 students attending 1,016 schools of various types to analyze this question. They concluded: "In general, with background characteristics controlled, Catholic school sophomores perform at the highest level, sophomores in other private schools next, and sophomores in the public schools lowest."[9] Their interpretation of these differences is that they represent the gain in achievement that a public school student could expect were he or she to attend a Catholic or other private school. However, Murnane (1983) points out that the crucial question is what the gain in achievement would be if the public school student *along with his public school peers* attended a Catholic or other private school–that is, what would be the gain in achievement if the Catholic school demographic composition mirrored that of the public schools. He finds substantially different results from those reported above, with the Catholic/public school gap being one-half of that reported by Coleman, Hoffer, and Kilgore (1981) and little or no difference between the other private schools and public schools.

Coleman, Hoffer, and Kilgore's analysis (1981) has been the subject of much criticism, ranging from their dependent variable and the way they handled missing data, to the variables used for controlling differences in the socioeconomic composition of private and public schools. Other researchers, using the same database, have reported varying results. Willms (1984) found that there are no differences in academic achievement for advantaged whites across public and private schools but small differences for minority and disadvantaged students, which may be partly explained by differential selection. His second study stresses the fact that there is no pervasive private schooling effect for the average child and that the range in school effectiveness within the private and public sectors far outweighs the differences between them.

Lee and Bryk (1989), in a thorough study of the effect of school composition and types of advanced courses on mathematics achievement, concluded that the private sector variable was not statistically significant.

However, a recent study by Chubb and Moe (1990) found that there were major differences between private and public schools and that students in private schools outperformed their public school counterparts. There has been considerable criticism of their study, one of the more important being that they *"never directly tested the differential effect of public and private schools on achievement."*[10]

A recent article by Evans and Schwab (1993) reanalyzes the *High School and Beyond* data and finds that Catholic schools are more effective than public schools. Their estimates suggest that a Catholic school senior will score about 2.4 points higher than a public school senior, with an average score of 30. They also find that the benefits of Catholic school education are concentrated among the less able students and that the difference between Catholic and public school test scores declines sharply as one moves up the test score distribution.

To summarize, there appears to be some evidence that less able students do better in private, particularly Catholic schools. However, the evidence does not appear to be overwhelming, and it is still an open question as to whether private schools are more effective than public schools.

The above studies are econometric studies based on nonexperimental data. The evidence from the only experiment in private/public school choice being conducted in Milwaukee is mixed. Choice students were ahead of other low-income Milwaukee Public School students in reading but significantly behind in mathematics in the first year. In the second year, the trend in reading was reversed with choice students being considerably behind in reading but about the same level in mathematics. Witte, Bailey, and Thorn (1992) attribute this fluctuation in achievement tests to attrition of high-achievers from the program and an influx of very low-achieving students in the second year. They warn, however, that the sample sizes are very small and that results should be interpreted with a great deal of caution.

Conclusions

The main objective of this paper has been to examine a number of questions related to educational vouchers and the likely initial response of families with school-aged children to the introduction of a voucher such as that proposed in California's Proposition 174. The theory and evidence presented here lead to a number of conclusions and several unanswered questions. In particular:

- Previous empirical literature provides evidence that families with higher parental incomes and/or education levels will be more apt to choose private schools than will other families. This suggests that, initially, voucher schemes like Proposition 174 may lower the average income and the overall demand for educational quantity/quality among families remaining in public schools.

- The estimated effects of income and education suggest that the windfall gains from introducing a voucher will tend to benefit higher-income and better-educated families.

- However, there is also econometric evidence to support the view that vouchers will benefit families who currently do not enjoy the same access to good quality, publicly subsidized public education enjoyed by other families because they reside in central cities.

- Econometric studies also find that households behave like smart consumers in general–the probability of choosing a private school rises as the "quantity/quality" of public schooling, as measured by variables such as test scores and per-pupil spending, declines.

- Empirical evidence on how many families would switch from public to private schools if offered a voucher is quite limited, principally because there is surprisingly little evidence on how the relative costs of private/public schooling actually affect private/public school choice.

- The beneficial effects of competition–a point highly stressed by proponents–on the quality of public schools and overall educational outcomes remains uncertain for two reasons. First, a large influx of students into private schools due to competition may cause a decline in achievement levels at such schools. Second, the evidence that private schools are, in themselves, more effective and of higher quality than public schools is rather mixed.

Overall, educational vouchers appear to hold promise as a vehicle for school reform, but the many unresolved questions suggest that we need to proceed with some caution and gather more information through demonstrations and experiments before launching a full-scale effort.

Notes

1. The California voucher plan also had two interesting but little discussed provisions. First, the plan encouraged the conversion of public schools into semiautonomous charter schools that would accept educational vouchers. This provision would allow substantial expansion of the charter school concept in the state. Second, the plan provided for open enrollment across school districts in the state, which presumably would foster greater competition among public schools. The law allowed first priority for local residents, however, and it is unclear whether districts would have substantial incentives to compete for students from adjacent districts.

2. For more detail, see Darling-Hammond and Kirby (1985) and Wells (1993).

3. Justice White, Committee for Public Education and Religious Liberty v. Regan, 444 U.S. 646, 662 (1980).

4. Chubb and Moe (1990), 6.

5. Levin (1990), 267.

6. Astin (1992), 257.

7. Coleman (1992), 260.

8. Witte (1992), 209.

9. Coleman, Hoffer, and Kilgore (1981), 173.

10. Witte (1992), 220.

References

Astin, A. W. "Educational 'Choice': Its Appeal May Be Illusory." *Sociology of Education*, 65, 4 (1992): 255–59.

Bryk, A. S., and V. E. Lee. *Catholic Schools and the Common Good*. Cambridge, MA: Harvard University Press, 1993.

Buddin, R., J. J. Cordes, and S. N. Kirby. *Public School Finance and Public School Choice: Examining the California Education Voucher Proposal*. Paper presented at the Association for Public Policy and Management Fourteenth Annual Research Conference. Washington, D.C., 1993.

Carnegie Foundation for the Advancement of Teaching. *School Choice: A Special Report*. Princeton, NJ: Carnegie Foundation, 1992.

Chubb, J. E., and T. M. Moe. "Choice Is a Panacea". *The Brookings Review* (summer 1990).

Coleman, J. S. "Some Points on Choice in Education." *Sociology of Education* 65, 4 (1992): 260–62.

Coleman, J. S., T. Hoffer, and S. Kilgore. *Public and Private Schools*. Chicago: National Opinion Research Center, 1981.

———. *High School Achievement: Public, Catholic, and Private Schools Compared*. New York: Basic Books, 1982.

Coons, J. E., and S. D. Sugarman. *Education by Choice*. Berkeley, CA: University of California Press, 1978.

Darling-Hammond, L., and S. N. Kirby. *Tuition Tax Deductions and Parent School Choice: A Case Study of Minnesota*, RAND, R-3294–NIE. 1985.

Evans, W. N., and R. M. Schwab. *Our Lady of Sacred Heart vs. PS 112: The Relative Efficiency of Catholic and Public Schools*. Mimeograph, 1993.

Gemello, J. M., and J. W. Osman. "Estimating the Demand for Private School Enrollment." *American Journal of Education* (1984): 262–79.

Friedman, M.. "The Role of Government in Education." In *Economics and the Public Interest*. Edited by R. A. Solo, 123–44. New Brunswick, NJ: Rutgers University Press, 1955.

Guerra, M., J. *Dollars and Sense: Catholic High Schools and Their Finances 1992*. Washington, D.C.: National Catholic Educational Association, 1993.

Hamilton, B. W., and M. K. Macauley. "Determinants and Consequences of the Private-Public School Choice." *Journal of Urban Economics* 29 (1991): 282–94.

Kealey, R. J. *United States Catholic Elementary Schools and Their Finances, 1991*. Washington, D.C.: National Catholic Education Association, 1992.

Kirby, S. N., and L. Darling-Hammond. "Parental School Choice: A Case Study of Minnesota." *Journal of Policy Analysis and Management* 8 (1988): 506–18.

Koppich, J. E. "Demography, Diversity, and Dollars: Rethinking School Finance Policy in California." In *Who Pays for Student Diversity*. Edited by J. G. Ward and P. Anthony. Newbury Park, CA: Sage Publications, 1992.

Lankford, H., and J. Wyckoff, "Primary and Secondary School Choice Among Public and Religious Alternatives." *Economics of Education Review* 11 (1992): 317–37.

Lee, V. E., and A. S. Bryk. "A Multilevel Model of the Social Distribution of High School Achievement." *Sociology of Education* 62 (1989): 172–92.

Levin, H. M. "The Theory of Choice Applied to Education." In *Choice and Control in American Education, Volume 1: The Theory of Choice and Control in Education* Edited by W. H. Clune and J. F. Witte, 247–84. London: The Falmer Press, 1990.

Levin, H. M. "The Economics of Educational Choice." *Economics of Education Review* 10, 2 (1991): 137–58.

Long, J. E., and E. F. Toma. "The Determinants of Private School Attendance, 1970–1980." *The Review of Economics and Statistics* 70 (1988): 351–56.

Martinez-Vazquez, J., and B. A. Seaman. "Private Schooling and the Tiebout Hypothesis." *Public Finance Quarterly* 13 (1985): 293–318.

Murnane, R. J. "The Uncertain Consequences of Tuition Tax Credits: An Analysis of Student Achievement and Economic Incentives." In *Public Dollars for Private Schools*. Edited by T. James and H. M. Levin. Philadelphia, PA: Temple University Press, 1983.

Peltzman, S. "The Effect of Government Subsidies-in-Kind on Private Expenditures: The Case of Higher Education." *The Journal of Political Economy* 81, 1 (1973): 1–27.

Schmidt, A. B. "Private School Enrollment in Metropolitan Areas." *Public Finance Quarterly* 20 (1992): 298–320.

Sonstelie, J. "Public School Quality and Private School Enrollments." *National Tax Journal* (Supplement) (1979), 343–53.

———. "The Welfare Cost of Free Public Schools." *Journal of Political Economy* 90 (1982): 794–808.

U.S. Bureau of the Census. *Statistical Abstract of the United States*: 1993, (113th Edition). Washington, D.C.: U.S. Government Printing Office, 1993.

Wells, A. S. *Time to Choose: America at the Crossroads of School Choice Policy*. New York: Hill and Wang, 1993.

West, E. G. and H. Palsson. "Parental Choice of School Characteristics: Estimation Using State-Wide Data." *Economic Inquiry* 26 (1988): 725–40.

Willms, J. D. "School Effectiveness within the Public and Private Sectors." *Evaluation Review* 8, 1 (1984): 113–35.

Witte, J. F. "Public Subsidies for Private Schools: What We Know and How to Proceed." *Educational Policy* 6 (1992): 206–27.

Witte, J. F., A. B. Bailey, and C. A. Thorn. *Second-Year Report: Milwaukee Parental Choice Program*. December 1992.

Young, T. W., and E. Clinchy. *Choice in Public Education*. New York: Teachers College Press, 1992.

10

Information, Prices, and Competition in the Child-Care Market: What Role Should Government Play?

Ellen B. Magenheim

Introduction

When child care is discussed by economists, it is usually discussed from the perspective of labor supply. That is, how will the availability of child care affect the decision of women to participate in the labor market? Ellen Magenheim's chapter takes an entirely different perspective. Her purpose is to examine the market for child care itself. She uses the theory of monopolistic competition in the analysis.

Magenheim examines both positive and normative issues. In the area of positive economics, there are the questions of the determinants of demand for child-care services, the nature of the supply response, and the determinants of the quality of child-care services. The main focus, however, is on normative or policy analysis. Here the question concerns the nature and magnitude of potential market failure in the child-care industry, and appropriate responses to it.

To some, the idea of regulation of child-care services may seem obvious, but regulation of many economists approach the idea of governmental regulation skeptically. Governments may intend one action and achieve another. Consider, for example, licensing of child-care centers. There are several possible effects of such licensing. First, licensing reduces the supply of such centers and so would tend to raise the price (this on the argument that licensing must exclude *some potential competitors). Indeed, economists*

269

regard some kinds of licensing as mostly a barrier to entry, *that is, its true purpose is to protect the market for those currently licensed. Licensing also potentially increases quality, but it increases quality to the level determined by a government bureaucrat, not to the level determined by the consumer. We would not tolerate such licensing to ensure quality in our choice of VCRs, but the governmental purpose in licensing child-care seems more important. Nonetheless, governmental regulation of quality necessarily reduces choice. Finally, inept government licensing may serve to mask ineptitude and low quality.*

Magenheim takes a different view. For her, the government may contribute positively to the provision of quality child care, and also may overcome potential market failure associated with informational asymmetries. What are these asymmetries? Information about prices and quality levels are not universally available, as assumed by many economic models. In the face of such informational asymmetries, government may have a role in sponsoring resource and referral agencies (R&Rs) or enhancing information availability through licensing and regulation. Magenheim examines a wide scope of literature on empirical questions relating to child care. One clear conclusion is that more work needs to be done and better data needs to be gathered to support policy conclusions in this important area and in the role the government may play in improving the operation of the child-care market.

The structure of the child-care industry most closely resembles the theoretical model of monopolistic competition. Relatively low barriers to entry and exit indicate that the market will be competitive, but differentiated products endow producers with some market power. Products can be differentiated along a number of dimensions, including location, quality, hours of service, legal status, and sponsorship. These characteristics have important implications for both the types and extent of competition that will be observed among child-care producers.

As an imperfectly competitive industry, the operation of which has implications for a variety of social goals and program, there is room for government intervention in the child-care market. This takes a variety of forms, from indirect financial supports (tax credits for child-care consumers) to direct financial supports (subsidies to providers) to regulation of staff/child ratios and safety requirements. The extent to which these forms of government intervention improve the efficiency and equity of the child-care market is a subject of considerable debate. One area in which it is agreed that the government is doing very little is in the area of information asymmetries.

Although standard analyses of monopolistically competitive markets do not focus on the role of information, they must be considered in any study of behavior in the child-care industry. In perfect competition we assume that all buyers and sellers have complete and perfect information and never make a mistaken decision due to misinformation. From the perspective of consumers, information problems in child-care markets are of two types: asymmetric information, in which the seller knows the quality of a good and the buyer does not, and imperfect consumer information about prices, which arises because price searching is costly. Both of these problems have important efficiency implications. Since it may be difficult or impossible for consumers to get full information about quality, providers may move toward producing a lower level of quality than they would in a world of perfect information in which consumers could effectively vote with their dollars. Search costs that prevent consumers from obtaining full information about prices may lead to firms charging prices above marginal costs and thus to a range of prices being offered within the same market for the same or very similar goods. The implications are that families purchasing child care may face higher prices, lower quality, and greater variation across both parameters than they would in a world of perfect information. Information shortages prevent consumers from exerting competitive pressure on product characteristics and prices.

To the extent that increased competition can lead to lower prices and higher quality (both with lower variance across providers) it is desirable to find cost-efficient ways to increase competition. Nevertheless, we do not know much about the nature of competition among child-care providers. Competition in child-care markets, as in any nonperfectly competitive market, can take the forms of price and nonprice competition. In this market, the latter appears to be the dominant mode of competition and proceeds along the lines of such variables as quality, legal status and sponsorship, and location and types of services offered. A more specific consideration is the extent to which providers compete with rivals offering related but not identical goods–for example, is it likely that for-profit centers are concerned with the characteristics of care offered by family day care homes or nonprofit centers, or neither?

This chapter examines, on a general level, the characteristics of the child-care market and the roles played by the government in that market and, at a more specific level, the nature of information problems and the government's role in solving them. The second section offers a sketch of the component elements and functioning of the child-care market. The third section is a discussion of the reasons for government intervention in the child-care market, the role of the public sector in the child-care market, and a review of the actual forms that intervention takes. The fourth section is a discussion of the problems of information availability in the child-care market and of the appropriate role for government involvement in information dissemination. The fifth section presents conclusions and suggestions for changes in government involvement in the child-care market.

A Review of the Component Elements and Functioning of the Child-Care Market

This review will focus less on the analytical details of past research and more on illustrating the types of questions being asked and the major findings. The literature on the economics of child care is relatively small and new. This is partially because, until recently, there has continued to be a lack of comprehensive data sets and because child care was not considered an interesting topic except by a very few economists (e.g., Robins and Spiegelman 1978; Robins and Weiner 1978; and Rose-Ackerman 1983, 1986). The bulk of the work has been done from a labor economics perspective with a focus on how child-care costs and availability affect women's labor supply decisions. More recently, work has expanded to include research on the organization of the child-care industry, cost structures and their relationship to quality, and the effects of regulations on child-care availability, among other topics.

Child-Care Costs and Labor Supply

There are significant negative effects of child-care costs on labor market participation of mothers of young children (Connelly 1992). Further, significant work-related costs are imposed on two-earner families. Middle- and upper-income women do not gain as much additional income as do lower-income women, suggesting that these mothers may work in part for noneconomic benefits (Hanson and Ooms 1991). Higher mother's wages are associated with an earlier return to work after childbirth, and higher family income is associated with a later return to work (Leibowitz, Klerman, and Waite 1992).

Demand for Child Care

As microeconomic theory predicts, the choice of a particular type of child care is negatively related to the price of that type of care (Hofferth and Wissoker 1990). Conflicting evidence exists regarding the extent to which quality is a good predictor of the type of care chosen (Hofferth and Wissoker 1990; Waite, Leibowitz, and Witsberger 1991), although one study reports that quality was cited more than other characteristics to explain child-care choice (Hofferth, Brayfield, Deich, and Holcomb 1991). The characteristics of care (for example, hours, location staff/child ratios) may matter more than the type of care (for example, center or family day care home) and no particular type of care appears to rank highest along all characteristics (Sonenstein and Wolf 1991). One reason for confusion in understanding the relationship between quality and child-care choices is uncertainty about what the characteristics of quality care are and whether parents can tell what constitutes quality care.

Child-care choices follow consistent patterns with relation to family income. Children from low- and high-income families are more likely to be in child-care centers than are children from middle-income families (Henriques and Vaillancourt 1988). Further, middle-income children are predominantly enrolled in for-profit centers, while higher- and lower-income children are more likely to be enrolled in nonprofit care (Hofferth, Brayfield, Deich, and Holcomb 1991). More generally, the higher the mother's wage and family income, the more likely is the mother to choose a center. Therefore, government policies that effectively raise income—such as subsidies, vouchers, and tax credits—will increase the use of child-care centers.

Child-Care Supply: Quantity and Quality

The supply of child care is highly diverse and varies along a number of different dimensions. The two major categories of care are child-care centers and family day care homes, in which a relatively small number of children are cared for in the provider's home. Centers can be publicly or privately sponsored, and private centers can be run on a nonprofit or for-profit basis. Family day care homes can be licensed or unlicensed (in some states, family day care homes with fewer than a threshold number of children are not required to be licensed; in other cases they simply do not comply with licensing requirements). There is an informal child-care sector, the size of which cannot accurately be estimated. One focus of research has been on determining if and in what ways care varies systematically by type of provider; for example, whether for-profit centers vary systematically from nonprofit centers.

Child-care centers receive a subsidy in the form of underpaid workers (Culkin, Morris, and Helburn 1991). Based on staff turnover, staff education, and level of developmentally appropriate activities, nonprofit centers offer higher quality than do for-profit providers. These differences, however, are not statistically significant and as much variation can be found among providers as across types of providers. The costs of nonprofit providers are higher than for-profit providers (Mukerjee and Witte 1993). There are two competing explanations for this: either the nonprofits are providing higher-quality care (Kagan and Newton 1989; Kagan 1991) and that higher quality costs more or the nonprofit providers are less efficient than for-profit providers of the same quality of care (Mukerjee and Witte 1993).

Monopolistic Competition in the Child-Care Market: Theory and Evidence

The theory of monopolistic competition describes a market structure that has some characteristics of perfectly competitive markets and some of oligopolistic or monopolistic markets. Like perfectly competitive markets, a monopolistically competitive industry has many participants and no effective barriers to entry or exit. The monopolistic competitor faces a downward-sloping demand curve due to the varying characteristics of products across providers and, therefore, does have some control over price.

The child-care market conforms closely to this description. There are a large number of providers operating within local markets. Potential entrants face regulations but, as is discussed in more detail below, these regulations are often only weakly enforced. Further, some types of providers operate in what is known as the "informal sector" without complying with regulations, and other types of providers, such as family day care homes with a small number of children or providers of in-home care, are not covered by regulations in many states. For these reasons, regulations do not appear to impose significant barriers to entry.

In the short run, the monopolistic competitor earns economic profits that offer an incentive for entry by producers with slightly differentiated products. New entry causes some customers to shift from their existing producer to the new entrant and demand curves facing each producer become more elastic over time. This process continues until a long-run equilibrium is reached. It is important to note that in long-run equilibrium, economic profits are zero but–unlike the outcome of perfect competition–firms are *not* producing at minimum average cost. That is, the long-run equilibrium is inefficient, since $P > MC$ and there is excess capacity since $P >$ minimum ATC. Some researchers describe this inefficiency as the price that society is willing to pay for product heterogeneity.

I turn now to evidence regarding the forms that competition can take in the child-care market and present findings regarding the incidence of these types of competition based upon *A Profile of Child Care Settings: Early Education and Care in 1990* (Kisker, Hofferth, Phillips, and Farquhar 1991), a national survey of child-care supply. All empirical data presented in this section, unless otherwise noted, come from this source.

Before discussing the extent of competition in the child-care markets, it is important to define the boundaries of the market, both in terms of what types of services are provided and what types of services are considered substitutable for one another. The types of care range from center care (for-profit, nonprofit, or public) to family day care homes (which are almost always private) and from providers offering care to children of all ages to providers specializing in the care of infants, toddlers, preschool, or school-aged children. Clearly, not all of these types of care are substitutable; for example, for-profit and nonprofit centers are potentially strong substitutes for each other while in-home care for a baby is not competitive with nursery schools. The significance here is the extent to which providers compete, that is, vary their price and nonprice strategies in relation to other providers.

In theory, the question of substitutability can be sorted out through estimation of cross-price elasticities. The empirical problem is that sufficient data for such estimation are not available. The underlying conceptual problem is that goods can only be substitutes if consumers know enough about the alternatives to consider them substitutes, which requires that information be available at a cost that consumers are willing to bear.

Finally, child-care markets are highly localized. Due to the nature of the good produced–child care while the parent(s) work(s)–the child-care industry as a whole appears to be composed of a large number of geographically small markets. Parents typically will not choose care, even of particularly desirable quality and price, at a location far from home. Thus, the appropriate market for analysis is a geographically compact set of producers and consumers. This condition is particularly important when discussing policies to increase information flows in order to increase competition and affect prices and quality; increasing information in one geographical market may have no impact on a different local market.

Prices

Substantial price variations are observed across geographical areas for the same type of care. Much of this cross-regional difference can be attributed to different input costs, particularly labor, and to different government regulations and standards that affect staff/child ratios or staff educational levels. But since competition does not extend across regions, what is of interest here are the determinants of price variation within regions across different suppliers. Theory predicts that a monopolistically competitive market will exhibit short-run variations in price across providers due, in part, to different cost structures associated with differentiated products. It also predicts that as consumer search increases, prices will converge.

Evidence from Kisker et al. (1991) indicates that there are a variety of determinants of price differences. Of the variable categories employed by Kisker et al. (1991), price levels were found to be determined by, most importantly, staff/child ratios, the age distribution of children in care, staff education and experience, years in operation, whether the provider is affiliated with a resource and referral agency, whether the provider is affiliated with the National Association for the Education of Young Children (NAEYC), and legal status (that is, for-profit or nonprofit). This applies only to those providers that charge fees, which not all do. The age of children, staff education, years in operation, and affiliation were all positively associated with prices. For-profit centers charge slightly lower fees than nonprofit providers, with the level varying with the type of for-profit center, that is, centers that are part of national chains charge less than those that are independent or part of local chains.

Surprisingly, Kisker et al. found that average fees charged by centers and regulated family day care homes are similar, with the former charging an average $1.59 per hour and the latter $1.64 per hour. More specifically, the survey addressed the fee adjustment policies of different providers and found that fees are adjusted depending upon the number of children from the same family who are cared for by the provider, the number of hours the child is in care, the child's age, the family's income, and whether the child's slot is subsidized by outside financial support. The extent to which fee levels are set or adjusted with respect to the behavior of rival providers was not documented.

Nonprice Competition and Product Differentiation

In general, products can be differentiated by brand image and advertising or by product quality, location of provider, or service. Many of these variables are applicable to analysis of product differentiation in the child-care industry. Child-care providers make choices regarding location, hours of operation, and type and quality of services provided. These choices are guided by the provider's objective function, whether that is to maximize profits or to fulfill an ideological objective, such as a commitment to a particular educational philosophy or to accessibility of quality care. What is reviewed here are the dimensions along which providers can compete (other than through price variation) and, to the extent possible, the patterns of provision among different types of providers. It should be noted that this discussion of nonprice competition is conceptually distinct from the discussion above of patterns of price competition since among the determinants of the latter were such variables as staff/child ratios that in turn relate to quality, a form of nonprice competition.

Providers may be structured as for-profit or nonprofit providers. I refer to this characteristic as legal status. In turn, for-profit providers can be independent or part of national or local chains. Kisker et al. (1991) reported that nonprofit centers are more common than for-profit centers, but that the latter are more common in the South and in suburban areas. A related form of differentiation is sponsorship; a sponsored provider is one that receives funding or direction from the sponsoring organization. While religious organizations are the most common type of sponsor, other sponsors include schools, employers, and Head Start. Choice of legal status and sponsorship are elements of product differentiation since they may serve as signals regarding the objectives of the provider. Consumers may interpret nonprofit status as a signal that the provider is more interested in providing high-quality care than in maximizing the return to shareholders or that a center sponsored by a religious organization will include a religious component in its educational program. While the latter is easily verifiable, the former is not, so signals may be an imperfect but nevertheless important element of product differentiation.

Given the localized nature of child-care markets, location is obviously an important way to differentiate the product. Kisker et al. (1991) described location using two indicators: whether the provider offers access to public transportation and whether the provider is located in an independent structure or as part of another structure (for example, school, religious organization, or employer). Location is an element of product differentiation as it affects the time-cost of consuming child care (depending on how long it takes parents to take their children to the provider) and also determines accessibility.

Since many families consume child care primarily in order to allow parents to work, the schedules and services offered by providers are important. Among the providers surveyed by Kisker et al. (1991), the vast majority of family day care homes operate on a full-time basis while about 67 percent of centers do. What is extremely rare is care offered during evenings and weekends. Other types of services that can be offered include serving meals (which is very common), offering care for sick children (which is rare), and offering other medical services, such as vision and hearing screening.

An important aspect of product differentiation, both from the perspective of consumers and child-care advocates, is quality differentiation, which, as noted above, is also intimately related to price variations. Although there continues to be debate about the constituent elements of quality child care, there is widespread agreement about a number of structural variables that are related to quality, including staff/child ratios, educational levels of the staff, and the rate of turnover among staff members (which, in turn, is inversely related to wage rates). The providers' choice in hiring and employment policies will serve as quality signals.

What is more difficult to assess is the "feeling" of the care provided; that is, whether the environment is nurturing and supportive or whether structural standards are not matched by emotional inputs from providers. While this sense of environment is cited a being important to consumers, it is difficult to define and measure. Thus, reputations built over time are particularly important in successfully differentiating the product as being care that is offered in a loving and nurturing environment.

Capacity and Responsiveness of Supply Changes

The standard model of monopolistic competition predicts that, in long-run equilibrium, the firms in the industry will have excess capacity. Further, one indicator of the extent of competition is the industry's ability to respond to changes in demand. Thus, it is important to examine capacity utilization and responsiveness of supply changes, both of which are examined below.

Evidence from Kisker et al. (1991) is inconsistent with some of the predictions of monopolistic competition models. That is, it appears that centers operate on average near full capacity (60 children on average) and that this result holds true across regions. Family day care homes also exhibit high rates of capacity utilization although lower than the rates for centers. In aggregate, these results suggest that suppliers have responded, as a group, to increasing demand although not to a degree that leaves excess capacity. Further, this does not account for capacity and capacity utilization in unlicensed providers. This ability to respond to demand changes more or less quickly can constitute another component of product differentiation; for example, a provider can develop a reputation for having openings when other child-care arrangements fall through. Research reviewed below indicates that responsiveness does vary by type of provider and may constitute a means by which providers differentiate themselves.

The issue of supply responsiveness is important not only for understanding how the child-care market operates but also from a policy perspective. If government policies, such as the Family Support Act (discussed below), cause substantial shifts in demand, it is important for policymakers to be able to anticipate how the supply side is likely to adjust to these changes and to design policy initiatives that compensate, if necessary, for effects on prices and quality. Studies by Rose-Ackerman (1986) and Kushman (1979) help to inform this issue.

Rose-Ackerman (1986) addressed the question of whether the industry is responsive to demand changes and other stimuli. Recognizing the heterogeneity of the industry, she considered whether that characteristic affects the capability of an industry to respond to increasing demand. Microeconomic theory predicts that the profits created by increases in demand should encourage firms to enter until profits are driven to zero. Theory, however, is not explicit regarding supply responses of nonprofit or public child-care providers who may face a different set of objectives and constraints than those facing for-profit providers. Rose-Ackerman looked to see whether demand is differentially responsive across different types of providers. She found that it is but not necessarily at the same quality level and theorized that this may be due to a "shortage of altruists" to run nonprofit centers.

Her paper explicitly looked at supply responsiveness and how it might vary across types of providers as well as at the related issue of specialization in types of care provided by different categories of providers. For example, she suggests that for-profit centers might specialize in providing low-quality care for middle- to low-income parents while nonprofit providers might specialize in high-quality care for higher-income families. Another aspect of this paper is her examination of the extent to which public intervention may affect outcomes in types of care provided; for example, by imposing quality regulations.

Data are limited, so a number of simplifying assumptions were made.[1] Rose-Ackerman (1) was unable to control for the size of the informal sector (which is generally thought to be substantial), (2) was unable to make a meaningful distinction between nonprofit and for-profit providers and so studied the industry as a whole, and (3) used states as the relevant market even while recognizing that "true" markets are actually more locally defined. She also assumed that the supply side of the market is competitive. Thus, price will equal cost, and an estimate of prices or costs can be used in the estimation. The estimated equations can be interpreted as demand equations.

She estimated a linear demand curve of the following form:[2]

$$q = a_0 + a_1k + a_2p + a_3SB + a_4x_4 \ldots + a_nx_n + a_n + 1^s \qquad (10.1)$$

where q = quantity of child-care center services demanded
k = children in public school preprimary programs
p = price of center care
SB = subsidized children in centers
s = availability of care by providers other than centers or public schools
$x_4, \ldots, x_n$ = determinants of overall demand for child care, for example, strength of job market for women, children in single-parent families.

She found that supply is responsive to demand conditions: the coefficients on female employment opportunities and percentage of children in single-parent families are both positive and statistically significant. She also found a positive and significant coefficient on public subsidies: that is, they have helped to foster the growth of the industry. These subsidies, however, are not distributed in connection with the prevalence of children in poverty, minority, or single-parent families or in connection with female labor force participation rates. Government initiatives instituted after this analysis was performed, most particularly the Child Care Development Block Grant (described in the third section), may have brought this allocation of subsidies more closely into line with the distribution of populations in need of child care.

Kushman (1979), too, examined this question but separated the industry into three supply sectors: proprietary (private for-profit), voluntary (private nonprofit), and public (government). He tested for supply sensitivity with respect to sets of variables appropriate for each sector. He found that public center care is responsive to costs to local taxpayers and not responsive to female labor force participation, while the for-profit sector shows the greatest responsiveness to female labor force participation. The nonprofit sector falls somewhere in between by responding to the local tax burden as well as labor force opportunities. Kushman concluded that these results reveal something about the objective functions of the different types of providers. While for-profit firms are profit-maximizers, responding to increases in demand, public and nonprofit providers are sensitive to other considerations–such as tax burdens and public support.

Kushman's analysis focused on the 100 counties of North Carolina in 1973. All child-care centers were classified as public, nonprofit, or for-profit, according to their sponsor. He assumed that there are no significant barriers to entry (an assumption consistent with the earlier discussion of child care as a monopolistically competitive industry), suggesting that supply responses will be rapid. The demand equations (the specific form of each is described below) are estimated using the tobit model. Although the standard econometric approach to estimating the demand equations would be to use ordinary least squares regression equations, Kushman could not estimate these equations using ordinary least squares analysis because approximately 25 percent of the dependent variable values were zero. Thus, he conducted a tobit analysis. This is an estimation technique that is used when the dependent variable is truncated at either or both high and low values (see, for example, Maddala 1986). In this case, the dependent variable is truncated at the lower end; that is, the lowest value for the demand response can be a zero response. The results are interpreted in the same way they would be if ordinary least squares were used.

The equation for the public sector estimates the demand for a good with externalities, assuming a collective choice process. The externalities are similar to those associated with education (and discussed more fully in the third section); that is, a well-educated and productive population. Other aspects of government provision of child care are equitable distribution of child care by income, labor market opportunities by gender, and licensed spaces in public centers per one thousand children 13 years old or younger.

Spaces in child-care centers are used to measure society's (rather than individuals') demand for the provision of child-care services. Independent variables are per capita income, the proportion of the population that is 13 years old or younger, the proportion of the population that is non-white, the proportion of women in the labor force with children younger than six years old, the average weekly fee charged by government centers, the average fee charged by nonprofit centers, the proportion of families receiving benefits under the Aid to Families with Dependent Children (AFDC) program, and the eligibility of the county for federal funds under the Appalachian Regional Program. (The Appalachian Regional Commission provides funds for child-care expenses incurred by workers in the Appalachia area.) Only two variables are statistically significant: demand is negatively related to the average fee and positively related to participation in the Appalachian Regional Program (which proxies the costs to local taxpayers).

The equation for the nonprofit sector estimates the sum of demand for the provision of subsidized care as expressed through tax and transfer programs, private contributions, and the demand for unsubsidized care. The dependent variable is the number of children in nonprofit centers per one thousand children. The independent variables are the same as in the earlier equation, although here their effect on demand operates through the market rather than through a collective choice process in the public sector. Significant variables are labor market participation rates, AFDC recipiency, and parental fees; the first two variables are positively related to demand and the third negatively related.

The model for the for-profit sector estimates demand for private, for-profit child-care services, and the dependent variable is children in for-profit centers per one thousand children. The same independent variables are used except for children since the number of children in for-profit centers will not affect the burden of local taxes or charity. With the exception of parental fees, all coefficients are significant and have the expected sign.

Thus, this analysis finds supply responsiveness that varies by type of producer. Public center care is responsive to the costs to local taxpayers; for example, availability of federal and state funds from AFDC or the Appalachian Regional Program can substantially increase the provision of care in government centers. Public center care, however, is not responsive to female labor force opportunities, whereas the for-profit sector is responsive to changes in this variable. Finally, evidence indicates that nonprofit care is responsive to labor force opportunities and to the cost of redistribution programs.

In aggregate, these findings indicate that different categories of suppliers produce different products and respond to different stimuli. Rose-Ackerman and Kushman both find that profit-maximizing firms respond most to new opportunities. However, since for-profit providers do not generally produce the highest-quality child care, this is a troubling finding for child-care consumers and advocates. If for-profit providers contribute the bulk of the supply response, this may lead to shortages in particular types of care but may put them in a stronger competitive position for capturing increases in demand. Considered in light of current policy initiatives, these are significant findings. For example, the Family Support Act (1988) requires AFDC recipients who are parents of children above three years of age to participate in training, education, or work, and such individuals receive subsidized care. (This is discussed in more detail below.) This policy calls for a substantial increase in demand for child care, some of which will be met through informal means and some through market activity. Kushman and Rose-Ackerman's findings that for-profit providers are most likely to be responsive to demand shifts coupled with evidence cited earlier that for-profit providers on average provide care of a quality inferior to that of nonprofit providers raises the troubling possibility that this population of new market demanders will be served more frequently by lower-quality providers than might be desirable. Policymakers could use these findings to consider ways to increase the supply responsiveness of nonprofit providers or to provide more high-quality public care, for example, by increasing the number of Head Start programs and extending them to become full-day programs.

Public Policy toward Child Care

The government is involved in the child-care sector in two general ways: first, by offering financial support or subsidies and, secondly, through regulations that directly or indirectly affect the supply of and demand for child care. The financial mode of intervention occurs both at the state and federal level, whereas regulations are almost completely promulgated and enforced at the state level. Like other service delivery sectors in the United States, such as health care and education, child care is provided and funded by both public and private sources and among the private sources are both for-profit and nonprofit participants. Forms of public support for child care include direct and indirect subsidies to producers and consumers and direct provision of services. The government is also involved in the child-care sector indirectly because legislation that deals with other issues, for example, welfare reform, can and does have implications for child-care supply and demand (as can other regulations such as zoning restrictions). Specific programs offering financial support or regulations and licensing are described below. Before turning to that discussion, however, I address the more general question of why the government should be involved in the market at all.

Why Should the Government Intervene in the Child-Care Market?

There are a variety of standard arguments for government intervention in a market, and many of these have implications for the child-care market. One variable that changes across the different arguments is who is the beneficiary. Some arguments for government intervention focus on the needs of the children, others on the needs of the parents, and still others on the needs of society at large.

Market Failures

Market failures arise when conditions prohibit a market from achieving the Pareto optimal outcomes that would obtain if the market were perfectly competitive.[3] Two of the reasons for market failure include existence of externalities and information asymmetries. An externality arises when a party suffers negative effects (a negative externality) or enjoys positive effects (a positive externality) from the decision without having been involved in the decision making. The standard economic example of a negative externality is air pollution, and the standard positive example is education. The entire society–not just the people who become educated– benefits from having a well-educated workforce that is more productive and behaves with more civic responsibility. One of the characteristics of an externality is that without government intervention, a nonoptimal amount of the good that generates the externality will be produced–that is, there will be too much pollution or too little education. This is because the marginal private and social costs (or benefits) do not coincide. Thus, the government intervenes in order to ensure that these costs (benefits) do coincide and that the socially optimal quantity of the good is produced.

The same argument that is used for public provision of education can be applied to child care, some forms of which are also referred to as early childhood education. To the extent that the government ensures–either directly through services or indirectly through financial support–that young children receive higher-quality care, the entire population benefits, assuming that these children perform better in school and become more productive citizens than they would otherwise have been. Obviously, this argument is most compelling for children from at-risk families and neighborhoods but should not be limited to them. The simplest way to state this externality argument for public support of child-care provision is to note that if it is appropriate for the government to provide education for children from the age of five, then it should be appropriate to do so for younger children. It is worth noting that this argument has been accepted in the vast majority of industrialized nations that offer some form of publicly provided early childhood education and child care.

One of the assumptions of a perfectly competitive market is that there is perfect information: no one ever makes a mistake from having inadequate or incorrect information about prices, quality, or other product characteristics. When this condition does not hold, there is the potential for all types of mistakes to be made and, at a more general level, for greater variations in quality and prices, lower average quality, and higher average prices than would prevail if more information were available. This is a market failure. Many markets suffer from this problem; for example, consumers of health care have much less information than do providers of health care (for example, doctors) who know much more about outcomes, costs, and probabilities. In the medical arena, what many consumers do is substitute trust in their provider for information that would allow the consumer to make an informed decision by herself. In the case of corporate securities, disclosure information is collected by the Securities and Exchange Commission with the purpose of providing consumers with adequate information for sound decision making. One possibility is for the government to provide full and accurate information. This possibility is discussed in greater detail in the fourth section of this chapter.

Quality Control

Markets in which it is difficult for consumers to evaluate quality or be sure that the environment is safe are sometimes characterized by self-policing. Examples include board certification for doctors and financial advisors. When such self-policing does not arise, or if it is incomplete, the government can intervene with regulations that affect the terms of operation for providers of the service. The role of government here is to specify conditions for safe and high quality child-care services and, if the rules are to have any practical meaning, to develop an enforcement mechanism.

The child-care market is very clearly a case in which it is difficult for parents to evaluate (or even to define) quality care. Since it is a highly fragmented industry with a high level of entry and exit, no formal system of self-policing has arisen and responsibility for monitoring quality and safety has fallen to a mixed and highly problematic system of public and private monitoring. Determining the implications of regulations for quantity supplied, prices, and quality of care is a complex problem and there is the potential for regulations to yield outcomes in conflict with original intentions, for example, to decrease supply while raising quality.

Needs of Families

The purpose of the Dependent Care Tax Credit (described in the next section) is, in part, to enable parents of young children to work by subsidizing the cost of child care. By assisting women in returning to the labor force after childbirth and allowing both single parents and dual-worker families to participate in the labor market and attend to the needs of children, government support allows greater participation in the labor market. This can have both private benefits for the income-earners and positive externalities for the economy at large.

An alternative perspective on helping families work arises in the context of welfare reform. Child care plays a role in enabling parents, particularly single parents, to participate in training or work programs that are intended to allow parents to become financially self-sufficient

Redistribution

While some forms of government support allow AFDC recipients to participate in training and work programs, another type of support can be directed at the category known as the "working poor." Families with earnings near the poverty level may be unable to purchase child care of even minimal quality without government support. Thus, the government can intervene to redistribute income from wealthier taxpayers to poorer workers and enable them to purchase better-quality child care. This redistribution will affect the welfare of both the recipient parent and child.

Forms of Government Involvement in the Child-Care Market

Government involvement in the child-care market occurs at both the federal and the state level and takes four basic forms: subsidies to providers, subsidies to consumers, direct provision of services, and regulations. The first three categories include both federal and state involvement while regulation is promulgated and enforced at the state level. It should be noted that all of these types of government sector involvement are relevant only to the formal sector of the market, whereas the informal sector of babysitters and unregulated family day care homes operates largely independently of government involvement, which is in itself an issue of policy concern.

The discussion that follows highlights the major forms of government participation in the child-care market, but it is not exhaustive. Rather, it is meant to highlight the largest programs most directly related to child care. However, there are many other programs that have some direct or indirect implications for child-care economics, such as the Women, Infants, and Children (WIC) Food Program; the Family and Medical Leave Act (1993); and the Dependent Care Assistance Program (DCAP).

Federal Funding of Child Care

Subsidies come through three programs: Head Start, the Child Care Food Program, and Title XX Social Service Block Grants. The Head Start program provides primarily part-time educational and developmental enhancement programs, which are supplemented by medical and nutritional services and include parent participation as well. Since the vast majority of Head Start programs are part-time, they are not really child-care programs but are often referred to as such during discussions of government involvement in the child-care market. Head Start funds are allocated to states based on the number of young children from low-income families. It is estimated that in 1989 more than $1 billion was allocated to Head Start grantees who provided services to approximately 450,000 children. On the basis of eligibility requirements, another approximately 1.8 million children were eligible.

The Child Care Food Program (CCFP) is administered by the U.S. Department of Agriculture. Funds are allocated to states, which, in turn, dispense funds to licensed child-care centers and family day care homes to provide healthy meals. Only licensed providers are eligible for CCFP funds. These funds are also allocated to states based on the number of children from low-income families. In 1992, funding through this program was valued at $1.2 billion.

A third major source of child-care funding is the Title XX Social Service Block Grants (SSBG). This program was initiated in 1977 under Title XX of the Social Security Act. Each state is allocated funds in proportion to the population, and no matching funds from the state are required. States have discretion as to how much to spend on different social services as well as on eligibility requirements for receipt. The only federal requirement is that the funds be allocated to meet the needs of the low-income population. This is not specifically a child-care program. The majority of states, however, do dedicate some SSBG funds to child care. In 1987, 45 states used SSBG funding, supplemented by state funding, for child-care services (Blank, Wilkins, and Crawley 1987). There are no reliable data on how much money was actually spent on child-care services through SSBG. Although this is one of the biggest child-care funding streams, it was estimated in a 1988 study that only 13 percent of the children deemed eligible on the basis of family income were receiving services from SSBG programs (Reismon, Moore, and Fitzgerald 1988).

On the consumer side, financial support provided directly to families comes in the form of federal and state child-care tax credits, support provided as part of the Family Support Act, the Child Care and Development Block Grant, and Title IV-A "At-Risk" program.

The Dependent Care Tax Credit allows for deduction from the tax bill of a portion of the child-care bill. The proportion is inversely related to income. According to the National Commission on Children, this credit was worth a total of $2.7 billion to taxpayers with children in 1991 (National Commission on Children 1993). Specifically, it allows a tax credit of between 20 and 30 percent of $2,400 for one child and $4,800 for two or more children of working parents. In 1981, the size of the credit increased, making this the largest federal program helping families with child-care costs. This is the single largest source of government spending on child care, and it was estimated that nearly half of all families with working mothers claim the deduction (Hayes, Palmer, and Zaslow 1990). Because of the way it is structured, this tax credit is primarily of benefit to middle- and upper-income families.

The Family Support Act (FSA), which is a major attempt to reform the welfare system, has far-reaching implications for child-care demand by low-income families as well as for families' ability to pay for child care. The increase in child-care demand arises because of the FSA's requirement that AFDC recipients, depending upon the age of their child(ren), participate in training, education, or work programs through what are called Jobs Opportunities and Basic Skills (JOBS) Training Programs. Parents of children three years of age and older are required to participate in training programs. In some states, parents of children younger than three may be required to participate in JOBS programs.

The FSA includes a child-care guarantee for parents in the JOBS program. Because in the original formulation there are no plans to increase supply, not all eligible parents could make the necessary child-care arrangements. In October 1989, federal regulations were issued for the FSA that allowed parents unable to make child-care arrangements to defer participation in work or training programs. Further, in order to expand the supply of care available to participants, the regulations were changed so as to allow participants to receive subsidies even when using informal care arrangements. This was controversial since it raises questions about the quality of care that participants might choose; informal care may be inferior to programs provided in centers, for example.

Financial support for child-care expenditures through the FSA takes several forms. It redefined the terms of the earned income disregard for families on AFDC: that is, parents on AFDC who are working can deduct from their income a portion of their expenditures on child care. Specifically, this disregard was increased to $175 per child per month for children older than two and $200 per month for children younger than two.

The FSA also includes transitional care provisions for parents who cease receiving AFDC benefits because of increased income. If a working parent has received AFDC in three of the prior six months, that parent is eligible for transitional child-care assistance, the specific terms of which are determined at the state level.

The culmination of a long and heated debate over child-care policy was the Child Care and Development Block Grant (1990). This legislation is aimed at increasing the quality and quantity of child-care available to families. Congress designated $732 million for child-care funding for fiscal year 1991, with projected increases of about $100 million per year. The term "eligible children" was defined to include children less than 13 years old with parents who are working or in job training programs and whose family income does not exceed 75 percent of the state median income, adjusted for family size. Three-quarters of the total funds are reserved for providing child-care services; the balance is to be used for a variety of purposes including developing before- and after-school care programs and increasing the availability and quality of care. Eligible approaches to improving the quality of care are broadly defined and include increased enforcement of regulations; enhanced provision of information about child-care through, for example, a resource and referral agency; or child-care staff training programs.

The Child Care Entitlement Grant, also known as the At-Risk Child Care Program, is directed at providing child care for the children of parents who are working and not receiving AFDC but who might be unable to continue working if subsidies were not available. These families are often referred to as the "working poor," some of whose income from work may be so low that the size of child-care costs may force them out of work and onto welfare benefits. Specific eligibility requirements are established at the state level, and parents typically pay some portion of child-care expenses on a sliding fee basis.

State Regulations

The other main form of government intervention in the child-care market is regulation and licensing. Child-care regulations are promulgated and implemented at the state level and vary considerably in terms of specific characteristics and level of stringency (see Morgan 1987; Adams 1990). Every state regulates child care and nearly every state regulates family day care homes. The most common types of regulations concentrate on staff/child ratios, caregiver qualifications, and health- and safety-related considerations. The mechanisms for enforcing the regulations include screening prospective providers (for compliance with background requirements and training), on-site inspections, and imposing penalties for violations (General Accounting Office 1994).

It is important to remember that not all child-care providers are covered by the regulatory framework. The first category of providers that are not regulated are what are known as exempt providers: in some states these include family day care providers who care for fewer than some minimum number of children (as specified by regulation) and child care sponsored by religious institutions. In addition, child-care providers operating in the informal sector, such as babysitters and family day care homes that are not registered or licensed (but should be according to regulatory standards), operate outside the framework of regulation. Thus, even if regulations were strictly enforced, not all children would be cared for in settings controlled by regulation.

There are two fundamental issues that arise with respect to regulations: To what extent do they affect quality, and to what extent do they affect supply? With regard to the first issue, there is considerable question as to the extent to which child-care regulations are enforced and thus the extent to which they affect behavior by producers and consumers. The consensus in the literature is that while regulations sometimes positively influence quality, they do not have the effect that they would have if they were strictly enforced. Kahn and Kamerman (1987) write, with regard to family day care homes, that many states do not have adequate staff to ensure that regulations are enforced, rendering them meaningless. Other researchers share that view. A recent survey conducted by the General Accounting Office reported that unsafe conditions were found in 29 percent of the 134 centers visited (General Accounting Office February 11, 1994), suggesting that regulations were not being enforced. This is not surprising given that the recent steady growth in demand for and supply of child-care services has not been matched by growth in enforcement capacity (Hayes, Palmer, and Zaslow 1990; Adams 1990). Thus, the issue of the effectiveness of regulation in imposing quality standards is an unresolved one, but indications are that it is not fully effective.

Another issue that arises with respect to licensing and regulation is the extent to which they impose barriers to entry. To the extent they do, policymakers are confronted with a difficult trade-off between quality (enforced through regulation) and quantity (reduced by regulation). In an attempt to gauge the effect of regulations on supply, Gormley (1991) focused on three aspects of child-care regulations–costliness, intrusiveness, and enforceability–to determine the extent to which regulations that fall into these three categories affect supply. Regulations he characterizes as costly are ratios, liability insurance requirements, and frequent inspections; intrusive regulations are ratios, liability insurance requirements, frequent inspections, and a ban on corporal punishment; and enforceable regulations are ratios, liability insurance requirements, frequent inspections, a parental visit right, and immunization requirements.

He conducted separate analyses for child-care centers and family day care homes. He employed ordinary least squares regression to estimate the effects of various state regulations on the number of child-care facilities in the United States. Data limitations made it impossible to simultaneously estimate supply and demand equations, which would be the most desirable approach to the empirical work. Instead, he employed reduced form equations to estimate the effects of regulations on the equilibrium quantity of child-care services while controlling for the effects of other independent variables that could affect either supply or demand.

The center analysis equation variables are mandatory staff/child ratios for 18-month-olds, a liability insurance requirement, the actual number of inspections per center per year, a corporal punishment ban, a parental right to visit, an immunization requirement for preschoolers, initial training for teachers, and mandatory handwashing procedures. In other words, these are the variables along which the fit of the straight line estimated in the regression equation can vary. Gormley found that two regulatory variables have an impact on the number of group day care centers per child: group day care centers are more likely to be found in states with higher staff/child ratios (that is, limits on size reduce the supply of child-care centers) and are less likely to be found in states that allow parents the right to visit group centers. This means that these are the ones among the independent variables found to have a statistically significant relationship to the dependent variables. The statistical significance tells us that there is great confidence that the coefficient on the independent variable, which measures the extent to which the value of the dependent variable moves with the value of the independent variable, has a true value different from zero. As Gormley notes, a parental visit right might reflect activist parents and, therefore, be a surrogate for other more costly regulations not included in his analysis.

The family day care home analysis equation variables include number of children under age two who can be cared for by one person, a general liability insurance requirement, the number of mandatory inspections per year times the percentage of homes inspected, a corporal punishment ban, a parental right to visit, an immunization requirement for preschoolers, a provider training requirement, and limitations on care for mildly ill children. His findings were that general liability insurance requirements reduce the number of regulated family day care homes and that elaborate home inspection systems reduce the supply of family day care providers. As Gormley notes, this is a problem since home inspection is a major component of many regulatory systems. Nevertheless, his findings are that most regulations do not have an effect on the number of child-care facilities.

Rose-Ackerman looked at another interesting possible effect of government intervention (1983). Noting that centers are playing a growing role in meeting demands for child care and that regulations vary substantially across states, she examined the relationship between receiving subsidies and racial segregation in centers. She employed the Taueber index to measure segregation. The index was originally developed for studies of segregated housing patterns. In this context, the Taueber index indicates what proportion of black children would have to change centers so as to leave each center with the same proportion of black children in all centers. Using Rose-Ackerman's notation, the Taueber index for black children versus children who are not black (TB) is measured as:

$$TB = \frac{1}{2} \sum_{i=1}^{n} \left| \frac{B_i}{B} - \frac{NB_i}{NB} \right| \tag{10.2}$$

where B_i =   the number of black children in center i,
        B =   the number of black children in the sample,
        NB_i =   the number of children who are not black in center i,
        NB =   the total number of children who are not black in the sample

and $i = 1, \ldots, n$, where n is the number of centers in
                    the sample.

Using the Taueber index she reported that centers that accept subsidized
children had a higher proportion of poor and black children than did other
centers. Forty percent of nonprofit centers that accepted subsidized children
had their entire budget paid by public subsidy whereas only 10 percent of
the for-profits that were eligible to accept subsidized children were financed
entirely by the government. Seventy-five percent of for-profit providers did
not even participate in the subsidy program. For-profit providers that
accepted subsidized children were more racially segregated than nonprofits.
Her evidence supports the hypothesis that quality standards that are costly
combined with subsidies lead to increased segregation in centers. Since this
is not a desirable outcome, she suggests alternatives: vouchers and proxy
shopping. A voucher system is one in which beneficiaries receive child-care
vouchers and can choose any provider, subject to the value of the voucher.
A proxy shopping system is one in which the government provides subsidies
to children at centers only if the centers are also serving children who are
not subsidized. This ensures that the subsidized children are getting the
same quality of care that other customers pay for. As Rose-Ackerman notes,
such a system would work only if unsubsidized consumers are willing to
place their children with providers that also provide child care for subsidized
children.

It is difficult to draw strong conclusions about the effects of government
intervention and regulation on the basis of only two studies that are not
directly comparable to each other. What they do suggest is that certain types
of regulations that are intended to raise quality, as considered by Gormley,
will have a significant effect on the supply of care provided by centers and
family day care homes. All else being equal, this would be expected to lead,
in turn, to higher prices. Rose-Ackerman's work further suggests that
regulations, in association with financial intervention, may lead to unexpected and undesirable outcomes. Together these studies suggest that
policymakers in the child-care field need to address the potential conflict
between the effect of regulations on quality and quantity as well as the
possibility of other undesirable outcomes, such as increasing segregation
across providers.

It is important to consider to what extent these funding and regulatory
structures address the reasons discussed above for government intervention
in the child-care market: that is, to address market failures, to ensure quality
and safety, to help families work, and to redistribute income. The conclusion
is that government interventions, at the state and federal level combined,
address all of these areas but address none of them adequately. To review,
subsidies to providers and consumers redistribute income and help families

work, regulatory specification and enforcement help to improve quality, and direct provision of services (such as through Head Start and the CCFP) help to create a well-educated and healthy population of children, with the attendant positive externalities. The lack of full regulatory enforcement, large numbers of children eligible for Head Start or subsidies but unable to receive them, and child-care costs that comprise a large proportion of the income of low-income families all speak to the inadequacy of the current policy framework in the child-care market. The rest of this paper addresses one particular area in which improved government involvement is needed: that is, to address the information problems that are a major problem in the child-care market.

You may have noted in reading about the types of government intervention in the child-care market that while all of the reasons for government intervention are addressed either explicitly (helping parents work) or implicitly (Head Start as a way to increase the positive externality), none directly address the problem of information asymmetries. Although in principle regulations that ensure quality and safety might obviate the need for some types of evaluative information, we saw that there is considerable question as to whether regulations are enforced. Second, even if regulations are enforced, they cannot solve all the different types of information asymmetries that arise. The implications of these information problems are explored below.

Information Problems in the Child-Care Market

Two general types of information problems arise in child-care markets: information asymmetries and costly search. Asymmetric information exists when the seller knows the quality of a good but the buyer does not. The situation arises in a number of other markets; for example, consumers of professional services in the medical and legal professions are often unable to determine the quality of care or services they are receiving at least until the services are completed. In these cases the asymmetry arises in part due to the technical nature of the product so that the consumer not trained in medicine or the law is not in a position to evaluate quality. In such instances, a consumer not trained in medicine or the law is not in a position to evaluate quality. In such instances, a consumer must rely on signals of quality, such as professional licensing and board membership, which may or may not accurately signal quality.

In child-care markets, quality signals may include education, licensing, and affiliation with a larger organization that has a reputation for providing quality care. These signals, because of a lack of agreement even among child-care professionals as to what constitutes quality care and because of the nature of regulations regarding licensing, may be imperfect in signaling quality (Magenheim 1992a). Quality signaling is further complicated by two other particular aspects of the child-care market. There is a high rate of entry into and exit from the industry, which makes it difficult for providers to develop reputations for providing quality care. Second, because families participate in the child-care market for a relatively short time (as compared to 60 years of buying cars and a lifetime of receiving medical care), the incentive to obtain enough education to understand quality in child care may be relatively weak.

Markets characterized by asymmetric information are also characterized by lower quality than would be offered if perfect information prevailed. By drawing on Akerlof's classic study of "the market for lemons" (1970), it can be shown that when there is asymmetric information, only the lowest-quality products will be sold. The used car market is one in which there are informational asymmetries between buyers and sellers. Only the seller knows if the car she is selling is a good one or if she is selling it because it is a "lemon." The consumer, who cannot tell if the car is a lemon, will only pay what a lemon is worth. Thus, if the seller knows that her car is a good one but all she can get is the "lemon price," she will not sell her car in the used car market, and, in the end, the only cars that will be sold in the used car market are lemons.

Akerlof developed a formal model to predict the quality of used cars that will be sold. He assumed that there are four types of cars: new and used cars and good and bad cars (lemons). Both new and used cars may be good or may be lemons. A consumer buys a car without knowing whether the car she is going to buy is good or a lemon. There is some probability q that it is a good car and another probability $(1-q)$ that it is a lemon. Over time, the owner is able to determine with accuracy whether her car is good or a lemon and will adjust the probabilities accordingly. But if she tries to sell her car, buyers do not know whether the car is good or a lemon: this is the information asymmetry. If there is no way credibly to indicate that her car is good (rather than a lemon) then she can only sell it at the lemon price; in the long run, owners of good cars will keep them, and the only cars in the market for lemons will be lemons in long-run equilibrium.

Schotter (1994) examined the problem of information asymmetry in the context of the market for car repairs, focusing on the question of what the equilibrium mix of honest and dishonest car mechanics will be. He established two propositions:

1   No all-competent and all-honest equilibrium exists: If consumers expect all car repairers to be honest then they will get only one estimate and accept it. As a result, some experts will lie because they know consumers will not bother to check on the validity of

the estimate. This is the same outcome as for used cars and is basically the service market equivalent of Gresham's Law except that here bad services (rather than money) drive out good.

2   An all-dishonest equilibrium exists: If the consumer knows that she will need a major repair she will only get one opinion because she knows that everyone will lie to her. Consequently, everyone will be dishonest.

This extreme outcome is not anticipated in the market for child care where information asymmetries are not complete. With a relatively small investment of time, a consumer can determine the major indicators of quality (that is, staff/child ratios, rate of staff turnover, group size, and educational level of staff and teachers) but cannot observe, at least not perfectly, the nature of interaction between providers and children during the course of the day. These unobservable quality indicators are important but unavailable to parents in judging quality. Further, there is evidence that families may not know the observable characteristics of the provider, for example, whether the provider is licensed (see, for example, Walker 1992).

Thus, following the same general argument as in the lemons market, if suppliers are unable to earn an adequate return on quality because consumers cannot determine the quality level accurately, high-quality providers may exit the market or lower the quality level they provide. The extent to which this will occur in the child-care market is limited by the heterogeneity of types of producers. Assuming that it is costly to provide higher-quality care, for-profit producers may be compelled to lower quality so that they can earn at least a normal rate of return. Nonprofit providers, however, do not face the same profit constraint and may be able to continue to produce high-quality care even if parents are unwilling to pay a "high enough" price for it. Ultimately, this could evolve into a situation in which nonprofit status becomes a credible signal for offering high-quality care. Nevertheless, there will be segments of the market in which lower-quality care will be offered than would have been offered if information were perfect.

Search Costs

If consumers do not have full information about prices and quality within the market, producers are able to charge a price higher than the perfectly competitive one. If a producer in a perfectly competitive market raises her price above the market price, she loses her entire market because all of her customers know that they can buy the same good elsewhere for a lower price. If these consumers did not know what other prices prevailed (that is, if the market were not perfectly competitive) then it is possible that the producer could maintain a price above marginal cost (that is, could exercise market power) and not be caught by consumers.

What is likely in the market for child care is that the reality is somewhere between these two extremes; that is, consumers probably have some information about prices charged by other child-care providers but not perfect information and producers, therefore, have some market power but not perfect monopoly pricing power.

The reason that consumers do not have perfect information about prices is that search is costly; therefore, one way to increase the amount of search in a market is to reduce the cost of information. An obvious means of doing this is through advertising. In a monopolistically competitive industry, such as child care, more consumer search leads to lower prices and a smaller dispersion in prices. Evidence of this has been found in the market for optometrists' services (Benham 1972). Whether more search will lead to a uniform price within a market depends on product characteristics. In one of the first articles on this topic, Stigler (1961) argued that the larger the amount of the consumer's intended expenditure, the more search was worthwhile and the more likely that competition would lead prices to be the same across providers. The present value of five years' of full-time child care and five years of after-school care is certainly on a par with a major expenditure like a car so that the initial child-care decision could be considered a major one. On the other hand, given that what constitutes appropriate care varies with the age of the child, breaking down the child-care decision into three or four decisions, lowers the cost of making a mistake in any one decision and, therefore, may lower the level of search investment the consumer is willing to make each time she switches child-care arrangements.

One complication can arise when considering the interactive effects of increasing search and lowering price and how that will affect quality. On one hand, better information will enable consumers to evaluate quality better, and better information will apply competitive pressure on producers to raise quality and make quality levels more consistent. An alternative argument has been made that lowering search costs and price will ultimately lead to lower quality. If prices fall due to more search, then producers are predicted to meet their increased demand by lowering the quality of the product they provide. In one notable example, it was argued that if optometrists were allowed to advertise they would meet increased demand by spending less time with each patient (Kwoka 1984). In the case of child care, a producer might meet increased demand by lowering her staff/child ratio. The likelihood of this outcome is enhanced by the low probability of being caught by regulators, even if her staff/child ratio were below the regulatory standard. This is most likely to be a short-run phenomenon; in the long run, the child-care provider could optimally adjust input levels to return to the initial quality level.

Information Problems in Child-Care Markets: Private, Public, and Joint Solutions

The two obvious solutions, even if they are only partial solutions, operating in the child-care market today are resource and referral agencies and licensing and regulations, both of which are considered in this section. In some markets characterized by asymmetric information and costly search, institutions develop that enable information to be produced more efficiently than a single consumer is capable of doing. For example, in the market for health care, which suffers from analogous types of information problems, there are licensing boards and professional societies that are intended to help overcome asymmetric information about quality. There is some question as to how effective such mechanisms are in the child-care market, and there is also a question as to how willing providers are to invest in such institutions and in signals such as education and licensing (Magenheim 1992a). Physician and nursing home referral services may provide information that helps consumers evaluate quality and economize on search costs. The institutional innovation within the child-care market that comes closest to serving these functions are resource and referral agencies (R&Rs). R&Rs are a relatively recent institutional development (for historical background, see Magenheim 1992b) in the child-care market, and they vary tremendously in terms of the services provided and in their sponsorship (that is, public or private, independent, or part of a private or public network). It should be noted that there has been substantial growth, fueled in part by increased public funding through the Child Care Development Block Grant, in state-administered R&R networks as well as growth in the variety of services provided by R&Rs.

Among the services typically provided by R&Rs are referrals for suppliers and demanders, supply creation and retention, and parent education. Thus, at least in theory, R&Rs address the specific types of information problems discussed above, and therefore their role in mitigating information problems in the child-care markets is reviewed below. Following that, roles that can be played by the government directly in solving information problems are considered.

What do R&Rs do? McConaghy and Siegel (1988) list a variety of services provided by R&Rs. They note three basic functions: parent consultation (assisting parents in search by explaining what constitutes quality and age-appropriate care and by offering a number of referrals), support for providers (including training, establishing and maintaining family day care home networks and helping providers obtain state licensing), and collecting data. They also note a wide variety of other activities, including publishing newsletters and sponsoring toy or book lending libraries. More recently,

TABLE 10.1   Participation with and Receipt of Referrals from R&Rs: Child-Care Centers by Geographic Region

Region	Program Listed with R&R (percent)	Fill Opening from R&R (percent)	Number
Entire Population	.67	.07	1,811
West	.88	.10	262
Mountain	.61	.04	71
West North Central	.66	.12	124
West South Central	.59	.06	191
New England	.78	.07	160
East North Central	.60	.06	311
East South Central	.45	.01	80
South Atlantic	.62	.06	447
Middle Atlantic	.71	.06	165

Region Codes: West = Washington, Oregon, California, Hawaii, Nevada, and Arkansas

Mountain = Idaho, Colorado, Arizona, New Mexico, Montana, Wyoming, and Utah

West North Central = Nebraska, Minnesota, North Dakota, South Dakota, Kansas, Missouri, and Iowa

West South Central = Texas, Oklahoma, Louisiana, and Arizona

New England = New Hampshire, Rhode Island, Connecticut, Maine, Massachusetts,and Vermont

East North Central = Wisconsin, Illinois, Indiana, Ohio, and Michigan

East South Central = Tennessee, Alabama, Kentucky, and Mississippi

South Atlantic = West Virginia, Virginia, North Carolina, South Carolina, Georgia, Florida, Mayland, Washington, DC, and Delaware

Middle Atlantic = New York, New Jersey, and Pennsylvania

Source: Author's calculations from data in *A Profile of Child-Care Settings* (Kisker, Hofferth, Phillips, and Farquhar 1991).

due largely to administrative needs growing out of the Family Support Act, some R&Rs have begun to work with states as monitors for licensing compliance or to administer voucher programs.

Of the 125 respondents to a survey conducted by the National Association for Child Care Resource and Referral Agencies (NACCRRA), 80 percent provide child-care referrals, consumer education, help for parents in obtaining public subsidies, assistance to child-care centers in establishing programs, and production of supply-and-demand data reports. Friedman and Kolben (1990) reported that of 103 respondents who provided information on the average number of child-care requests from parents, 10 percent handled more than 500 requests per month and about 50 percent handled between 100 and 500 requests per month. Forty-seven percent of survey respondents help to run financial support programs such as scholarships.

It is worth noting what R&Rs do not do. While they do provide referrals, they do not make recommendations to parents. Also, any particular R&R will only offer some subset of the services listed above. Finally, they will most likely not be able to be of help to unlicensed family day care homes

TABLE 10.2   Participation with and Receipt of Referrals from R&Rs: Family Providers by Geographic Region

Region	Program Listed with R&R (mean)	Fill Opening from R&R (mean)	Number
Entire Population	.90	.22	547
West	.95	.26	139
Mountain	.81	.33	18
West North Central	.93	.18	79
West South Central	.76	.34	32
New England	.97	.34	64
East North Central	.91	.14	87
East South Central	.00	.00	11
South Atlantic	.81	.10	93
Middle Atlantic	.95	.29	24

Note: See Table 10.1 for region codes.

Source: Author's calculations from data in A Profile of Child Care Settings (Kisker, Hofferth, Phillips, and Farquhar 1991)

(unless such homes are seeking to become licensed), particularly if the R&R is publicly funded. This means that a nontrivial segment of the supply side of the child-care market is not involved in the R&R system either through receiving help in filling vacancies or as a type of referral that a parent might receive.

Although the economic theory reviewed above primarily focuses on the relationship between information intermediaries and price and quality levels, such outcomes are relevant only if participants in the child-care market actually use the information intermediaries. The emphasis in the literature on R&Rs is on how they serve the needs of demanders, but it is also important to consider their relationship to suppliers. By enabling suppliers to fill vacancies more quickly (and therefore to operate more consistently at their efficient scale of operation) and to receive information about demand changes, R&Rs are in a position to provide valuable information and assistance to suppliers as well as demanders. Therefore, in this section I will review the evidence on the extent to which both demanders and suppliers use R&R services, and then I will consider possible explanations for the observed patterns.

It is important to note that the patterns documented below, in terms of who is using R&Rs and to what extent, may be changing over time, fueled in large part by funding and provisions of the Child Care Development Block Grant. According to NACCRRA, state proposals included requests totaling $19 million for R&R services in 36 states (NACCRRA 1993). It appears that there may be a shift occurring toward more public funding of R&RS and more participation of these services in providing care for low-income families, although this funding is still at a very low level.

Perhaps it should not be surprising that demanders report that family and friends are by far the most important source of information for finding child care. What is surprising, however, is the extent to which R&Rs do not play a role in helping families find care. Evidence of the reliance on social networks as information sources for child-care referrals is documented in Powell and Eisenstadt (1982); Bogat and Gensheimer (1986); and Kisker, Maynard, Gordon, and Strain (1989). Focusing specifically on welfare recipients, Ward and Porter (1991) found similar results in their study of child-care arrangements of 627 welfare recipients who participated in New York State's welfare reform demonstration program. More than half of the women in this study, like the women in Kisker et al.'s (1989) study, relied on family and friends as primary sources of referrals. While slightly over one-fifth of the mothers obtained referrals from R&Rs, close to 30 percent received information from program counselors, making R&Rs the least-used of major information sources.

Ward and Porter's findings suggest that providing information and counseling may be an important component of increasing the effectiveness of R&R services. One pattern that emerged from focus group discussions is that some women choose care with relatives, rather than investigating and choosing formal institutional care, because the latter are unfamiliar and the benefits unknown to these women. When parents were provided with information about center care, as well as access to center care, they were more likely to choose that option for that child, even when the parents had characteristics of parents who more typically choose relative care. More generally, it may be that R&R referrals must be supplemented by education and information in order to be effective. Similar findings are reported in Porter (1991).

The single most comprehensive source of evidence regarding consumer use of R&Rs is the *National Child Care Survey, 1990* (Hofferth, Brayfield, Deich, and Holcomb 1991), which indicates that R&Rs play a relatively small role in helping demanders find care. When asked about how they had located their current caregiver, 66 percent of respondents cited friends and relatives, consistent with the results reported above. Formal sources were used by a much smaller percentage of respondents: specifically, 9 percent located care by following up on a referral from an R&R. Interestingly, these patterns are reported to hold across demographic variables.

Kisker, Maynard, Gordon, and Strain (1989) report the methods that child-care centers and family day care homes in Camden, Newark, and South Chicago use to fill vacancies. The role played by R&Rs is a small one: in Camden and South Chicago, no centers reported using R&Rs and in Newark 3.9 percent did. Obviously, this may be due to lack of R&R resources.

Suppliers did rely on a range of services that varied across sites, the most popular of which were waiting lists, referrals from social service caseworkers, advertising, and bulletin boards. Referrals from family and friends played a dominant role in how family day care providers fill vacancies. More than half of all family day care providers did not take any action to fill empty slots, and less than 5 percent use a waiting list.

Evidence from Kisker et al. (1991) shows that the majority of providers are active in trying to fill vacancies: 97 percent of centers and 94 percent of family day care homes report that they take steps to fill vacancies. What is surprising is that although very high percentages of both types of providers are listed with R&Rs (see tables 10.1 and 10.2) very low percentages actually report filling vacancies with referrals from R&Rs. Specifically, 67 percent of centers are listed with R&Rs but only 7 percent report filling vacancies with referrals from R&Rs; the corresponding numbers for family day care providers are 90 percent and 22 percent. The alternative most heavily relied on by centers is personal referrals, with formal and informal advertising and publicity employed by smaller numbers of centers. Family day care providers follow similar patterns.

Thus, we see low reliance on R&Rs among suppliers and demanders. From the perspective of demanders, perhaps information intermediaries make more sense in instances when the information asymmetries are more obvious. A consumer who is not medically trained herself does not imagine that she can evaluate the quality of medical care delivered in a nursing home and so may rely on an intermediary to evaluate the quality for her. But since the person searching for child care is typically a parent or guardian, she, therefore, knows something about child care. Further, since there is less of an obvious technical component to child care, the need for institutional assistance in determining quality may be less obvious to consumers (if not less real).

Interacting with these factors that may decrease reliance on R&Rs is the fact that what R&Rs do is give referrals but do not make recommendations. No doubt this is in part because of legal constraints. Nevertheless, parents still must invest in searches by visiting sites and making a decision independently–such steps may be costly in terms of time and difficult for parents unfamiliar with formal definitions of quality or whose decisions are tightly constrained by provider hours, services, location, and price. Some of the studies cited indicate that an important part of increasing the effectiveness of R&R services is information and education; parents who are given help in making informed decisions appear to be more likely to use the referrals than those who are simply given a list of names to call.

It is difficult, given available information, to sort out how much of this low reliance among suppliers is due to availability of R&Rs and how much to supplier perceptions of the usefulness of R&Rs. The fact that such a high proportion of survey respondents are listed with R&Rs indicates that there are R&Rs available, but it could be that these R&Rs cover a wide geographic range and therefore may not be able to meet the specific needs of a given center at a given time. That is, since parents do not typically travel far to child-care providers, an R&R serving a broad area may not be able to provide a center with names of parents within its immediate market area.

Coupled with availability may be the level of information dissemination about R&R services. The data show that the western region has high listing rates and relatively high utilization rates. No doubt this is driven in part by the inclusion of California, which has a very strong statewide network of R&Rs that are actively involved in outreach programs to suppliers and demanders.

Other possible approaches to ameliorating information problems that have been used in other industries, particularly in the health care industry—which is similar to the child-care industry in a number of ways—include professional associations, referral services, and licensing. As discussed in Magenheim (1992a), these are not completely effective signals of quality or sources of information in health care and may be even less effective in child-care markets.

Government Roles: Licensing, Regulation, and Information Services

Purely governmental efforts to solve information problems (unlike the mixed public and private activities represented by R&Rs) can take a variety of forms ranging from promulgation and enforcement of licensing requirements and regulations to providing information directly. The evidence noted above suggests that licensing requirements and regulations are not sufficient, at least as currently implemented, for ensuring that parents have full and accurate information about child-care choices. Obviously, if regulations were fully enforced and penalties were sufficiently severe to ensure compliance, they would go a long way toward enabling parents to make assumptions about the characteristics of the care that they are purchasing. This is not currently the case.

It is worth considering what it would take for the government to become a more effective information intermediary. It would require both meaningful regulation (that is, regulation, that if enforced, would actually ensure quality child care) as well as an effective and credible means of enforcing these regulations. It would also need a structure in which consumers could more easily find out which providers are licensed and by what licensing means and could check for licensing violations or other problems There are currently no consistent and convenient mechanisms either for reporting violations or for checking on violations, so this potential source of information about quality is not being exercised.

Further, all of this discussion focuses on child care provided in *licensed* family day care homes and centers. As noted earlier, this ignores two large classes of providers. First, there are unlicensed group providers who operate outside of the regulatory framework and, therefore, about which virtually no information is available. Second, it ignores in-home care by nannies and babysitters and exempt family day care homes, for which there are another large set of problems regarding safety and reliability and also about whom very little information is available. A recent article in the *Washington Post* (23 February 1994) documented the rise in private investigative services researching the backgrounds of babysitters and nannies, but such services are costly, and many consumers, either for financial reasons or due to lack of information or availability, will not be able to take advantage of such services.

The alternative or additional role that the government can play is to facilitate information flows between consumers and producers and other interested parties. The government is already doing this to some degree through R&R networks that are partly or fully funded by the public sector. These R&Rs were traditionally community-based organizations with funding from foundations, private businesses, and other sources. As noted above, currently the only government funding explicitly for this purpose is included in the Child Care Development Block Grant, of which a small percentage is dedicated to quality improvements—one form of which can be an R&R agency or network. Increased public funding for the information dissemination and education roles of R&Rs would help to ensure that such services are provided on an expanded basis for all consumers and producers. Public investment in information could generate benefits in excess of the initial investment by increasing the efficiency of the child-care market. Increasing efficiency should yield lower prices, higher quality, and reduced variance. This, in turn, will have both private and public benefits, as discussed above.

Conclusions and Policy Relevance

It is important to be explicit about the problems that arise due to insufficient information in child-care markets. As noted repeatedly above, to the extent that inadequate information leads to less than desirable levels of consumer search, prices may be higher and quality lower than would prevail if the level of competition increased as a result of enhanced information flows. Who bears the burden for these outcomes? On one hand, all consumers do to the extent that they pay more for lower-quality care. On the other hand, this may pose a greater problem for lower-income consumers. Higher-income consumers may be seen to have more alternatives in terms of care purchased because they can buy better-quality care even if the price is higher than it would be in a competitive market. The cost of search is higher, however, for high-income consumers who, if they view child-care quality as a normal good, may limit their searches and thus exacerbate the lack of competitive pressure on firms. Alternatively, if high-income consumers have a high-income elasticity for child-care quality, they may be more willing to invest in searches to find quality care. Whichever interpretation is accepted, the burden of less competitive child-care markets will fall more heavily on lower-income consumers who may be less able to search extensively for good care or may have a more limited portfolio of substitutes from which to choose. Further, since markets are geographically limited, a program that encourages more search or more efficient search by higher-income consumers may not affect the price and quality combinations facing lower-income consumers who live in different communities than higher-income consumers and thus participate in essentially different markets.

It is also important to note that, although this chapter has concentrated on the issue of improving information flows in child-care markets, improved information is not an end in itself. The reason to try to improve information flows is to increase the efficiency of the operation of the child-care market so as to reduce prices and raise quality on average and to reduce the variance in these parameters across child-care providers. If this outcome is realized, it would address—at least in part—the government's obligation to help families work, generate positive externalities, and ensure that child-care services are safe and of high quality.

There are really two issues here from a public policy perspective: first, what mechanisms can be implemented to increase information flows in child-care markets and second, who should be responsible for financing and supplying them? The answer to the first question is not obvious—clearly R&Rs have a role to play in this regard and that role is rapidly changing and developing. Further, licensing and regulations have the potential to be an integral element of enhanced information flows but need, in some cases, to be tightened and in all cases to be enforced more stringently. The question of responsibility involves two other issues: the existence of externalities and the desirability of redistribution. If the benefits of increased information flows are purely private then that weakens the case for government involvement. But the benefits are not purely private—to the extent that the efficiency of the market is increased, more children can experience better-quality child care, and the external benefits of a better-educated and more productive labor force will be enjoyed by all citizens.

Although higher-income consumers face problems with information availability in child-care markets, they are also more likely to enjoy employer-provided R&R services and other child-care related benefits (Magenheim 1993) and to have more choices with respect to the types of care they can purchase. Lower-income consumers, with much more constrained options, face a greater problem in finding quality care, which is a particular problem since children from low-income families in poor neighborhoods may potentially enjoy the greatest benefit from being in high-quality child-care settings. Thus, the government has a clear redistributive role to play in ensuring that children from low-income families are able to experience quality child care and that their parents are able to obtain child care that allows them to work or participate in training programs.

Given that the R&R movement has grown without large-scale intervention by the government, a reasonable question is whether the government needs to intervene by increasing the level of public funding or whether it would make sense for the government to intervene only with regard to the needs of low-income consumers. The question of the funding of R&Rs is important for two reasons: first, with regard to the question of accountability within R&Rs and, second, with regard to the mix of services R&Rs will provide. Funding will influence to whom the R&R is accountable and whose interests it will be serving. For example, there may be trade-offs between making referrals that enable a parent to find care quickly, and referrals that enable her to find high-quality care (perhaps more slowly). The exact way in which the R&R deals with this trade-off may depend on who is funding the R&R (for example, the parent herself, an employer, or the state). Further, conflicts of interest may arise with the private providers of information. For example, if an information source is affiliated with a set of providers, the information could be used to create or steer demand toward the funding providers, as sometimes occurs in health markets. While this could be wealth increasing for providers, its effects on consumer welfare are more problematic. The issue here is not whether the services themselves are provided by a public or private provider but who provides the funding to the provider. That is ultimately what will determine whether or not there is a conflict of interest. If, however, R&Rs are publicly funded, they will not face these potential conflicts.

It is increasingly common for R&Rs to administer government child-care voucher programs or to be involved in other public programs. On the one hand this makes sense given many R&Rs' central position among community organizations providing social services. On the other hand, these activities take R&Rs away from their basic information dissemination role, and, in the vast majority of communities, there are no alternative institutions that can take on that function. Public funding that is expressly targeted at supporting the information function of R&Rs would ensure that reliable information is available.

From a political perspective, increasing the supply of information may offer a means for being responsive to families' demands for help with raising children while not becoming directly involved in the actual provision of child-care services or even being seen as encouraging nonfamilial care. An alternative, of course, is for the government to become the direct provider of child care as is the case in any number of other industrialized countries.

The debate over health care reform and the strong resistance to a single-payer system is indicative of the characteristic U.S. reluctance to have government directly provide social services, choosing instead to restrict its participation to regulation and some funding for those in particular need as occurs in a wide variety of service delivery areas. That reluctance is likely to be amplified in the case of child care, a service that has traditionally been provided by the family and that raises all sorts of highly charged issues regarding the roles of women in society, family structure, and "family values." Thus, it is not realistic to expect universal public provision of quality child-care services in the foreseeable future.

This paper has considered in detail only one of the numerous areas in which there may be room for government intervention in the child-care market. While information is a particularly pressing problem as more parents enter an increasingly tight market for child care, there are other important issues including accessibility and affordability, ensuring adequate quality, and the role that child care will play in welfare reform. Returning to the reasons for government intervention, including market failures, externalities, and redistribution, there is much more research needed regarding the appropriate role of the government in the child-care market.

Bibliography

Adams, G. *Who Knows How Safe? The Status of State Efforts to Ensure Quality Child Care.* Washington, D.C.: Children's Defense Fund, 1990.

Akerlof, G. "The Market for 'Lemons': Quality Uncertainty and the Market Mechanism" *Quarterly Journal of Economics* (1970): 488–500.

Benham, L. "The Effect of Advertising on the Price of Eyeglasses," *Journal of Law and Economics* (1972). 337–52.

Blank, H., A. Wilkins, and M. Crawley. *State Child Care Fact Book 1987.* Washington, D.C.: Children's Defense Fund, 1987

Bogat, A., and L. K. Gensheimer. "The Role of an Information and Referral Service in the Selection of Child Care," *Children and Youth Services Review 1986* 8 (1986): 243–56.

Connelly, R. "The Effect of Child Care Costs on Married Women's Labor Force Participation," *Review of Economics and Statistics* (1992): 83–90.

Culkin, M., J. Morris, and S. Helburn, "Quality and the True Cost of Child Care," *Journal of Social Issues* (1991): 71–86.

Friedman, D. A., and N. Kolben, *Child Care Resource and Referral: 1989 Survey Findings.* Rochester, MN: National Association for Child Care Resource and Referral Agencies, 1990.

General Accounting Office. "Child Care Quality: States' Difficulties Enforcing Standards Confront Welfare Reform Plans." Testimony before the Subcommittee on Regulation, Business Opportunities, and Technology of the Committee on Small Business, House of Representatives, 11 February 1994.

Gormley Jr., W. "State Regulations and the Availability of Child-Care Services," *Journal of Policy Analysis and Management* 10, 1 (1991): 78–95.

Hanson, S., and T. Ooms. "The Economic Costs and Rewards of Two-Earner, Two-Parent Families," *Journal of Marriage and the Family* (August 1991): 622–34.

Hayes, C., J. Palmer, and M. Zaslow, eds. *Who Cares for America's Children?* Washington, D.C.: National Academy Press, 1990.

Henriques, I., and F. Vaillancourt. "The Demand for Child Care Services in Canada," *Applied Economics* (1988): 385–94.

Hofferth, S., A. Brayfield, S. Deich, and P. Holcomb. *National Child Care Survey, 1990.* Urban Institute Report 91–5. Washington, D.C.: Urban Institute Press, 1991.

Kagan, S. "Examining Profit and Nonprofit Child Care: An Odyssey of Quality and Auspices," *Journal of Social Issues* (1991): 87–104.

Kagan, S., and J. W. Newton. "For-Profit and Nonprofit Child Care: Similarities and Differences," *Young Children* (November 1989): 4–10.

Kahn, A. J., and S. B. Kamerman. *Child Care: Facing the Hard Choices.* Dover, MA: Auburn House Publishing, 1987.

Kisker, E. E., S. Hofferth, D. Phillips, and E. Farquhar. *A Profile of Child Care Settings: Early Education and Care in 1990.* Vol. 1. Washington, D.C.: U.S. Government Printing Office, 1991.

Kisker, E. E., and R. Maynard. "Quality, Cost, and Parental Choice in Child Care." In *The Economics of Child Care,* David Blau, editor. New York: Russell Sage Foundation, 1991. 127–143.

Kisker, E., R. Maynard, A. Gordon, and M. Strain. *The Child Care Challenge: What Parents Need and What Is Available in Three Metropolitan Areas.* Princeton, N.J.: Mathematica Policy Research, 1989.

Kushman, J., "A Three-Sector Model of Day Care Center Services," *Journal of Human Resources* 14 (1979): 543–62.

Kwoka, J., "Price Advertising of Optometric Services," *The American Economic Review* (March 1984): 211–16.

Liebowitz, A., J. Klerman, and L. Waite. "Employment of New Mothers and Child Care Choice: Differences by Children's Age," *Journal of Human Resources* (winter 1992): 112–33.

Maddala, G. S., *Limited-Dependent and Qualitative Variables in Econometrics.* Cambridge: Cambridge University Press, 1986.

Magenheim, E. "The Market for Child Care: What Mainstream Economics Ignores." Manuscript, 1992a.

——"Resource and Referral Agencies: Can They Solve the Information Problems in Child-Care Markets?" Manuscript, 1992b.

——"Employer-Provided Child-Care Benefits," chapter 13 in *Trends in Health Benefits.* Washington, D.C.: U.S. Government Printing Office, 1993.

McConaghy, E., and P. Siegel. "The Challenge for Child Care Resource and Referral Services." Paper presented at the NACCRRA Preconference Session NAEYC 1988.

Morgan, G. *The National State of Child Care Regulation, 1986.* Watertown, MA: Work/Family Directions, Inc., 1987.

Mukerjee, S., and A. Witte. "Provision of Child Care: Cost Functions for Profit-Making and Not-for-Profit Making Day Care Centers," *Journal of Productivity Analysis* (1993): 145–63.

National Commission on Children. *Just the Facts: A Summary of Recent Information on America's Children and Their Families.* Washington, D.C.: NCC, 1993.

Porter, T. *Just Like Any Parent: The Child Care Choices of Welfare Mothers in New Jersey.* New York: Bank Street College of Education, December 1991.

Powell, D., and J. Eisenstadt. "Parents' Searches for Child Care and the Design of Information Services," *Children and Youth Review* 4 (1982): 239–53.

Reismon, B., A. Moore, and K. Fitzgerald, *Child Care: The Bottom Line—An Economic and Child Care Policy Paper.* New York: The Child Care Action Campaign, 1988.

Robins, P., and R. Spiegelman. "An Econometric Model of the Demand for Child Care." *Economic Inquiry* (1978): 83–94.

Robins, P., and S. Weiner, ed. *Child Care and Public Policy.* Lexington, MA: Lexington Books, 1978.

Rose-Ackerman, S. "Unintended Consequences: Regulating the Quality of Subsidized Day Care." *Journal of Policy Analysis and Management* (1983): 14–30.

——"Altruistic Nonprofit Firms in Competitive Markets: The Case of Day-Care Centers in the United States." *Journal of Consumer Policy* (1986): 291–310.

Schotter, A. *Microeconomics: A Modern Approach.* New York: Harper-Collins College Publishers, 1994.

Sonenstein, F., and D. Wolf. "Satisfaction with Child Care: Perspectives of Welfare Mothers." *Journal of Social Issues* 47, 2 (1991): 15–31.

Stigler, G. "The Economics of Information." *Journal of Political Economy* (June 1961): 213–25.

Waite, L., A. Leibowitz, and C. Witsberger. "What Parents Pay For: Child Care Characteristics, Quality, and Costs." *Journal of Social Issues* 47, 2 (1991): 33–48.

Walker, J. "New Evidence on the Supply of Child Care: A Statistical Portrait of Family Providers and an Analysis of Their Fees." *Journal of Human Resources* (winter 1992): 40–69.

Ward, A, and T. Porter, *No Choice But Home: Child Care and Welfare Reform.* New York: Child Care Inc., 1991.

Notes

1. It is worth noting that there are very few nationally representative child-care data sets, so this is a problem in many studies, not just this one.

2. The regression equation is estimated by finding the "best-fitting" straight line that fits all of the observations. Typically, no straight line fits all of the observations exactly, and the fit of the straight line differs also along different variables. Coefficients of regression equations are called statistically significant if, accounting for this variability along the dimension of the particular variable, the mean value of the coefficient differs sufficiently from zero so that there is great confidence that the true value is different from zero.

3. An outcome is Pareto optimal if no economic agent can be made better off without making someone else worse off. General equilibrium in a perfectly competitive economy is Pareto optimal.

Contributors

Joseph J. Cordes is a professor of economics at The George Washington University, where he also serves as Chair of the Department of economics and the director of the Ph.D. program in public policy. From 1989 to 1991, Professor Cordes seved as Deputy Assistant Director for tax analysis at the Congressional Budget Office. Professor Cordes has published numerous articles in scholarly journals on regulatory policy, technology policy, public expenditure analysis, and tax policy. His recent research interests include the economics of education and the voluntary provision of public goods.

Sheila Nataraj Kirby is a senior economist at the RAND Corporation, Washington, D.C., and an adjunct professor of economics at The George Washington University. Dr. Kirby's major areas of specialization are military manpower issues with particular emphasis on reserve manpower, economics of education and intellectual property issues. She is the author of several RAND monographs and journal and book articles on these subjects.

Richard Buddin is an economist at the RAND Corporation, Santa Monica, California and a visiting associate professor of economics at the University of California at Los Angeles. He received his Ph.D. from UCLA with a specialization in labor economics and econometrics. He has published extensively in the areas of personnel tranining, promotion, and job mobility. His recent research interests have also included the economics of education and health care.

Alain C. Enthoven is the Marriner S. Eccles Professor of Public and Private Management in the Graduate School of Business at Stanford University. He holds degrees in economics from Stanford, Oxford (where he was a Rhodes Scholar) and MIT. The positions he has held include economist with the RAND Corporation, assistant secretary of defense, and president of Litton Medical Products. In 1963, he received the President's Award for Distinguished Federal Civilian Service from John F. Kennedy. He is a member of the Institute of Medicine of the National Academy of Sciences and a fellow of the American Academy of Arts and Sciences. He is chairman of the Health Benefits Advisory Council for CalPERS, the California state employees' medical and hospital care plans, former chairman of Stanford's University Committee on Faculty/Staff Benefits, and a consultant to Kaiser Permanente. His latest book is *Theory and Practice of Managed Competiton in Health Care Finance*.

Paul G. Farnham is Associate Professor of Economics at Georgia State University. Since 1990, he has also been a visiting health economist with the Office of the Associate Director, HIV/AIDS at the Centers for Disease Control and Prevention (CDC).

While at the CDC, Dr. Farnham has worked on projects analyzing the economic impact of the AIDS epidemic on business and applying economic analysis to the evaluation of HIV prevention strategies. He has published in a variety of journals including *Inquiry, Public Health Reports, Southern Economic Journal* and *Public Finance Quarterly*. Dr. Farnham received his B.A. degree in economics from Union College, Schenectady, New York, and his M.A. and Ph.D. degrees in economics from the University of California, Berkeley.

Thomas E. Getzen is Professor of Health Administration at Temple University, director of the International Health Economics Association, past chair of the Health Economics Committee of the American Public Health Association, and has been a visiting professor at the Centre for Health Economics, University of York, United Kingdom. He serves on the board of Covenant House Health Services and is the finance and audit director of the Mustard Seed Corporation. Dr. Getzen received his B.A. in literature from Yale University and his master's degree in health administration and Ph.D. in economics from the University of Washington.

Charles R. Hulten has been a professor of economics at the University of Maryland since 1985. He received his undergraduate and Ph.D. degrees from the University of California, Berkeley (1965 and 1973, respectively). He is also a research associate of the National Bureau of Economic Research and Chairman of the Conference on Research in Income and Wealth. He was senior research associate at the Urban Institute (1978–1985) and assistant professor of economics at the Johns Hopkins University (1971-1978). He has also been a visiting professor of economics at the European Institute of Business Administration (1992) and a visiting scholar at the American Enterprise Institute (1988–1992). His research interests include the areas of productivity analysis, infrastructure, economic growth and capital formation, tax policy and the measurement of economic depreciation. He serves on the editorial board of the journal *Economic Inquiry*.

Ellen B. Magenheim is Associate Professor of Economics at Swarthmore College. This article was written while she was the Visiting Scholar at Child Trends, Inc., in Washington, D.C. (supported with funding from the William and Flora Hewlett Foundation). She received a B.A. in history from the University of Rochester and the M.A. and Ph.D. in economics from the University of Maryland. Her research interests include corporate mergers, pensions, and the economics of the child-care industry, and she has consulted to the U.S. Department of Labor and the Rockefeller Foundation.

J. M. Pogodzinski is Associate Professor of Economics at San Jose State University. He was born in Detroit, Michigan, and attended Cornell University as an undergraduate. He received his M.A. and Ph.D. degrees in economics from the State University of New York at Stony Brook. While in graduate school he was an exchange student in Poland. He has also served on the faculties of Purdue University and Georgia State University. In 1993 he was awarded a fellowship at the Lusk Center for Real Estate Development, School of Urban and Regional Planning, at the University of Southern California, Los Angeles, and was a visiting scholar in the Department of Economics, The George Washington University, Washington, D.C. for the 1993–1994 academic year. He was a consultant on aid to Poland for the U.S. Agency for International Development. He was also a consultant to and a senior housing economist with Abt Associates, Inc., and participated in housing policy research in Zimbabwe. His main interests are urban public finance issues and East European economies. He has published papers in a variety of journals including *Journal of Urban Economics, Land Economics, Journal of Public Economics,* and *Economics of Planning.*

Ellen P. Roche is the Director of Mortgage Markets and International Research at Fannie Mae, the Federal National Mortgage Association. Dr. Roche is responsible for research and publications on housing finance including the development and publication of the first issue of the *Journal of Housing Research,* "Mortgage Markets in the Year 2000," and for conceptualizing and directing comparative research on housing finance in Europe and the United States that resulted in several conferences and articles published in the journals. Her current projects include a pilot study for a panel survey on the behavioral reasons for default and an analysis of the relationship between savings and homeownership. Dr. Roche earned her Ph.D. from the University of Maryland with concentrations in public finance and industrial organization. Dr. Roche earned her bachelor's degree from Cornell University and a master's of Public Administration from the Maxwell School at Syracuse University. Dr. Roche is a member of Women in Housing and Finance, the American Economics Association; and the American Real Estate and Urban Economic Association.

Robert M. Schwab received his Ph.D. from Johns Hopkins in 1980 and then joined the University of Maryland where he is now a professor of economics. He spent 1987–88 as a Gilbert White Fellow at Resources for the Future and has been the Department of Economics' director of graduate studies since 1991. His primary field of research is public economics with an emphasis on state and local government. He has written recent papers on education, teenage pregnancy, infrastructure, land taxation, tax amnesties, and life cycle tax incidence.

David L. Sjoquist is Professor of Economics, a senior associate, and associate director of the Policy Research Center, College of Business at Georgia State University. He also serves as executive director of both the Urban Study Institute Project and the Research Atlanta Project. Sjoquist is an expert on state and local taxation and urban poverty. His fields of interest include public finance, urban and regional economics, micro-economic theory and competitive strategy. He has coauthored several books and written numerous articles. His education includes the University of Minnesota (M.A.; 1966; Ph.D., 1971) and University of St. Thomas (B.A., 1964). He is a member of the American Economic Association, Southern Economic Association, National Tax Association, and Public Choice Society.

Carolyn L. Weaver is Resident Scholar and Director of Social Security and Pension Studies at the American Enterprise Institute. She has written widely on social security and disability policy, has testified frequently on Capitol Hill, and served on several public advisory councils dealing with these issues. Her fields of interest are public economics, labor economics, and political economy. Before joining AEI, Dr. Weaver was a Senior Research Fellow at the Hoover Institution. She has also been a member of the economics faculties of Tulane University and Virginia Tech, where she received her Ph.D., and subsequently was a Research Associate of the Center for Study of Public Choice. From 1981–1984, Dr. Weaver served as the chief professional staff member on social security and disability legislation for the U.S. Senate Committee on Finance. Dr. Weaver was born in Washington, D.C., and received her undergraduate degree from Mary Washington College.

Appendix B

NATIONAL PET-RELATED ORGANIZATIONS

ANIMAL HEALTH TRUST
Lanwades Farm
Kentford
Suffolk
CB8 7UU
Tel: 01638 751000
Fax: 01638 555606

**ASSOCIATION FOR THE STUDY
OF REPTILIA & AMPHIBIA**
PO Box 73
Banbury
Oxon
OX15 6RE

**ASSOCIATION OF PET
BEHAVIOUR COUNSELLORS**
PO Box 46
Worcester
WR8 9YS
Tel: 01386 751151
Fax: 01386 751151

**ASSOCIATION OF PET DOG
TRAINERS**
Peacocks Farm
Northchapel
Petworth
West Sussex
GU28 9JB
Tel: 01428 707234
Fax: 01428 708190
E-mail: guarddog@u.genie.co.uk
Website: www.apdt.co.uk
Enclose an s.a.e. please

BLUE CROSS
Field Centre
Shilton Road
Burford
Oxford
OX18 4PF
Tel: 01993 822651
Fax: 01993 823083

BRITISH CHELONIA GROUP
PO Box 2163
London
NW10 5HW

**BRITISH HEDGEHOG
PRESERVATION SOCIETY**
Knowbury House
Knowbury
Ludlow
Shropshire
SY8 3LQ
Tel: 01584 890801

**BRITISH HERPETOLOGICAL
SOCIETY AND YOUNG
HERPETOLOGICAL CLUB**
c/o Zoological Society of London
Regent's Park
London
NW1 4RY
Tel: 020 8452 9578

BRITISH HORSE SOCIETY
Stoneleigh Deer Park
Kenilworth
Warwickshire
CV8 2XZ
Tel: 01926 707700
E-mail: enquiry@BHS.org.uk
Website: www.bhs.org.uk

**BRITISH SMALL ANIMAL
VETERINARY ASSOCIATION**
Woodrow House
1 Telford Way
Waterwells Business Park
Quedgeley
Gloucester
GL2 4AB
Tel: 01242 862994
Fax: 01452 726701
E-mail: adminoff@bsava.demon.co.uk
Website: www.bsava.ac.uk

**BRITISH VETERINARY
ASSOCIATION**
7 Mansfield Street
London
W1M 0AT
Tel: 0207 636 6541
Fax: 0207 436 2970
E-mail: bvahg@bva.co.uk
Website: www.bva.co.uk

**BRITISH VETERINARY NURSES
ASSOCIATION (BVNA)**
Unit D12
The Seedbed Centre
Cold Harbour Road
Harlow
Essex
CM19 5AF
Tel: 01279 450567
Fax: 01279 420866

**CANINE PARTNERS FOR
INDEPENDENCE (CPI)**
Homewell House
22 Homewell
Havant
Hants
PO9 1EE
Tel: 02392 450156
Fax: 02392 470140
E-mail: cpi@cpiuk.org
Website: www.cpiuk.org

**CHILDREN IN HOSPITAL AND
ANIMAL THERAPY
ASSOCIATION (CHATA)**
Sandra Stone
87 Longland Drive
Totteridge
London
N20 8HN
Tel: 0208 445 7883
Fax: 0208 445 7883

COMPANION ANIMAL WELFARE COUNCIL (CAWC)
43 Brook Lane Field
Harlow
Essex
CM18 7AU
Tel: 01279 639212

DOGS FOR THE DISABLED
The Old Vicarage
London Road
Ryton-on-Dunsmore
Coventry
CV8 3ER
Tel: 01295 252600
Fax: 01295 252668
E-mail: xnw47@dial.pipex.com
Website: www.vois.org.uk

FELINE ADVISORY BUREAU
Taeselbury
High Street
Tisbury
Wiltshire
SP3 6LD
Tel: 01747 871872
Fax: 01747 871873
Website: www.fabcats.org

THE GOVERNING COUNCIL OF THE CAT FANCY
4–6 Penel Orlieu
Bridgwater
Somerset
TA6 3PG
Tel: 01278 427575

THE GUIDE DOGS FOR THE BLIND ASSOCIATION
Hillfields
Burghfield Common
Reading
RG7 3YG
Tel: 0118 983 5555
Fax: 0118 983 8223
E-mail: guidedogs@gdba.org.uk
Website: www.gdba.org.uk

HEARING DOGS FOR THE DEAF
London Road (A40)
Lewknor
Oxford
OX9 5RY
Tel: 01844 353898
Fax: 01844 353099
Website: www.hearing.dogs.co.uk

THE KENNEL CLUB
(Breed Rescue Society Information)
1 Clarges Street
Piccadilly
London W1Y 8AB
Tel: 0870 60 66750
Website: www.the-kennel-club.org.uk

NATIONAL CANINE DEFENCE LEAGUE
17 Wakely Street
London
EC1V 7LT
Tel: 020 7837 0006
Fax: 020 7689 0482
Website: www.ncdl.org.uk

NATIONAL DOG WARDEN ASSOCIATION (NDWA)
Sue Bell
NDWA
Tewkesbury Borough Council
Gloucester Road
Tewkesbury
GL20 5TT
E-mail: sbell@NDWA.co.uk

NATIONAL OFFICE OF ANIMAL HEALTH LTD (NOAH)
3 Crossfield Chambers
Gladbeck Way
Enfield
Middlesex
EN2 7HF
Tel: 020 8367 3131
Fax: 020 8363 1155

ORNAMENTAL AQUATICS TRADE ASSOCIATION (OATA)
PO Box 1860
Unit 5, Narrow Wine Street
Trowbridge
Wilts
BA14 8FJ
Tel: 01225 777177
Fax: 01225 775523
Website: www.ornamentalfish.org

PEOPLE'S DISPENSARY FOR SICK ANIMALS (PDSA)
Head Office
Whitechapel Way
Priorslee
Telford
Shropshire
TF2 9PQ
Tel: 01952 290999
Fax: 01952 291035

PET ADVISORY COMMITTEE (PAC)
Westminster Strategy
1 Bedford Avenue
London
WC1B 3AU
Tel: 020 7255 5475

PET FOOD MANUFACTURERS' ASSOCIATION (PFMA)
Suite 1/2
12–14 Henrietta Street
Covent Garden
London
WC2E 8LH
Tel: 020 7379 9009
Fax: 020 7379 8008/3898

PET HEALTH COUNCIL
Thistledome Cottage
49 Main Street
Sewstern
Grantham
Lincs
NG33 5RF
Tel: 01476 861379
Fax: 01476 861336

PETS AS THERAPY
3 Grange Farm Cottages
Wycombe Road
Sanderton
Princes Risborough
HP27 9NS
Tel: 0870 240 1239

RABBIT CHARITY
PO Box 23698
London
N8 0WS
Tel: 020 8888 0001
Fax: 020 8888 8868
E-mail: info@bunny.org.uk
Website: www.bunny.org.uk

ROYAL COLLEGE OF VETERINARY SURGEONS
Belgravia House
62–64 Horseferry Road
London
SW1X 8QP
Tel: 020 7222 2001
Fax: 020 7222 2004

SOCIETY FOR COMPANION ANIMAL STUDIES (SCAS)
(see Blue Cross)

SUPPORT DOGS
Val Strong
The John Fisher Centre
Trianco House
Thorncliffe Park Estate
Chapletown
Sheffield
S35 2PH
Tel: 0114 257 7997
Fax: 0114 257 7997